SIKHISM AND WOMEN

SIKHISM AND WOMEN
History, Texts, and Experience

edited by

DORIS R. JAKOBSH

OXFORD
UNIVERSITY PRESS

OXFORD
UNIVERSITY PRESS

YMCA Library Building, Jai Singh Road, New Delhi 110001

Oxford University Press is a department of the University of Oxford. It furthers
the University's objective of excellence in research, scholarship, and education by
publishing worldwide in

Oxford New York
Auckland Cape Town Dar es Salaam Hong Kong Karachi
Kuala Lumpur Madrid Melbourne Mexico City Nairobi
New Delhi Shanghai Taipei Toronto

With offices in
Argentina Austria Brazil Chile Czech Republic France Greece
Guatemala Hungary Italy Japan Poland Portugal Singapore
South Korea Switzerland Thailand Turkey Ukraine Vietnam

Oxford is a registered trade mark of Oxford University Press
in the UK and in certain other countries

Published in India
by Oxford University Press, New Delhi

© Oxford University Press 2010

ISBN-13: 978-0-19-806002-4
ISBN-10: 0-19-806002-5

Typeset in Plantin STD 10.5/12.6
by Sai Graphic Design, New Delhi 110 055,
Published by Oxford University Press
YMCA Library Building, Jai Singh Road, New Delhi 110 001

Contents

Acknowledgements

This book could never have come to fruition if it were not for the encouragement and support of all of the contributors. I am especially grateful to Eleanor Nesbitt who offered invaluable insight and her seemingly vast patience to the process. Thank you. To my spouse, Paul Roorda, my love and gratitude, as always. To my children, Jessen and Kaira, you are my joy.

This book is dedicated to the memory of Hew McLeod— friend, mentor, guide, gentleman scholar.

Doris R. Jakobsh
Waterloo, Ontario, Canada

INTRODUCTION
Sikhism and Women
Contextualizing the Issues

Doris R. Jakobsh and Eleanor Nesbitt

IDENTITY WITHIN SIKHISM

At first glance, it would appear that the topic at hand, namely, Sikhism and women, is a straightforward categorization. Moreover, the raison d'être of this volume too seems almost simplistically clear: it is an exploration of Sikh women's social and religious lives and experiences. A casual reader may expect within its pages a finely tuned 'capturing' of the essence of Sikh womanhood. If only it were so simple. For the terms 'Sikhism' and 'women', in and of themselves, are highly complex constructions; questions of 'who is a Sikh' and what constitutes Sikh behaviour and identity have long perplexed the Sikh community as well as scholars of Sikhism.[1] Religion, according to Elizabeth Castelli, is not an 'innocent' category. It is rather, a mediated discursive space, particularly when looking at religious discourse and practice; these two realms 'oscillate endlessly back and forth, each reflecting and reinscribing the other's claims' (Castelli 2001: 4). This issue becomes all the more problematic in light of the emergence of modern perceptions of religion stemming largely from debates within Christian communities and European colonizers encountering other cultural forms, rituals, practices, and texts in the 'contact zone' of the imperial frontier

(Ballantyne 2006: 43, see also Green and Searle-Chatterjee 2008: 1–23).[2] Further, the ethos of the 'Age of Enlightenment' played a significant role in the formulation of what was perceived to be *religion* and what was understood to be *religious*.

In an Enlightenment age of classification and taxonomies, Protestants increasingly imagined 'religion' as a series of propositions or beliefs that could be simply summarized and even conveyed in the form of a chart or diagram. In this form, religion could be identified as distinct and self-contained, something that could be separated from economics or politics, a definition that has recently been identified as an important move toward the essentialized and increasingly privatized vision of the cultural practices we denote as 'religion' (Ballantyne 2006: 42–3).

Moreover, as Harjot Oberoi's seminal work on Sikh identity formation during the nineteenth and early twentieth centuries has shown, British and Sikh (alongside other religious communities') increasing preoccupation with texts and scriptures and definitions played no small part in the heightened and politicized communal dynamics of colonial Punjab. For even the 'idea' of religion as a 'systematized sociological unit claiming unbridled loyalty from its adherents and opposing an amorphous religious imagination, is a relatively recent development in the history of the Indian peoples' (Oberoi 1994: 17). Ibbetson, the commissioner of the 1881 census in Punjab had earlier noted:

But on the border lands where these great faiths meet, and especially among the ignorant peasantry whose creed, by whatever name it may be known, is seldom more than a superstition and a ritual, the various observances and beliefs which distinguish the followers of the several faiths in their purity are so strangely blended and intermingled, that it is often impossible to say that one prevails rather than other, or to decide in what category the people shall be classed (Ibbetson 1883: 101).

The British penchant for classification is here shown as utterly challenged by the fluid understandings of religiosity of the Punjab masses. Only terms like 'superstition' (or perhaps, 'folk beliefs' in a more contemporary manifestation), which are highly pejorative within the linear and rational worldview espoused by the British colonizers, (and still utilized by many contemporary writers), and which refer to 'alternate' or 'non-Sikh' practices that have 'crept' into what was perceived as 'true Sikhism', could account for the vast array of the practices that simply evaded the classificatory needs of the British administration.

The British gaze toward the last state of the Indian sub-continent to be conquered, particularly in relation to the Sikhs and Sikhism, found a great deal that was familiar. Through what Jakobsh has termed elsewhere the 'politics of similarity', the British imagined and actively promoted kinship ties to the Sikhs, for they saw in them a reflection of themselves, though an earlier, less civilized, less refined likeness (Jakobsh 2003: 57–9). What was especially disturbing to the colonizers was the variance of what constituted 'the Sikh'. 'This translated into censure when variations of Sikh identity did not fit into British attempts to create a powerful Sikh military machine' (ibid.: 60). When the Singh Sabha reform movement was inaugurated by Sikhs in the late nineteenth century to return Sikhism to what they considered to be the 'pristine purity of the age of the Sikh gurus' and to conclusively establish what was 'true Sikhism', the British were highly supportive of their efforts. As a result, what Ballantyne has called the 'reformation trope' of Sikh and British endeavours set in motion a tendency to 'abstract "religion" from the complex set of kinship, economic and political relationships that were central to Punjabi life' (Ballantyne 2006: 44).

The question of Sikh identity plagued the reformers, particularly given Sikh minority status in Hindu-dominated India, and the fluidity of boundaries, at times merging, at times separating 'religious' affiliation in Punjab. Swami Dayanand, the founder of the reformist Arya Samaj movement in the nineteenth century, among many others, simply considered Sikhism as part and parcel of the larger Hindu milieu. Finding ways to counter this perception became the dominant focus of the Sikh reformers. It was to the order of the Khalsa that the Singh Sabha reformers turned for their inspiration in the movement to insist on Sikh uniqueness within the wider milieu, as well as rejuvenate what was understood to be a degenerate Sikh tradition. The reasons for this are not difficult to understand, namely, increasingly, many Sikhs were rejecting the Khalsa identity as normative. Reformers made colossal attempts to stem the tide of those unwilling to undergo initiation into the Khalsa, citing that this state of affairs was responsible for the degeneration of the Sikh community.

As Oberoi has succinctly noted, the Singh Sabha discourse of the regeneration of a 'fallen' tradition was and still continues, to be the benchmark of modern Sikhism today, continuing 'to hold a profound fascination for the adherents of the faith' (Oberoi 1994: 306). The means by which the Singh Sabha divested what was (and some would add, still is) a highly amorphous, heterogeneous tradition into an increasingly homogeneous one, namely the Khalsa Sikh or Tat Khalsa (true Khalsa), is important to coming to an understanding of the complexity surrounding issues of Sikh identity today. For Singh Sabha reinterpretation and adaptation of the Sikh tradition had far-reaching effects that went far beyond the colonial time frame. The reforms they put in place in their 'purification process' are reflective of what the many Sikhs today understand to be the essence of 'true' Sikhism.

However, the notion of a 'true Sikhism' also bears the stamp, by its very nature, of acknowledging that there exists that which is *not* true Sikhism. And it is in this arena that what is often construed as the opposing worlds of 'religion', 'culture', or 'ethnicity' come to the fore (Hall 1996: 297). Paul Bramadat notes that

ethnicity and religion are inextricably linked, so much so that it is often virtually impossible to tease them apart. We do not assume that we can determine precisely which parts of a person or group's identity or motivations are derived from religious sources, and which are derived from ethnic sources...[yet] people regularly speak as though there is an obvious division between the concepts of religion and ethnicity (or religion and culture) (Bramadat 2005: 18).

Similar to Kamala Nayar's observations in this volume, Jakobsh's experience in teaching students in an introductory Sikhism course may shed some light on the issues at hand, for it is particularly in the arenas of caste and gender issues that the 'culture' and 'religion' confusion becomes evident for students. Sikh students often speak of Sikhism as being 'casteless', in its *true* form, yet riddled by caste issues, due to *cultural* norms; similarly, they proclaim that Sikhism is truly egalitarian when it comes to women and men, yet insist that it is due to the negative effects of Punjabi *culture* that many Sikhs do not live according to Sikh principles in this regard. When asked where Punjabi cultural norms end and Sikh principles begin, students are at a loss. As is evident in the contributions in this volume, this 'loss' is not only confined to students; many scholars too find themselves in 'murky territory' when attempting to circumscribe these issues. For Jakobsh's students, often, when referring to harmful social problems within the Indo-Canadian community, culture is identified as the perpetrator; when positive attributes are being referred to, then Sikhism as 'religion' is viewed as being relevant.

At the heart of this issue are the continuing effects of the Enlightenment ethos alluded to earlier, where religion came to be classified as utterly distinct from cultural practices, economics, politics, and kinship issues; in other words, religion came to be addressed as abstract theoretical constructs as opposed to being 'the product of complex acts of translation, codification, and social reform' that outlined core beliefs. Ballantyne calls for a move beyond this 'chief heritage of the colonial period, that is the notion of "religion" as a self-contained field', to a richer, more textured understanding of the many strands that constitute Sikh identity (Ballantyne 2006: 43–4, 172).

Oberoi has warned that while many historians (and one could add scholars of religion) 'think, speak and write about Islam, Hinduism and Sikhism...they rarely pause to consider if such clear-cut categories actually found expression in the conscious-ness, actions and cultural performances of the human actors they describe' (Oberoi 1994: 1). This point is driven home in an important essay by Ron Geaves where he notes that his recent fieldwork on the cult of Baba Balaknath indicates that many of the worshippers define themselves as *Sikh*, despite the fact that their primary loyalty is to a Hindu folk deity. Their allegiance stems from historical extended family networks (*biradari*s), or from the deity's reputation for healing. While supportive of Oberoi's findings within the eighteenth and nineteenth centu-ries, Geaves notes that the kind of eclecticism Oberoi dismisses as being largely a *historical* phenomenon is still very much alive in contemporary Punjab. The range of diversity within a larger Sikh identity includes numerous sects, many of which are led by living gurus and godmen (or, as they are often called, *ba-ba*s), Sikh ascetics, Sanatan Sikhs, Sikhs as worshippers of miracle saints and other miraculous sites, alongside Sikhs who do not perceive their Sikh identity as religious but rather as an ethnic identity. Through fieldwork, rather than an exclusive focus on texts, an additional focus on the 'borders of traditions' alongside the mainstream is allowed for, leading to a richer and more authentic understanding of what constitutes Sikhism (Geaves 1998: 28). Here, specifically focusing his critique on scholarly religious studies texts, he argues:

[These texts] do not describe the complexity and variety of forms of Sikh identity but rather present the Khalsa as the definitive and discrete Sikh world religion…By presenting Sikhism in a particular way…I am unwittingly guilty of aiding the Khalsa in representing itself as the definitive form of Sikh tradition. It may be necessary to re-examine the definition of a Sikh in order to incorporate the diversity of Sikh identity. Essentially, this definition needs to recognize the common ethnic dimension to Sikh identity which may then manifest a variety of religious forms which should equally demand our attention (Geaves 1996).

Fluidity, defying clear-cut boundaries of religious identity, continues strongly not only in Punjab but also in the Punjabi diaspora which similarly provides strong challenges to simplistic notions of Sikh identity. Eleanor Nesbitt's ethnographic studies over two decades in the Midlands of Britain (Nesbitt 1980, 2000, 2004a) have highlighted the role of cross-cutting allegiances and influences in Sikhs' understandings of what 'being Sikh' means. Salient among these are caste (*zat-biradari*) and the appeal of spiritual masters (known as *sant*s or babas) (Tatla 1992). At times these allegiances and influences converge, as for example in the largely Ramgarhia caste membership of the Namdhari Sikhs, followers of a living Guru, Satguru Jagjit Singh. In other instances caste tradition affects cultural, and so religious, practice in ways that differentiate that community from others. This, as outlined below, was certainly the case with the Bhatra Sikhs of Nesbitt's fieldwork in Nottingham (Nesbitt 1980, 1981).

According to Nesbitt, at times, those who regard themselves as Sikh are written off as 'non-Sikh' by (other) Sikhs. This is particularly evident when groups (such as the Namdharis) openly regard a living master as Guru, and is liable to happen when any (Sikh) sant or baba appears to critics to be accepting veneration due only to a Guru. The consequences in the diaspora, no less than in Punjab, can be fatal as in the killing in Southall of Mahraz Darshan Das, the leader of the controversial Sachkhand Nanak Dham that took place in 1987 (on Sachkhand Nanak Dham, see Cox and Robinson 2006).

As Nesbitt's additional fieldwork in Coventry disclosed (Nesbitt 1990a, 1990b, 1991, 1994), in two other zat-biradaris, the Ravidasi and Valmiki communities, members themselves vary in how, and how strongly, they define themselves. 'Valmiki' and 'Ravidasi' are the honorific designations which most members prefer to the caste labels which are still used pejoratively among UK Punjabis. Both communities have a history of stigma and oppression in Punjab. Young Valmikis and Ravidasis in Coventry variously term themselves 'Sikh', 'Hindu', and 'Hindu Punjabi' (Nesbitt 1991, 2004b). Ritual practice within and between families varies, regarding, for example, whether a house-warming ceremony centres on the Guru Granth Sahib or a *havan* (sacred fire) and whether images of Hindu deities or Sikh Gurus predominate in the house; but all worshipped (according to caste) in either Valmiki or Ravidasi places of worship. In each of these Coventry temples the Guru Granth Sahib is also installed, although in the Valmiki temple the *Ramayana* is equally venerated. As these examples indicate, any imagined boundary between 'Hinduism' and 'Sikhism' becomes utterly challenged. The clear-cut boundaries of what constitutes 'Sikhism', generally presented from the perspective of 'normative' Khalsa identity, simply do not suffice when the actual diversity of ethnic, cultural, and religious practices is more closely examined.

CONTEXTUALIZING 'SIKH WOMEN': ISSUES OF IDENTITY

If the construct of what constitutes 'Sikhism' is problematic, theorists have increasingly pointed to terms such as 'gender' and 'woman' as also highly mediated and unstable constructs. These terms, according to Judith Butler, are troublesome 'because both...gain their troubled significations only as relational terms...' (Butler 1999: xxix). She continues by asking whether being 'female' is a 'natural fact or a cultural performance' (ibid.: xxviii–xxix), largely on the basis of Simone de Beauvoir's groundbreaking insistence that women 'become'; they are not 'born' (de Beauvoir 1973: 301).[3] By its very nature then, if 'woman' is a process of 'becoming', and thus an ongoing, discursive practice that is 'open to intervention and resignification' (Butler 1999: 43), we must ask ourselves, to what extent is this question applicable to another classification, that of 'Sikh woman'?

This question is beautifully elucidated in a retelling of a classroom dialogue event that took place in a recent course on Sikhism taught by Jakobsh. She posed the following question to her students, the majority of whom were Sikhs (the question was addressed to both males and females): 'What *one* word would you say best defines or characterizes what you think about when you envision the concept of "Sikh women"?' The answer was most fascinating. After some discussion the overwhelming majority pointed to the Punjabi/Sikh notion of 'honour' or '*izzat*' as the one word that best characterized 'being' Sikh and female. Izzat is a 'multivocalic term defying simple translation…it is central to a whole complex of emotionally charged values including honor, respect, reputation, shame, prestige, and status…[Central to izzat is] power, reciprocity, *protection of one's social domain*' (editor's italics) (Dusenbery 1990: 242–3). Needless to say, this is not a novel phenomenon. As Dhavan in this volume shows, family honour as it has historically been symbolized within two repositories—women and the turban worn by Sikh males—and has long defined social reality for Sikhs, both for women and men. It is thus perhaps not surprising that it is to this arena of 'social domain' that the young women in the class related most closely. What is most interesting is just how central to, and consistent with, their negotiated identities izzat is, despite the complexity of its very definition. Izzat, *not* Sikh scriptural references, *not* Sikh ritual acts, *not* the Punjabi language, *not* an extensive litany of rules and regulations, *not* 'the homeland' or one's *pind* [village] (though this too, without doubt, is intimately tied to notions of honour) is at the forefront of *being* a female Sikh for some first, second, and third generation Canadian Sikhs! Needless to say, the Sikh male students, while agreeing that honour was indeed central for their female counterparts, quickly noted that this was not the central concept defining their own understanding of Sikh 'maleness'. Notwithstanding the small sample size of this informal survey, highly artificially chosen, the response of these young women in terms of community norms and expectations is significant (see also McLeod 1997: 245–9). Veena Das' important essay 'Masks and faces: an essay on Punjabi kinship' first published over thirty years ago, is still remarkably relevant today in terms of its ability to capture current Punjabi kinship and marriage patterns and expectations of women within kinship networks. Her work too supports the claims of these students. According to Das, women—particularly daughters—are the *repositories* of honour; 'dishonourable conduct on the part of the daughter can ruin the honour of the family forever, leaving parents 'unfit to show their face' to the *biradari* [kinship group]. It is often said that it is the duty of the father to kill an errant daughter rather than allow her to smear the good name of the family' (Das 1976: 15). While the killing of unmanageable daughters is obviously not carried out by the majority of parents / fathers, Das' words do point to the supreme position that izzat holds within the Punjabi milieu.[4] Certainly the centrality of izzat among Sikhs is not confined to Canada or Punjab; Satwant Kaur Rait's recent study of Sikh women in the UK also addresses the fundamental role played by this notion of 'honour' in contemporary British society (Rait 2005: 53).

Theorists have pointed to the need to locate specific 'moments' or, to use Oberoi's phrase 'ruptures, rapprochements and transitions' (Oberoi 1996: 35) and specific 'structures' within history or culture that are particularly significant in the congealing process or the 'becoming' for female identity formation. Jakobsh in *Relocating Gender in Sikh History: Transformation, Meaning and Identity* (2003), identifies several time frames within Sikh history that have served as specific 'moments' of gender construction. The Singh Sabha reform movement stands out in this regard, given that these reformers set the ground rules as well as the agenda for prevailing notions of gender in the early twentieth century.

In many ways the Singh Sabha movement at large can be understood as a Sikh Renaissance; the movement is unparalleled in terms of the intellectual activity that took place (Barrier 1975: 219–52). Within the context of the debates taking place, similar to those within other reform movements within the colonial milieu—Hindu, Sikh, and Muslim—women became *sites* on which larger political, even communal, claims were made (Uberoi 1996; Forbes 1996). The success of the newly educated Sikh elite owed an immeasurable debt to the power of the printed word and access to the print culture introduced by American Presbyterian missionaries in Punjab in 1836. A major focus of the reform movement was to decentralize and de-legitimize the traditional bearers of Sikh authority, namely guru lineages, saints or holy men, caretakers of Sikh shrines, *Gianis* and *Bhais*—bearers of Sikh culture in that they ran Sikh educational institutions (Oberoi 1994: 108–38).What separated the 'new' and the 'old' bearers of tradition was the British educational advantage of the latter, and their level of expertise, and thus control over print culture so effectively taught to them by their Christian missionary teachers. '[B]y gaining proficiency in the mechanics of print culture, members of the new elites—lawyers, teachers, journalists, the rural gentry—appropriated both the channels of communication and, more importantly, the signifiers these generated'. Having the power associated with control of print culture allowed for important inroads into the production of the specificities of Sikh identity that these new elites were in the process of constructing (Sayers 2003: 19).

VIRTUAL IDENTITY CONSTRUCTION

Jakobsh has recently identified the internet as an important arena of study vis-à-vis Sikh identity and gender construction. She posits that the World Wide Web must be understood as a specific and significant (albeit virtual) *site* of contemporary Sikh gender construction (Jakobsh 2004, 2006; see also Kapur and Misra's essay in this volume). This has become increasingly the case within the American milieu since 9/11 when many Sikhs were mistakenly identified as turban-wearing Muslims. One of the first victims of the anti-Muslim backlash in the USA was a Sikh, Balbir Singh Sodhi, who was shot to death at his gas station in Mesa, Arizona. His crime? Wearing a turban that mis-identified him as a sympathizer with Osama Bin Laden. One of the outcomes of this tragic event has been a proliferation of organizations, largely based online, that serve as virtual databases on all matters 'Sikh'—history, religion, culture.

Others serve as human rights centres, 'watchdogs' per se which keep track of abuses facing Sikhs within the USA in particular, but also in Europe and Asia. According to I.J. Singh, a Sikh observer, the

most attractive silver lining to emerge from the crisis of 9/11 has been the fantastic initiatives of young Sikhs who are growing up in the diaspora...

They are products of this culture and understand how to pull its levers of power and tweak the system. I am pointing primarily to the role of the Sikh Coalition, the Sikh Mediawatch and Resource Task Force (SMART) and a host of similar smaller groups (I.J. Singh 2003: 211).

Many of these sites are the creations of Sikh technocrats, namely Sikhs who are skilled in the technological wherewithal to create, manage, and update highly sophisticated, user-friendly websites. In essence then, largely on the basis of their technological skills, these individuals have become 'new authorities', similar in many ways to their Singh Sabha counterparts, of Sikhism as it is presented online. As Jakobsh has noted elsewhere, the question arises, to what extent are these 'new authorities' on Sikhism actually *constructing* Sikh identity online (Jakobsh 2004: 127–42)? Complex questions of Sikh identities quickly come to the fore, namely, *which* Sikh identity is being presented as normative?

The question of privileging specific identities has been addressed within another context by Marcia Hermansen, namely, that of Islam in America. She notes that

increasingly, in recent years I have seen…quite a number of Muslim youth in America are becoming increasingly rigidly conservative and condemnatory of their peers (Muslim and non-Muslim), their parents, and all who are not within a narrow ideological band of what I will define as internationalist, 'identity' Islam…they are moving in a direction that negates interpretation and diversity altogether and…privileges certain external markers of identity… (Hermansen 2003: 306).

Further, she identifies 'the genie of identity Islam' as one way of asserting a 'true' Muslim identity through rigid understandings of gender difference (ibid.: 315, 318). This notion of 'identity Islam' within the context of understanding it as an active process of eliminating diverse identities within the larger rubric of Islam, is perhaps useful in addressing similar directions within the Sikh tradition, namely, what could be labelled as 'identity Sikhism'. If one conducts an image search on the World Wide Web on 'Sikh women' the results are rather astonishing. Many, if not most, images are of Sikh women wearing turbans. On one particular site, the question is asked:

Q: What is the appropriate head covering for Sikh women? Are there particular colors and designs accepted by Sikhism?

A: *The most common head covering for Sikh women is the round turban and a chunni (headscarf)*...Some Sikh women wear both, while some wear either turban or chunni...The main purpose of the head covering is to cover the head. The choice of colors is totally up to the individual [italics the editor] (Real Sikhism).

This citation is remarkable in its very definitiveness and in its erroneousness. For the 'most common head covering for Sikh women' is *not* the turban; women wearing turbans (a male-Sikh signifier) are a tiny minority within the Sikh populace.

This focus is highly reminiscent of the Singh Sabha movement's attempts in the nineteenth century to conclusively carve out 'Sikh' ritual space and distinct Sikh identity markers for their womenfolk, with a view to separate Sikh women unambiguously from their Hindu and Muslim counterparts. As Jakobsh has noted, though initially focusing on the construction of the 'hyper-masculine' male, reformers eventually turned to Sikh female identity within their reform initiatives. Their attempts to reformulate Sikh female identity included a novel focus on a ritualized naming process, and, the creation of novel ritual space for women, including full initiation into what had been an overwhelmingly male prerogative, the Khalsa order (Jakobsh 2003, especially 'Redefining the Ritual Drama').

The tradition of a minute number of women wearing turbans also has its genesis during this era. A marginal voice, eventually banished from the Sikh Panth as too radical by the Tat Khalsa, was Teja Singh Bhasaur, the leader of the Panch Khalsa Diwan. Teja Singh Bhasaur advocated, in the name of the strict egalitarianism espoused by his organization, that *both* women and men were required to wear uncut hair and turbans. Those women who did not agree to wear the traditional male headgear were simply refused initiation (Jakobsh 2003: 213–14; Barrier 1970: xvi–xxvii). The Panch Khalsa Diwan soon thereafter disintegrated but, clearly, at least Bhasaur's radical mandate, requiring initiated women to don turbans, is being newly espoused within the contemporary milieu.

In terms of the correlation between the Singh Sabha authorities and the 'new authorities' of the twenty-first century, both were and are making every effort to go beyond the active construction of the male gender to also include that of the female. One must question 'the legacy of this use of images as a means of controlling populations today' (Sturken and Cartwright 2000: 22)? For, as noted earlier, what is poignant about this process of identity construction is the fact that turbaned Sikh women are unequivocally *not* representative of Sikh female identity; in India, as well as in the diaspora, by far the majority of Sikh females who are *amritdhari* (that is, who have been initiated into the Khalsa order) instead cover their hair with the traditional Indian chunni or scarf. Non-orthodox[5] (in the sense of non-amritdhari) Sikh women generally do not cover their hair except within the bounds of gurdwaras, or, wherever the Guru Granth Sahib, Sikh sacred scripture, is enshrined. However, if one were to judge Sikh women's identity markers from a number of websites created by western Sikhs, it would appear that the turban for women is in fact normative.[6] Similarly, as to how Minoo Moallem has posited the veil within contemporary Islam as 'metaphor', the turban, within 'identity Sikhism' signifies 'as a system of symbolic and material marking' (Moallem 1999: 133–4). The turban, similar to the veil for Muslims, distinguishes Sikhs from non-Sikhs, the 'devoted' from the not-so-devoted (Mahmood and Brady 2000: 47).[7]

According to Brian Axel's study of the Sikh separatist organization known as the Khalistan movement and its use of corporeal images online, it is in the archiving of these images through the internet that a particularized Khalistani Sikh subject is created. Similarly here, within the process of identity construction taking place, through the repeated 'visuality and iconicity' of the specific image, a 'globalized domain of images', or 'transnational domain of visual images', which Axel labels the 'diasporic imaginary', is created (Axel 2004: 35).

Thus, even though only a minority of Sikhs worldwide are amritdhari, and indeed only a minority of Sikhs in the Diaspora are even *kesdhari* (keeping their hair uncut, though not initiated), and even though within the amritdhari minority only very small numbers of Sikh women wear turbans, it is these particularized identity markers that have the potential, through persistent and repetitive usage on the internet, to become the primary identity markers of 'what it means to be Sikh'. These carefully constructed images are not *only* available within the online context, yet clearly, the boundlessness of the internet is an accelerated catalyst in the active construction of Sikh identity taking place. In the process, the image of the turbaned Sikh woman, for instance, despite the fact that it incontrovertibly does not mirror the realities of Sikh women worldwide, is cast instead as normative. The image below, entitled 'Wake Up Call For Sikhs' is an excellent case in point.[8]

Fig. 1 'Wake Up Call For Sikhs'
Source: http://www.mkhalsa.com/art/imageg/singhneelossofrehat.gif

The artist, Manoj Singh Khalsa, notes: 'Before Sikhi, most were some type of [H]indu, then they discovered the wonders of Sikhi. But somewhere down the line, someone forgot to pass it on and I guess they ended up right where they started'. What is fascinating about this image is the call to legitimacy through a 'self-styled' historical lens, alongside the sense of 'urgency' within the text accompanying the image. The 'great grandmother' being held up as normatively turbaned would have been virtually non-existent one hundred years earlier; moreover the 'break in rehat', vis-à-vis the turban, has simply never existed.

Roland Barthes' notion of the term *myth* in referring to the value systems and beliefs inherent in advertisements and images is useful in this regard. For Barthes, 'myth is the hidden set of rules and conventions through which meanings, which are in reality specific to certain groups, are made to seem universal and given for a whole society' (Sturken and Cartwright 2000: 19–20). Barthes argues that a French advertisement for Italian pasta and sauce is as much about the 'myth' about Italian culture as it is about the product itself, and he gives the name of 'Italianicity' to the concept that is constructed through the image and the text (Barthes 1977: 34). In essence then, what is innocuously presented as normative becomes mythologized because it is 'historically and culturally specific, not "natural"'. Sturken and Cartwright continue that

to explore the meaning of images is to recognize that they are produced within dynamics of social power and ideology...Images are an important means through which ideologies are produced and onto which ideologies are projected...The most important aspect of ideologies is that they appear to be natural or given, rather than part of a system of belief that a culture produces in order to function in a particular way (Sturken and Cartwright 2000: 19–22).

This concept is, I believe, helpful in coming to an understanding of the process of Sikh identity construction taking place online, both for male and female Sikhs. Images of the amritdhari body, 'Khalsa-isms' per se, complete with external insignia such as uncut hair and turban, have become mythologized, not because they are representative of Sikh identity at large but because they constructed in such a way, over and over again, as to *seem* universal and representative. Axel's understanding of the 'transnational domain of visual images' on-line that are part and parcel of 'a diasporic imaginary' echoes the process of myth making as envisioned by Barthes (Axel 2004: 35–6). And, clearly, there are ramifications of Sikh identity construction emanating from a diasporic Sikh consciousness as opposed to those from within the Sikh structures of authority in India. Power dynamics associated with Sikh identity construction are changing; diasporic 'imaginings', repetitive narratives outlining 'true' Sikh identity, are taking hold largely due to the internet. And, the key players in Sikh internet sites are western Sikhs, both converts to Sikhism known as 3HO Sikhs or Sikh Dharma of the Western Hemisphere, and, Indian Sikhs who have made their home for up to three or four generations in diasporic homelands. Most are based in North America or the UK.

Certainly this is not unique to the Sikh diasporic experience. As Radhika Gajjala's important work on South Asian feminist ethnography and the internet has shown, 'narratives are often appropriated and reappropriated in various ways within the hegemonic frameworks that favor "Western" structures of thought and cultures' (Gajjala 2004: 39). In the case at hand, western structures include those that are grounded in the available technologies; in the nineteenth century, these hegemonic frameworks were built upon the educational advantages offered by the British and the subsequent and wholehearted consumption of print culture. In the twenty-first century, effective exploitation of digital media and the boundlessness of the internet have enabled the formation of new loci of authority, largely western-based. These new authorities are aptly taking up the challenge of representing, constructing and furthering their own visions of Sikh identity.

Representing 'Sikh Women'

Jhutti-Johal, in this volume, addresses the problematic issue of the representation of Sikhs. Jhutti-Johal, citing Lee, notes that 'more recently, minority communities, at least, have increasingly come to feel threatened by the attention of outside researchers' (Lee 1993: 140). And without question, the homogenization of women's experience across borders, across race, ethnicity, class and caste, and religion is indeed fraught with difficulties. Theorists have pointed to the contemporary feminist identity crisis as largely tied to a process of deconstructing the category of 'woman' by acknowledging and critiquing the white western woman's complicity in the formation of an ethnocentric and imperialist order. The question is, ultimately, whether western women's agendas are 'irredeemably beset by ethnocentrism' (Jeffery 2001: 473) thus precluding western women from studying and commenting on the realities of their non-western counterparts. Kumari Jayawardena has focused on this very issue in noting that while every woman has the *right* to address 'women's oppression and exploitation everywhere' (Jayawardena 1995: 10–11), what is truly at the heart of the matter is an unquestioning 'universalism' that *only* takes gender into account in a critique of the injustice to which women are subjected. Recognition of the inherent plurality and diversity in cultures and within women's experiences must be at the forefront of any inquiry into women's realities across borders, race, economics, class, and religion. Suma Chitnis continues that each specific context—in this case, the South Asian context—must be taken into account in any discussion of women's identity issues:

Quite apart from this pragmatic consideration, the articulation of the distinctiveness of the Indian context is important, in as much as a recognition of differences of context of each country or culture, and a careful consideration of the implications of these differences, is necessary from the point of view of bringing greater depth to an understanding of the problems concerning gender discrimination (Chitnis 2004: 9).

The birth of nationalism, in this case, within the Indian context, including male reformers roles as *initiators* of the 'women's reform' efforts across India, as well as their impressive efforts in championing the cause of women must be understood as integral to historical and even contemporary studies of women in India. And certainly, this was the case within the Sikh reform movement in Punjab (Jakobsh 2003; Malhotra 2002).

But there is more at stake to the 'insider' and 'outsider' debate than simply 'having to *be* one to know one'. As Stuart Hall has demonstrated 'people's multiple sources of social identity crosscut and overlap one another in complex, shifting and contradictory ways. People cannot be neatly boxed in by one identity alone (Hall 1992: 273–325). Further, Paul Gilroy's important analysis of cultural politics in the Afro-Caribbean diaspora identifies 'rhetorical strategies' that are used to produce understandings of 'cultural insiderism' and distinctions between essentialist and hybrid cultural identities (Gilroy 1993: 83–4). In line with Gilroy's notion of strategizing identities, Parlo Singh, an Australian woman of Sikh origin has written of the difficulties of 'claiming' and 'negotiating' her own hybrid identity, requiring her to persistently negotiate what she is saying and how she is doing so (Singh 1994: 92–100). Maira's work (2002) on young South Asians in New York City has also commented on the ambiguity women represent in their 'sullying of the categories of authenticity and hybridity'. In this regard, Hall offers the somewhat helpful notion of 'new ethnicities' based on a reconfigured understanding of difference as 'positional, conditional and conjunctional' (Hall 1996: 443–7), while Caroline Wright has alternately called for a 'multi-dimensional conception of standpoint'. Race, ethnicity, class, age, gender,

sexuality, nationality, descent, language, politics—all make the
'difference' to what we 'know' (Wright 1997: 86). Wright, citing
Yuval-Davis, warns that essentialist notions of difference are
problematic because 'anyone who can claim to be a member
of the grouping can claim to represent it to outside agencies
and benefit from it, no matter how different she/he is in terms
of class, power, gender etc., from the majority of the people
claimed to be represented' (Wright 1997: 86; Yuval-Davis 1993:
6). The question then becomes 'how *much* of one does one have
to be to know one'?

A controversial issue has recently come to the fore that adds
practical import to this discussion and is addressed briefly by
Jhutti-Johal in this volume, and earlier by Jakobsh (2006), namely,
the 'women and *sewa* issue' that centres around the Harmandir
Sahib, also known as the Golden Temple in Amritsar. There, in
2003, two British, highly educated, highly devoted, amritdhari
'hybrid' Sikh women sought the right to take part in a specific
ritual activity known as the *sukhasan* procession, during which
the Guru Granth Sahib is laid to rest for the night within the
shrine. But they were denied access to these and other activities,
because they were women and because 'tradition' denied them
the right to take part in the procession. They however took
public issue with what they considered to be an overt and highly
discriminatory refusal of their rights as Sikh women. Petitions,
both on and offline were signed,[9] (largely initiated by western
Sikhs), conferences were organized, and heated discussions took
place, particularly based on the world wide web. As Jakobsh has
noted, the issues raised by the 'sewa' controversy point to an
apparent divide between Sikh women of the diaspora and Sikh
women in Punjab. 'These questions are largely raised by women
in the West and have been given impetus by western Sikhs...This
in and of itself adds considerable complexity to what appears to
be an issue of human and women's right for those advocates for
religious reforms in the diaspora.' It would appear that the fact
that millions of Sikh women in Punjab and India at large have
not raised their voices in protest in this regard is significant.

But the issue is now being raised as unjust by a handful of Sikh women in
the West... One must wonder whether the issue of cultural hegemony raised
earlier is perhaps also applicable in this situation? Certainly the influences
of the 'West' are often maligned, particularly by Diaspora Sikhs attempting

to uphold Punjabi Sikh values, practices and customs in the raising of their children. Yet it would appear that it is precisely western values of equality, feminism and post-modern responses to authority, here combined with a distinctly minority-based interpretation of Sikh egalitarianism, that are driving the momentum in birthing a new resistance movement and ethos within Sikhism; at least, Sikhism in the diaspora. (Jakobsh 2006: 191–2)

The ambiguities surrounding the issue of representation, or 'who speaks for Sikh women', and mistrust of women associated with 'the West', despite the fact that the women calling for changes were firmly ensconced *within* the Sikh tradition, is also brought to the fore by one of Jhutti-Johal's interviewees in this volume:

Our practices in the past have never caused us any trouble or problems. Why is it that all of a sudden they seem so wrong? Our religious activities and our participation have worked nicely to date. Why change a system that has worked so well? The young women are trying to be modern and copy women in the West but they don't realize that our system and values work for us and that by demanding these changes they are causing problems for themselves but also the women who accept the traditions and practices (Jhutti-Johal *this volume*).

Moreover, as Patricia Jeffery has pointed out, this dilemma extends far beyond a simple critique of 'western feminism' or 'western privilege', but extends to Indian scholars as well, who are themselves in a highly complex situation, needing to confront their own position of privilege within India. They too are in a situation in which they must 'combine respect for the local with a belief in the universal standards of women's rights. Is it possible to draw selectively on western feminist agendas without mimicking the inappropriate' (Jeffery 2001: 474)?

For the most part, the study of women in Sikhism (which, in and of itself, is minimal) has ignored the contributions of critical feminist approaches to the study of women in religion. As Jakobsh has noted elsewhere, writings focusing on women in Sikhism have been firmly embedded within the realm of apologetics (Jakobsh 2003). The 'Golden Age' of Sikh women during the Guru period is iterated and reiterated; scriptural passages highlighting women's equal access to liberation, along with injunctions against women's impurity, are consistently upheld. When the issue of inequality is raised, the raison d'être for those inequalities is quickly deflected to the religious milieu surrounding Sikhism. Upinder Jit Kaur notes that the 'deviances'

found between the Sikh ideal and lived reality have everything
to do with the detrimental influence of Hinduism. 'The right
of Sikh woman to equality with man was foreclosed by the
Hindu society...She is still a lesser person...though her lot is
comparatively better than that of women belonging to other
major Indian religions' (Kaur 1990: 314–15). Nikky Singh has
also pointed to 'the overwhelming Hindu and Islamic presence
[which] has over the centuries reinforced and even today
continues to reinforce the patriarchal values which are difficult
to break' (Singh 1993: 51).

These examples serve to show a common means of confronting
inequalities between men and women in Sikhism, namely, the
tradition's decline into patriarchal norms has everything to do
with the influence of the 'other'. Another approach has been to
show the Sikh tradition as *unique* in the history of religions vis-
à-vis its position of women. According to 'Gateway to Sikhism',
a popular Sikh internet site:

A Sikh woman has equal rights to a Sikh man. Unlike Christianity, no
post in Sikhism is reserved solely for men. Unlike Islam, a woman is not
considered subordinate to a man. Sikh baptism (Amrit ceremony) is open
to both sexes. The Khalsa nation is made up equally of men and women. A
Sikh woman has the right to become a Granthi, Ragi, one of the Panj Pyare
(5 beloved)... Christian women must change their names after marriage.
The concept of maiden and married names is alien to Sikh philosophy
('Sikhism & Women, 2007').

While the article makes clear its intent to present the position
of women in Sikhism as superior to other traditions, in this
case, Christianity and Islam, another important and equally
common approach becomes evident (see also Mahmood and
Brady 2000: 43). The article notes unequivocally that women
have the *right* to become *granthi*s (gurdwara caretakers), *ragi*s
(musicians), and *panj piare* ('beloved five'),[10] but it certainly
says nothing about the fact that women rarely, if ever, become
granthis or panj piare. Moreover, in many gurdwaras a married
Sikh female is not allowed to partake in the *amrit* (initiation)
ceremony unless she is accompanied by her husband. Further,
while women are encouraged to cook, clean, and wash dishes
for the Sikh communal meal (*langar*), they are not permitted
to enter the *sanctum sanctorum* of the temple, a special room,
known as the *Sach Khand*, where the Guru Granth is placed

(Kaur 2007). While the occasional woman may indeed break cultural barriers and become one of the 'beloved five' in local gurdwaras, she will generally do so only in the company of an all woman *panj piarian*.[11] Perhaps, on a more significant plane, at the most sacred of Sikh shrines, the Harimandir Sahib, otherwise known as the Golden Temple, women are not included when *prasad* (sanctified food) is distributed to the panj piare, the first five individuals who are given prasad before it is distributed to the remaining participants (ibid.).

By and large, writings that have accentuated the egalitarian ethos of Sikhism have done so on the basis of selected hymns within the sacred scripture of the Sikhs that reflect, particularly Guru Nanak's, insistence that *all* can attain direct liberation, men or women. This then is upheld as 'proof' that Sikhism, uniquely so, is fully egalitarian with regard to gender. Nonetheless, while Guru Nanak's soteriological teachings *are* doubtlessly 'egalitarian', Oberoi posits that the early Sikh movement

had shown little enthusiasm for distinguishing its constituents from members of other religious traditions and establishing a pan-Indian community. Sikh notions of time, space, corporeality, holiness, mythology, kinship, societal distinctions, purity and pollution, gender, sexuality and commensality were firmly rooted in Indic cultural [and one could add, religious] thinking (Oberoi 1996: 36).

And it is here that the ideology of Sikh egalitarianism, based on selected scriptural references, and relatively recent historical critical writings of scholars of Sikhism begin to clash. For 'its supporters, an ideology represents the proper, and even the natural, arrangement of society' (Lorenzen 1996: 3). For some, the raison d'être of this 'clash' is western analytical models and the scholarly traditions emanating from them. Critics of these so-called 'western' models insist that to come to an understanding of Sikhism, 'Sikh realities from a subjective faith point of view of the Khalsa values and ideals' must form the basis of study (Sodhi 1995: 342). Gurdarshan Singh Dhillon adds that that the 'proper' study of Sikhism is 'beyond the domain of Sociology, Anthropology and History' (Dhillon 1994: 4). Sikhism, then, can only be understood from a scriptural basis, and, according to this line of thinking, as '*sui generis*, standing above and beyond the limitations of historical and cultural contingencies...' and as having a 'transhistorical essence' (Tite 2004: 341). It thus follows that because scripture, the Adi Granth, contains, as it is often posited, an explicit (though this is arguable) posture of egalitarianism, then the case is clear: *Sikhism is at its core egalitarian vis-à-vis the role and status of women and men*. And it is this supposed 'core' that has been utilized to buttress any critique of practices or attitudes that are *anti*-egalitarian, including anti-woman tendencies within Sikh religious institutions, Sikh rituals, Sikh history, and Sikh cultural and religious practices in general; in other words, any discriminatory, misogynistic practices or attitudes are by their very nature 'outside' of Sikhism.

Butler's warning about that which 'travels under the sign of "clarity"' is highly relevant in this regard. She questions what the price would be of 'failing to deploy a certain critical suspicion when the arrival of lucidity is announced' (Butler 1999: xix). For in the clear privileging of 'text' over 'practice', an understanding of religion as dynamic, not static is discounted, alongside a core feature of religion as 'communitas', as living, fluid, transformative organism. To return to a point made early on: religion is neither an innocent nor a neutral entity. But religion *can* be, though highly problematically, 'detached from the specific historical contexts, social frameworks, political struggles, and institutional constraints that have produced it' (Castelli 2001: 6). In other words, it is often understood as separable from other aspects of social life.

REPRESENTING DIVERSITY

Constance Elsberg's essay in this volume on 3HO Sikhs addresses specific gender issues relating to converts to Sikhism, whose historical contexts and social frameworks are radically divergent from ethnic Punjabi Sikh women. Similarly, Nesbitt's studies of UK Sikh communities, particularly those that stand on the 'margins' due to caste or adherence to specific religious leaders, also offer important insight into how and why 'difference' may be constructed vis-à-vis gender. With regard to the sant phenomenon, among the *sangat* (congregation) at the Ajit Darbar, a 'sant gurdwara' in a line continuous from the eighteenth-century exorcist, Vadbhag Singh (see McLeod 1991: 132) women are not allowed close to the *nishan sahib* (the Khalsa flag that flies above a Sikh gurdwara) during its annual cleansing and adorning at Vaisakhi, because of the pollution attributed to menstruation. Meanwhile, in Nanaksar gurdwaras, in which one or other of the competing successors to Baba Nand Singh of Kaleran is honoured, the *bahingam*s, entourage of the baba, must be male and celibate (Nesbitt 1985: 1997).

As regards the correlation between caste and gender, in Nesbitt's early studies focusing on Bhatra gurdwaras in Nottingham, married women observed complete *gungat* that is, they covered both head and face with the *chunni* (scarf). This was because, as married women, they were required (like wives in parts of rural north India today) to keep their faces hidden in the presence of their male in-laws. Moreover, girls were expected to leave school at the age of sixteen, if not earlier, to marry soon after and not to go out to work. (Serving in a home-based off-license facility, viewed as an extension of domestic space, was however, allowed), (Nesbitt 1980, 1981). By contrast, at the same time, women in the other local Sikh communities—the Jats and Ramgarhias—were being encouraged to further their education and to secure outside employment. Marriage-related customs too, and the weight of gold jewellery which many wore, likewise differentiated the Bhatras from the other local Sikhs. However, during the three decades since the study of Nottingham Bhatras, Nesbitt's Bhatra informants from elsewhere in the UK have indicated some changes with regard to expectations of women. Moreover, the rate of change has differed from one city to another. (Nesbitt's informants note that in some cities the adverse gossip if, for example, a woman goes out to work, is reportedly greater than in another.)

In addition to recognizing diversities of time and place, an analytical approach to caste-related divergence in UK Sikh women's experience also requires us to take into account factors which include the different migration histories of the zat-biradaris concerned, as well as the way in which concepts of izzat, of being a good and honourable Sikh, and of relative caste status, interact. The fact that Bhatras have lived in Britain longer than any other Sikh community may have a bearing on the maintenance of tradition. (Bhatra men arrived between World Wars I and II, whereas the Jats' substantial migration commenced in the 1950s and the pioneers of Ramgarhia settlement arrived mainly in the 1960s and 1970s.) Arguably (although we know of no research on this) certain customs and assumptions had been held in these other communities but had weakened before their migration to the UK. It can also be argued that although both Ramgarhias and Bhatras were subject to being viewed as lower caste by the numerically and (in Punjab) economically dominant Jat community, their coping strategies were different. Residence in the countries of East Africa had already given the Ramgarhias a sense of relative security or superiority in relation to the Jats, whereas Bhatras' main response may have been to assert their commitment to Indic tradition and, symbolically and centrally, the modesty and compliance of their women.

STUDYING WOMEN IN SIKHISM

The question then remains, to what extent can we speak of 'Sikh women'? How can one study, learn about, understand 'Sikh women'? First and foremost, since there is no 'seamless category of woman' (Butler 1999: xxix, 7), there can be no seamless category of 'Sikh womanhood'. The possibilities for further collaboration are endless. They could include a study of texts and scripture, but, one hopes, would move beyond the privileging of text to focus on women's ritual and symbolic lives also; women's health and sexual identities; occupational patterns and traditions; marriage and kinship groups; village connections and urban and rural differences shaping Punjabi Sikh society. They could also focus on Sikh women as artisans and artists, musicians and actors. Moreover, given the long-standing tradition of Sikh migration from Punjab and other parts of India, one could expect an examination of transnational and migration patterns as they pertain to women. Studies could, and should, aim at enlarging Sikh women's space and their role as agents of change while at the same time recognizing and identifying Sikh women as victims of patriarchal norms, and sexual and domestic violence.

This field of study is new and scholarship on Sikh women is in its infancy. Some crucial exploratory forays have been made, and have been gathered together in this volume. When the editor initiated discussions with scholars about a potential volume on 'Sikh women', the immediate and most pressing issue was that of simply locating and identifying those scholars who have worked in some manner within this realm. Given that scholarly attention to Sikhism in general has been scant, particularly within North America where Jakobsh is situated, it was not an easy task! But as the discussions continued, and more connections within North America, the UK, and India were made, (largely via the internet) a groundswell of interest in the project also grew. This volume is the result of those discussions and connections. The contributors span the globe, and come from a remarkably wide spectrum of academic disciplines. They were invited to draw from these diverse disciplines and areas of expertise to enable a rich, textured, and layered 'weaving' of perspectives on Sikh women. This multi-disciplinarity is one of the ways in which this volume is unique. The essays included draw attention to the diverse backgrounds and socio-religious contexts from which each contributor writes. This question of voice is important in developing an understanding of the experience of women who are Sikh and of the literary and social representation of woman in Sikh society. Of the fifteen contributors (all but one female) nine are of South Asian background. The writers of this introduction, both of northern European background, currently live and work in Canada and the UK. These multiple perspectives, within a paradigm of western scholarship, are perhaps the greatest strength of this highly varied collection. The multiplicity of disciplines included is also, arguably, an inherent weakness of the volume, making a 'thematic flow' difficult, to say the least. How does one contain such a plethora of diverse perspectives *and* disciplinary methodologies within an adequate *and* manageable thematic?

In an attempt to navigate this complex issue, the volume is roughly divided into three sections, namely, textual studies, Sikh women in India, and Sikh women in diasporic contexts. Unavoidably, the categorizations often overlap; some of the essays refuse to 'fit neatly' within one or other of the somewhat arbitrarily imposed boundaries. Nikky Singh's piece is an excellent case in point. While she herself is very much a western Sikh feminist writer, and her 'call' to change is directed largely toward a western audience, the dominant focus of her essay is on her own experiences upon the death of her mother in Punjab, India. In a sense, her essay merges elements of all three of the thematic categories outlined above—scriptural and historical reflections, alongside both diasporic and homeland narratives. Similarly, chapters focusing on Sikh women in Indian and diasporic contexts are largely ethnographic studies, but some of the contributions are also tied in some way to historical and textual analysis. In a volume as diverse as this one, finding an adequate 'fit' within any one section has been an exigent process!

THE CONTRIBUTIONS

Sikhism, Women, and Textual Studies

By focusing on gender in her discussion of the Dasam Granth (the eighteenth-century volume second only to the Adi Granth as a Sikh religious text), Robin Rinehart places at centrestage the issues at the heart of persistent controversy about the volume's authorship. As Rinehart explains, it is the prominence of the goddess Durga (and other Hindu deities), together with the *Charitropakhian*, the multitude of stories of relationships involving deceitful women, that fuel speculation that these sections at least could not be the work of the putative author, Guru Gobind Singh. After outlining the Guru's life, Rinehart maps the content of the Dasam Granth, including the *Charitropakhian*, and notes why recent translators have omitted these stories. She approvingly summarizes Nikky Singh's innovatively feminist interpretation of the tenth Guru's affirmation of female power through his selection as metaphor (if not as deity) of Durga, the goddess most powerful in both creation and destruction. For Rinehart, however, Singh's interpretation needs to be balanced by critical attention to the *Charitropakhian*, intended as they apparently were as cautionary tales for men, and to the male commentary on these, since these assume women to be ensnaring temptresses.

For Purnima Dhavan, the challenge to the will of a Sikh chief's widow, Rani Bagberi, in 1810, provides a springboard for an investigation of the attitudes and behaviour of Sikh chiefs in the eighteenth century. Dhavan argues that, despite the egalitarian emphasis discernible in the creation of the Khalsa, in fact 'the eighteenth century Khalsa chiefs were no more egalitarian than the other new warrior groups of the period.' Dhavan discusses the masculine norms exemplified within eighteenth-century texts, such as *rahitnama*s (Codes of Conduct). The code of masculine honour (izzat), which was at potential risk from women, grew stronger and the proportion of Sikhs from the Jat caste also grew. As Dhavan observes, 'notions of caste and honor were tightly woven together' and the honour of a Sikh ruler 'was particularly symbolized by the protection and exchange of two repositories of his family's honour—women, and the turbans worn by its men'.

Anshu Malhotra's discussion of female infanticide during the colonial period is emotively linked to the continuing destruction of unborn girls in the twenty-first century. Her opening reference to her paternal grandmother's survival binds the centuries together, whilst her detailed analysis refuses to be content with general or easy explanations. The British administrators' and legislators' interventions are revealed as playing contradictory roles—by banning without enforcing implementation of the ban and by classification which could (in the case of the dowry expenses sanctioned by law in 1870) sharpen the very competition between families that was conducive to reducing the number of daughters. In interpreting the story of Guru Nanak's grandson, Dharam Chand, authorizing the Bedis to kill their daughters, Malhotra deftly identifies the interplay of complex social dynamics.

Bhai Vir Singh, 1872–1957, was the most prominent of the intellectuals in the reformist Singh Sabha movement and it is his notions of Sikh identity, community, and nation in three of his novels that provide Christine Fair's focus. The central characters of these Punjabi historical novels, all set in the eighteenth century, are 'extraordinary women who cook, clean, nurse, kill and die for their faith and the Panth'. This chapter's interest lies not only in its examination of the historical context and narrative roles of Sundri, Sheel Kaur, and Satwant Kaur respectively, but also in the juxtaposition of the 'second life' of these novels, in translation in the US during the 1980s, a period in which Sikhs, not least in the diaspora, were ideologically afire with the idea of a 'Sikh nation' and when their children's links with Punjab were weakening. On the grounds that the novels' first readers were almost certainly men, Fair questions Nikky Singh's interpretation of Sundri as a novel 'written for women to

provide a "role model for defiance"'. More fundamentally, Fair
discloses Singh's reading of Sundri as a 'paradigm of Sikh ethics'
as simplistic since her 'heroism is manifest at the expense of the
very women she is *supposedly* [Fair's italics] inspiring'. Instead,
Fair contends, Bhai Vir Singh's 'use of a female protagonist is
intended to chastise and question the masculinity of Sikh men',
whilst also advocating 'social reform with respect to women'.
As well as defining Hindu, Muslim, and Sikh communities the
novels, Fair argues, also help to define Punjab for young Sikhs
in diaspora.

Sikh Women in India

Woman as cultural producer, rather than as cultural product, is
the focus of Michelle Maskiell's essay, as she traces the history of
designing, embroidering, and uses of *phulkari* (literally 'flower-
work') textiles stitched and worn by Punjabi women. Maskiell
charts the transition of phulkari, an artifact shared in the
nineteenth century by Sikh, Muslim, and Hindu women, from
the skilfully crafted trousseau items to the subject of nostalgic
colonial and urban Punjabi writers on Punjab's rural folklore.
She charts the phulkari's 'morphing' in the twentieth century
from an outdated fabric that was no longer worn to, increasingly,
an item for display and an art form that is often interpreted as
an important element of *Sikh* heritage. The tendency for later
connoisseurs' interpretations to impose their own concerns on
the original embroiderers is suggested in Maskiell's discussion of
women's agency which concludes with reference to an exhibition
in New York City in 2006.

Lines from a song sung on the eve of a marriage open Nicola
Mooney's ethnographic study of gender disparity for Jat Sikh
women. While the song evokes the daughter's status as 'foreigner'
and the property of another in her parental home, this chapter's
title, 'Lowly Shoes on Lowly Feet', is a reminder of a formerly
commonplace idiom with which men refer to women. On the
basis of her fieldwork among Jat Sikh grandmothers, mothers,
and daughters-in-law, Mooney highlights the divergence between
expected social norms and the 'possibilities for gender equality
in Sikhism'. In disclosing the different perspectives of women of
different generations she takes account of the changes wrought

by increasing levels of education and urbanization. Central to her analysis (as in so many analyses of women's roles in South Asian communties) is the complex of marriage, izzat (honour and reputation) and *sharam* (modesty and propriety). In her conclusion Mooney notes that while women's lives have in some respects improved, the obligations of marriage and family life, and the very circumscribed opportunities for pursuing education and career look set to continue.

Research by Preeti Kapur and Girishwar Misra provides further confirmation of the continuing stereotyping and conditioning of gender roles, as revealed in matrimonial advertisements for brides and bridegrooms that appeared in two newspapers, the *Tribune* and *Ajit*. Kapur's and Misra's interviews with middle-class, urban Sikh women provided further data. The authors note the dominant images of men (in terms of appearance—whether as 'turbaned', 'clean-shaven', or one who 'trims his hair' or who is a 'non-trimmer' and of women (as fair-complexioned and 'homely') plus the importance of caste and family background. Education and professional training 'have added on another layer of identity approved by the community' but these in no way supersede the traditional expectations, although matrimonial sites on the internet suggest a more flexible match-making process than previously. The authors suggest a tension between actual changes to women's identities and the apparently unchanging requirements of their domestic role in the family.

Sikhism, understood as a complex and multilayered religion, has played a significant and often complicated role in the formation of identity, in social relations, and in the power structures of millions of women. While many academics have tended to present 'religion' in wholly negative terms, understanding religion to be principally responsible for the ideological and institutional restraints placed *upon* women, and religious affiliation or allegiances signifying 'false consciousness' (Castelli 2001: 5), religion also represents for many women, including the writers of this essay, a source of liberation, consciousness-raising, spiritual healing, and a deep commitment to a spiritual home or community. In the words of Rita Gross, one of the pioneering voices within the wider milieu of women in religions, 'misogyny is not the whole story of any religion' (Gross 1996: 74). This is perhaps best portrayed by Nikky-Guninder Kaur

Singh, arguably a pioneer of Sikh feminist thought, who, as a Sikh herself, explores what she considers both 'the feminist vision of Guru Nanak' as well as the discriminatory practices faced by Sikh women today, both in gurdwaras and, more widely, in Sikh society. Central to Singh's moving chapter 'Why Did I not Light the Fire?' is her experience of the funeral of her mother in Punjab. Implicit in the sub-title ('The refeminization of ritual in Sikhism'), and eloquently articulated in the text, is a contrast between that which is uplifting for women and that which undermines Sikh women's emancipation. Stirred to deep reflection on the implications of her own painful experience of exclusion from roles reserved for male relatives, Singh evokes instead what she calls a 'pattern of inclusivity' in Kartarpur, the settlement established by Guru Nanak. While gender egalitarian funeral rites during the time of the gurus cannot be historically established, she points to other 'excellent paradigms of women leading Sikh institutions' during these time periods. Invoking western feminist writers, the chapter is a clarion cry for Sikh women to be 'full members of the Sikh community', and to read and indeed translate the scriptures 'from our perspective'. She also calls for other Sikh rites of passage, notably marriage, which is so degradingly entangled with dowry and the devaluing of women, to be 'refeminized'. Singh includes a few hopeful pointers to potential change.

Sikh Women in Diasporic Contexts

Jagbir Jhutti-Johal conducted interviews among a small pool of Sikh women in the north and south of Britain and in villages in Punjab in order to discover their perceptions of their roles in gurdwaras. Her chapter reports a variety of views, differentiated to some extent by the age of the interviewees. A stronger dichotomy appears between the general acceptance by the women in Punjab of the dominant role of males in gurdwaras and the readiness among UK women to question this. But Jhutti-Johal notes in the UK sample too a general 'apathy on issues of gender inequality in gurdwaras' as compared to the women's concerns about marriage, career, and education.

The psychosocial pressures on Sikh women in Vancouver are explored by Kamala Nayar, whose analysis indicates that the tensions are complex, with women experiencing contradictory pulls between 'tradition' and 'modernity' exacerbated by the sudden relocation of many of these women from village Punjab into a modern metropolis. Moreover, as noted earlier, contra- diction between traditional Punjabi culture and the tenets of the Sikh religion, and confusion over the relationship between culture and spiritual teaching, compound the pressure. For this generation parents' 'double standard in relation to the treatment of brothers or male cousins' and the attraction of fitting into a western lifestyle contribute to younger women's strategy of 'living a double life' and its attendant feelings of 'anxiety, guilt and alienation'. At the same time, for some Canadian-born Sikh women the emphasis of scriptural teaching on gender equality provides some impetus towards change.

Inderpal Grewal focuses on 'the production of Sikh women from Punjab as refugees' in the USA during the 1990s. The con- struction of these women as 'victims of violence' and 'victims of human rights violations', Grewal presents as exemplifying 'knowledge production' in transnational discourse on human rights. She notes the particular concern of 'cultural feminism' with foregrounding the sexual abuse suffered by these victims. Unlike male Sikh applicants for asylum, women could not suggest their political agency if their 'narrative' for asylum as refugees was to be credible in the USA. In discussing the 'sud- denness and the number' of similarly-worded applications for asylum, Grewal reports the significance of rape—the experience of it or threat of it—in establishing the 'credibility' of the wom- en's cases, together with the 'impetus of proving that they were not terrorists'. In the discourse surrounding these women, she identifies the American 'experts' homogenized representa- tion of 'the Sikh' and how, in contrast to the 'passive "Asian woman" of the US state narrative', Human Rights NGOs (Non- governmental Organizations) in India instead depict Sikh women as 'courageous' and 'stoic'.

The women of Sikh Dharma and its related organization, 3HO, the Healthy, Happy, Holy Organization, are Constance Elsberg's subject. Elsberg charts the emergence of Yogi Bhajan's eclectic movement in North America in the 1970s from his yoga classes and ashrams, and the appeal of his 'Grace of God Meditation' to women followers. She notes the creation of the

Khalsa Women's Training Camp at which 3HO/Sikh Dharma 'ideas about the nature of women and women's experience were formulated', with Yogi Bhajan emphasizing the creative power of women who are calm, centred, and 'graceful'. His followers took on board not only the harsh criticisms of women, as voiced by Bhajan, but also the practice of arranged marriages which he advocated. Changes during and beyond the 1990s analysed by Elsberg include the increasing number of women in leadership roles in organizations and businesses associated with 3HO.

The disciplinary framework of Margaret Walton-Roberts' study of transnational immigrant networks linking Canada and India is that of critical population geography. She considers why geographers—unlike anthropologists—have only recently begun to engage with transnationalism and notes the ways in which 'gender has been underplayed in the transnationalism literature'. Walton-Roberts' exploration of Punjabi marriage migration networks draws upon her fieldwork in the Doaba region of Punjab and an understanding of Punjab's patriarchal marriage norms (including dowry and the preference for male offspring). She comments on the keenness of many rural families for their daughters to marry NRIs (Non-Resident Indians), an enthusiasm shared by the young women, themselves and she demonstrates how the practice of selecting spouses has become globalized. Her examples suggest 'what a critical population geography, attuned to issues of gendered transnational processes' (and freed from such exclusive dependence on numerical data), might contribute to current debates.

Continuing this transnational theme is a focus on the paid work of women in ten transnational Jat Sikh families (linked with Punjab, Tanzania, and Britain) that Kanwal Mand provides. Although paid employment is not the reason for the women's migration, in Britain it is a norm, owing to the high cost of living, and it is regarded as part of being a 'good' wife. This contrasts with the prevailing situation in Tanzania, where women's employment is seen to reflect negatively on the ability of men in the household to support them. Sikh women's paid work in Britain, Mand argues, also makes it possible for them to negotiate further travel, sometimes including an element of tourism.

Concluding Remarks

This volume has, through varied contours and disciplines, begun an important undertaking. In providing a snapshot of the field as it stands now, in opening up perspectives on Sikh women not yet published before, and in identifying areas ripe for further study, this collection of essays seeks to spark the scholarly imagination and serve as a catalyst for further inquiry and research. And such research is much needed. While the field of Sikh Studies is well established, there is currently no organized or recognized 'group' of scholars working specifically on feminist and gender issues within Sikhism. By drawing together academics with shared interest in Sikh women—scholars who, up until now, have been pursuing their work in relative isolation of each other—this pioneering volume has succeeded in opening up a vital conversation and cleared the path for further discussion and dialogue. It is crucial that this conversation continue: that analytic theories specific to Sikhism and women be developed, that further ethnographic and textual studies be pursued, that interdisciplinary collaboration be fostered, and that yet-isolated scholars with an interest in Sikhism and women be encouraged to bring their insights to the table.

Finally, each contributor must be lauded for agreeing to participate in this publishing venture. Scholarly analysis of women within religion is, in some ways, a sensitive and even challenging endeavour. More so than in most areas of academic inquiry, those choosing to pursue this field of study risk facing the resistance and sometimes censure of certain groups within the religious community.

Notes

1. The preparation of this book coincided with a period of sporadic unrest in Punjab surrounding the controversial leader, Baba Gurmit Ram Rahim Singh who has millions of followers, many of whom are Sikhs, of the lowest castes and women. This leader and his organization (as well as many others throughout Punjab) highlight the question of 'who is a Sikh'? (Walia 2007; Jodhka 2008: 54–7; and Baixas and Simon 2007).

2. The notion of 'contact zone' is originally that of Pratt (1991). Green and Searle-Chatterjee (2008) also offer critical analysis of 'religion' and especially 'world religion'.

3. An important study on South Asian youth culture in New York shows a fascinating case in point. Sunaina Marr Maira addresses how remix music, dance, and style in the lives of *desis* in New York are actually sites of 'becoming' male and female (especially 'To be Young, Brown and Hip', 29–82).

4. A recent and highly publicized case, the subject of the Canadian Broadcasting Corporation's The Fifth Estate's documentary film, *The Murdered Bride* directed by Vic Sarin, which tells the story of a young Canadian woman, Jaswinder Kaur Sidhu who, because she went against the wishes of her family in marrying a young man of a lower caste in India, was then allegedly killed, on order by her parents, aired 6 February 2006 (Sarin 2006).

Moreover, a recent poll for the British Broadcasting Corporation's (BBC's) Asian Network, surveying 500 South Asians in the UK, including Sikhs, Hindus, Muslims, and Christians, reveals that 10 per cent of those surveyed would condone the murder of someone who put the family's honour in disrepute ('One in 10 "backs honour killings"'). http://www.redhotcurry.com/archive/news/2006/honour_killings.htm. For the implications of caste in izzat and 'honour killings' see Waughray 2009: 198–9.

5. Both Sikh and non-Sikh writers apply the adjective 'orthodox' to Sikhs, usually as a synonym for *amritdhari* (that is, for a Sikh who has been initiated into the Khalsa, the nucleus of Sikhs committed to observing a certain discipline that includes the five outward signs of Sikh allegiance). The words 'orthodox' and 'orthodoxy' are potentially misleading, since they imply a value judgement and come from the context of Christianity in which 'right belief' was, historically, crucial for salvation and neither spiritual discipline nor identity involved maintaining physical signifiers of commitment to one's faith. The term may also, ironically, include those who *appear*, through the wearing of the 5Ks, to be following the tenets of the Khalsa order, but who in actual practice reject the mandate of *initiation* into the Khalsa. These Sikhs are generally known as kesdhari Sikhs.

6. While there are no statistics available on Sikh women wearing turbans, it is highly likely that their numbers, in terms of actual representation, are higher within diasporic contexts than within Punjab, the heartland of Sikhism.

7. Mahmood and Brady's ethnographic study of North American Sikh women adds an important dimension to this discussion, namely, women wearing the turban do so as a form of agency in their demands for gender equality (Mahmood and Brady 2000: 47).

8. The image is reproduced with permission from the artist, Manjot Singh Khalsa, and can be found at http://www.mkhalsa.com/art/images/singh neelossofrehat.gif. Permission granted via email, 28 April 2007.

9. One young woman in particular, a student in a course on Sikhism taught by Jakobsh in 2003, took this issue to heart and circulated a petition around the University of Waterloo campus, calling for an end to discriminatory practices at the Golden Temple.

10. The institution of the 'five beloved ones' stems from the institution of the Khalsa brotherhood by Guru Gobind Singh in 1699, when five men volunteered their lives for their beloved master. Today, the five who administer initiation into the Khalsa order are also called 'five beloved ones'.

11. This is not the case among 3HO/Sikh Dharma converts, where women are highly vocal about their participation as 'panj piare'. They also play substantial roles as musicians in the performance of kirtan. See Elsberg this volume and Jakobsh 2008).

REFERENCES

Axel, Brian (2004). 'The Context of Diaspora', *Cultural Anthropology*, Vol. 19, No. 1, (February) pp. 26–60.

'Badal: IG-level Officer Conducting Probe', *Tribune News Service*, 10 May 2007, http://www.tribuneindia.com/2007/20070519/punjab1.htm#1, accessed on 12 May 2007.

Baixas, Lionel and Charlène Simon (2008). 'From Protesters to Martyrs: How to Become a "True" Sikh', *South Asia Multidisciplinary Academic Journal*, Vol. 2, http://samaj.revues.org/index1532.html, accessed 15 April 2009.

Ballantyne, Tony (2006). *Between Colonialism and Diaspora: Sikh Cultural Formations in an Imperial World*, Durham and London: Duke University Press.

Barrier, N. Gerald (1970). *The Sikhs and their Literature: A Guide to Tracts, Books and Periodicals, 1849-1919*, Delhi: Manohar.

—— (1975). 'The Sikh Resurgence, 1849-1947: An Assessment of Printed Sources and Their Location', in W. Eric Gustafson, Kenneth W. Jones (eds), *Sources in Punjab History*, Delhi: Manohar, pp. 219–52.

Barthes, Roland (1977). 'Rhetoric of the Image', in Stephen Heath (ed. and tr.), *Image, Music, Text*, New York: Hill and Wang, pp. 32–51.

Bramadat, Paul (2005). 'Beyond Christian Canada: Religion and Ethnicity in a Multicultural Society', in Paul Bramadat and David Seljak (eds), *Religion and Ethnicity in Canada*, Toronto: Pearson Longman, pp. 1–29.

Bulbeck, Chilla (1998). *Re-orienting Western Feminisms: Women's Diversity in a Postcolonial World*, Cambridge: Cambridge University Press.

Butler, Judith (1999). *Gender Trouble: Feminism and the Subversion of Identity*, New York and London: Routledge.

Castelli, Elizabeth (2001). 'Women, Gender, Religion: Troubling Categories and Transforming Knowledge', in Elizabeth Castelli (ed.), *Women, Gender Religion: A Reader*, New York: Palgrave, pp. 3–25.

Chitnis, Suma (2004). 'Feminism: Indian Ethos and Indian Convictions', in Maitrayee Chaudhuri (ed.), *Feminism in India*, Delhi: Kali for Women, pp. 8–25.

Cox, L. and C. Robinson (2006). 'The Living Words of the Living Master: Sants, Sikhs, Sachkhand Nanak Dham and the Academy', *Journal of Contemporary Religion*, Vol. 21, No. 3, pp. 373–87.

Das, Veena (1976). 'Masks and faces: an essay on Punjabi Kinship', *Contributions of Indian Sociology*, Vol. 10, No. 1, pp. 1–30.

de Beauvoir, Simone (1973). *The Second Sex*, tr. E.M. Parshley. New York: Vintage.

Dhillon, Gurdarshan (1994). 'Review of *The Construction of Religious Boundaries*', *Sikh Press*, Vol. 4, No. 33 (May), pp. 1–15.

Dusenbery, Verne A. (1990). 'On the Moral Sensitivities of Sikhs in North America', in Owen M. Lynch (ed.), *Divine Passions: The Social Construction of Emotion in North America*, Delhi: Oxford University Press, pp. 239–61.

Forbes, Geraldine (1996). *Women in Modern India*, The New Cambridge History of India, IV.2, Delhi: Cambridge University Press.

Gajjala, Radhika (2004). *Cyber Selves: Feminist Ethnographies of South Asian Women*, Walnut Creek: CA, ALTAMIRA Press.

Geaves, R.A. (1996). 'Baba Balaknath: An Exploration of Religious Identity', *DISKUS WebEdition*, Vol. 4, No. 2, http://web.uni-marburg.de/religion swissenschaft/journal/diskus/geaves.html, accessed on 8 March 2007.

—— (1998). 'The Borders between Religions: A Challenge to the World Religions Approach to Religious Education', *British Journal of Religious Education*, Vol. 21, No. 1, pp. 20–31.

Gilroy, Paul (1993). *The Black Atlantic: Modernity and Double Consciousness*, Cambridge: Harvard University Press.

Green, N. and M. Searle-Chatterjee (2008). 'Religion, Language, and Power: An Introductory Essay', in N. Green and M. Searle-Chatterjee (eds), *Religion, Language, and Power*, London: Routledge, pp. 1–23.

Gross, Rita (1996). *Feminism and Religion: An Introduction*, Boston: Beacon Press.

Hall, Stuart (1992). 'The Question of Cultural Identity', in Stuart Hall, David Held and Tony McGrew (eds), *Modernity and its Futures*, Cambridge: Polity Press, pp. 273–325.

—— (1996). 'New Ethnicities', in D. Morley and K.H. Chen (eds), *Stuart Hall: Critical Dialogues in Cultural Studies*, London and New York: Routledge, pp. 441–9.

Hermansen, Marcia (2003). 'How to Put the Genie Back in the Bottle: "Identity" Islam and Muslim Youth Cultures in America', in Omar Safi (ed.), *Progressive Muslims: On Justice, Gender and Pluralism*, Oxford, UK: Oneworld Publications, pp. 303–19.

Ibbetson, D.C.J. (1883). *Report on the Census of the Punjab, 1881, Vol. 1*, Calcutta.

Jakobsh, Doris R. (2003). *Relocating Gender in Sikh History: Transformation, Meaning and Identity*. Delhi: Oxford University Press.

—— (2004). 'Constructing Sikh Identities: Authorities, Virtual and Imagined', *International Journal of Punjab Studies*, Vol. 10, No. 1 and 2, (January), pp. 127-42.

—— (2006). 'Sikhism, Interfaith Dialogue and Women: Transformation and Identity', *Journal of Contemporary Religion*, Vol. 21, No. 2 (May), pp. 183–99.

—— (2008). '3HO/Sikh Dharma of the Western Hemisphere: The "Forgotten" New Religious Movement?', *Religion Compass*, Vol. 2, pp. 1–24.

Jayawardena, Kumari (1995). *The White Woman's Other Burden: Western Women and South Asian during British Colonial Rule*, New York and London: Routledge.

Jeffrey, Patricia (2001). 'Agency, Activism and Agendas', in Elizabeth A. Castelli (ed.), *Women, Gender, Religion: A Reader*, New York: Palgrave, pp. 465–91.

Jodhka, Surinder S. (2008). 'Of Babas and Deras', *Seminar*, 581 (January), pp. 54—7.

Kaur, Gurdev. 'Role of Sikh Women in the 21st Century', http://www. sikhnarimanch.com/content.asp?id=7812636&cat=10&parentid=0, accessed on 2 April 2007.

Kaur, Upinder Jit (1990). *Sikh Religion and Economic Development*, Delhi: National Book Organization.

Khalsa, Manjot Singh, 'Sikh Art', http://www.mkhalsa.com/art/, accessed 10 March 2007.

Lee, R.M. (1993). *Doing Research on Sensitive Topics*, London: Sage Publications.

Lorenzen, David (ed.) (1996). *Bhakti Religion in North India: Community Identity and Political Action*, Delhi: Manohar.

Mahmood, Cynthia and Stacy Brady (2000). *The Guru's Gift: An Ethnography Exploring Gender Equality with North American Sikh Women*, Mountain View, CA: Mayfield Publishing.

Maira, Sunaina Marr (2002). *Desis in the House: Indian American Youth Culture in New York City*, Philadelphia: Temple University Press.

Malhotra, Anshu (2002). *Gender, Caste, and Religious Identities: Restructuring Class in Colonial Punjab*, New Delhi: Oxford University Press.

McLeod, W.H. (1997). *Sikhism*, London: Penguin.

—— (1991). *Popular Sikh Art*, Delhi: Oxford University Press.

Moallem, Minoo (1999). 'Transnationalism, Feminism and Fundamentalism', in Caren Kaplan, Norma Alarcón, Minoo Moallem (eds), *Between Woman and Nation. Nationalisms, Transnational Feminisms, and the State*, Durham and London: Duke University Press, pp. 320–48.

Nesbitt, E. (1980). 'Aspects of Sikh Tradition in Nottingham', unpublished M Phil thesis, University of Nottingham.

—— (1981). 'A Note on Bhatra Sikhs', *New Community*, Vol. 9, No. 1, pp. 70–2.

—— (1985). 'The Nanaksar Movement', *Religion*, Vol. 15, pp. 67–79.

—— (1990a). 'Religion and Identity: The Valmiki Community in Coventry', *New Community*, Vol. 16, No. 2, pp. 261–74.

—— (1990b). 'Pitfalls in Religious Taxonomy: Hindus and Sikhs, Valmikis and Ravidasis', *Religion Today*, Vol. 6, No. 1, pp. 9–12.

—— (1991). *'My Dad's Hindu, My Mum's Side are Sikhs': Issues in Religious Identity*, (Arts, Culture, Education, Research and Curriculum Paper), Charlbury: National Foundation for Arts Education. Available online at http://www.art.man.ac.uk/CASAS/pdfpapers/identity.pdf

—— (1994). 'Valmikis in Coventry: The Revival and Reconstruction of a Community', in R. Ballard (ed.), *Desh Pardesh: The South Asian Presence in Britain*, London: C. Hurst and Co., pp. 117–41.

—— (1997). 'The Body in Sikh Tradition', in S. Coakley (ed.), *Religion and the Body*, Cambridge: Cambridge University Press, pp. 289–305.

—— (2000). *The Religious Lives of Sikh Children: A Coventry Based Study*, Monograph Series, Leeds: Community Religions Project, University of Leeds.

Nesbitt, E. (2004a). *Intercultural Education: Ethnographic and Religious Approaches*, Brighton: Sussex Academic Press.

—— (2004b). 'UK Valmikis and the Label "Hindu"', in J. Leslie and M. Clark (eds), *Creating a Dialogue: Text, Belief and Personal Identity (Proceedings of the Valmiki Studies Workshop 2004)*, London: SOAS, pp. 25–31.

Oberoi, Harjot (1994). *The Construction of Religious Boundaries. Culture, Identity and Diversity in the Sikh Tradition*. New Delhi: Oxford University Press.

—— (1996). 'The Making of a Religious Paradox. Sikh, Khalsa, Sahajdhari as Modes of Early Sikh Identity', in David Lorenzen (ed.), *Bhakti Religion in North India. Community Identity and Political Action*, Delhi: Manohar, pp. 35–66.

'One in 10 "backs honour killings"', 2006, BBC News, 4 Sept. 2006, at http://news.bbc.co.uk/1/hi/uk/5311244.stm, accessed on 4 April 2007.

Pratt, Mary Louise (1991). 'Profession 91', New York: MLA, pp. 33–40.

Rait, Satwant Kaur (2005). *Sikh Women in England. Their Religious and Cultural Beliefs and Social Practices*, Stoke on Trent: Trentham Books.

RealSikhism, http://www.realsikhism.com/faq/headcovering.html, accessed on 2 May 2007.

Sarin, Vic (2006). *Murder Unveiled*, Documentary film, Force Four Entertainment Inc., first aired by Canadian Broadcasting Corporation's *The Fifth Estate*, 6 February 2006.

Sayers, Matthew R. (2003). 'Tat Khalsa Use of Non-Traditional Educational Tools in the Ascendancy of the Khalsa Sikh Identity', *Sagar*, Vol. II (Fall), pp. 19–36.

'Sikhism & Women: Some Questions and Answers', at http://allaboutsikhs.com/articles/sikhism&women.htm, accessed on 2 April 2007.

Singh, I.J. (2003). *Being & Becoming a Sikh*, Toronto: Centennial Foundation.

Singh, Nikky-Guninder Kaur (1993). *The Feminine Principle in the Sikh Vision of the Transcendent*, Cambridge: Cambridge University Press.

Singh, Parlo (1994). 'Generating Literacies of 'Difference' from the Belly of the Beast', *Australian Journal of Language and Literacy*, Vol. 17, No. 2, pp. 92–100.

Sodhi, Surinder Singh (1995). 'Eurocentrism vs. Khalsacentrism', in J.S. Mann, S.S. Sodhi, G.S. Gill (eds), *The Invasion of Religious Boundaries: A Critique of Harjot Oberoi's Work*, Vancouver, BC: Canadian Sikh Study and Teaching Society.

Sturken, Marita and Lisa Cartwright (2000). *Practices of Looking. An Introduction to Visual Culture*. Oxford: Oxford University Press.

Tatla, D.S. (1992). 'Nurturing the Faithful: The Role of the Sant among Britain's Sikhs', *Religion*, Vol. 22, No. 4, pp. 349–74.

Tite, Philip L. (2004). 'Naming or Defining? On the Necessity of Reduction in Religious Studies', *Culture and Religion: An Interdisciplinary Journal*, Vol. 5, No. 3, pp. 339–65.

Uberoi, Patricia (1996). 'Introduction: Problematising Social Reform, Engaging Sexuality, Interrogating the State', in Patricia Uberoi (ed.), *Social Reform, Sexuality and the State*, Delhi: Sage Publications, pp. ix–xxvi.

Walia, Varinder, 'Dera Chief can't be Summoned: Vedanti', *Tribune News Service*, 10 May 2007, http://www.tribuneindia.com/2007/20070519/punjab1.htm#1, accessed on 12 May 2007.

Waughray, A. (2009). 'Caste Discrimination: A Twenty-First Century Challenge for the UK Discrimination Law?', *The Modern Law Review*, Vol. 72, No. 2, pp. 182–219.

Wright, Caroline (1997). 'Representing the 'Other': Some Thoughts', *Indian Journal of Gender Studies*, Vol. 4, No. 1, pp. 83–8.

Yuval-Davis, Nira (1993). 'Beyond Difference: Women and Coalition Politics', in Mary Kennedy, Cathy Lubelska and Val Walsh (eds), *Making Connections: Women's Studies, Women's Movements, Women's Lives*, London: Taylor and Francis and Women's Studies Network, pp. 3–10.

The Guru, The Goddess

The Dasam Granth and Its Implications for Constructions of Gender in Sikhism

Robin Rinehart

The lives and teachings of Guru Nanak and his successors shape the framework of the early history of the Sikh religion. The declaration of the tenth Guru, Guru Gobind Singh, that the Gurus' teachings, along with other compositions, compiled in a granth or book, should henceforth be accorded the status of 'Guru' highlights the fact that the ten Gurus and the Guru Granth Sahib are indisputably central to Sikhism. But there is another 'granth' associated with Guru Gobind Singh, and its status is far less clear than that of the Guru Granth Sahib.

Most popularly called the 'Dasam Granth' or 'book of the tenth', this lengthy compendium of compositions, totalling 1,428 pages in most standard printed editions, has been controversial throughout its history. While some have argued that Guru Gobind Singh is the author of the entire text, others have concluded that he wrote only portions of it; still others have decided that Guru Gobind Singh composed none of it, and that the entire Dasam Granth is part of a conspiracy to discredit Sikhism. The controversy largely swirls around two issues. The first issue is the text's extensive attention to Hindu mythology, such as several sections about the goddess Durga, alongside descriptions of the lives of Krishna, Rama, and other gods that comprise a substantial portion of the Dasam Granth.[1] Many

Sikh thinkers have been troubled by this material because of the possibility that the Hindu myths could be understood as an endorsement of the worship of Hindu gods and goddesses rather than the monotheistic theology of normative Sikhism. The second issue is the lengthy portion of the Dasam Granth called *Charitropakhian* which includes hundreds of stories about men and women, many of them engaged in illicit relationships, with particular emphasis on women who deceive their husbands in order to pursue other men. This section is troubling to many readers because its content does not immediately appear to warrant inclusion in a religious text, particularly due to the graphic nature of some of its passages.

Viewing the Dasam Granth through the lens of gender adds yet another layer of complexity to understanding the text and its history, for gender is a central component of these two controversial issues: gender with respect to the nature of divinity because of the goddess mythology, and, gender with respect to the nature of men's and women's inherent natures and behavioural inclinations as described in *Charitropakhian*. This essay will introduce the Dasam Granth, focusing particularly on the gender issues raised by different portions of the text. It will also consider the extent to which women have participated in the transmission and interpretation of the Dasam Granth.

GURU GOBIND SINGH AND THE DASAM GRANTH

Certain aspects of Guru Gobind Singh's life as reported in Sikh biographies are important for understanding the origins of the Dasam Granth as well as the different ways people have interpreted its contents. Guru Gobind Singh was born in Patna (in the modern Indian state of Bihar) in 1666. He moved to the Punjab with his family in 1672, settling at Anandpur. When his father, Guru Tegh Bahadur, was killed in Delhi in 1675, the young Gobind assumed leadership of the Sikh community or *panth*. At first, his mother and uncle helped him in his new role, and then as he grew older he assumed full leadership. Most biographical sources concur that in Anandpur, Guru Gobind Singh continued his education in the languages of Braj, Persian, the Gurmukhi script, and, according to some sources, Sanskrit (Chhibbar 1972: 99, verses 6–10). This is important because most of the Dasam Granth is in the Braj language, with other portions in Punjabi and Persian. Guru Gobind Singh was married to Jito in 1677, and Sundari in 1685. Jito gave birth to three sons, and Sundari gave birth to one son.[2] All four sons were killed in 1704.

Guru Gobind Singh had, like his father, what is typically described as a royal court at Anandpur. According to many accounts of his life, as part of his retinue he sponsored court poets, the traditional number being fifty-two. The existence of these court poets is central to arguments about the Dasam Granth, because some Sikh commentators have attributed particular sections to the court poets rather than Guru Gobind Singh.

Guru Gobind Singh and his followers came into conflict with neighbouring kingdoms, and left Anandpur for some time, establishing a fort at a site that came to be known as Paonta. There the Guru stayed for several years, from 1685 until 1688, and some biographical sources describe this as a time of great literary composition in his life. For example, Bhai Santokh Singh's 1843 *Suraj Prakash* states that Guru Gobind Singh would spend several hours a day composing or translating (from Sanskrit) poetry on topics such as Krishna's activities as an *avatar* or divine descent (Singh 1999: 384).[3] There are passages in the Dasam Granth itself which make reference to the place and time they were composed; for example, the *Krishna Avatar* section states that its author composed the passage at Anandpur and that it was based on the tenth chapter of the *Bhagavat Purana*, a Sanskrit text which describes the life of Krishna.

Military conflict with neighbouring kings continued on and off for the rest of Guru Gobind Singh's life. He maintained an army, recruiting soldiers from various places and backgrounds. Guru Gobind Singh by nearly all accounts was fascinated with weapons and apparently often encouraged his male followers to be armed at all times.[4] This ongoing military activity as well as the diverse nature of his army are important for how people have understood the Dasam Granth, which includes a section devoted solely to the description and praise of weapons, as well as detailed descriptions of many battles. Some commentators have also suggested that some of the most controversial portions of the Dasam Granth, which describe men and women engaged in illicit affairs, may have been used as the basis for moral teaching to the Guru's armed forces, and were not intended for general circulation.

One of the most significant events in the Guru's life is his establishment of the Khalsa order in Anandpur in 1699, which provided the basis for subsequent rites of initiation. The rite of initiation into the Khalsa typically involves recitation of certain parts of Dasam Granth such as its opening section, the *Jaap*. Accounts of the establishment of the Khalsa vary in their details, and there are some traditions that bear directly on controversies about the Dasam Granth. For example, Kesar Singh Chhibbar's 1769 *Bansavalinama* reports that Guru Gobind Singh worshipped the goddess before establishing the Khalsa. More recently, some historians of Sikhism have argued that this did not happen, or that Guru Gobind Singh used goddess worship as a means of attracting the attention of the people who lived in an area in which such worship was popular, or that rather than actually worshipping the goddess, the Guru was in fact trying to show the futility of goddess worship and the ways in which Hindu Brahman priests exploited people through the performance of elaborate rituals.[5] Compositions that relate goddess and other types of Hindu mythology are often the focus of arguments for and against Guru Gobind Singh as author of some or all of the Dasam Granth; those who accept Guru Gobind Singh as author of the entire text typically argue that he had specific reasons for addressing Hindu mythology, such as appealing to a wider audience or inspiring his warriors (but not advocating devotion to Hindu deities); others have argued that Guru Gobind Singh did not author such compositions and that instead they must be attributed to poets he sponsored in his court.[6]

Meanwhile, after the establishment of the Khalsa, disputes with neighbouring kings continued, which led to the first siege of Anandpur. Guru Gobind Singh and his followers left Anandpur in 1699. They were able to return in 1702, but were still caught up in the machinations of local kings and their rivalries. Some of those local kings sought the assistance of the forces of the powerful Mughal Empire which then ruled much of north India. After a second siege of Anandpur, Guru Gobind Singh left the town at the end of 1704. Mughal officials had promised him and his family safe passage, and the family separated. All four of Guru Gobind Singh's sons were killed at the end of 1704. In

1708, Guru Gobind Singh was stabbed and died several days afterwards.

According to some accounts, when the Guru and his followers left Anandpur, a great deal of written material was lost. This detail factors into later arguments about the compilation of the Dasam Granth and whether the material it contains was meant to comprise a single collection. Many Sikh commentators have noted a passage in Kesar Singh Chhibbar's *Bansavalinama* which reports that Guru Gobind Singh believed that his compositions and those of the Adi Granth (to become known as the Guru Granth Sahib) should be kept separate, because his writings were for amusement (*khed*) (Chhibbar 1972: verse 389).

CONTENTS OF THE DASAM GRANTH

The different sections of the Dasam Granth vary widely in content. Additionally, early manuscripts do not all contain exactly the same sections in the same order, and the titles of some sections vary. Many recent printed editions of the text, both in the original languages and in modern Punjabi or English translation, do not follow the exact same ordering and do not include all the sections of the text. The majority of the text is in the Braj language, with several sections in Punjabi and Persian. The main portions are each described briefly below.

Jaap. ('Spoken Prayer'; the title is derived from a verb meaning 'to pray or to recite quietly'). While the exact dating of this composition is uncertain, most commentators consider it to be one of the Guru's first compositions. It is one of the least controversial portions of the Dasam Granth. As its title suggests, it may be seen as parallel to Guru Nanak's *Japji*, the opening composition of the Guru Granth Sahib.[7] The 199 verses of the *Jaap* offer praise to a formless, all-pervading god. Many Sikhs know it by heart and recite it daily. It is worth noting that while the notion of a formless god may in theory be understood to transcend distinctions such as male/female, the language of the text is masculine in gender, and most English translations refer to this god as 'He'.

Akal Ustati ('Praise of the Timeless One'). Most commentators believe that this section is incomplete, and some have speculated that there are parts of this text that are later interpolations or may actually belong in other parts of the Dasam Granth. *Akal Ustati* describes God as *Akal Purakh* or the Timeless Primal Being or Lord, and *Sarbloh* or the 'Lord of all Steel'. This lord is also described as manifesting in various other gods and goddesses, as well as in people of different religious affiliations such as Hindu and Muslim. While there are occasional references to Muslim practices and Islam's sacred text the Qur'an, the preponderance of references are to Hindu mythology; the Lord is described as manifesting, for example, in the form of a goddess who slays demons. As in many compositions of the earlier Sikh Gurus, ritualism is criticized as an ineffective means of gaining knowledge of God.

Bachitra Natak ('The Wondrous Drama'). This section includes a portion called *Apni Katha* ('My Story'). *Apni Katha* is one of the most fascinating sections of the Dasam Granth. It is an autobiographical narrative in which the author (who, depending on one's perspective, may or may not be Guru Gobind Singh) relates his lineage going back to the beginning of creation, and his birth in the Sodhi lineage, which includes the family of Rama and Sita, hero and heroine of the Hindu epic the Ramayana. In *Apni Katha*, Guru Nanak is mentioned as a member of the Bedi clan, whose lineage is traced back to Kusha, the elder twin son of Rama and Sita. The Bedi and Sodhi clans are both part of the *Kshatriya varna* (the so-called 'warrior' or 'princely' caste). Prior to Guru Nanak's birth, the Bedis had fallen on hard times, and the members of the different varnas or castes did not perform their traditional occupations. *Apni Katha* then details the passing on of the guruship to the next eight Sikh Gurus, noting that the ninth, Guru Tegh Bahadur (Guru Gobind Singh's father), was martyred to protect *dharma* (proper religious practice, righteousness in general), particularly the sacred threads and *tilak*s or forehead marks of Hindus.

Next Guru Gobind Singh explains that he was deep in meditation, absorbed in devotion to God at Mount Hemkunt, when he was ordered by God to take birth in the *kaliyug* or age of iron, which in classical Hindu mythology is the fourth and last era of each cycle of creation when dharma is at its weakest. God explained to him that throughout history he had created various people who started their own religious paths (including Muhammad), but that people still pursued self-interest over devotion, and therefore he charged Guru Gobind Singh with spreading dharma. A reader familiar with Hindu mythology is likely to hear echoes of the Bhagavad Gita (part of the epic Mahabharata), a dialogue between the god Krishna and the warrior Arjuna, in which Krishna explains to Arjuna why it is proper to fight in a just war. In the Gita, Krishna explains that as the supreme lord he chooses to incarnate himself in various forms whenever dharma is in a state of decline.[8] Confusion of caste responsibilities is a typical example of dharma gone astray. How Sikh readers and listeners have interpreted this passage, however, has varied. The degree to which Sikhism has incorporated Hindu traditions is a matter of great debate. While some historians of Sikh religion have argued that Sikhs have often shared many beliefs and practices with their Hindu neighbours, more recent Sikh historians have emphasized the distinct character of Sikh practice and belief, particularly emphasizing that Sikhism does not accept belief in avatars or incarnations. *Apni Katha*'s description of Guru Nanak highlights the fact that it was he who propagated dharma in the Kaliyuga.

Apni Katha goes on to criticize those who take pride in their specific religious garb and practices, or who believe that God can be confined to a particular text. Then, the Guru describes his birth in Patna and the nurses who looked after him, his return to the Punjab, his assumption of a leadership role, his hunting expeditions, and various battles with local kings in the Punjab. The text covers events up until the late 1690s. Towards the end of this section, the author mentions that God allowed him to recall his previous births.

Chandi Charitra Ukti Bilasa ('The sport of Chandi's life is told'). This is the first of three portions of the Dasam Granth focused on the goddess. It is a retelling of the tale of the goddess Durga slaying the buffalo demon Mahisha and other demons, as recounted in the Sanskrit *Markandeya Purana*. The composition which follows it, *Chandi Charitra II*, tells the story again.

Var Sri Bhagauti ji ki, Var Durga Ki, or *Chandi di Var* ('the ballad of Bhagauti, Durga, or Chandi'). In the Punjabi language, this is yet another account of the exploits of the goddess. Like the first two, it details events similar to those related in the Sanskrit portion of the *Markandeya Purana* known as the *Devi-*

Mahatmya or *Durga Saptasati*. The first part of this composition is part of the frequently recited *ardas* prayer or petition. There is some controversy over the translation of the term '*bhagauti*' which occurs in the first line: 'I first recall Bhagauti, and then I focus my attention on Guru Nanak'. Etymologically bhagauti appears to be the feminine form of a word for Lord or God, that is, Goddess, so that one might translate the first phrase of this line as, 'I first recall the Goddess'. However, many Sikh commentators translate the word bhagauti as 'sword'. The term is thus part of the ongoing debate about whether reverence for a goddess is implied in the Dasam Granth; those who argue against this possibility tend to accept the translation of 'bhagauti' as 'sword' rather than 'goddess'. Whatever position one takes on this debate, however, it is notable that there are three separate compositions focusing on goddess mythology in the Dasam Granth.

Gian Prabodh ('The Awakening of Knowledge'). Many Sikh commentators have concluded that this portion of the text is incomplete. *Gian Prabodh* begins with a number of verses praising God. A later section includes a conversation between the soul and God, and there are many references to Hindu texts and mythology, particularly the epic Mahabharata.

Chaubis Avatar ('The Twenty-four Avatars'). This lengthy section describes various incarnations of the Hindu god Vishnu, including Brahma, Rudra, Rama, Krishna, the Buddha and the future avatar, Kalki. The verses on Krishna and Rama comprise the longest portion of the *Chaubis Avatar*, and both it and the section on Rama include passages frequently cited by Sikh commentators in which the author states that he does not worship Hindu gods. For example, verse 434 of the Krishna section reads, 'I do not begin by propitiating [the Hindu god] Ganesha, nor do I ever meditate on Krishna or Vishnu'. Verse 863 of Rama section states, 'The Puranas speak of Rama, and the Qur'an of Rahim, but I don't believe in either of them'. Sikh commentators have often cited these passages as evidence that although the Dasam Granth tells the stories of various Hindu gods, it does not advocate their worship.

Brahma Avatar ('The Avatars of Brahma') and *Rudra Avatar* ('The Avatars of Rudra, that is, Shiva'). Here, avatars of Brahma

and Rudra are presented, although both were previously described as avatars of Vishnu.[9]

Shabad Hazare (literally 'Thousand Words'; 'Selected Compositions'). There are nine hymns in this section, each composed
with a particular *raga* or melody, as are the verses in the Guru
Granth Sahib. *Shabad Hazare* is not found in the earliest manuscripts of the Dasam Granth (Jaggi 1966: 206). Some of these
hymns are thematically similar to poetry about the god Vishnu
and his incarnations.

Savaiye. The title refers to the particular type of poem in this
section. These thirty three verses may be used in the Khalsa rite
of initiation. They praise a god who is beyond the imaginings
of Hindu texts such as the Vedas and the Puranas, and beyond
the reckoning of the Qur'an as well. The verses challenge those
who worship specific avatars or incarnations and who display
their religiosity publicly without true knowledge of the mystery
of god.

Khalsa Mahima ('Praise of the Khalsa'). This text is not found
in the earliest manuscripts of the Dasam Granth. It is a short
passage containing Guru Gobind Singh's address to a Hindu
Brahman priest explaining why alms were given to Sikhs rather
than Brahmans after a sacrifice to the goddess at Naina Devi.
(The Naina Devi or 'eye goddess' temple near Anandpur is
related to a Hindu goddess myth in which different portions of
the goddess' body fell to earth, Naina Devi being the site where
the goddess' eye fell.)

Shastra-nam-mala ('Garland of the Names of Weapons').
This section, over 1,300 verses long, praises various weapons
such as the sword, noose, discus, and matchlock rifle, describing them as symbols of God's power. Terms for weapons are
listed and praised, particular weapons used by various gods in
battles against demons are noted, and there are riddles about
weapons.

Charitropakhian (*Pakhyan Charitra, Tria Charitra*) ('An
Account of Behavior/Deeds'; 'The Behavior of Women'). This is
perhaps the most intriguing part of the Dasam Granth, and to
many readers the most troubling. It is also the longest section
of the text. It contains over 400 *charitra*s ('deeds, behaviour';
'character studies'). The frame story is related in the second
charitra. A celestial nymph (*apsara*) fell in love with King Chitra

Singh, married him, and bore a son. But she later returned to her heavenly abode, and the stricken king sought a human look alike to replace his beloved wife. When he found one and married her, the new wife tried to seduce his son, explaining to her stepson that his father didn't satisfy her. The king's son refused his father's new wife's advances; when the king learned what had happened, he first thought of killing his son, but his ministers explained that it is difficult to understand the charitra of women. The king then put his son in jail, and each morning would have him released and brought to his court to hear a minister tell various other charitras. Thus, the context of *Charitropakhian* is that it is a male narrator relating stories about women and men for a male audience, from a male perspective.

The charitras that follow include traditional romance tales well known in the Punjab such as the stories of Hir and Ranjha, Sohni and Mahiwal, Krishna and his amorous exploits with the cowherd girls or *gopi*s, and the tale of Yusuf and Zulaikha. A substantial number of the charitras, however, describe married women who concoct schemes that allow their lovers to visit them without their husbands knowing, such as by having their lovers disguise themselves as yogis, sadhus or fakirs, and then taking them into the home. Characters in these tales also delight in opium, drinking liquor, and gambling.

Charitras twenty-one through twenty-three are sometimes said to relate an incident from Guru Gobind Singh's own life but this is a matter of debate among Sikh commentators. These three charitras are set in Anandpur, and concern a rich man's wife who tries unsuccessfully to seduce the Raja of Anandpur. She lures the raja by having her servant promise the raja that he may learn a special *mantra* or prayer if he accompanies him (the servant). The rich woman, tormented by desire, tries to convince the raja to become her lover, but he refuses, explaining that he is an honourable married man. The woman then threatens to poison herself if the raja doesn't accede to her wishes, and finally in frustration she shouts that he is a thief. The raja then runs away, leaving behind his shoes and a robe, and is caught and beaten by people who think he is a thief. The woman then concocts a ruse that allows the raja to be freed, but the next day she angrily displays the clothing he had left behind. In the meantime, the raja announced that these items had been stolen, and requested that his subjects find out who took them. The woman is then brought to him as an alleged thief, the king assures her that because she is a woman he will let her free, and he eventually grants her a pension.

Many printed editions of the Dasam Granth, such as the one published in 1995 by the Publications Bureau of Punjabi University, the *Shabadarth Dasam Granth Sahib*, omit the *Charitropakhian* section entirely on the grounds that it is not suitable material for inclusion in a religious text. Surindar Singh Kohli's 2005 translation of the Dasam Granth omits this section as well.

Much of the debate regarding the authorship of the Dasam Granth centres on the *Charitropakhian*. A key element in the dispute is the author's use of pen names such as 'Ram' and 'Shyam'. Commentators who argue that Guru Gobind Singh did not compose the *Charitropakhian* have cited the use of such names as compelling evidence that this is the work of one or more of Guru Gobind Singh's court poets. Those who believe that Guru Gobind Singh did write it sometimes argue that the stories were meant particularly for Guru Gobind Singh's troops who were away from their wives and families during battle, and that the stories served as entertainment as well as the basis for moral edification. They also argue that Guru Gobind Singh himself used different pen names such as Ram and Shyam.

Zafarnama/Hikaitan. The *Zafarnama* ('Letter of Victory') is a Persian letter to the Mughal emperor Aurangzeb which Guru Gobind Singh is said to have composed in 1706. In the letter, he chastizes the emperor for reneging on a sworn oath to guard the Guru and his family safe passage from Anandpur. Instead, they were attacked. Virtually all commentators agree that this is an authentic composition of Guru Gobind Singh.

The *Zafarnama* is grouped with the *Hikaitan*, which are of a completely different nature. The *Hikaitan* are twelve stories along the lines of the *Charitropakhian* (indeed, many are Persian versions of the same tales). Some suggest that these tales were sent along with the letter because they would be instructive for Aurangzeb; another explanation is that they were grouped together in the Dasam Granth simply because they are both in the Persian language.

The Compilation of the Dasam Granth

How did such a diverse array of compositions come together? Sikh history ascribes the compilation of the Dasam Granth to the Sikh scribe and scholar Bhai Mani Singh, some twenty years after Guru Gobind Singh's death in 1708. Many sources state that during the turbulent times of conflict with local kings in the area surrounding Anandpur, written material was lost as the Guru and his followers moved or had to flee during battles. It is not clear whether the compositions that now comprise the Dasam Granth were compiled together during Guru Gobind Singh's lifetime, or whether they were meant to be part of a single text (Jaggi 1966: 29–34). As noted previously, Kesar Singh Chhibbar's *Bansavalinama* reports that when Guru Gobind Singh was presented with the possibility of combining the Adi Granth (which subsequently became known as the Guru Granth Sahib) with his own compositions, he distinguished between the Adi Granth and his own work which he termed entertainment (khed), and declared that the two should remain separate (Chhibbar 1972, verse 389: 136).

Bhai Mani Singh was responsible for preparing the final version of the Guru Granth Sahib in 1706 under Guru Gobind Singh's direction, which included the addition of Guru Tegh Bahadur's compositions. He later served as the head official at the central Sikh sacred site, the Golden Temple in Amritsar. There is an early Dasam Granth manuscript associated with him, as well as a letter to Guru Gobind Singh's widow Mata Sundari, but many Sikh scholars have questioned the authenticity of these documents. Additionally, Sikh scholars have debated the authenticity of opening passages of some sections of the Dasam Granth which state that they are the words of the tenth Guru, typically with a phrase such as '*sri mukhvak patshahi das*' or 'from the mouth of the revered tenth Guru'. Whatever the exact circumstances of its authorship and compilation, however, multiple manuscript versions of the Dasam Granth were in circulation by the mid-to-late eighteenth century, and many Sikhs appear to have taken the text as the authentic work of Guru Gobind Singh, granting it a place of honour in gurdwaras alongside the Guru Granth Sahib.

Interpretations of the Dasam Granth

Historians of Sikhism generally agree that throughout the eighteenth century, there was a wide range of practices among Sikhs, and that in many cases, people combined aspects of Sikh practice with traditions more closely associated with Hinduism. Goddess worship is especially popular in Punjabi Hinduism, and therefore was one of the Hindu practices pursued by some Sikhs in the eighteenth century. In such an environment, the goddess mythology components of the Dasam Granth likely seemed less problematic.

However, the Dasam Granth became an important focus of the reform movements that arose within Sikhism in the nineteenth century. Sikhs in different towns and cities established branches of the Singh Sabha, and Singh Sabha reformers typically sought to establish clear distinctions between Hinduism and Sikhism, urging Sikhs to give up practices associated with Hinduism. Kahn Singh Nabha (1861–1938), author of the celebrated 1898 book *Ham Hindu Nahin* [We Are Not Hindus], presented an account of the Dasam Granth in his 1930 encyclopaedia *Gurushabad Ratnakar Mahan Kosh*. According to the Dasam Granth entry in this text, the Dasam Granth was sent to Damdama Sahib after Bhai Mani Singh's martyrdom in 1737. But Sikh leaders were unsure of what to make of it. Some thought it should remain as a single text, but others suggested that it be separated into two parts, one with those compositions of the tenth Guru which seemed in keeping with the sentiments of the previous Gurus, and another containing the rest of the text. But there was no consensus, and the debate was solved in an intriguing way. Matab Singh stopped at Damdama Sahib on his way to Amritsar, where he had heard that Massa Ranghar was defiling the Golden Temple with illicit activities. Matab Singh planned to kill Massa Ranghar, and he suggested to the leaders debating the Dasam Granth that if he succeeded in his mission, the Dasam Granth should be kept as it was, and that it should be divided if he were to be killed (Kahn Singh Nabha 1990: 616). Since he was indeed successful, the Dasam Granth remained as a single text. Note, however, that this solution did not address the substance of the issue—whether or not the material in the Dasam Granth constitutes a coherent whole. It is also noteworthy that these debates involved male Sikh leaders; we do not know what female Sikhs might have thought about the Dasam Granth during this era.

Since the rise of the Singh Sabha movement, there have been a number of studies of the Dasam Granth arguing for particular interpretations of its history and authenticity. Sikh organizations have established committees to research and make pronouncements on the text, often reaching different conclusions. For the most part, publications on the Dasam Granth have been written by male scholars. Thus, although much of the text concerns the female gender, whether as goddess or human, the historical record preserves very few female voices participating in the debate.

One of the few female voices in the literature concerning the Dasam Granth is that of Nikky-Guninder Kaur Singh of Colby College in Maine. In several publications, she has explored the issue of the goddess mythology in the Dasam Granth.[10] In the chapter entitled 'Durga Recalled: Transition from Mythos to Ethos' in her book *The Feminine Principle in the Sikh Vision of the Transcendent,* Singh argues that Guru Gobind Singh did compose the sections of the Dasam Granth that describe the mythology of the goddess. She believes that scholars who have challenged Guru Gobind Singh's authorship 'are unable or perhaps unwilling to recognize the relevance of this female mythological figure for the religious vision of Guru Gobind Singh' (Singh 1993: 122). At the same time, she argues against those who believe that Guru Gobind Singh's focus on the goddess is indicative of a Hindu influence on his thought, 'for Durga is being recalled as a figure of myth and literature; she is not invoked as a goddess by the Guru' (ibid.: 122).

Like other commentators, Nikky Singh also argues that Guru Gobind Singh composed both spiritual and heroic poetry. Thus one function of the stories of the goddesses' battles with demons is to 'infuse new vigor into a listless society' (ibid.: 120). To exhort a passive people to action, 'he picked themes from the ancient epics and mythology of India to produce new verse charged with martial fervor' (ibid.: 121).

The argument that Guru Gobind Singh used goddess mythology to inspire his armies in battle but did not endorse actual worship of the goddess is quite common among commentators

who accept that Guru Gobind Singh composed these portions
of the Dasam Granth. Nikky Singh, however, goes on to build
a more complex argument about the particular choice of the
goddess and her battles out of all the possibilities afforded by the
myths of the vast Hindu pantheon. She suggests that those who
challenge Guru Gobind Singh's authorship of the goddess tales
may have a 'not fully conscious fear of "female power", "goddess
worship", and "polytheism"' (Singh 1993: 123). By choosing
to tell the story of goddess, Guru Gobind Singh acknowledged
woman's power in society, the goddess serving as a 'model of
moral force and martial prowess for both men and women'
(ibid.: 126–7). Thus, she believes, the goddess Durga becomes a
model for both men and women through her independence, her
creative and destructive power, and her extraordinary physical
strength (ibid.: 127–9). For Nikky Singh, the fact that Guru
Gobind Singh chose to tell and retell the tale of a goddess who
vanquishes demons reflects an overall positive valuation of the
female gender in Sikhism:

[Durga] symbolizes the moral power to overcome an oppressive system.
Her aggression is indeed healthy; her anger is indeed purifying. This
affirmation of female power by Guru Gobind Singh illustrates the overall
positive attitude towards women in Sikh speculation. Guru Nanak likewise
affirmed that there is nothing inferior or insidious about woman. Neither a
hindrance nor a negative influence, she is necessary for the continuance of
society and for the preservation of its ethical structure (ibid.: 131).

Nikky Singh also addresses the use of the term bhagauti. She
interprets it as 'a metaphor within a metaphor'; that is, she argues
that for Guru Gobind Singh the sword was a metaphor for the
transcendent deity, and that the sword was also a metaphor for
Durga and her female power. By making the wearing of a sword
as one of the obligations of those initiated into the Khalsa, the
metaphor of the sword (with its attendant associations of female
power) also became a concrete part of Sikh ritual and a sign
of Sikh identity. Nikky Singh further argues that the regular
recitation of the line 'I first recall bhagauti' in the ardas prayer
is another way of linking the sword, female power, and the
transcendent God in everyday religious practice (ibid.: 142–3).

In the conclusion to his review of *The Feminine Principle*, W.
Owen Cole notes accurately that Nikky Singh's overall study of
the feminine principle in Sikhism is 'a restatement of Sikh theo/

alogy' (Cole 1995: 399–400). Nikky Singh's interpretation of Guru Gobind Singh's use of goddess mythology, in particular, represents a new direction in the analysis of this material, for even among those Sikh commentators who accept Guru Gobind Singh as the author of the goddess stories, while the general consensus has been that the Guru used these tales to incite bravery, none has gone on to make the assertion that the fact that the Guru chose a goddess is itself a significant indicator of the Guru's views on gender and a positive valuation of women. In the context of Sikh theology, especially with respect to the issue of the role of gender in conceptualizing the deity, Nikky Singh's work is pioneering.

The assertion that Guru Gobind Singh's use of the sword/ Durga metaphor for the transcendent, enacted in the wearing of the sword and in Sikh liturgy, is indicative of a positive valuation of female power, however, becomes more complex if one views it in light of the material in *Charitropakhian* and the ways Sikh commentators have explained it. First of all, Sikh commentators have commonly treated *Charitropakhian* as an extended consideration of the character of women (indeed an alternate title is *Triyacharitra* or 'character studies of women'). Second, it is worth noting that many commentators simply avoid this section of the Dasam Granth entirely, whether by omitting the text itself from edited versions of the Dasam Granth, arguing that it was meant only for a specific male audience, or summarily dismissing it as inauthentic. Whatever view one takes on the authorship of *Charitropakhian*, the fact that it addresses character—both male and female—makes it a compelling source of evidence about Sikh notions of gender. Given however, that many Sikh commentators reject the authenticity of the text, we cannot assume that it presents a vision of gender that all Sikhs would accept.

There is an interesting gap between how writers summarizing *Charitropakhian* have characterized it and what emerges from a more careful reading of the individual charitras. While a substantial number of the charitras do indeed portray women as deceitful, there are others which show resourceful, heroic women. And, even in the cases in which women are deceiving their husbands as they pursue involvements with other men, it is not they alone who are responsible for the deceit—there are of course necessarily other men involved, in fact men who know that they are becoming involved with married women. Pritpal Singh Bindra (2002), who recently translated *Charitropakhian* into English, makes this point in the subtitle of his translation: *Tales of Male-Female Tricky Deceptions from Sri Dasam Granth.* For the most part, however, this portion of the Dasam Granth has been characterized as a text primarily focused on the deceit of women.

This persistent assessment of *Charitropakhian* itself suggests something about the ongoing construction of gender in Sikh scholarship and interpretation. In a situation in which a male and a female engage in an extramarital relationship, it is somehow the woman who is held responsible for the deceit. This suggests the presupposition that women fulfil the role of temptresses who are defined primarily by their sexuality, a sexuality which they use to ensnare males. It is as if the men who engage in illicit relationships with women are somehow less responsible for their actions.

In addition, the characterization of the *Charitropakhian* as primarily a text about deceitful women, coupled with the fact that there is so little detailed discussion of the actual contents of *Charitropakhian*, suggests that commentators may be linking notions of a dangerous female sexuality with a related set of ideals regarding female modesty, and the notion that sexuality, licit or illicit, should not be discussed openly. When, for example, commentators argue that Guru Gobind Singh could not possibly have composed *Charitropakhian* because it is inconceivable that the Sikh Guru would even consider addressing such matters in the potentially public forum of a written text, the underlying value they are expressing is that sexuality is not a matter for public discussion and that it is separate from matters of spirituality.[11]

Given that *Charitropakhian* is a male-authored text presented to a male audience with women as one of its primary subjects, it is also possible to read it as reflecting a male assessment of the female gender. Although the stories as a whole do not present a uniform assessment of female character, key themes emerge. One is the notion that women are willing and able to be deceitful, whether in order to deceive their husbands or for more noble pursuits such as outwitting thieves.[12] Another is that women are capable of fighting valiantly in battle, often disguising themselves as men to do so (indicating yet again their skill at deceit; in this instance, in deceiving men into thinking they are battling other men rather than women).[13]

The inclusion of many classic love stories (which generally end tragically), such as that of Hir and Ranjha, which originated in the Punjab, suggests an acknowledgement of the power of love between men and women. Still, much of the advice dispensed throughout *Charitropakhian* suggests that men should always be wary of women and their motives; men are frequently cautioned against giving their hearts to women or revealing secrets to women because of women's generally sneaky natures. The flip side to this, of course, is the presumption that men are vulnerable to manipulation and easily deceived, although male commentators have not made mention of this point.

And there are women who put their cleverness to positive use. Charitra 100, for example, describes a queen who was able to defeat a demon who had managed to outwit various male religious leaders. The stories in *Charitropakhian* do not devalue women's intelligence by any means; they do suggest, however, that women may not always put their intelligence to good use and that men therefore must be ever wary of them.

CONCLUSION

In many ways, the Dasam Granth and its history illustrate what Doris R. Jakobsh has called 'the guiding principle in Sikh history with regard to women'—silence (Jakobsh 2003: 8). While key aspects of the Dasam Granth relate to construction of female gender whether in divine or human form, females themselves have had little role in the transmission and public discussion of the text. With respect to the portion of the Dasam Granth most directly concerned with females, *Charitropakhian*, we find a male-authored text tailored to a male audience presenting a male assessment of females. The omission of *Charitropakhian* from so many editions of the Dasam Granth is itself a clear illustration of silence. Nonetheless, reading the text through the lens of gender may provide a clearer picture of Sikh theology and the role of gender in understanding divinity. Nikky Singh's work shows that the Dasam Granth's goddess mythology can provide the foundation for a feminist theology in Sikhism. Given the ongoing controversy over *Charitropakhian* and whether or not it should even be published, however, it seems far less likely that Sikh commentators are likely to turn to it as a resource for shaping a contemporary Sikh vision of conceptions of gender.

NOTES

1. For a detailed analysis of the relationship between the Dasam Granth and the Sanskrit *Puranas* on which they appear to be based, see Jaggi (1965).

2. Some sources also mention Mata Sahib Kaur as a third wife. However, some Sikhs have argued that in fact Jito and Sundari were the same person, and that the Guru was not married to Mata Sahib Kaur. See, for example, http://www.sikhpoint.com/community/articles/GuruGobindAnd3Wives.php.

3. *Suraj Prakash* is a short version of Bhai Santokh Singh's voluminous *Sri Gur Pratap Suraj Granth*, which describes the lives of the ten Gurus and subsequent Sikh history.

4. The importance of weaponry is evidenced in later Sikh tradition. Early sources related to Khalsa tradition mention five weapons, and one of the Five Ks is the *kirpan* or sword.

5. One of the first to make the argument that Guru Gobind Singh sought to demonstrate the futility of goddess worship was Giani Gian Singh, in his 1880 *Panth Prakash*; for an English summary see Macauliffe (1990: 64–5). See also Banerjee (1976: 21–9) and Gupta (1984: 263–5).

6. For a detailed summary of arguments for and against Guru Gobind Singh as author of the Dasam Granth, see Jaggi (1966: 12–90).

7. Grewal and Bal (1967: 74–5) suggest that the Jap may be modelled on the Sanskrit text *Visnu Sahasra Nama* or 'thousand names of Visnu', which is part of a genre of Sanskrit texts listing various names and epithets of Hindu gods and goddesses.

8. The classic statement is *Bhagavad Gita* 4:7, in which Krishna proclaims, 'Whenever righteousness [*dharma*] falters and chaos threatens to prevail, I take on a human body and manifest myself on earth' (Mitchell 2000: 73).

9. In many early manuscripts of the Dasam Granth, the compositions *Bachitra Natak, Chandi Charitra Ukti Bilasa, Chandi Charitra 2, Chaubis Avatar, Brahma Avatar*, and *Rudra Avatar* are all described as being part of the *Bachitra Natak Granth* (see Jaggi 1965: 272).

10. For two early versions of this analysis of Guru Gobind Singh and the goddess, see Nikky-Guninder Kaur Singh (1989 and 1990). She makes a similar argument in chapter four of her 1993 book *The Feminine Principle in The Sikh Vision of the Transcendent*. See also her 2005 book *The Birth of the Khalsa: A Feminist Re-Memory of Sikh Identity*.

11. The relationship between attitudes about female sexuality and gendered understandings of the deity has been an important topic in the feminist critique of religion in general. For example, Plaskow (1990) argues that resistance to adopting female imagery for God in Judaism, in addition to the more familiar male imagery, stems from the presupposition that women are fundamentally

defined by their sexuality and their reproductive abilities. If one associates women with sexuality more than men, using female imagery for God is to associate sexuality with God, a troubling move to many. See especially her chapter 'Toward a New Theology of Sexuality'.

12. In Charitra 32, for example, a wife cleverly outwits a band of thieves from robbing her home while her husband is away.

13. See, for example, Charitras 57, 96, 102.

REFERENCES

Banerjee, A.C. (1976). 'Guru Gobind Singh and the Shakti Cult', *The Sikh Review*, Vol. 24, No. 268 (April).

Bindra, Pritpal Singh (2002). *Chritro Pakhyaan: Tales of Male-Female Tricky Deceptions from Sri Dasam Granth*, 2 vols, Amritsar: B. Chattar Singh Jiwan Singh.

Chhibbar, Kesar Singh (1972). *Bansavalinama Dasan Patshahian ka*. Rattan Singh Jaggi (ed.), *Parkh: Research Bulletin of Panjabi Language and Literature*, Vol. 2, Chandigarh: Punjab University Press.

Cole, W. Owen (1995). Review of *The Feminine Principle in The Sikh Vision of the Transcendent. Bulletin of the School of Oriental and African Studies*, Vol. 58, No. 2, pp. 399–400.

Grewal, J.S. and S.S. Bal (1967). *Guru Gobind Singh (A Biographical Study)*, Chandigarh: Department of History, Panjab University.

Gupta, Hari Ram (1984). *History of the Sikhs: Volume 1 (The Sikh Gurus, 1469–1708)*, New Delhi: Munshiram Manoharlal.

Jaggi, Rattan Singh (1965). *Dasam-Granth ki Pauranik Prshthabhumi*, Delhi: Bharati Sahitya Mandir.

—— (1966). *Dasam Granth da Kartritav*, New Delhi: Panjabi Sahit Sabha.

Jakobsh, Doris R. (2003). *Relocating Gender in Sikh History: Transformation, Meaning, and Identity*, New Delhi: Oxford University Press.

Kahn Singh Nabha (1990). *Gurushabad Ratnakar Mahan Kosh*, Delhi: National Book Shop.

Macauliffe, M.A. (1990). *The Sikh Religion: Its Gurus, Sacred Writings and Authors*, Vol. 5, Delhi: Low Price Publications.

Mitchell, Stephen (tr.) (2000). *Bhagavad Gita: A New Translation*, New York: Three Rivers Press.

Singh, Bhai Santokh (1999). *Suraj Prakash*, Amritsar: Chhattar Singh Jivan Singh.

Singh, Nikky-Guninder Kaur (1989). True Significance of Guru Gobind Singh Recalling Durga, *The Sikh Review*, Vol. 37, No. 7, pp. 9–23.

—— (1990). 'Guru Gobind Singh's Idea of Durga in His Poetry: The Unfathomable Woman as the Image of the Unfathomable Transcendent One', *Ultimate Reality and Meaning*, Vol. 13, pp. 243–67.

—— (1993). *The Feminine Principle in The Sikh Vision of the Transcendent*, Cambridge: Cambridge University Press.

—— (2005). *The Birth of the Khalsa: A Feminist Re-Memory of Sikh Identity*, Albany: State University of New York Press.

Tracing Gender in the Texts and Practices of the Early Khalsa

Purnima Dhavan

In 1810, Rani Bhagberi, the widow of Karam Singh, the chief of the tiny rural estate of Mani Majra created a will leaving her possessions to her two grandsons through the female line. When she died a few years later the male relatives of her husband raised questions about the validity of her will. Mani Majra was close to the important Sikh states ruled by the Phulkian family including Patila, Nabha, and Jindh and its chiefs had long had alliances with these states. Since the Phulkian and other smaller states of the Cis-Satluj area had signed a treaty with the East India Company in 1809 the British were eager to settle the claims of the estate (Farooqi 1986: 17–18). The Sikh chiefs of the area, however, began to take sides in the dispute. Sensing that a feud over this dispute could grow, George Birch of the nearby Karnal Agency was charged with investigating the competing claims on the estate. Central to this dispute was the legal position of daughters and widows in the inheritance laws of the Sikh ruling families. As the petitions and counter-claims piled up in the Agency offices in Karnal it became increasingly clear that there was no consensus among the neighbouring Sikh chiefs about the legal and social rights due to the women in the ruling families. In fact, even the question of whether to follow Sikh customs or the customs of the caste groups to which the rulers belonged was under dispute (Birch 1921: 1–34).[1]

The adopted heirs of Rani Bhagberi cited precedence in Sikh custom allowing women to inherit their husbands' estates. Rani Ratan Kaur, Bhagberi's daughter-in-law even flatly stated the futility in trying to find a customary precedence since succession through much of the eighteenth century in Sikh-ruled areas was chaotic and 'everything went by strength' (ibid.: 26). Strongly implied through much of this petition is the theme that any 'custom' to which Rani Rattan Kaur's rivals laid claim were newly invented depending on the whims and powers of the chiefs concerned. In contrast, the male kin of Rani Bhagberi's husband began by asserting the difference between Sikh custom and that of the ruling families of the Phulkian and Bhaikiyan clans. Bhai Lal Singh, the primary claimant against Rani Bhagberi's designated inheritors asserted in his petition to Birch: 'I argue on the customs of my caste. If I was to quote what belongs to others, it would form a volume, and I have nothing to do with Sikh customs' (ibid.: 24). The Bhaikiyan family's caste status in these documents was unclear. Bhai Lal Singh had previously claimed that the curtailment of a widow's rights to her husband's property rested on the authority of Guru Ram Das, the fourth Guru of the Sikhs, who had adopted the Bhaikiyan ancestors and asked them to follow the Khatri caste's rules of inheritance, disallowing women from inheriting (ibid.: 15). In another document, however, Lal Singh claimed that as Rajputs the family did not let women inherit (ibid.: 30). At the heart of Lal Singh's claims was the caste status of his family and he variously claimed that they were Khatri—of the same caste as the Sikh Gurus—and later that they were Rajputs (ibid.). There was even the concession that in Sikh 'institutes' women were allowed to inherit, but that custom had never been adopted by the Bhaikiyan families (ibid.: 22). Lal Singh ended his petition by roundly disparaging both the character of women and their capability for governing (ibid.). The interpretation of different rights and duties for men and women and even a gendered understanding of rights, duties, and status referred to by the litigants in this case clearly depended on conflicting ideas of both caste and religion.

The disputed claims to the Mani Majra estate are a reminder that when some families took the *khande ki pahul* or sword initiation and became Khalsa Sikhs they did not completely abandon their older social practices and caste identities. The last half of the eighteenth century was an extremely chaotic period for Sikhs in Punjab. The fortunes and influence of individual chiefs and their extensive caste *biradari*s (kinship networks, literally brotherhoods) waxed and waned in dramatic and unpredictable ways. As this paper will demonstrate, gendered understandings of collective honour and reciprocity among the men in landholding groups became an important way of preserving and extending the fragile social coalitions in this period. How Khalsa men acted as warriors and members of a new ruling order in public was as important to the preservation of this new paradigm as the restraints put on the behaviour and autonomy of Khalsa women. Embodying the collective honour of their natal families and those into which they married, elite Sikh women were subject to new rules of decorum and more circumscribed rights. As the Mani Majra case indicates, the ability of women to negotiate and resist these new norms was somewhat limited since this required the support of these very same social networks whose status now dictated a more circumscribed role for elite women. Such cases emphasize the need to understand the changing attitudes towards categories such as gender and caste in Sikh history not only through prescriptive texts, but also actual social practices. It is particularly important to pay attention to the evolving social practices of the Khalsa in the late eighteenth century, since such an approach reveals that the casteless society described by the prescriptive sources often used by scholars, did not in fact exist in Punjab at that time.

Relying on prescriptive literature in religious texts to understand Sikh ideas about gender in the eighteenth century poses clear problems since they often describe an ideal rather than reality. There are also other problems associated with the textual sources for this period. Since these works represent multiple authors with differing social visions, focusing on different texts leads to entirely different, even contradictory, readings of the normative traditions represented within these texts. The dating and authorship of the Dasam Granth, the scripture attributed to the tenth and last Guru of the Sikhs, remains controversial and it is not clear how much of it was authored by the tenth Guru or by other writers (McLeod 1999: 79–82; Singh 1969: 61–7). Another source for information about Sikh understandings of gender is the *rahitnama* literature (codes of conduct), which attempted to define an appropriate code of conduct for the new Khalsa, but most of these texts date to the period after Guru Gobind Singh's assassination in 1708. It is also not clear how much actual influence these rahitnama texts from the eighteenth and early nineteenth century had on the wider Sikh population. Some scholars have navigated the textual problems by attempting to analyse texts most closely associated with the last Guru, and thus considered more authoritative, such as the *Bachitra Natak* and *Chandi Charitra*, while expressing some skepticism about those that were clearly authored after his death, such as the *Pakhyan Charitra*. Following this strategy, Nikky-Guninder Kaur Singh's critical analyses of the incorporation of the feminine in Sikh scripture identified a crucial paradox in contemporary Sikh cultural understandings of gender—while there was ample evidence of an inclusive ontology and theology in Sikhism, Singh argued that the exegetical practices and social structures in modern Punjab is a reinforced rather than weakened patriarchy (Singh 1993: 11–15). Doris R. Jakobsh's analysis of gender in the eighteenth-century Sikh tradition looks more broadly at other texts associated with the new Khalsa such as the The *Chaupa Singh Rahit-nama* and the other portions of the Dasam Granth such as the *Pakhyan Charitra*. The *Chaupa Singh Rahit-nama* clearly positions men as the normative members of the new warrior community, while women occupy an ambivalent secondary place. Jakobsh has pointed out that the prescriptive literature of the early Khalsa viewed women in a far more negative light as they were excluded from the initiation rite of khande ki pahul, the bearing of weapons, and seen as a danger to the disciplined moral behaviour of the warrior-saints of the Khalsa (Jakobsh 2003: 42–4).

Both major studies of gender in the Sikh tradition mentioned above derive their arguments from a close reading of the prescriptive texts of the Khalsa, including the scripture attributed to the tenth Guru, the Dasam Granth, and the rahitnamas. We know relatively little about how gender was constructed in the actual social practices of the eighteenth-century Khalsa. While the prescriptive texts of the Sikh tradition were an important influence on the understanding of appropriate conduct for Sikh men and women, the existing notions of appropriate *kshatriya* or warrior codes of behaviour also began to affect the social behaviour of Sikh rulers. This mix of practices was not restricted to the prominent Sikh ruling families alone. As the case of Rani Bhagberi indicates, the social practices of politically prominent families such as that of the Phulkians would be adapted and adopted by the chiefs of smaller rural estates such as Mani Majra.

My argument will demonstrate that while Sikh chiefs struggled to implement the egalitarian notions regarding caste implicit in the creation of the Khalsa in the early parts of the eighteenth century, by the late eighteenth century most chiefs were in favour of establishing a hierarchical order in which they alone emerged as rulers, patrons, and patriarchs. These attempts generated some tension with the egalitarian ideals of the Khalsa and led to the elaboration of ceremonies in which the symbolic equality of the participants was emphasized—such as ceremonies involving turban exchanges. At the same time honour feuds proliferated as a growing emphasis on appropriate masculine conduct and warrior caste status created a need to zealously guard even the slightest perceived insult to a chief's honour. Increasingly, by the close of the eighteenth century, the emerging code of masculine honour for Khalsa warriors dictated that social and political alliances were to be preserved through the elaborate conduct of ceremonies of patronage and marriage and policed by the constant threat of feuds. In such circumstances, gender roles within the Khalsa ruling order became polarized.

As we shall see, while the political order in Punjab was in flux, there existed some latitude in how Sikh men and women, particularly those from the ruling families, could navigate the restrictions placed on their rights and duties within the evolving order by creatively interpreting caste or religious customs. As the nineteenth century began and the various states in Punjab were absorbed by Ranjit Singh's growing empire in the west and the East India Company's territories in the east, this latitude evaporated. Khalsa men had less political autonomy but laboured under the continued pressures of maintaining a hyper-masculine identity in order to maintain an imperiled social and political status. Khalsa women could no longer use the elite privileges of their families to create a limited autonomy in relation to property and contractual rights; gradually their role as subordinate and dependent figures in their families became even more circumscribed under colonial rule.

TEXTUAL TRADITIONS AND SOCIAL PRACTICE

The Sikh construction of sovereignty and warrior identity both owed much to the critique of Mughal political authority and its excesses during the period of the Sikh Gurus. Guru Gobind Singh, the creator of the warrior Khalsa order, had long opposed the Mughal Emperor Aurangzeb's rule as tyrannical. In his compositions such as the *Zafarnama,* which would later be included in the second Sikh scripture, the Dasam Granth, the Guru detailed the abuse of power under Aurangzeb's rule (Sri Dasam Granth Sahibji 1391).[2] According to the theology associated with the tenth Guru, worldly power was an instrument of divine power and a means of creating *dharam* or moral order on earth. Its use for any other purpose, particularly for self-gratification, was both vainglorious and short-lived. Thus, even the Mughal Emperor's authority, would be used and subverted by divine will and dharam would be restored on earth. Sikhs were urged to discern between different types of power, legitimate and illegitimate, to support virtue and resist tyranny:

You alone determine who has the right to rule, whether it will be the descendents of Baba (Guru Nanak) or Babar (founder of the Mughal Dynasty),
Discern between the rightful rulers by their characteristics.
Those who do not give freely to Baba eventually have it appropriated by Babar,
One who builds his own house through plundering others will be punished.
(Sri Dasam Granth Sahibji 1988: 71).

It is clear reading the *Bachitra Natak,* the section of the Dasam Granth from which the preceding quote is taken, that the 'dharam' referred to in this text is not the conventional caste order of Brahminical texts. The gift of governance is not according to caste, but through the capability of the ruler. In early Khalsa texts, the idea of priests or any type of spiritual deputies as custodians of dharam is firmly rejected, and emphasis

placed on a personal effort towards moral salvation. According
to Sainapati, writing in 1711, when Guru Gobind Singh created
the Khalsa in 1699 he reaffirmed Sikh rejection of caste and
priestly authority. The office of *masands*—who claimed to be
deputies of the Guru—was abolished and the new initiation
ceremony emphasized the more egalitarian aspects of inclusion
and governance of the new community (Ganda Singh 1967:
23–4).[3] The Guru himself took the *pahul* initiation from the first
five initiates, and all swore to recognize no other authority other
than that of the Guru. Men who wished to become Khalsa Sikhs
were initiated through a ceremony called khande ki pahul. The
initiate had to drink sweetened water stirred by five other Khalsa
Sikhs holding a double-edged sword (*khanda*). Communal consumption of food and drink between members of the Khalsa
destroyed the earlier caste identities of the Khalsa initiates; they
were also highly visible after initiation since they were expected
to maintain uncut hair (*kes*) and carry weapons at all times.[4]

Early Khalsa literature, the Dasam Granth and the first
rahitnamas and *gurbila*s (celebratory narratives of the last Guru's
life), clearly viewed world power as corrupting. The virtue of
the Khalsa warrior could only be protected through constant
humility and a life of service to the Khalsa community. The
Khalsa warrior was to bear weapons at all times, avoid all evil
impulses such as pride, lust, greed, anger, and attachment to
worldly pursuits.[5] He was to be the embodiment of a disciplined
and virtuous masculinity never seeking to be thought better than
his Khalsa brethren (Bhangu 1995: 214).[6] While these early texts
established the basic framework upon which later constructions
of Sikh masculinity and honour would be constructed, they posed
a problem to Sikh rulers attempting to create a political system
using older social hierarchies such as caste. If all in the Khalsa
were to be equal, how would political hierarchies function?

This Khalsa Sikh model of masculinity and the insistence on
the egalitarian brotherhood of men, of course, contrasted sharply
with the masculinity associated with nobility or *mirzai* prized
in the aristocratic circles of the Mughal court during the late
seventeenth century. Rosalind O' Hanlon's research indicates
that by the latter half of the seventeenth century concepts of
masculinity were beginning to change in the Mughal nobility.
The Mughal noble who also aspired to be a *mirza* attempted

to distinguish himself from the rising classes of merchants and new nobility that were emerging throughout the Mughal Empire with the expansion of trade. The new mirza's refined dress and consumption patterns, according to O'Hanlon, reflected not only the ability to consume more expensive luxury goods, but also an aesthetic and restrained eye for appropriate colours, flavours, fabrics suitable for each occasion and season (O'Hanlon 2004: 75–6). Unlike the older modes of nobility in which Mughal aristocrats were expected to live a life of service to the empire, the new mirzas avoided the appearance of toadying to the emperor or higher nobility, instead they attempted to cultivate an independent existence dedicated to a life of aesthetic and spiritual refinement lived in the company of peers with similar tastes in dress, music, cuisine, and modes of consumption. These expensive tastes were a source of tension with the older Mughal expectations of military service and absolute fidelity to the Emperor. The emergence of these newer forms of mirzai were not unsurprisingly accompanied by scorn and stigmatization from other Mughal social circles, particularly those who viewed it as a deviant and effeminate perversion of older norms, but also from the emerging sense of an entirely different sort of masculinity prized by the warriors of the emerging Sikh and Afghan powers (O'Hanlon 1997: 8–12).

While the idea of a disciplined masculinity associated with martial conduct, humility, and service to the Khalsa community contrasted sharply with the supposed self-indulgence of more aristocratic circles, it also posed problems for the Sikh chiefs who came to power in the mid eighteenth century. Political power implied that the chief was at the apex of a hierarchy. Sikh chiefs frequently made appeals to a shared caste origin to build solidarity within their kinship groups and claim a nobler descent (Griffin 1998: 2).[7] Yet, at the same time, the chiefs could not appear to be displaying pride or claiming precedence over other Khalsa Sikhs. Most Sikh chiefs came to power as leaders of bands of cavalry called *misl*s. These had evolved from the raiding parties and war bands formed during the period of Sikh rebellion against the Mughals in the first part of the eighteenth century (Grewal 1994: 82). Although the new Khalsa rejected caste pride, its very *creation* generated deep divisions along caste lines in some parts of the Sikh community (Deol 2000: 27). The presence of lower-caste Jats in the early Khalsa and the inclusion of rituals such as khande ki pahul that broke caste observances were of much concern to the higher caste Khatri traders who were prominent in the Sikh community. The poet Sainapati recounts how shortly after news of the Guru's creation of the Khalsa reached Delhi, Khatri merchants had deep disagreements about complying with the new forms and abandoning older caste practices. Some favoured obeying the Guru's decree, while others worried that observing rituals that broke their caste identity would lead to a complete social boycott by fellow Khatris and they would lose face in their caste community and suffer the loss of the livelihood as well (Singh 1967: 32–3). For Sainapati, those preoccupied with preserving the status of their families (*kul*) were blind to their actual losses: 'wrapped in the illusion of *kul* they lose everything'. Social interaction with such persons, according to Sainapati was to be avoided (ibid.: 43). Sainapati is among the first Sikh writers to emphasize the necessity of avoiding social contact with those who did not observe the Khalsa rahit or rules of conduct.

Unfortunately, for much of the eighteenth century, Jats who became Khalsa Sikhs found that the need for caste solidarity was not merely a matter of social convenience but actual survival. Between 1709 and 1715, large numbers of Jats joined the peasant rebellion led by Banda, a *Vasihnav* monk who claimed to be the last Guru's deputy. In the aftermath of Banda's rebellion after 1715 both Mughal and Afghan authorities authorized officers to hunt down Sikhs, setting monetary rewards for Sikhs captured or killed and conducting house-to-house searches in order to arrest and punish Sikhs and those who harboured them (Rai 1811: 60, 64).[8] As Mughal–Sikh conflict intensified in the early part of the eighteenth century, more and more Jats joined the Sikh Khalsa. Why would they choose to do so? The heavy-handed tactics of the Punjab governors led to a greater sense of solidarity among Jat kinship groups. Also, as their ethnic rivals such as the Manj Rajputs and Bhattis formed alliances with the Mughal officers, Jats also closed ranks. Since the new Khalsa provided a way of defending territory and organizing against these groups, young Jat men began to join the Khalsa in larger numbers in the eighteenth century (Dhavan 2003: 49–50).[9]

Within the Sikh misls and through the institutions connected with the main Sikh shrine at Amritsar that was used as a base by all the Sikh misls, young Jats were instructed in the niceties of Khalsa Sikh behaviour. As Sikh power over parts of Panjab solidified in the mid eighteenth century, new rahitnamas cautioned new Sikhs to be particularly attentive to their roles as representatives of a new warrior order. This was particularly stressed in the care given to the maintenance of arms and other outward markers of Khalsa identity such as uncut hair, or kes. The literature from this early period endeavours to remind the new Khalsa of their mission and duties. The *Nasihat Nama* of 1718 attributed to Nand Lal attempts to define Khalsa conduct in terms of one who is steadfast in battle and never turns his back, one who controls the five evil impulses (lust, anger, pride, greed, and attachment to worldly things), avoids Brahminical rituals, and embraces Sikh practices (McLeod 2003: 284). That this advice is addressed to a male audience becomes clear with the following injunction against viewing women with lustful eyes, marrying daughters to men who were not Khalsa Sikhs, or accepting any bride price for a daughter or sister given in marriage (ibid.: 281). Sexual discipline rather than gender equity appears to be the intended goal of the few sections of this work that mention women, in fact the role of a patriarch in arranging marriages or functioning as a model of chaste masculinity is affirmed. Much like Sainapati's work, this rahitnama or code of conduct also attempts to separate recruits from older caste observances and alliances, redirecting their energies to a future in which these would be unimportant. Khalsa Sikhs are constantly reminded of the future that awaits those who put their faith in the Guru:

Hear this truth, Nand Lal
I shall establish my rule.
I shall merge the four castes into one
I shall have people repeat 'Praise to the Guru.'
My Sikhs shall ride swift horses and fly like hawks
Muslims once sighted shall be defeated
One Sikh will confront a host of 125,000
Spiritual liberation awaits that Singh who fights
Banners shall wave, grand elephants shall parade
Music shall resound at every gate.

The mighty host shall discharge their guns.
When they do the Khalsa shall arise and all enemies of the truth shall be
overthrown (McLeod 2003: 285).

Soon after the suppression of Banda's rebellion, Khalsa Sikhs
reestablished control over the main Sikh shrine at Amritsar
and began the first attempts to preserve Guru Gobind Singh's
legacy. It was during this chaotic period that the Dasam Granth,
the scripture associated with Guru Gobind Singh was compiled
sometime between 1721 and 1738 (ibid.: 61–2). According to
a recent study by Jeevan Deol, this text is the meta-narrative
that grounds Khalsa identity in a larger cosmological universe
shared with those who were not part of the Khasla, yet reserved
the role of the warriors who would restore order to the world
to the Khalsa alone (Deol 2000: 39–40). It is within this
larger cosmological universe that a literature different from
the rahitnamas emerges in that it does not seek to emphasize
the differences among Khalsa Sikhs, *Sahajdharis* (those Sikhs
who did not did not take pahul [initiation]) and non-Sikhs.
Instead it attempts to place Guru Gobind Singh's life within
the *Puranic* stories about Hindu Gods and Goddesses familiar
to the majority of South Asians. By doing so, the text read as a
whole suggests that just as these incarnations and emanations
of the divine took human birth to save humanity from evil, so
also the Guru takes birth to continue the cosmic struggle of
good over evil (ibid.: 33). In this wider cosmological struggle the
Khalsa would continue this mission after Guru Gobind Singh's
death. The hymns to Goddesses such as Chandi, found in this
text, appear to have inspired other authors to frame the tenth
Guru's life within a cosmology that posited his struggle against
internal and external foes as a cosmic struggle for good over
evil. For authors such as Koer Singh writing at the end of the
misl period, the Khalsa continued the Guru's struggle, and thus
the older mythology of the Puranas found in the Dasam Granth
also became a justification of the moral legitimacy of Khalsa rule
(Singh 1999: 101–2).[10]

The Khalsa as Creators and Preservers of Social Order

Since the new Khalsa rulers claimed to be restorers of dharam,
and through this function, the latest in a long line of warrior

dynasties, it comes as no surprise that older notions of masculine honour and appropriate warrior conduct were absorbed into the cultural practices of the Khalsa elite. Gender norms were inevitably linked to ideas of caste and religion. The role of caste as a marker of status, the basis for matrimonial and political alliances, and, as the rubric for patronage between ruler and ruled would be invoked in many of the new customs favoured by the Khalsa rulers, often with uneasy accommodation with older Sikh norms. Notions of caste and honour were tightly woven together, both in the prescriptive texts of the Sikhs of the late eighteenth century, but also in their actual deeds and words. The honour, or *izzat*, of a Sikh ruler was particularly symbolized by the protection and exchange of two repositories of his family's honour—women, and the turbans worn by its men. Women occupied a site of dual symbolism within the new culture of the Khalsa rulers, first as repositories of their families' honour, but also as the secondary category in reference to which the masculine identity of the Khalsa warrior was created (Jakobsh 2003: 40–9).[11]

The increasing political successes of the Khalsa chiefs in the late eighteenth century brought issues of honour and caste identity into sharper focus. As the Sikh misls gradually gained territories and developed into hereditary chiefdoms, the caste identities of the new ruling families underwent a slow transformation. The new ruling families re-centred their caste identities into the Kshatriya/Rajput genealogies associated with more established ruling houses. The Patiala rulers as well as the descendents of Jassa Singh Ahluwalia traced their families back to the old Rajput rulers of Jaisalmer (n.a./d., *Waqa-e Khandan-e Rajgan-e Patiala*, Diwan Ramjas 1897: 82–4).[12] Such moves were not a radical departure for Jats, since the story of the Jats' Rajput origins were well established in oral traditions, and the Jat–Rajput boundaries in Panjab were ambiguous (Ibbetson 1974: 17, 90).

The new emphasis on Kshatriya culture, however, could only succeed with the tacit acceptance of and cooperation by the extended kin branches of the chief's families. Misl chiefs recruited soldiers from within their own natal or collateral branches, or through their caste biradaris (kin networks) in their home territories (Kaur 1980: 14). That these Jats were not always Khalsa

Sikhs is indicated by the practice of requiring new recruits to take pahul (Bhangu 1995: 220). The re-centring of caste identity and the extension of a new warrior masculinity could not be achieved though the individual endeavours of the chief's family alone. To succeed, it needed the tacit acceptance and public participation of a much larger social network. The importance of such ties might explain why the prohibitions against associating with non-Khalsa Sikhs, and relinquishing older caste associations and practices gradually fade away from the Khalsa literature of the late eighteenth century. In particular, prohibitions against marrying Sikhs who had not taken the Khalsa pahul loosened, and it became more important to consider the relative status of each family. For example, in the later rahitnama of Chaupa Singh, the injunction against caste prejudice and pride is modified in connection with marriage alliances; Khalsa Sikhs are instructed to arrange marriages in a way that will not bring dishonour to their families (McLeod 1987: 150).

Women were now seen as symbols of a clan's honour and became highly important in sealing political relationships through marriage alliances, but such exchanges needed to be carefully calibrated to preserve the honour of the family. Weddings, in which the izzat of one family was entrusted to another, could thus be events fraught with the possibility of dishonour. Every effort was taken to cater to the comfort of the groom's family, and any embarrassment suffered by the guests became a public humiliation of the bride's family. Thus, Chaupa Singh warns Sikh women not to sing the 'coarse' songs generally sung at weddings, or indulge in the customary ridiculing or mockery of male guests, which was the customary privilege of the bride's female relatives (ibid.: 189).

One famous incident of a feud sparked during wedding festivities offers us an example of the heightened sensitivities of such occasions. In 1774, Gajpat Singh, the ruler of Jind, one of the minor Phulkian states, was celebrating the nuptials of his daughter, Raj Kaur, with Mahan Singh Sukarchakia. All the Phulkian chiefs were assembled for the event, and the groom also bought a retinue of some 10,000 horsemen and pack animals. These animals were put to pasture on land belonging to the bride's relative, the Phulkian chief of Nabha. Yakub Khan, the agent of the Nabha chief, attacked the groom's party, offending the dignity of Gajpat Singh, the bride's father. This event was felt to be so offensive by Gajpat Singh, that he not only blamed Yakub Singh, but his own relative, and soon after the wedding, Gajpat Singh used a ruse to lure both Yakub Khan and the king of Nabha into his kingdom, and tortured and put to death the agent. The Nabha ruler was only released after the Phulkian chief of Patiala intervened (Griffin 1998: 313–25; Rai 1811: 121–2).

It is not clear if the incident was due to miscommunication between Yakub Khan and his employer, the rule of Nabha, or if the public insult offered to the bride's father was intentional. But regardless of the actual reason for this feud it is clear that Gajpat Singh felt the humiliation of the incident keenly. During such public festivities the extended kin of the bride were expected to show solidarity and support. Sharing the costs of hospitality was an expectation and the public flouting of this unwritten code—whether intentional or not—endangered not only the status of the bride's father as a generous host but also his sense of masculine honour as a warrior, if the insult was allowed to pass without retribution.

Many historians of the Sikhs have lamented the seemingly petty and pointless feuding of the minor Sikh chiefs, without analysing the cultural place of feuding in the misl system (Singh 1991: 184). A brief examination of both the system of reciprocal gift exchanges and feuding will reveal that both practices were linked to the creation and extension of a new masculine warrior identity by Khalsa Sikhs. The public nature of such exchanges and feuds, and the participation of a chief's kin networks in such exchanges were crucial to the wide-scale reinterpretation of warrior identity not just for the immediate family of the chief, but also to wider kinship group to which the chief belonged. It was not only a means of creating solidarity within certain groups, but also a demand to be treated with respect as a social equal by another chief.

The most significant marker of this extended participation in the new warrior culture was the system by which newly conquered land and its income were distributed by the chief. The gifting of strips of land or *patti*s to the subordinates of the chief, entitled the grantee to act as a leader or *sirdar* of soldiers in his own right. While still acknowledging the authority of the granting chief, the income from such grants allowed the *pattidar*, or recipient, to participate in a shared warrior culture and acquire honour as a patron of other soldiers and holy sites himself. The revenue system of the Sikhs, thus, was also a means of distributing honour or izzat. The independence of such lesser chiefs was widely recognized, even by Sikh rulers who had achieved the political supremacy over other chiefs (Forster 1798: 287). Generosity was a virtue expected of rulers. Thus the defeat of lesser chiefs in war could not end in complete public humiliation, since such a move would be damaging to the reputation of the conqueror. Even as Ranjit Singh began to conquer large parts of the Punjab in the nineteenth century, these values were still important, and in most cases after defeating another Sikh chief, Ranjit Singh provided the defeated chief with a symbolic grant that enabled the chief to continue to maintain a semblance of his former lifestyle. More importantly, the soldiers of that chief were often incorporated into Ranjit Singh's army. When the powerful Bhangi chiefs were defeated, Ranjit Singh publicly presented the Bhangi Sirdar with a *jagir* (revenue from an estate) promising that 'he would always look after and protect him and his dignity' (Garret 1970: 16).

Similarly another important ceremony used by the Khalsa chiefs was the ceremonial exchange of turbans in public between two chiefs. Such an exchange was usually undertaken to seal a compact—and since turbans in South Asian culture also symbolize a warrior's honour or izzat—the chiefs involved in the ritual were publicly entrusting each other with one another's honour in a public expression of that trust. The participants' mutual recognition of each other as social equals was also an important component of this ritual. One such exchange took place between Jassa Singh Ahluwalia and Charhat Singh Sukerchakia in the mid eighteenth century (Ramjas 1897: 148). At this time these rulers and their associates were powerful rivals with their bases in the eastern and western parts of Punjab respectively. Another turban exchange took place nearly a half-century later between their descendants Bhag Singh and Ranjit Singh in 1802, and both swore on the Guru Granth Sahib, the Sikh scripture, to maintain their friendship (Griffin 1998: 519). By this time, Bhag Singh Ahluwalia's family had comparatively less power, but his links to the now legendary Jassa Singh made him a powerful and symbolically useful ally.

The symbolism of the turban exchange becomes clear when compared with the *khilat* ceremony used by the Mughals. Unlike the khilat ceremony which symbolized the subordination of a lesser chief into the symbolic dress/body-politic of the Emperor, the turban exchange was a public acknowledgement of the equality of rank between chiefs (Hambly 2003: 36).[13] Even in cases where the actual power of one chief was considerably more than that of the other, as in the case of Ranjit Singh and Bhag Singh Ahluwalia, the public acknowledgement of an alliance had to also be accompanied by the symbolic acknowledgement of the other chief as a brother warrior, not a subordinate. The honour and masculine identity of each chief had to be acknowledged in order to preserve the collective honour and status of the Khalsa brotherhood as a ruling order. The turban had become a symbol of the honour of the Khalsa as a whole.

The importance given to the turban in the later period makes sense when one thinks of its relationship to kes or uncut hair in the early Sikh texts as one of the key outward identifiers of Khalsa Sikhs. The *Chaupa Singh Rahit-nama* warns: 'A Gursikh should not fight a scuffle with another person, for in doing so he may sully and defile his kes. Ensure that the dignity of your kes is protected' (McLeod 1987: 155). This advice is supplemented by the warning that pulling another Sikh's turban, or knocking off the turban is a serious offence against the Khalsa code or rahit (ibid.: 177). As a symbol of the warrior status of the Khalsa Sikh, and an emblem of his masculinity, the kes had to be guarded in other ways as well. Khalsa Sikhs were prohibited to let a woman groom their kes, or appear in the company of women with their kes untied (ibid.: 187). In a similar vein, a Khalsa Sikh was also to avoid eating a woman's leftover food, dancing, wearing red clothes, or applying black collyrium to his eyes (ibid.: 178, 180).[14] Clearly by the mid eighteenth century the rahit was developing into a more complex and gendered code of behaviour.

The gendered worldview of the mid-eighteenth-century Khalsa culture is also reflected in the prohibition by Chaupa Singh against women reading the Guru Granth Sahib in public, or a man doing the same in the company of women (ibid.: 187–8). That the Khalsa identity was primarily believed by mid-eighteenth-century Sikhs like Chaupa Singh as appropriate

for men alone is clear. According to Chaupa Singh, it was a
violation of the rahit to give the sword baptism to a woman, or
for a woman to abuse, berate of fight with a man (ibid.: 186,
188). Thus, in the world of the eighteenth-century Sikhs, the
Khalsa culture was that of hyper-masculine men, while women
served as symbols of the family's honour, to be guarded and
defended by the men of their community. It is notable that
Chaupa Singh's rahitnama is the only text from the eighteenth
century that emphatically denies the ritual of khande ki pahul
to women. Later texts from the nineteenth century offer a
variety of initiation rites for women ranging from the standard
two-edged sword (khanda) initiation, to the use of different
swords or knives (McLeod 2003: 244–5). This indicates that
Chaupa Singh's instructions represent only one among many
different views on the subject. The variety of advice regarding
the initiation practices for women suggests that unlike the ritual
for men there was no standardized ritual for women. Although
this indicates the ambivalent position of women in this culture,
it also suggests that this very ambivalence did leave a space for
women to claim inclusion in the Khalsa to a limited degree. After
all, there would be little need for Chaupa Singh to so roundly
criticize the practice unless its very presence was alarming to
men such as him. The discrepancy within the rahitnamas also
brings into question the authority that the writers of these texts
claimed. It would be far more accurate to see these rahitnamas
as reflecting diverse views within the Khalsa Sikh community,
rather than describing an actual historical reality.

Women from ruling families did occasionally contest the increasingly circumscribed roles into which the warrior ethos of
the Khalsa rulers placed them; however, in each of the cases
that have come to light women gained authority only through
their status as the sisters, wives, and widows of ruling Sikhs. In
other words, similar to the ways in which the social status of
men either through a claim to higher caste, as rulers, or as part
of the Khalsa brotherhood was linked to their sense of masculine
honour, women in ruling families could use their social status
and kinship ties to claim a limited authority in society as 'hon-
ourary men'. This was not an option open to non-elite women.
Exceptional circumstances allowed women to assume power,

however, as soon as the emergency passed, patriarchal control was quickly restored. Other than the well-known example of Sada Kaur, Ranjit Singh's early mentor and mother-in-law, the Patiala court offers numerous examples of such temporary assertions of authority. For example, when the Afghan ruler Ahmed Shah Abdali's armies threatened Patiala, its ruler Alha Singh was away in Monak and had left the administration of the province in the joint hands of his wife Mata Fatoh and his heir and grandson Amar Singh, who was quite young. Mata Fatoh quickly realized that the odds were against the Patiala forces and started negotiations with Abdali's officers (n.a/d, *Tazkira-e Rajgan-e Phulkian, Halat-e Rajgan-e Patiala,* f. 8b, *Waqa-e Khandan-e Rajgan-e Patiala,* f. 11 a–b).[15] Towards the end of the eighteenth century, during the minority of Raja Sahib Singh, the queens of Patiala had greater power (Griffin 1998: 55–6). Even after Sahib Singh assumed power his ineptness endangered the kingdom and he asked his sister Sahib Kaur to assume control over the administration. Sahib Kaur was able to use her own abilities as a commander to rescue her natal state from the incursions of the Marathas and also her husband from the aggressions of his own family. Yet the eventual jealousy of her brother finally drove her away from Patiala and to a premature death in 1799 (ibid.: 75–85).

Such fierceness in the defence of women, yet indifference to 'womanly wiles' were desirable traits for warriors in other cultures as well. It is interesting to note that during Ahmad Shah Durrani's invasion of Panjab, one of the Afghan clerics in his retinue took note of this aspect of the new Sikh warrior culture. Qazi Nur Muhammad, in his *Jangnama,* refers to the Khalsa Sikhs through much of his book as *sag* or dogs, yet in the last part of his composition he points out that, in fact, he judges Sikhs to be worth adversaries: 'They are soldiers who are like roaring lions. If you desire to learn the science of war, learn it from them' (Muhammad 1939: 156). He reluctantly admits that they are men of honour, who never attack those who would be considered '*namard*', or not men. In particular, Nur Muhammad notes that they never capture women, and to them all women are old hags (ibid.: 158–9). This evaluation of desirable warrior traits is strikingly similar to Doris R. Jakobsh's observation that from the eighteenth-century Khalsa perspective, all those who did not take the Khalsa baptism 'were not true men; they were either womanly (those men who refused to heed the Guru's call), or women' (Jakobsh 2003: 48).

The violent and short lives of the Sikh chiefs did provide opportunities for women in their families to assume power occasionally; however, the preference for male successors was never subverted. It is not surprising that despite the active resistance of some women, in the end, the newer norms of courtly behaviour for the women in these families were dominant. In Patiala where the queens had long played critical roles in ruling, especially during the regency of minors, the trend towards closing these avenues to power was particularly noticeable. When Maharajah Karam Singh ascended the throne of Patiala, his attempts to modernize the state would further curtail the rights of his female relatives. In 1820 on the advice of Sayad Barkat Ali Khan of Awadh, who was experienced in the new 'modern' traditions of colonial rule, the queens were asked to remain in *purdah* (veiled seclusion) for the first time in the history of the state (Srivastava 1991: 6). Further negotiations later in the nineteenth century would lead to the barring of women from succession in 1837 and their exclusion from Councils of Regency in all state affairs after 1858 (Griffin 1998: 247, 252). Within this larger context, it is perhaps not surprising that Rani Bhagberi's will, which initiated the dispute narrated at the beginning of this paper, was settled against the wishes expressed in her will, in favour of her husband's male descendents (Birch 1921: 32).

CONCLUSION

Throughout the eighteenth century, Khalsa identity was radically transformed as the political fortunes of the Khalsa improved. Although scholars have emphasized the singularity of the Khalsa as a distinctive religious order, particularly in its emphasis on an egalitarian brotherhood of Sikhs, and, its opposition to caste hierarchies, in actual practice the eighteenth-century Khalsa chiefs were no more egalitarian than the other new warrior groups of the period such as the Afghans and the Marathas. This trend is particularly noticeable in the preoccupation with issues of masculine honour that permeates the later-eighteenth-century Khalsa texts and rituals. The growing emphasis on appropriate masculine conduct within Sikh courtly culture put a premium on rituals of exchange and ritualized feuding. The constant feuds and the rituals of alliances that often ended these feuds reinforced the warrior credentials of these new ethnic and caste groups. These customs also built cohesion among the Khalsa Sikh elite by disseminating masculine ideals and cultural norms that were simultaneously close to older warrior cultures and to some aspects of Jat practices. Extensive recruitment of soldiers and patronage through caste networks helped to extend the ranks of Sikh landholders and warriors.

At the same time; however, the creation of new social hierarchies clearly clashed with the expressed religious beliefs of the wider Sikh communities. This preoccupation with status and honour, however, was not uncritically accepted by all Sikhs. For some Sikhs they were signs of moral perversion, a sign of a new obsession with *Singhi* or rule, rather than *Sikhi*, or fidelity with the teachings of the Sikh Gurus. In one text from the 1760s, the *Bansavalinama*, the self-aggrandizing behaviour of Sikh chiefs is represented as a sign of a coming apocalypse. Kesar Singh Chibbar, the author of this text, reaffirms the older Sikh belief that Sikh values of brotherhood and service were incompatible with worldly rule (Chibbar 1997: 128–9).[16] Such criticism, however, was rare. By and large, later Khalsa histories and rahitnamas attempted to legitimize Sikh rule as one foretold by the last Guru and a reflection of God's moral order or dharam. It comes as no surprise then, that when Sikh reform movements began in earnest in the nineteenth century the 'decadent' and 'Hinduized' practices of the Sikh elite would be among the first to be criticized by Sikh reformers.[17]

NOTES

1. By the time the investigation of claims began the adopted son and one grandson of the Rani were also deceased, and the widow of one grandson, Rattan Kaur, also had a claim on the estate.

2. All page numbers in the Dasam Granth are now standardized. All citations henceforth will use the standard chapter, verse and page format from the following edition, Sri Dasam Granth Sahibji 1988.

3. Sainapati, the author of *Gursobha*, a text generally dated to 1711 emphasizes the corruption and abuse of authority by masands as a primary reason for the founding of the Khalsa.

4. The historical development of Khalsa identity and ritual is a source of contention among scholars. For a generally accepted historical overview see Grewal 1994: 76–8. Pashaura Singh (1999), among others, has argued for a slow development of the markers of Khasa rahit.

5. These virtues are mentioned in several eighteenth-century rahitnamas including those attributed to the companions of the last Guru such as Nand Lal and Prahlad Rai, and Desa Singh (McLeod 2003: 284, 289, 300–1).

6. Several stories praise Sikhs who were known for humble service to the Khalsa, see for example the story of how Nawab Kapur Singh was granted his title by his fellow Sikhs for his humility.

7. This might explain the common origin stories of Rajput descent found in the chronicles of later Sikh ruling families.

8. Khushwaqt Rai's *Tarikh-e Ahwal-e Sikhan* was completed in 1811. Multiple copies of this work exist in archives in India, Pakistan, and the United Kingdom. References in this work are to the copy made for the Khalsa College Archives in 1934 by Pal Singh from a nineteenth-century manuscript in the Punjab Public Library at Lahore (Suri 1956: 8).

9. I discuss the motives for young Jats joining the Khalsa during this time of persecution in chapter 2 of my dissertation, 'The Origins and Growth of the Eighteenth-Century Khalsa *Panth*'. A more extensive discussion of the case of the Phulkian families can be found in Chapter 2, 'Re-reading Alha Singh: Rebel, Rajah, *Sirdar*, and Sikh'.

10. It is striking that these stories about the Guru and the Devi only appear in the later gurbilas narratives from the mid eighteenth century onwards.

11. In this reading I concur with Doris R. Jakobsh's argument regarding a gender duality in the later Khalsa although the evidence of extending it to an earlier period is more tenuous.

12. These genealogies appear to have been written in the nineteenth century after Sikh rule was established, although they have reference to earlier oral histories.

13. See Hambly's notes on Babar's use of *khilat*. By contrast, according to Bhangu, Khalsa Sikhs were uncomfortable accepting a khilat and jagir from the Mughals in 1739 due to the connotation of subservience implied in the ritual (Hambly 2003: 213).

14. The red colour might be a reference to the robes of Sadhus or monks, in this case emphasizing the Khalsa man's obligation to avoid the extremes of either celibacy or debauchery, but aim for a disciplined and chaste life as a married householder.

15. This incident was important enough to be mentioned in both chronicles of the royal family.

16. Chibbar's own work, however, is not immune from the criticisms about caste pride that he levels at Sikh chiefs since through much of his work he emphasizes his own Brahmin heritage and his caste superiority over mere Jat peasants or Kshatriya warriors.

17. See for example, the pamphlets for the later reform period such as those authored by Bhai Kahn Singh Nabha (1973). A more extensive study of this reformist critique can be found in Oberoi (1994).

REFERENCES

Bhangu, Rattan Singh (1995). *Prachin Panth Prakash*, Bhai Vir Singh, ed. New Delhi: Bhai Vir Singh Sahitya Sadan, 1935, reprint 1995.

Birch, George (1921). *Selections from Note-Books kept by* Captain G. *Birch, Assistant to Agent to the Governor-General, Karnal Agency, 1818–1821,* Lahore: Superintendent, Government Printing, Punjab.

Chibbar, Kesar Singh (1997). *Bhai Kesar Singh Chibar Krit Bansavalinama Dasan Patshah Ka,* Piara Singh Padam, ed., Amritsar: Singh Brothers.

Deol, Jeevan (2000). 'Eighteenth Century Khalsa Identity: Discourse, Praxis, and Narrative', in Christopher Shackle, Gurharpal Singh, and Arvind-Pal Mandair (eds), *Sikh Religion, Culture, and Ethnicity,* Sussex: Curzon Press, pp. 25–46.

Dhavan, Purnima (2003). 'The Warriors' Way: The Making of the Eighteenth-Century Khalsa Panth', Unpublished Dissertation, University of Virginia, Charlottesville.

Farooqi, Bashir Ahmed (1986). *British Relations with the Cis-Sutlej States, 1809–1823,* New Delhi: Nirmal Publishers.

Forster, George (1798). *A Journey from Bengal to England, Through the Northern Part of India, Kashmir, Afghanistan, and Persia, and Into Russia by the Caspian Sea, Vol. 1,* London: R. Fauler.

Garret, H.L.O. (1970). *Events at the Court of Ranjit Singh, 1810–1817,* Patiala: Punjabi University Press, 1935, reprint, 1970.

Grewal, J.S. (1994). *The New Cambridge History of India, Vol. II.3: The Sikhs of the Punjab,* Cambridge: Cambridge University Press, 1994.

Griffin, Lepel H. (1998). *The Rajas of the Punjab, Being the History of the Principal States in the Punjab and their Political Relations with the British Government,* New Delhi: Munshilal Manoharlal, 1870, reprint 1998.

Hambly, Gavin (2003). 'The Emperor's New Clothes: Robing and Robes of Honour in Mughal India', in Stewart Gordon (ed.), *Robes of Honour: Khilat in Pre-Colonial and Colonial India,* New Delhi: Oxford University Press, pp. 31–49.

Ibbetson, Sir Denzil (1974). *Punjab Castes,* Lahore: Mubarak Ali Publishers, 1882, reprint 1974.

Jakobsh, Doris R. (2003) *Relocating Gender in Sikh History: Transformation, Meaning, and Identity,* New Delhi: Oxford University Press.

Kaur, Joginder, fw. (1980). *Ram Sukh Rao's Stri Fateh Singh Partap Prabhakar (A History of the Early 19th Century Punjab),* Patiala: Punjabi University.

McLeod, W.H. ed. (1987). *Chaupa Singh Rahit-nama,* Dunedin: University of Otago Press.

McLeod, W.H. (1999). *Evolution of the Sikh Community,* in *Sikhs and Sikhism,* New Delhi: Oxford University Press, 1976, reprint 1999, pp. 79–82.

—— (2003). *Sikhs of the Khalsa: A History of the Khalsa Rahit,* New Delhi: Oxford University Press.

Muhammad, Qazi Nur (1939). *Qazi Nur Muhammad's Jang Namah, Giving an Account of the Seventh Invasion of Ahmed Shah Durrani,* Ganda Singh, ed., Amritsar: Khalsa College Amritsar, Sikh History Research Department.

n.a./d, *Tazkira-e Rajgan-e Phulkian, Halat-e Rajgan-e Patiala, Waqa-e Khandan-e Rajgan-e Patiala*, Patiala State Archives, M/859.

Nabha, Bhai Kahn Singh (1973). *Hum Hindu Nahin*, in Gurdit Singh Giani (ed.), Amritsar: Shri Guru Singh Sabha Shatabdi Committee.

O'Hanlon, Rosalind (1997). 'Issues of Masculinity in North Indian History: The Bangash Nawabs of Farrukhabad', *Indian Journal of Gender Studies*, Vol. 4, No. 1, pp. 1–19.

—— (2004). 'Manliness and Imperial Service in Mughal North India', *JESHO*, Vol. 42, No. 1, pp. 47–93.

Oberoi, Harjot (1994). *The Construction of Religious Boundaries: Culture, Identity, and Diversity in the Sikh Tradition*, New Delhi: Oxford University Press.

Rai, Khushwaqt (1811). *Tarikh-e Ahwal-e Sikhan*, SHR 1273, Sikh History Research Library, Khalsa College Amritsar. Ms. Copy made in 1934.

Ramjas, Diwan (1897). *Tarikh Riyasat Kapurthala, Vol. 1.* Lahore: Guru Gobind Singh Press.

Singh, Ganda, ed. (1967). *Kavi Sainapati Krit Gursobha*, Patiala: Punjabi University, 1967.

Singh, Khushwant (1991). *A History of the Sikhs, Vol. 1: 1469–1839*, New Delhi: Oxford University Press, 1963, reprint 1991.

Singh, Koer (1999). *Gurbilas Patshahi 10*, Pataila: Publication Bureau, Punjabi University.

Singh, Mahip (1969). *Guru Govind Singh aur Unki Hindi Kavita*, New Delhi: National Publishing House, pp. 61–7.

Singh, Nikky-Guninder Kaur (1993). *The Feminine Principle in the Sikh Vision of the Transcendent*, New York: Cambridge University Press.

Singh, Pashaura (1999). 'Formulation of the Convention of the Five Ks A Focus on the Evolution of the Khalsa Rahit', *International Journal of Punjab Studies*, Vol. 6, No. 2, pp. 155–170.

Sri Dasam Granth Sahibji (1988). ed., Giani Mahendra Singh Rattan, Amritsar: Bhai Chattar Singh and Bhai Jiwan Singh.

Srivastava, S.P. (1991). *Art and Cultural History of Patiala*, New Delhi: Sundeep Prakashan.

Suri, Vidya Sagar (1956, 1947). *Some Original Sources of Punjabi History*, Lahore: Punjabi University Historical Society.

Shameful Continuities[*]
The Practice of Female Infanticide in Colonial Punjab

Anshu Malhotra

I will begin this essay by relating an account that comes from my paternal grandmother. She was born sometime in the first decade of the twentieth century in Satghara, in the Okara *tahsil* (division) of Montgomery district of western Punjab. The fourth daughter of a well-established moneylender in an area nurtured by the British and developed as part of the imperial Canal Colonies project (Ali 1988: 8–61), she survived the murderous onslaughts of a 'son-preference' culture to tell the story of her father's flirtation with modernity by keeping her alive. With pride she used to relate to us the surprise and awe expressed by her father's colleagues and friends that he had decided to keep a fourth daughter alive! *Lalaji, aih kurri vi rakh lai je?*—Lalaji you've kept (alive) this girl too? Besides telling us something of her father's benign nature (though he may not have been so with his debtors if we are to believe the accounts of British administrators), this story tells us a little more of the fate of the third and fourth daughters even among the more affluent families of rural colonial Punjab. While the anecdote indicates to us how sections of the indigenous elite had the will to please the colonial masters who persisted with an anti-female infanticide reform through much of the nineteenth and early twentieth centuries, (though it remained more rhetorical than practical in its import and impact), the incident also shows the precarious position of girls permanently placed on the cusp of uncertainty.

The word permanent has been used here advisedly for the saga of female infanticide as a practice has a *longue duree* in the cultural context of Punjab, with its latest manifestation in the form of female foeticide in our times. Having said that, I may hasten to add that before we indict all Punjabis as '*kurri maars*' (daughter slayers) it may be worth remembering that the practice may have been followed by different groups at different times for separate reasons, and also that the practice seemed to have increased during the British period and persisting thereon. The colonial context, however, is the subject of this essay.

The latest 2001 Census again hints at a rise in the practice of doing away with female foetuses, with the imbalance in the child sex ratios today being indicative of not only the use of modern technologies to abort unwanted foetuses, but also undoubtedly driven by newer family planning norms. It must also be borne in mind that the doing away with some girls does not, of course, mean doing away with all daughters, especially in the context of colonial Punjab, and perhaps even applicable at present. At the same time the continual history of female infanticide/ foeticide over a fairly long period of time, shows a culture's proclivity of devaluing female life (though once again this must be qualified by saying that many women and girls are held in high regard), placing them a notch or perhaps several notches below men/boys, a reality poignantly fictionalized by Shauna Singh Baldwin in her novel *What the Body Remembers*. In this story Roop, the young second wife of a rich Sikh, having learnt of the vicissitudes of womanhood the difficult and painful way, thinks she will make the lesson of female devaluation easier for her daughter by teaching her bodily discipline, and the need for the effacement of the body, early in her tender life. Her resounding slap to her daughter, on a pretext which to the little girl was incomprehensible, and the girl's plaintive '*mein ki kita*' (what have I done?) stay with the reader for a long time. In a novel set in colonial and pre-Partition Punjab, but also covering the trauma and the sheer enormity of that dislocation, Roop teaches her daughter shame, secretiveness, and never to compare herself with her brothers (Baldwin 1999: 274–5). Today we need to probe the ingenuous 'mein ki kita' (what have I done?) in order to not only make sense of an egregious practice of the past and its new *avatar* amidst us in the form of foeticide, to unravel the paradox of worshipping some girls and killing a few,[1] but to also hope for the elimination of this horrendous practice in the future. We need to make sense of how some daughters could be valued—for instance a sister of many brothers[2]—how moral social norms put good treatment of a daughter and a good marriage for her on the scale of charitable behaviour, while the lot of many women remains sorry and, of some unwanted ones, indeed sordid.

I will argue in this essay that there is ample evidence of the fact that infanticide was prevalent among many communities in colonial Punjab, the period of study here. The body of the essay will look at the attempts of the colonial state in intervening on the question of female infanticide and the repercussions thereof. The colonial state by picking out the social elites, publicizing their customs, and indeed recognizing them through these, tended to impart to these customs a fixity that may not have been present earlier. In this context, the association of infanticide with hypergamous marriages, and more significantly with *kanya dan* (the highest form of marriage in the brahmanical context that required the gifting of a virgin daughter to the groom) and dowry marriages, created routes to social mobility that developed through the further degradation of women and girls. British attempts at social engineering were conducted within what they believed to be the mores of the Hindu caste society, imparting rigidity to what were more fluid practices. As the state's power of collation, enumeration, and categorization of its Punjabi populace grew, it was forced to recognize widespread prevalence of infanticide among not only those whom they recognized as social elites, but also the agricultural Jats of Punjab, and among them too the Jat Sikhs whom the state tended to lionize as agriculturists and as Khalsa Sikhs (Malhotra 2002: 24–34). The Jats, in any case, were the mainstay of the government's source of revenue and the pride of its 'martial' army. Therefore, the state was in a dilemma over asserting its moral high ground by putting a stop to infanticide or to resort to only some desultory measures while leaving the Jats alone, with infanticide going on unchecked. There are, at the same time, clear indications of the practice on the increase during the British period, and it is the cultural reasons for this inflation that the present essay tries to explore. Though the accent is on the colonial period and the essay points to many convoluted paradoxes of the colonial state's policy, the idea is to also look at the indigenous response to the social situation as it emerged at that time.

'Figuring' Out Punjab's Missing Girls

'Buri nazar vale tere ghar larrki hove' (O evil-eyed one, may your house be cursed with the birth of a daughter) read the graffiti on the back of a truck in Haryana, a witty play on the more familiar *'buri nazar vale tera munh kala'* (O evil-eyed one, may your shameful face be darkened).[3] The innocuous phrase meant to ward off the onlooker's evil and jealous eye by shaming the person (*kala* [black] evoking the darkened visage in a ritualistic shaming), here becomes a curse for those with the envious eye by wishing them daughters as progeny, against the much-desired and celebrated birth of sons. This humorous and succinct witticism works as a successful message only because the ethos it evokes mirrors the cultural norms of the society.

To underscore the relatively long history of infanticide/ foeticide in Punjab, it may be gainful to do a quick comparison between the figures for the missing girls yielded by the 2001 Census in relation to those available in some of the censuses undertaken by the British. What to some are the shocking revelations of the 2001 Census, the female/male ratio in the age group of 0–6, of 927 girls per 1,000 boys for the whole country, has been in fact, a secular trend over the last censuses. This figure is, of course, very decent in comparison to the statistical anomaly displayed by some regions, derided with the acronym *demaru* (daughter eliminating/killing) states by Ashish Bose (2001). Punjab features prominently in these rightly stigmatized states, with only 874 females to 1,000 males in the juvenile sex ratio. In Fatehgarh Sahib, infamous for the lowest juvenile sex ratio in the country, the figures plummet to 754/1,000, with Khamano block teetering at 628 females to 1,000 males (M. Grewal 2004). This sorry saga becomes more wretched still when we see the urban, and relatively more affluent areas 'leading' the trend in not only Punjab and Haryana, but also in

Delhi, where the ignominious statistic of 762 females to 1,000 males in the juvenile sex ratio comes from upmarket south Delhi (Nayar 2004). Thus the utilization of increasingly sophisticated reproductive technologies readily available on the market, and the government's lethargic record of action on the available MTP or Medical Termination of Pregnancy Act (1972) and the PNDT or the Prenatal Diagnostic Techniques Regulation and Prevention of Misuse Act (1994)[4] have contributed to strengthening the bias against the girl child in Punjab.

The 2001 Census, taking its cue from the then government in power, led by the right-wing Bharatiya Janata Party (BJP), also 'insightfully' provided religion-based data. While the stereotypical outcry of the BJP spokesperson on the 'Muslim growth rate' may have landed the party with egg on its face (the Muslim growth rate in fact had declined more than the Hindu growth rate, 3.5 per cent as against 2.9 per cent) (Raghuraman 2004), on the sidelines were also the atrocious figures that appeared for the Sikhs. The Sikhs showed the lowest sex ratio among all the major religious communities, at an abysmal 893 females to 1,000 males, with its child sex ratio standing at a reprehensible 786 (Bagga 2004). What the religion-based sex ratios do not reveal are, of course, the regional trends, for example, the child sex ratio among the Hindus in Punjab is also a low 821 (ibid.). It is important to note that the Sikhs in the post-Partition Indian Punjab are the dominant community, forming over 60 per cent of the population of the state (*Census of India* 1991: 4) as compared to about 14 per cent in 1931 in pre-Partition Punjab (*Census of India* 1931: 290–1) and therefore the trends visible in Punjab today are necessarily theirs, but not exclusively so.

The revelations of Sikh sex ratios have led intellectuals and journalists to highlight the contrast between the supposedly 'egalitarian' ideals of the Sikh community in relation to women and the degradation of their condition as indicated by the statistics. For example, an editorial in *The Times of India* in 2004 carried a quote by Guru Nanak, illuminating the need to respect women's maternal role,[5] followed by a discussion of the most recent abominable figures showing that only 5 per cent of girls received treatment for liver transplants as against 95 per cent boys in the capital's elite Apollo Hospital. The article then further discussed the appalling sex ratios for the Sikhs, despite fairly good literacy rates among them (*The Times of India* 2004).

I do not here wish to discuss the inherently egalitarian nature of the Sikh religion or otherwise, which has recently received some degree of scholarly attention,[6] but point out that this myth, first propped up and developed by the British, may not necessarily lead to any useful results. British ethnographers and compilers of census reports liked working with socially divisive but manageable communities/categories that imparted them with less complicated knowledge, but also perpetuated myths and artificial divisions in society. One fruitless experiment was carried out by the British in Punjab in 1901, when they tried to work out why the Sikhs had such low female to male child sex ratios, as when H.A. Rose, continuing to deal with the conundrum as the Superintendent of the Census Operations in 1911, wrote that '...no people in India treats its women better than do the Sikhs as a body. Sikh women have considerable liberty and receive a measure of education' (*Report on the Prevalence of Female Infanticide in the Punjab*, 1911).

This insistence on the part of the British of looking upon the Sikhs as a community more inclined to treat their women well is all the more surprising since infanticide was first 'discovered' by the British among the Bedis, the descendants of Guru Nanak, settled in Dera Baba Nanak as early as 1851. In the early days of the Raj in Punjab, the British, tuned in to pick out the 'natural leaders' of a society, the 'notables' with whom they could do business, and yet establish their own cultural and moral superiority, saw infanticide as a high caste/class phenomena across Punjab. The social elites indicted for the crimes were not only the Khatris (especially the Bedis among them), the Rajputs, Aroras, but also the Muslims, Brahmans, and some Jats (Montgomery 1853). The horrific practice of infanticide and of consistent neglect of little girls took its toll upon the female child in Punjab. This was brought out time and again by the adverse sex ratio data, as knowledge about the natives was compiled in statistics that showed the precarious life of girls. In 1911, for instance, it was calculated that among the 0–5 age group there were only 914 girls per 1,000 boys among the Hindu Khatris and 931 among the Sikh Khatris. The figures were even more imbalanced among the Jats, and it was the Jats who came under increasing scrutiny for female infanticide as the nineteenth century progressed. Among the Hindu Jats it was calculated that there were only 839 girls per 1,000 boys, while the figure declined still further with Sikh Jats, the returns showing only 694 girls under five (*Report on the Prevalence of Female Infanticide in the Punjab*, 1911). The Report also mentioned the religion-based data collected in the earlier two census operations. The figures for Hindus over the 1891 and 1901 censuses remained steady at 841; the Sikhs showed a decline from 778 to 766, while the figures showed a marginal improvement for Muslims from 871 to 879 (ibid.). The parallels with the present situation in Punjab are striking, and point to a regional malaise even though the religious and caste constitution of Punjab has changed dramatically since 1947. It may be noted that the figures for Muslims follow the regional trend. However, the British never considered infanticide a 'Muslim' problem, and none of the reports discussed the question in terms of a 'Muslim' community, as they did, for example, with the Bedis or the Sikh Jats. Though some reports worked on the premise of 'caste' categories, for instance the Rajputs or the Jats, which ought to include the Muslims among them, the focus was invariably on the Hindus or the Sikhs. This was another manifestation of the blinkered way in which the colonial state worked, its preconceptions sometimes more important than the obvious that the data stated. However, the arguments that the British proceeded with, or placed, in this essay, must work for the Muslims of Punjab as well, though there is little specific information to go by.

NATIVE ADDICTION AND BRITISH SERENDIPITY: REPORTING INFANTICIDE IN COLONIAL PUNJAB

While the census figures, even if not wholly reliable or accurate for the colonial period, reveal the anomalous position of missing girls in Punjab of the past and the present, they, of course, do not tell us why this situation prevailed in that area. To understand the fact of the missing girls in Punjab we need to don an interpretive cap, though much of what might be said will remain in the domain of conjecture. The copious compilations of the British amateur ethnographers-cum-administrators are an important source here, but only when used in tandem with an anthropological and a historical insight into Punjabi culture and rituals, and the place of women in Punjabi society.

The British discovered the 'crime' of infanticide very early upon their arrival in Punjab and used metaphors of intoxication and disease while reporting its practice. They pointed to the natives' 'addiction' to it, or their being 'infected' with it, as for example in the reports made by Major Herbert Edwardes from Jullunder, and by Major Lake from Gurdaspur in 1851, military men in their new civilian jobs, just two years after the complete conquest of Punjab (Montgomery 1853; Browne 1857: 108–29). The serendipitous discovery of barbaric crimes amongst the natives can be seen almost as a ritual among the British administrators, who came armed with their moral righteousness along with the superiority of their forces, ready to decimate the arms and the morale of their opponents. Thus, infanticide had only recently been discovered among the Chauhan Rajputs of Mainpuri in the North Western Provinces and its replication in Punjab only confirmed the need for intervention by the British in the social fabric of the newly conquered. Undoubtedly, the British sought legitimization of their rule through pronouncements on the uplifting rectitude ushered in by them. This was evident in the grandiose meeting organized by the British in Amritsar on the occasion of Diwali in 1853 where all the defeated, subdued, and the otherwise pliant chiefs, *sardar*s and notables were invited to pay homage to the new power, and receive in turn the message of moral uprightness from the British, represented in the meeting by the Judicial and the Financial Commissioners of Punjab (Browne 1857: 153–64; Montgomery 1853).[7] Both the venue of the meeting, the city holy to the Sikhs only recently unseated by the British, and the occasion of Diwali, when the city was to be draped in the glory of the new rulers, was carefully chosen to underline the unassailable power of the British. Those who were seen to have challenged the onward march of British supremacy were deliberately left out, as for example Bedi Bikrama Singh, not only viewed as seditious in the past, but also considered to be indifferent if not hostile to British reformist efforts on the question of female infanticide. Assembled on the occasion were also the more receptive leaders of the 'daughter-slaying races' who now had to pledge their disavowal of this practice (ibid.).

It may be noted here in passing that the repeated references to the methods employed by the native society in snuffing out the life of female infants, encountered in periodical reports of the state on the issue, started with Robert Montgomery's *Minute on Infanticide* in 1853. They served to further point to the savage customs of the Punjabis, their ingenuity employed in both crushing a helpless life, as well as their deception of the British by evading indictment and therefore punishment, when they were liable for the same in some areas of Punjab after the mid-1880s. Here is a sample of such reportage coming from T.J. Kennedy, the Deputy Commissioner of Ludhiana in 1895:

The method of killing the daughters is so cunningly contrived that it is very difficult to detect. In some cases a wet piece of linen is spread over the infant's face and suffocates it, in others again a dose of opium is administered, and, as opium is very commonly given to infants, it is easy to say the child has died from an accidental overdose; but the common practice is simply to omit attending to the elementary needs of girl children and allowing them to perish of neglect. Thus, for instance, when they are born they are placed face downwards on the floor, and this very often kills them, or their mother does not give them nourishment and allow them to gradually perish of emaciation, or, if they contract fever or other epidemic diseases, no remedies are administered, or they are purposely exposed to cold and die of bronchial affections (sic). In such cases it is difficult and almost impossible to bring home guilt to the parents of the children who are directly responsible for the mortality (*High Proportion of Male to Female Births in Peshawar District and the Crime of Female Infanticide in Certain Districts of Punjab*, 1896).

The most 'chilling' of these reports, both literally and figuratively, came from the 1914 *Note on the Female Infanticide*. The report pointed to both the cruelty of the practice and suggested its history among the Punjabis, even if probed and unearthed by the not entirely disinterested British. The reminiscences of Munshi Bakhshi Ram Das Chibbar, a Muhiyal Brahmin, was quoted to affirm the practice among the Muhiyals. He had remembered how when he was eight years old, he had been wakened one night and taken to the room where his mother had given birth to a baby girl. The child was placed in his arms and then a midwife had poured a jarful of water on her head that had been chilled by putting it on the roof on a cold December night. The baby's face had instantly turned blue, and she had gasped once and died.[8]

The reporting of infanticide among the Bedis, first noted by Edwardes, was significant, for the Bedis (with the exception of Bikrama Singh) were seen as respected religious leaders of the Sikhs, being the descendants of the first Guru, Guru Nanak. The Sikhs were in turn viewed as important, not only as the immediate predecessors of the British, but also because the British came to admire their religion, especially its martial values. Thus, if the Bedis could be persuaded to give up infanticide, it was hoped others would follow suit, even though by the time of the Amritsar meeting many others were charged with the crime including the Rajputs, Khatris (Lahorins and Sarins), Brahmins, Jats, and Muslims (Browne 1857).

The British in Punjab, but probably elsewhere too where infanticide was found, spoke of two primary reasons why infanticide was practised. They linked infanticide of girls to the deleterious effect of 'pride' and 'poverty' of the Punjabis that led some to kill their daughters at birth, though one reason may predominate over the other among different castes. Pride, it was felt, did not allow some to marry their daughters beneath their station, while leaving them unmarried was thought to bring disgrace to the girl and her family. This practice of hypergamy, that is, marrying a daughter into a family of superior status, was seen as an established practice among many castes in Punjab. The unfortunate outcome of this practice, it was felt, was that it left a surplus of unmarried girls amongst the highest castes who were removed through infanticide. The other reason, the reports had suggested, was that of poverty, for the marriage of a daughter required parents to spend lavishly on the celebration of the ceremony, and also to provide her with a large dowry. Thus, to avoid becoming poor, it was concluded, many parents destroyed their girls (Montgomery 1853).

Did this thesis work? Or was this a hypothesis fabricated out of the imagination of the British dilettantish ethnographers being taken for a ride by the cunning patriarchs of various communities (but especially the Bedis), manoeuvring to escape individual responsibility for what amounted to murder, as has been alleged recently (Oldenburg 2006: 82–120)? Undisputedly, the stories being proffered to the British by the 'notables', the male heads of various caste and religious groups required by the British as sources of information and as agents of carrying forth new programmes, were stitched together for maximum mileage in terms of enhancing status and reputation, both before the new rulers and their own society. The fluidity of circumstance engendered by the new conquest, that too by a power adept at storing and fossilizing information, presented unique opportunities to lay claims for uplifting status, if we agree that traditionally caste status was fixed or manipulated in relation to the political power (Dirks 1993: 42–52). That the processes of enumeration and collation ultimately lost the inherent flexibility of the system did not take away the desire among people for social benefit from political affiliation. It also needs to be pointed out that in the context of the widespread prevalence of infanticide in the Punjabi society, as the British were to realize once their triumphal trumpeting of power in Punjab gave way to more routine matters, one or the other reason to understand the phenomenon was perhaps not adequate to explain its prevalence among a wide cross-section of people. This inconvenience, though, did not stop them from putting forward the same arguments in every report, in all probability to prevent degeneration into utter confusion.

I will firstly argue that the myths embedded in the content of some of the stories collected by British officers, howsoever motivated by extraneous reasons, must be analysed for what they may yield about the social mores of the Punjabi society. Thus, I am not inclined to dismiss these tales out of hand as merely yarns sewed to ensnare trusting but dim-witted foreigners. This especially pertains to the complex question of hypergamy discussed here in the context of the Bedis and the Darbari Jats. Secondly, I will argue that the practice of infanticide, widespread in the Punjabi society in the colonial period, may have actually increased as the pressure of maintaining and enhancing social status received a fillip not only because of the practice of the British to ossify social categories, but also because they tended to recognize elites through their rituals and customs, as mentioned earlier. Their attempts at social engineering and meddling in some instances, combined with ineptitude and the desire not to overly displease the revenue-paying 'martial' Jats, increasingly seen as the main perpetrators of infanticide as the nineteenth century wore on, created situations where the practice of doing away with female infants came to be on the rise. In this context, historian Veena Talwar Oldenburg's argument for the 'masculinization' of Punjab's economy under the British, that is, the creation of absolute property in land in the hands of a male patriarch, and in its timely revenue payments that required supplementary income from the army, works when one looks at the Jat dominated landscape of Punjab. Having a girl, according to Oldenburg, became more unattractive than ever before with female infanticide resorted to with impunity in order to achieve the family of choice (Oldenburg 2002: 41–72). However, if we see the continuous history of infanticide/foeticide from the pre-colonial to the post-colonial period, then arguments that emphasize economic reasons, I believe, can only make sense in conjunction with an understanding of the cultural context and milieu of the Punjabi people.

A Question of Status? Bedi Khatris and Darbari Jats

So what was the story offered by the Bedis to explain rampant female infanticide among them, as Herbert Edwardes claimed, for a period of 300 years (Montgomery 1853)? It may be mentioned in passing that the practice of infanticide was condemned at various times by the Sikh Gurus and evidence of injunctions against it are available for the third Guru, Amar Das, whose guruship began in 1552 and the tenth Guru, Gobind Singh, who began his guruship in 1675 (Jakobsh 2003: 29, 40; Grewal 2002: 51). In the nineteenth century, the Namdhari or Kuka movement, often interpreted as millenarian in a pre-modern sense (Oberoi 1992: 157–97), also spoke against female infanticide with its Guru Ram Das censuring those indulging in the practice (Jakobsh 2003: 110). So the antiquity of the practice, said to be initiated by the Bedis in the following tale, was of fairly long standing in Punjab.

The Bedi story ran as follows: Dharam Chand, a grandson of Guru Nanak, was said to have had two sons, Mihr Chand and Nanak Chand, and a daughter. The girl, at the right age, was to be married to a Khatri boy. On the occasion of the marriage, the groom's party in many ways humiliated the bride's family, which included the forcible widening of the doorway to the bride's house in order to admit the litter of the boy. The bride's brothers, who went to drop her off some distance at the time of her *rukhsat* (departure), were also outraged when they were taken much farther than etiquette required, returning back weary and footsore. The indignant Dharam Chand, taking this as the last straw in a string of unwarranted humiliations, is said to have bade all the Bedis to kill their daughters as soon as they were born rather than bear such affronts. His sons, horrified at the import of his curse, prayed to him to withdraw such a cruel injunction. Dharam Chand is said to have replied that if the Bedis were true to their faith, and abstained from lies and strong drink, God would only gift them with male children. Dharam Chand, the saga goes, took the burden of the crime of female infanticide upon himself, and it was said that from that day on his head literally fell on his chest and he walked about as one bearing a heavy weight upon his shoulders.[9]

How may we interpret such a polyvalent story, a semiological delight? One historian has seen in this saga merely an attempt by the clever Bedis to be recognized as the true descendants of first Guru, Guru Nanak (Oldenburg 2006). That Guru Nanak was a Bedi Khatri is not an issue of debate among historians at all, and it therefore seems unlikely to have been a cause of major concern to anyone at the time (McLeod 1996b: 19, 34–67, 1996b: 89–90) though the question of which particular lineal descent among them may be seen to be carrying forward the right tradition may have been a more complex issue. The tale, of course, cannot be taken at its face value, as a relation of actual events having occurred in a specific order. Rather, the story belongs to the domain of the myth, its significance imbricated in the varied signs it carries. At the same time, this fable, taken as a variable mix of fact and fiction, truth and legend,[10] nevertheless, assumed its salience from its use as a justifying myth for what was an opprobrious practice condemned by the Gurus. The outstanding motif in this story, rich in symbolic value, seems to be that of honour, compromised for Dharam Chand when the groom's litter forcibly broke through his entrance or when his sons faced humiliation by the groom's party. If we see the marriage ceremony as showcasing the honour of the families involved, then the forcible entry of the litter (much as the subsequent violation of the daughter's virginity) can be viewed as an assault on the Bedis' honour.[11] Honour, in the Punjabi society under discussion, can be said to have a peculiar quality of being embedded in women's bodies, but augmenting male pride. Societies deeply concerned with honour and shame, as Peter Burke has reminded us, are especially bothered by the maintenance of facades, here perceived to be irredeemably damaged (Burke 1987: 3–14).

The tale was also clearly linked to the idea of hypergamy, with which were bound notions of marrying a daughter in the upward direction within broad endogamous caste units. The rules of hypergamy, however, are seen to create a problem on the two ends of the caste, leaving a surplus of unmarried women at one end and that of marriageable men at the lowest levels. The rules of endogamy are often breached at the low levels, where men may marry women outside their caste (Dumont 1980: 116–18). Recent reports of grooms from parts of north India, predominantly Haryana buying brides from as far as Bengal and Assam, or caste Gujaratis from Mehsana buying brides from tribal areas, is an indication of the continuance of these practices (Kaur 2004: 2595–603; Mahurkar 2004: 62–4). Hypergamy has been seen as an aspect of societies preoccupied with the question of status (Tambiah 1973: 93). The sociologist Declan Quigley defines hypergamy as a desire to further increase one's status among a prestigious and a powerful group by allying with those established as more powerful (Quigley 1995: 87–113).[12] Parents, therefore, looking for a suitable match for their daughters may adopt hypergamy as an appropriate way to enhance their own status by making this alliance. At the same time it needs to be emphasized that scholars mostly speak of a 'tendency' towards hypergamy in north India. Often, the actual situation may be of what anthropologists prefer to call isogamy, which is, marrying within the same status group. Denzil Ibbetson, in 1881, did note a tendency towards hypergamy among the highest castes in Punjab, but tried to show that it was isogamy, or marriage between groups of equal status, that was the established practice amongst most groups including the high castes (*Census of Panjab—1881*: 356).

Whether a marriage was in effect hypergamous or isogamous, hierarchy was nevertheless built into the rituals of high caste marriage. This was the hierarchy between the wife-givers, the family and clan of the bride, and the superior wife-takers, the relations of the groom. A number of anthropologists have spoken of the establishment of this hierarchy at the time of the marriage itself, as performed in the rituals and ceremonies of the marriage, even if two families of equal status were involved. Thus, Paul Hershman in his study of a village in Punjab showed how the ceremony of *milni*, (from the word *milan*, a meeting) when at the time of marriage the two clans were formally introduced to each other, ritually put the wife-givers in inferiority to the receivers (Hershman 1981: 194).[13] Gift-giving, before and during the ceremony, were an intrinsic aspect of the rituals associated with marriage, an important obligation that had to be fulfilled by the family of the bride. In such an ideal marriage, the bride herself was the most perfect gift, that of a virgin, who's gifting formed the central ritual in the ceremony of kanyadan (Fruzzeti 1990). However, it was not gift-giving that seemed a problem to Dharam Chand, the British positing that it was pride alone that was the cause of the downfall of Bedi daughters (Browne 1857: 114).

The falling of Dharam Chand's head upon his chest, again, can be interpreted in different ways. While the Bedis, accosted by the colonial state for their cruelty to infant daughters, preferred to present it as a penitent posture for advocating a heinous crime, it can well be taken to show a permanent humiliation that the marriage of a daughter had brought upon the Bedis' shoulders. In a sense, the motif of humility, on the part of the bride's family, can be said to be the central symbolism of hypergamous marriages. However, in Dharam Chand's case the question was perhaps a little more complex than that. The Bedis, it seems possible by Dharam Chand's time, considered themselves to be higher within the Khatri hierarchy than they were hitherto held, as they were the descendants of the founder of the Sikh faith. The Bedis belonged to the subsection of the Bunjahi Khatris, perhaps below the Bari and the Dhaighar in the internal ranking of the Khatris. Thus Nanak himself is said to have married within his Khatri subdivision as he married a Chona woman, and so did all the Gurus, Khatri by caste, marry within their subscribed categories (McLeod 1996a: 83–104). The attempts by his followers to upgrade their status, one can speculate, may have led to tensions, for in another version of the story related by Major Abbott, it was said to be Dharam Chand's son Mihr Chand who fixed the match of his daughter with the son of a Bari Khatri of Batala, and subsequently faced humiliation (Browne 1857: 117). This humiliation must have been especially galling since the Bedis may have now considered themselves as foremost among the Khatris. Female infanticide can be said to have been adopted as a strategy for upward mobility, for doing away with a daughter meant never having to bow before anyone, even one nominally held superior.

In fact, one may further speculate, that as the character of the Sikh movement began to change in the seventeenth century, with the Jats outnumbering the Khatris, and the movement becoming militant in nature, the need to preserve a ritual superiority from the Jats may have manifested itself to some high placed Khatris within Sikhism. Muzaffar Alam, for instance, has discussed the tensions arising within the Sikh movement between the trading community of the Khatris with their additional interest in providing service to the Mughal administration, and the upwardly mobile cultivating class of Jats, seen to be responsible for the rising militancy in the movement, and pitted against the Mughal state (Alam 1986: 134–75). It is plausible that in this context some Khatris may have adopted certain social practices meant to enhance their ritual status that may have included female infanticide. Thus too the Sodhis, the descendants of the gurus from the fourth Guru onwards, belonging to the subdivision of Sarin Khatris, were said to be also following the practice of female infanticide (Browne 1857: 117).

A third concern that the story displays is an overtly reformist one—an exhortation to the Bedis to stay away from lies and liquor, and to remain steadfast in their faith. Is it possible that between the many rival and guruship claiming branches of the families of the Sikh Gurus, many of whom accepted revenue-free grants from the Mughal state (Grewal 2002: 62–3) and later Ranjit Singh's Empire, a falling of moral and spiritual standards had occurred? It is important to note that the reward for moral uprightness in the Bedis' tale was the birth of male children, the birth of girls being viewed as a punishment for a sinful life. So while the Gurus exhorted against the practice of infanticide, among many of their followers and descendants, female infanticide was viewed as one possible way to achieve a high ritual status. The practice of female infanticide in our tale was made ethically acceptable, with no repugnance attached to its continuance, by being made a reward for a life of rectitude. It may be worth noting here, that Edwardes' report also spoke of those Bedis who preserved their daughters being treated as common sweepers by the rest of the community (Montgomery 1853; Browne 1857: 116). While this may or may not have been the fate of the more kind-hearted Bedis, and we hear of one Punjab Singh, a Bedi of Mukundpur who had two daughters, and one Baba Sampuran Singh with a daughter (though the British claimed these were preserved at their behest), it is the ritual falling of status that has been underlined here (Browne 1857: 162; Montgomery 1853).[14] It needs to be emphasized that the various strands of the Bedis' story are sewn together by the common theme of the devaluation of female life, whether one speaks of the desire for status enhancement or looks at sons as rewards for a good and simple life. This devaluation, moreover, can exist independent of the question of marriage and its specific mode employed by a family at a given time, as the reformist aspect of the Bedis' story makes clear. It is this cultural fabric that exults in women as mothers of sons, rather than as mothers of daughters.

Interestingly, even for the Jats, among whom the practice of female infanticide seemed rampant during the colonial period, for which one must look for other reasons than hypergamy, the question of social eminence was nevertheless important for a number of groups. Among many important Jat families, a replication of the process seen under the Bedis and the Khatris is visible, with the additional social burden of distinguishing themselves from the rest of the Jat community where women were seen to work in the fields and were often 'bought' in marriage. At a time when a major enquiry into the practice of female infanticide in Punjab was again initiated in 1895, T.J. Kennedy, the Deputy Commissioner of Ludhiana reported a set of eminent Jats called '*Sahu log*' (big/rich people). They claimed to have fallen from a Rajput status because their ancestors were said to have made 'misalliances' with Jat women. They emphasized that they now kept their women in seclusion, a claim disputed by other Jat families, who, however, conceded that their women did not go to the fields for labour as other Jat women, as well as confessing to a certain degree of pre-eminence for them in the village. These Sahu log, the Garehwal and Shiru Gil Jats prominent among them, apparently practised female infanticide. Kennedy noted that in some Garehwal villages, not a single girl was allowed to survive, while at the same time paradoxically writing that the girls of the Sahu log were sought in marriage by the 'best families of Sardars and even by Rajas', and that they did not marry them to men of inferior tribes, nor did they receive money for them (*High Proportion of Male to Female Births in Peshawar District and the Crime of Female Infanticide in Certain Districts of Punjab*, 1896). A process of sanskritization seemed to be in progress here, with latent conflict visible in the disclaimers of the villagers to the pretensions of the Sahu log, even though they made concessions to their social prestige. Similarly among the Gils, Kennedy noted a division between the 'Shiru Gil' and the 'Jalli Gil' ('false Gils' as the term *jalli* seems to imply?)[15] with the elevated status of the former based on the fact of murder of infant daughters, while the latter preserved them. A division between the 'Sahu' and 'Kame' (low class?) Jats[16] was also made along similar lines. This *fin de siecle* report of Kennedy, unlike Edwardes' mid-nineteenth-century jottings, does not clarify if such a process of upward movement among some Jats was a new phenomenon or an old one, though as mentioned earlier, the colonial period did see a rise in infanticide. However, the point to note is that the pattern adopted for making a social statement was a familiar one in Punjab.

By exploring another such story brought to light by J.M. Douie, the Deputy Commissioner of Jullunder, at the same time, the point about an older pattern of gaining social prestige in a new environment becomes further clarified (*High Proportion of Male to Female Births in Peshawar District and the Crime of Female Infanticide in Certain Districts of Punjab*, 1896). Like Kennedy's Sahu log, Douie mentioned 'Darbari' Jats in the Jullunder district, who felt obliged to marry their daughters within the category of Darbari families. The following story Douie picked up from the Ferozepur and Hoshiarpur Settlement Reports, placed in the latter by a 'native' Extra Assistant Commissioner. This story related how Emperor Akbar married the daughter of Mahr Mitha, a Dhariwal zamindar of Dhulah Kangar in Patiala.

The tale began with the Emperor setting eyes on the girl at a well in her village. While carrying two pitchers of water on her head, she at the same time caught a young buffalo that had escaped its owner by putting her foot on the rope attached to its head and held the animal without losing her balance, until its owner came to claim it. The Emperor, delighted and impressed with her strength and courage, married her in the hope of having children as brave as her. The Extra Assistant Commissioner noted that the girl's father's consent was sought by the creation of a 'Darbari Panchayat' of which Dhula Kangar was the head. Darbari families were meant to be descendants of thirty five Jat and thirty six Rajput families, who countenanced the marriage by sending representatives to Delhi. The Darbari families included those of 'Mussulman' Rajputs, and there were apparently thirty-six *makan*s or 'headquarters' of the Darbaris.

Again, this story, a caste and status myth for Darbari Jats, displays many interpretive possibilities, a few of which will be looked at to iterate the argument. The reference to the establishment of marital relations with the most eminent of Mughal Emperors, said to have initiated the policy of establishing marital relations with Rajputs in a bid to consolidate his Empire, is the central theme here. It may be noted that the Darbari Jats were elevating their status both by associating themselves with the Rajputs, as well as Akbar's court, and in this myth, at least, had no qualms of being related either to 'Mussulman' Rajputs or the 'Mussulman' king. On the other hand, it is these relationships that allowed their elevation to the status of the 'Darbaris', a name derived presumably from association with Akbar's court. Importantly, a number of origination myths of castes in Punjab relate some sort of relationship with Akbar and his court, a case in point being the division between the 'Lahorin' and 'Sarin' Khatris, the latter having accepted widow remarriage, it was claimed, at the behest of the king (and the Shariat) unlike the former group (Browne 1857: 122–3).[17] It is worth bearing in mind that Akbar's reign was viewed as a relatively benevolent one in Punjab, and it is only under his successors that conflict came to Punjab, and for instance the misfortunes of the Sikh Gurus began (Grewal 2002: 60–1).

What does the tale tell us of the unnamed daughter of Mahr Mitha? Unlike the unnamed Bedi daughter who had no role

to play in the turn of events,[18] it is the actions of the Darbari
daughter that unfolded the affair that led to the elevation of a
whole group. So while there was appreciation in the story of her
admirable qualities—later a Jat woman's labour was made much
of in colonial ethnography (Darling 1925: 38)—paradoxically,
these very qualities and their success meant that at least some
Darbari girls could never nurture them. The juxtaposition in this
narrative of the positive attributes of the ruddy Jat woman, and
her wilful oppression among the hypergamous status seeking
Jats, reveals sharply the dilemma that the colonial state found so
difficult to unravel. Why did the Jats practise female infanticide
when they needed the labour of the Jat woman in the field? Or
indeed when they could fetch, as British officers observed, fancy
prices by selling them?

SOCIAL INTERVENTIONISM AND ADMINISTRATIVE INERTIA: PERSISTENCE AND SPREAD OF INFANTICIDE

The practice of hypergamy, whether adhered to ideologically or practically, led to the degradation of the female child, a
cultural trait of Punjabi life explored in the last section. In the
British reports on the subject of infanticide, hypergamy was
said to work in conjunction with marriages that required massive expenditure, both on the ceremonial and on providing a
dowry. This expense allegedly led to the ruination of high status
groups who resorted to female infanticide in order to escape
this situation. The arguments that will be placed in this section
are as follows. Marriages with large expenses were indubitably
an aspect of Punjabi life, especially associated with the brahmanical kanyadan form of marriage. However, Punjab had only
a few communities that were brahmanical in their orientation,
though heeding some high caste practices was no doubt a well-
established method of status enhancement. Punjab had other
marriage forms that were prevalent as well, especially among
the Jats (Ibbetson 1974), who often practised exchange or *vatta-
satta* marriages (an example of a *vatta* marriage would be where
a bride's brother might be married to her husband's sister, a
bargain that is the basis of such marriages ensuring brides for
eligible young men and reciprocity in the treatment of married

sisters) and commonly accepted money on the marriage of a daughter. On the pretext of putting an end to infanticide, a proclaimed goal of the colonial state in its early years in Punjab, the British tended to intervene in the social customs of the people, recognizing high status groups through the customs and rituals they observed. What followed was an increased pressure to follow high caste practices in order to make claims of eminence, a theme that will be examined here.

However, older practices did not disappear in Punjab, though the rise in dowry marriages can be traced to this period (Sharma 1980: 138). What emerged then was a fairly complex situation where money was often accepted for the hand of a daughter while pretensions to high caste practices was maintained by a simultaneous bestowal of dowry, as I have discussed elsewhere (Malhotra 2002: 47–81). In fact, this was also a time when trade in women was on the rise in Punjab and selling and buying of women was common enough, extensively commented on by the British administrators, who often hoped that the increased demand for women and high prices for their persons should lead to an end to infanticide, a misplaced notion as figures for infanticide did not come down (Darling 1925: 55–61). While the many female infanticide practicing people bought women from lower castes, the barter of women also grew in the market due to the changing political economy, inflation in epidemic disease and famines, as well as ecological transitions put in place by the Raj (Malhotra 2002: 47–81).

The audacious interventionism in the social life of the people advocated by the British when they first came to Punjab was visible in the statement of P. Melville, Secretary to the Chief Commissioner of Punjab, who wrote to the Government of India in 1853 in connection with female infanticide:

...we must effect a radical change in the feelings, the prejudices, and the social customs of the people themselves. It must no longer be considered a disgrace to have a son-in-law, to marry a daughter into any but a class socially above that of her family. But, above all, the people must be taught to reduce the expenditure hitherto considered necessary by the bride's family. The personal influence of British officers, the knowledge that they take an active interest in the matter, a desire by the people to stand well in the eyes of their rulers, and lastly, the fear of punishment, will doubtless, from year to year, operate in diminishing the crime (Montgomery 1853).

It was this attitude of active interventionism that had led to the calling of the meeting of the important men of Punjab in 1853 in Amritsar mentioned earlier. In the resultant fanfare, among the things that the British chose to discuss was the amount various social groups ought to spend on a marriage. Separate agreements were signed on this occasion with the Hill Chiefs, Bedis, zamindars (landowners) and *lambardar*s (village headmen). The agreement with the lambardars tried to fix the expenditure that could be undertaken by the various categories among them at the time of marriage. Those in 'easy circumstances' were allowed to spend Rs 1–125; those in middle station Rs 125–250; and 'persons of substance' could spend up to Rs 500 (Montgomery 1853). This degree of social gradation among the lesser 'notables' of Punjab must have, one can conjecture, far from lessening marriage expenses led to a competitive spirit, not only to declare one's financial wherewithal but also to be recognized by the state as such. Despite having no effect, the logic of sumptuary proclamations was to stay with the colonial state for a long time in Punjab, as will be subsequently discussed.

At the same time two other intrusions into the lives of the Punjabis were recorded. The Bedis, with the backing of the Raja of Kapurthala, were exhorted to marry Bedi girls within the subcastes of the Bunjahi Khatris, encouraging both recognition and perpetuation of caste practices. Secondly, agreements with Khatris, Brahmans, zamindars, and Muslims sought to coax them into marrying their daughters by the age of twelve, announced in an appropriately imperial mien:

We also engage that no girl shall be allowed to remain unmarried after the age of twelve; that no person shall, from mercenary considerations... be allowed to cancel a betrothal....That in the event of any person not effecting the marriage of his daughter after she has attained her twelfth year...we will bring him to the notice of the authorities (ibid.).

The intention of reform displayed by the state here, one assumes, was to put a stop to the breaking off of betrothals, so that inflation in dowry demands would not follow.[19] It was perhaps also to ensure a marriage at a 'decent' age for the girl, according to the state perceived 'native' customs, in order to prevent the accruing of disgrace to her family, or conversely, to inhibit the intention of selling off girls in marriage by some people. In either case, the level of state intercession was enormous, and when combined with its programme of collecting and collating ethnographic information, it must have led to a new competitive spirit of one-upmanship in Punjab. It might be noted that this manner of intervention in the lives, customs, and rituals of the Punjabis remained an important aspect of the state's policy, especially where the question of female infanticide was concerned. Far from shying away because of the lack of success in such matters, the colonial state continued with its obdurate stand.

In the mid 1880s, when nine villages in Jullunder district were reported to be practising female infanticide, massive investigation was launched by the state to understand the phenomenon and bring it under check (*Prevalence of Female Infanticide in the Jullunder District*, 1884). Though mortality even among male infants was very high, mortality among female infants was seen to be noticeably higher. So in Rurka, for instance, 46.1 per cent of the boys died, the figure was at 63.2 per cent for girls. In Dosauj and Kulaita, more than 80 per cent of the infant girls were reported to have died, whereas the figure for boys stood between 35 per cent (Kulaita) and 40 per cent (Dosauj). The Jat castes accused of practising infanticide were also many, not just the highest on the social scale. In Kulaita and Chak Andian villages, for example, all Jats of castes Sahota, Sindhu, Dhaliwal, Chokar, Bhut, Koman, Munderah, Malli, Jhaj, Dhunu, and Kukar were meant to be practitioners of infanticide (Montgomery 1853). Act VIII of 1870 was put into operation in these villages, an act that used the hierarchy of the offices of the village *dai*s or midwives, *chowkidar*s or watchmen, *patwari*s or a minor village-level revenue administration officers, and lambardars, to record extensive information. Thus infant births, deaths (especially of infant and minor girls), pregnancies among women, and marriages of women in the village, were to be noted. Any expense incurred on the maintenance of Registers for storing this information, or in connection with any other aspect of the Act, was to be levied from the villages, recoverable as an arrear of land revenue (ibid.).

While Act VIII of 1870 had been devised for the North Western Provinces, its application in Punjab was with a difference, the primary one being that here an additional restriction on marriage expenses was introduced, as that was felt to be a major reason for practising infanticide in the state (ibid.). An extensive

chart of expenses to be incurred during the *shadi* or the marriage
ceremony (that seemed to include the dowry) was worked out:

Table 3.1: Marriage Expenses

Milni	Rs	1
Kamins' lag	Rs	2
Lag on the occasion Phera	Rs	2
Marriage feast	Rs	25
Khat	Rs	51
Vessels	Rs	10
Jewels	Rs	15
Cloth and clothes	Rs	8
Expense of lagis	Rs	15
Total	Rs	129

Additionally on *muklawa* or the ceremony when the bride
actually went to her marital home, sometimes undertaken even
a few years after the shadi, a sum of Rs 30 was allowed to be
spent (Montgomery 1853).

There is no information on how this chart of expenses was
worked out, though conferring with male patriarchs was a
favourite way of gathering information. It is the detailed nature
of the chart that is of interest, the state deeming it within its
jurisdiction to monitor intimate social and cultural aspects of
people's lives, albeit for the larger cause of improving their lot.
However, though the state through its particularly intrusive
paternalist interference tried to create a normative standard of
expenses, it perhaps lacked the will or the ability to implement
it. Thus, on the one hand, by the very process of setting up
norms it released the demons of social competition that sought
to exceed those norms, on the other, its lack of follow-up action
on implementation ensured excess of expenditure on the part
of those pushing the boundaries for social recognition. This
quixotic situation was underscored by J.M. Douie, the Deputy
Commissioner of Jullunder in 1895, the nine villages where Act
VIII was implemented coming under his jurisdiction, when he
observed:

...what can be more galling to the pride of the Jats in the proclaimed
estates than that village menials can, and in some cases do, spend more on
weddings than they themselves are permitted to do. At Kuleta (Kulaita)
the zaildar complained to me that a blacksmith will now spend Rs 500 on

his daughter's marriage and hire a band to add to the pomp of the nuptial procession (*High Proportion of Male to Female Births in Peshawar District and the Crime of Female Infanticide in Certain Districts of Punjab*, 1896).

And Sir Dennis Fitzpatrick, the Lieutenant Governor of Punjab in the same year endorsed the importance of Douie's point, telling us that at least some British officers realized the element of social competition that they were unwittingly introducing.

At present a man objects to having a daughter, because among other reasons he has to ruin himself in providing the cost of her marriage. In so far as our law took effect he would object to having a daughter, because, when it came to marrying her, he would have to be content with having her marriage celebrated in a manner that would be humiliating to him, unless indeed he chose, in addition to incurring ruinous expenditure as at present, to go to jail besides for disobeying the law (ibid.).

Female infanticide, in the meantime continued unabated, as reports on the issue in 1896, 1901, 1911 and again in 1914 made clear. One unresolved issue, as far as the British observers were concerned, was why this practice persisted when many Jats actually 'sold' daughters. As already posited, it is the degraded situation of girls that is underlined whether one speaks of the practice of infanticide or of accepting money for their hand. For many in Punjab it probably meant that if a girl escaped infanticide and survived neglect, she could be married to someone willing to pay money for her hand. Similarly, brides for the men of the households could also be 'bought', whether from one's own caste or from castes below one's own social standing. The deep alienation of daughters from Jat and other households can only be imagined in these situations. For others, the daughters not earmarked for extermination could be married well, their marriage made an occasion for splurging and gaining social prestige. For yet others, surviving daughters could be married while accepting money from the groom's party, yet a charade of high caste practices could be maintained by insisting on a kanyadan marriage and by conferring a dowry on the daughter, especially in the colonial state when such a route to upward mobility was recognizably available. And for vast others, daughters were to be preserved, whether to be married well or even exchanged in marriage. Punjab, one can say, perhaps always presented a spectrum of social possibilities, as far as upkeep of daughters was concerned. However, the colonial period, with its cultural agendas, released social energies that tended to look at daughters' marriages as easy routes for upward mobility.

The British, as we move into the twentieth century, began to lose interest or any degree of seriousness in changing the condition of infanticide as Douie's or Fitzpatrick's statements already indicate. In fact, from the beginning, the colonial state displayed enthusiastic interest in devising plans to bring an end to infanticide, but proved to be extremely lethargic in ensuring the success of those grand plans. Towards the end of the nineteenth century and the turn of the next, as more extensive spread of infanticide was seen in the society and made obvious by each subsequent report, the British officers also fought the charge of inaction on their part. Perhaps the very nature of the issue, an aspect of the intimate cultural life of the Punjabis, was difficult to control, once social and economic changes were set into motion by the colonial state. Reports on infanticide in the early twentieth century tended to disclose two anomalies. Firstly, discovery of infanticide among more and more castes and social groups was made. *The Report on the Prevalence of Female Infanticide in the Punjab* 1911, for instance, once again recalled all the 'tribes' and 'castes' of Punjab that indulged in female infanticide, going through all the theorized causes for its prevalence, from hypergamy to marriage expenses. However, it added a section on 'other castes', where infanticide was deduced to be prevalent. These were the lower caste groups among especially the Sikhs, which included the Lobanas, the Mazhabis, and the Chuhras. Were these the latest castes to join in the bandwagon of status enhancement through an established practice?

Secondly, and contradictorily, the growth of 'trade' in women seemed to suggest to many British officers that the practice of infanticide must come to an end. This was a wilful delusion, existing more in the realm of hope than a consequence of a hard look at reality. However, such belying optimism tended to open an exit route to the state from messy social concerns that offered no comforting solutions. Moreover, Jats, seen to be the worst offenders in the matter of infanticide, were, as already pointed out, too important as revenue payers and as regular recruits in the army to be pushed into a corner by the state. Unsurprisingly, on the eve of the First World War, C.A. Barron, the chief secretary to the Government of Punjab, presented a buoyant picture to the Government of India. He noted that the practice of

...female infanticide is now insignificant in the Punjab and cannot be considered a factor in the Hindu and Sikh females to males in the Province, which must be attributed to other causes, especially as the present undoubted demand for women in the marriage market greatly reduces one of the main incentives to infanticide (*Note on the Female Infanticide in the Punjab by Superintendent of Census Operations with Reference to Disproportionate Number of Males and Females Amongst Hindus and Sikhs in that Province*, 1914).

Barron was echoing the views of Lieutenant Colonel F. Popham Young, the Commissioner in the notorious Jullunder Division, who tried to help the state to withdraw from this sticky situation. He wrote:

...the fact remains that daughters are now bought and sold throughout the Punjab with a callous disregard of their feelings and their human rights. We cannot attempt a social reform which must come as a prelude to a finer conception of the relations which should subsist between the sexes. In the present we may at least derive some satisfaction from the fact that regarded as livestock the value of females is appreciating, with the result that their lives in infancy are less likely to be sacrificed than heretofore (ibid.).

While the suspected villages in Jullunder were to remain under surveillance, presumably to retain the facade of paternalistic reform, the colonial state had clearly prepared the ground for its withdrawal from a vexing issue. The clarion call for changing the social mores of the natives made with such élan in mid nineteenth century had given way to more practical considerations in the second decade of the twentieth. While this could be viewed as conceding their own failure at uplifting native morals, the British would of course never concede that their interference in the first place may have in fact worsened the situation.

CONCLUSION

This essay has tried to make a case for speaking of cultural continuities in Punjab where the question of female infanticide/foeticide is concerned. I have argued that it is perhaps not enough to look at only the economic and legal changes introduced by the British, though these were without doubt important ingredients in widening the net of the practice, to understand why some daughters in Punjab were devalued. It has posited that there were certain cultural values already in place in Punjab, which tended to upgrade social status by degrading infant female life. This neither meant that all female infants suffered a terrible fate, nor did it mean that some were not cherished. Nonetheless, it did point to a disturbing trend. However, the essay has also argued that the colonial state had its own agendas of establishing cultural and moral superiority that led it to a cultural interference of an unprecedented level in Punjab. Its paternalistic concern for infant female life encouraged the state to not only find reasons for the practice of infanticide, but also to highlight the customs of the upper castes who they assumed followed the practice. The massive intervention of the colonial state in suitably modifying cultural practices and rituals of the people added an element of social competition, the deleterious effects of which included a growing culture of dowry and kanyadan marriages, as well as higher rates of female infanticide, spreading among more and more social classes. Thus the colonial period definitely added and sharpened a cultural trait visible in Punjab on the eve of the colonial rule.

It is to our shame that we have not given up aspects of this abhorrent practice or the devaluation of the female foetus/infant/child that it underscores. The survival of the ethos is underlined by the figures discussed earlier, but its essence is brought out in the narration of this anecdote. On 7 November 2001, the then Punjab Chief Minister, Parkash Singh Badal's son Sukhbir Singh Badal was 'blessed' with the 'gift of a son' after two daughters. The Akalis celebrated the birth of the Akali 'heir'. One of the advertisements released by the then reigning party of Punjab read: 'Sons are like sweet fruits, may God bless everyone with sons' ('Akalis Go Gaga Over the Birth of Badal's Grandson', 2001). Sons are deemed in this ethos as the only true inheritors of a father's (parents'?) patrimony. The similarities with Dharam Chand Bedi who wished to bless the Bedis with only sons are not difficult to find.

Notes

* This essay emerges from a paper that was presented at the seminar on 'Social Transformation in the Punjab during the Twentieth Century', organized by the Institute of Punjab Studies at Chandigarh on 7–9 September 2005. I

would like to thank all the participants in this seminar, especially J.S. Grewal, Indu Banga, and Harish Puri for their comments.

1. Worshipping girls is, for example, visible in rituals like the *kanjak* in which virgin pre-pubertal daughters are worshipped in honour of the virgin goddess Durga.

2. Punjabi names for girls like Veeranvali or Bhravanvali (both names indicating a sister of many brothers) in the colonial period are indicative of how a sister of many brothers was cherished. A brother of many sisters was also very precious especially if born after the birth of sisters, and was regarded as the solace of parents in their old age. However, he was considered to be 'burdened' with sisters, and there are no celebratory names to underline his sisterly status.

3. Harish Puri's observation during the seminar on Social Transformations in North-Western India held by the Institute of Punjab Studies, Chandigarh, 7–9 September 2005. The ubiquitous Indian trucks are famous for their pithy graffiti, in this case an apposite social comment.

4. In the badly hit area of Khamano for example, only one diagnostic centre had been booked under the PNDT Act till February 2004 (Grewal 2004).

5. 'It is through woman that order is maintained. Then why call her inferior from whom all great ones are born'. A similar point is made by K.S. Singh in his foreword to the *People of India* volume on Punjab (K.S. Singh 2003: xiv).

6. Doris R. Jakobsh has discussed the ambivalent attitude of Guru Nanak towards women, as well as the turn towards 'hyper-masculinization' in the Sikh community after Guru Gobind Singh (Jakobsh 2003: 22–49).

7. Presumably the Judicial Commissioner was Robert Montgomery, who also compiled *The Minute on Infanticide*.

8. This account was taken by Hari Kishan Kaul, the Superintendent of Census Operations from Russell Stracey's 'History of the Muhiyals' in *Note on the Female Infanticide in the Punjab by Superintendent of Census Operations with Reference to Disproportionate Number of Males and Females Amongst Hindus and Sikhs in that Province*, 1914.

9. This story is repeated in many reports on infanticide in Punjab. For one example, see Browne 1857: 115–16.

10. On myths see McLeod 2000: 70–90.

11. Paul Hershman has noted that in Punjabi the term *sala* (wife's brother) is seen as a terrible abuse because it carries the opprobrium of having been given a sister to violate (Hershman 1981: 191–2).

12. Quigley also notes that hypergamy is likely to be visible in a society that has access to political power. The case of the Bedis discussed subsequently suggests access to 'spiritual' power, which may have paved the way for close ties with political powers.

13. Also see Madan 1975: 217–43; Vatuk 1975: 157–96. For a slightly different perspective see Raheja 1988.

14. Montgomery also reported that after British intervention, in Dera Baba Nanak, 61 females, all under the age of four were preserved, as against 450 male children.

15. While the term Shiru Gil seems to refer to the caste name Shergil, Jalli seems to be a term of opprobrium.

16. It is highly possible that the distinction 'Kame' may have referred to 'lower class' Jats. The word *kamin* refers to low caste agricultural labour working in the fields for the Jats.

17. Another myth of the origin of the Sarin Khatris related to their acceptance of widow remarriage in Alaudin Khalji's court, unlike the other Punjabi Khatris who refused to countenance this. The word Sarin was thus derived from having accepted the position of the *Shariat* (Malhotra 2002: 84–5).

18. Though in Major Abbott's version of the story it is her less than considerate treatment in her in-laws' home that provoked her father's wrath (Browne 1857: 117).

19. Lahori Khatris, for instance, were accused of breaking off betrothals in order to make larger dowry demands (Browne 1857: 123).

REFERENCES

Primary Sources

Census of India (1933). 1931-Vol.XVII-Punjab, Lahore.

Census of India (1991). Series. 20-Punjab-Part IV-B(ii)-Religion.

Census of Panjab-1881, Report by D.C.J. Ibbetson (1883) Superintendent of Government Printing, Calcutta.

High Proportion of Male to Female Births in Peshawar District and the Crime of Female Infanticide in Certain Districts of Punjab (1896) Home-Sanitary-7/49-B, September (National Archives of India, hereafter NAI).

Kaul, Hari Kishan (1914). *Note on Female Infanticide*, Home-Police-64-B, February (NAI).

Montgomery, R. (1853). *Minute on Infanticide in the Punjab*, Lahore, Oriental and India Office Collection.

Note on the Female Infanticide in the Punjab by Superintendent of Census Operations with Reference to Disproportionate Number of Males and Females Amongst Hindus and Sikhs in that Province (1914) Home-Police-64-B, February (NAI).

Prevalence of Female Infanticide in the Jullunder District (1884). Home-Police-27/30-A, May (NAI).

Report on the Prevalence of Female Infanticide in the Punjab (1911). Home-Police-38/39-A, January (NAI).

Rules for the Suppression of Female Infanticide Amongst Jat Residents of Certain Villages in Jullunder District (1885). Home Department Proceedings, July (NAI).

Current Newspapers and Weeklies

'Akalis Go Gaga Over the Birth of Badal's Grandson' (2001). *The Times of India*, 7 November.

Bagga, Chirdeep (2004). 'Census Shocker: Child Sex Ratio Takes a Fall', *The Times of India*, 8 September.

Bose, Ashish (2001). 'Without My Daughter: Killing Fields of the Mind', *The Times of India*, 25 April 2001.

Grewal, Manraj (2004). 'Missing Miss Punjab', *The Sunday Express*, 15 February.

Mahurkar, Uday (2004). 'Brides Wanted', *India Today*, 11 October, pp. 62–4.

Nayar, Mandira (2004). 'Girl Child Day? No, Its Missing Girl Child Day...,' *The Hindu*, 25 September.

Raghuraman, Shankar (2004). 'Muslim Growth Rate Much Lower', *The Times of India*, 8 September.

The Times of India (2004). 20 September.

'Without Women' (2001). *The Times of India*, 6 November.

Secondary Sources

Alam, Muzaffar (1986). *The Crisis of Empire in Mughal North India: Awadh and the Punjab 1707–1748*, New Delhi: Oxford University Press.

Ali, Imran (1988). *The Punjab Under Imperialism 1885–1947*, Princeton, New Jersey: Princeton University Press.

Baldwin, Shauna Singh (1999). *What the Body Remembers*, Delhi: Harper Collins Publishers India.

Browne, John Cave (1857). *Indian Infanticide: Its Origin, Progress, and Suppression*, London: W.H. Allen and Co.

Burke, Peter (1987). *The Historical Anthropology of Early Modern Italy*, Cambridge: Cambridge University Press.

Darling, M.L. (1925). *The Punjab Peasantry in Prosperity and Debt*, London: Oxford University Press.

Dirks, Nicholas B. (1989). 'The Invention of Caste: Civil Society in Colonial India', *Social Analysis*, No. 25 (September), pp. 42–52.

—— (1993). *The Hollow Crown: Ethnohistory of an Indian Kingdom*, Cambridge: Cambridge University Press.

Dumont, Louis (1980, 1970). *Homo Hierarchicus: The Caste System and Its Implications*, Chicago: University of Chicago Press.

Fruzzeti, Lina (1990, 1982). *The Gift of a Virgin*, New Delhi: Oxford University Press.

Grewal, J.S. (2002, 1994). *The Sikhs of the Punjab* (Revised Edition), New Delhi: Cambridge University Press.

Hershman, Paul (1981). *Punjabi Kinship and Marriage*, New Delhi: Manohar.

Ibbetson, D.C.J. (1974). *Punjab Castes* (a reprint of the chapter on 'The Races, Castes, and Tribes of the People' in the Report on the Census of Punjab published in 1883), Government Printing, Lahore, 1916, (Reprint, 1974, New Delhi: B.R. Publishing Corporation).

Jakobsh, Doris R. (2003). *Relocating Gender in History: Transformation, Meaning and Identity*, New Delhi: Oxford University Press.

Kaur, Ravinder (2004). 'Across-Region Marriages: Poverty, Female Migration and the Sex Ratio', *Economic and Political Weekly*, 19 June, pp. 2595–603.

Madan, T.N. (1975) 'Structural Implications of Marriage in North India: Wife-Givers and Wife-Takers Among the Pandits of Kashmir', in *Contributions to Indian Sociology* (ns), Vol. 9, No. 2, pp. 217–43.

Malhotra, Anshu (2002). *Gender, Caste and Religious Identities: Restructuring Class in Colonial Punjab*, New Delhi: Oxford University Press.

McLeod, W.H. (1996a, 1968). *Guru Nanak and the Sikh Religion*, New Delhi: Oxford University Press.

—— (1996b, 1976). 'Caste in the Sikh Panth', in his *The Evolution of the Sikh Community: Five Essays*, New Delhi: Oxford University Press.

—— (2000). 'The Sikh Struggle in the Eighteenth Century and its Relevance for Today', in his *Exploring Sikhism: Aspects of Sikh Identity, Culture and Thought*, New Delhi: Oxford University Press.

Oberoi, Harjot (1992). 'Brotherhood of the Pure: The Poetics and Politics of Cultural Transgression', *Modern Asian Studies*, Vol. 26, No. 1. pp. 157–97.

Oldenburg, Veena Talwar (2006). 'Questionable Motives, Flimsy Alibis: Reinvestigating the Murder of Female Infants in Colonial Punjab', in Avril A. Powell and Siobhan Lambert-Hurley, eds, *Rhetoric and Reality: Gender and Colonial Experience in South Asia*, New Delhi: Oxford University Press.

—— (2002) *Dowry Murder: The Imperial Origins of a Cultural Crime*, New Delhi: Oxford University Press.

Quigley, Declan (1995, 1993). *The Interpretation of Caste*, Oxford: Clarendon Press.

Raheja, Gloria G. (1988). *The Poison in the Gift*, Chicago: University of Chicago Press.

Sharma, Ursula (1980). *Women, Work and Property in North-West India*, London: Tavistock Publications.

Singh, K.S. (2003). *People of India Volume XXXVI Punjab*, Anthropological Survey of India, New Delhi: Manohar.

Tambiah, S.J. (1973). 'Dowry and Bridewealth, and the Property Rights of Women in South Asia', in Jack Goody and S.J. Tambiah, eds, *Bridewealth and Dowry*, Cambridge: Cambridge University Press.

Vatuk, Sylvia (1975). 'Gifts and Affines in North India,' *Contributions to Indian Sociology*, Vol. 9, No. 2, pp. 157–96.

The Novels of Bhai Vir Singh and the Imagination of Sikh Identity, Community, and Nation

C. Christine Fair

This chapter examines three novels of Bhai Vir Singh: *Sundri*, *Bijai Singh*, and *Satwant Kaur* and the ways in which they shaped notions of Sikh identity, community, and nation. Bhai Vir Singh, the 'Father of the Punjabi novel', authored them during the Singh Sabha movement, in which he was a crucial player. Singh intended the novels to reform and empower the Sikh community in the late nineteenth and early twentieth centuries. This is the period that I call the first 'life' of the novels. The second 'life' of these novels is realized in the 1980s when they are translated into English and distributed by Sikh booksellers in the United States. Sikh community groups used these translations to educate and invigorate young Sikhs settled and raised in countries outside of the Punjab. I argue here that these novels in some measure provide narratives that facilitate the imagination of a Sikh world and its inhabitants with the Punjab as its origin.

I expound on the important features that distinguish the first lives of these novels and contextualize the texts and their author in the Singh Sabha period. I will examine how the narratives serve to delineate Sikh, Hindu, and Muslim identities and establish ideological and political connections between these three groups. Crucially, the central figures of these novels are extraordinary women who cook, clean, nurse, kill and die for their faith and the *panth* (Sikh community). Therefore, I will explore the narrative functions of these heroines and the ways in which women are posited as the root of the family, panth, *qaum* (literally, 'people who stand together), community, and nation. Later, I turn to the second 'life' of these novels, manifest in the translation endeavours in the 1980s. Notably, the translations appear during this time frame, contemporaneously with the agitations for Khalistan. Hence, it is very difficult to view these translations outside of the political environments to which they are rooted. Having situated these novels in their contemporary contexts, I explore those narrative features that are both useful for imagining the Sikh world and particularly easy grist for the mills of transnational nationalisms.[1]

BHAI VIR SINGH AND THE POLITICAL NOVEL

The Punjabi novel, in its conception, was a vehicle for Singh Sabha ideology and Vir Singh was the foremost writer of the Singh Sabha movement. As the project and ideology of the Singh Sabhas have been documented elsewhere (Oberoi 1994, 1988; Kapur 1986; McLeod 1989; Fox 1985), my notes here will be brief. The first Singh Sabha was established in 1873, in response to four Sikh students at the Mission School in Amritsar who had announced their intention of taking Christian baptism. The second followed in 1879 in Lahore and several satellites followed. Within the Singh Sabhas, the Tat Khalsa emerged as a specifically religious reformist sector and promulgated historiographies and doctrine that brought great change both in the ways that Sikhs viewed themselves, and the way that non-Sikhs came to imagine Sikhs.

The Singh Sabhas, and the Tat Khalsa in particular, sought to forge a new and distinct identity for the Sikh panth, distinguishing Sikhs from what they decided was Hindu, and to homogenize a polyphonous tradition by squelching dissent within. The identity propounded was specifically that of the Khalsa,[2] instituted by the tenth guru, Guru Gobind Singh on Baisakhi in 1699 at Anandpur. The Singh Sabhas began Sikh newspapers for the purpose of spreading polemical material and promoting Punjabi as the sacred language of the Sikhs. In 1894, Bhai Vir Singh began the Khalsa Tract Society to disseminate polemic religious material. In 1908, the Khalsa Handbill Society was founded to reach areas that were not accessible to or influenced by the Singh Sabha chapters. These endeavours were blatant co-optations of the Christian Missionary enterprises and were commonplace features of nineteenth-century religious/reform movements in South Asia. In 1902, the Chief Khalsa Diwan (CKD) came into existence to coordinate the efforts of the various Singh Sabha satellites.[3]

Bhai Vir Singh, though he is most known for his poetry, wrote four novels in the Punjabi language that have been considered outstanding examples of Punjabi fiction. *Sundri* (1898/1899),[4] *Bijai Singh* (Parts I and II, 1900), (Dulai 1975: 49); *Satwant Kaur* (Part I in 1900, Part II in 1927), (Khosla 1984: 'Chronology') and a fourth novel *Baba Naudh Singh* (serialized from October 1917 to December 1921), which is unrelated to the trilogy that the first three comprise (Khosla 1984: 14; Oberoi 1994: 332).[5] The first three are historical accounts, with similar ideological agendas and historical contexts.[6] Vir Singh, in writing this trilogy, claimed to have had numerous motivations, all of which were coincident with Singh Sabha objectives, including encouraging Sikhs to embrace their heroic and important past, expunge corruption from their religious practice, and embrace 'orthodox' Sikh teachings and cultivate the Punjabi language as the sacred language of the Sikhs (Dulai 1975: 50–1).[7]

THE NOVELS AND THEIR HEROINES

The three historical novels are situated in the eighteenth century, depicting the bravery of the Khalsa Sikhs as they struggled against Mughal oppression. Importantly, for their future re-deployment in the Sikh world in the 1980s, they occupy the historical space between the death of the tenth Guru, Gobind Singh, and the establishment of the Khalsa Raj under Maharaja Ranjit Singh. Hence the target readers, Sikhs, would know that the martyrdom and valour would eventually come to fruition with the establishment of the Khalsa Raj. As he explained in the introduction to *Bijai Singh*, this is a particularly important period of time for Khalsa history. It is a period of Khalsa–Sikh martial skill and bravery, a period from which Sikhs should derive pride and therefore aspire to the Khalsa. Hence, by writing these novels, Sikhs will be proud to be Khalsa Sikhs. This historical location is important because it was Guru Gobind's Khalsa that is believed to have been subject to Mughal persecution. Faced with the Mughal intentions to annihilate the Khalsa, Vir Singh narrated how the Khalsa Singhs, by tenaciously clinging to their Khalsa identity, survived extinction. Vir Singh hoped to inspire such loyalty to the Khalsa at the turn of the twentieth century.

THE NOVELS

Sundri

This novel narrates the experiences of a young girl, Surasti, who is the daughter of a wealthy Hindu family in a quotidian Punjabi village. The narrative begins when the recently-married Surasti is kidnapped by a Mughal Nawab before she goes to her in-laws. Her father and husband beg the Nawab for her release, but, to no avail. However, when Surasti escapes the Nawab and returns to her maternal home, her family sends her away fearing the reprisals of the angry Nawab. Meanwhile, her brother, Balwant Singh has returned to the village after taking *amrit* (initiation) and joining the ranks of the Khalsa fighting the Mughals in the forest. Furious with his family's decision, he takes Surasti to the forest with him. However, en route to rejoin the Khalsa, they are captured by the same Nawab. Surasti is to be converted to Islam and become the Nawab's wife and Balwant is to convert as well. However, the Khalsa army storms in and rescues both upon which they all return to the Khalsa camp. Surasti then requests that she stay and serve the Khalsa, *as their sister*, in the forest. Soon thereafter, Surasti takes amrit and becomes Sundri. Most of the text subsequently involves Sundri eluding the lustful Nawab and exhibiting behaviour that Vir Singh believes is the model for contemporary Sikh women.

One day, Sundri stumbles across a wounded Muslim soldier, who, upon recovery, kidnaps her for the Nawab. Her honour, virginity, and faith are saved by her own piety and a timely rescue by her brother. The narrative digresses into historical mode, featuring a host of historical figures such as Lakhpat Rai, Kaura Mal, and Surat Singh. The use of historical characters gives the illusion that the book is not fiction, but a historical account. (This illusion is further fostered by the use of footnotes. All three of the novels use these techniques to elide fact and fiction.) There are numerous plot twists, all of which are generally used to demonstrate the ruthlessness of Muslims, the pusillanimity of Hindus and the valour and piety of Sikh men and women in the keeping of their faith. In the end, Sundri is wounded and seriously ill and again in the care of the same licentious Nawab. This time, once she is rescued by her brother and the other Singhs, she dies. Up to her death, Sundri exhibits extreme piety and desire for the Guru Granth Sahib. In her last breath, she exhorts her brothers to continue the fight.

This text discursively articulates distinct Hindu, Muslim, and Sikh communities. Muslims are notable for their ruthlessness, killing and kidnapping women, and torturing and killing Khalsa Sikhs because they refuse to accept Islam. Hindus are weak and effeminate and return their abducted daughters to their captors—after grovelling at the feet of the captors fails. They refuse to help the Khalsa openly or sell food to the Khalsa; but they do *accept* the help of the Khalsa in time of need. Sometimes they collude with the murderous Mughals. Sikhs are brave and valiant. The Khalsa army, much smaller in number than their Mughal foes, succeeds in miraculous victories. They are the antitheses of Muslims and Hindus and remain firm in their faith under the most difficult of circumstances.[8] These categories or identities are not necessarily static or fixed by birth. For instance, an effeminate Hindu can become a mighty Singh (lion) by taking amrit and becoming a Khalsa Sikh. Examples of the amrit transformation abound: Balwant, Surasti turned Sundri, a hapless Kshatriya couple who endured the tribulation of captivity.

Sundri is a model of piety and sacrifice which Sikh women should strive to imitate and she is a tool by which men are incited to heroic behaviour. Much of *Sundri*'s narrative is interrupted by various authorial exhortations for women to reform themselves and abjure heterodox Sikh religious practice such as believing in charms, worshiping at shrines, and languishing in luxury and comfort. I contend that these exhortations clearly demonstrate

a significant contempt for his female contemporaries whom Vir
Singh posits as the root of corruption, which he believed permeated the Sikh community.[9] Thus, Sundri's heroism is manifest at
the expense of the very women she is *supposedly* inspiring. In fact,
Vir Singh considered the contemporary women of the qaum to
be lax, superstitious, apostate, and spoiled, leading themselves
and their *sons* and *husbands* to hell. In this novel, women are exhorted to save the panth by taking amrit and becoming Singhnis
like the fictional Sundri who saves herself by leaving her Hindu
roots behind and embracing the Sikh future. Notably, Vir Singh's
use of a female protagonist chastises and questions the masculinity of Sikh men. While Sundri is clearly domestic (cooking,
nursing, fetching water), she also has a decidedly militant mode.
She lives in the forest with the Khalsa. When she is attacked
by a group of Turks, she kills one with her dagger before she is
captured again. In the final analysis, what man could possibly
compare himself favourably to this protagonist Sundri?

While Vir Singh, in this novel evinces disgust with the
behaviour of his female contemporaries, Vir Singh *did* advocate
social reform with respect to women. The novel chastises those
who practise female infanticide and reminds the reader that the
Gurus gave women equal rights. While men who mistreat women
and consider them their inferior are discredited in the novel, Vir
Singh forcefully exhorts women to be pure and faithful.

Bijai Singh

This novel chronicles the trials and tribulations of Bijai Singh and
his wife Sheel Kaur at the hands of a host of historical characters
like Mir Mannu. Like Sundri, Bijai Singh is not born into a
Sikh family. Rather, Bijai Singh is born Ram Lal, the son of the
historical Diwan Lakhpat Rai. By taking amrit, the scrawny Ram
Lal is transfigured into the courageous, albeit humble, Singh.
His conversion to Sikhism turns his family upside down and
he leaves the house with his *sahajdhari* Sikh (non-Khalsa) wife
Sheel Kaur, and their son. Upon striking out, his wife is injured
in the first round of battle. She is superficially hit in the belly, and
Bijai Singh must stay behind the Khalsa Dal to care for her. The
narrative weaves in and out of their various bouts with captivity

and separation. Upon her capture, manoeuvred by a corrupt pandit, Sheel Kaur becomes the object of ubiquitous Mughal lust. Her life is spared as she is targeted to become his wife, pending coerced conversion that awaits all three of them. She is imprisoned with her son, while Bijai is sent to a separate cell. This is the beginning of their separation. Much of the narrative takes place during this separation, allowing both Sheel and Bijai to be the alternating protagonists of the story.

Sheel and her son are imprisoned with other women and children who are hideously tortured.[10] Often, the author enters the narrative to laud the strength of these women; true Singhnis would rather see their husbands and sons killed than forsake their faith. These women, as opposed to Bhai Vir Singh's contemporaries, are not superstitious or bent on engaging in Hindu rituals. Mir Mannu wants Sheel as his wife and tortures her sister Singhnis to convince her to accept his offer. For several chapters, the exploits of Sheel Kaur's spiritual strength are narrated. When the narrative returns to Bijai Singh, he is saving women from Muslim atrocities. Though he has heard that his wife has become Mir Mannu's bride, he does not believe it, for, '[i]t is impossible for a Sikh woman to live with violated honour' (Duggal 1983: 109). He proceeds to get her back. However, Mir's wife begins to desire and pursue Bijai. This is a strange inversion of the predatory Muslim male sexuality that underlies and compels the narratives of the trilogy. Mir's wife, the Begum, is the only woman in this trilogy who pursues her sexual desires. Finally, upon escaping, Bijai Singh dies as a consequence of battle wounds. Sheel Kaur too dies upon uttering her last words: 'Nanak, they alone are true *Sati*s who die with the sheer shock of separation' (ibid.: 165). The novel concludes with Vir Singh informing his audience that Bijai's orphaned son grows to be a great hero.

Like *Sundri*, much of this volume is comprised of didactic authorial musings. The narrator specifically explains to the reader that they should learn from Sheel Kaur, whether they be man or woman. The narrator, referencing Sheel's various predicaments, cautions Sikhs to beware the lure of other, clearly false, religions and to remain steadfast to the truth of Sikh precepts. At various places in the novel, the narrator reminds Sikh women that it is their sacred duty to protect their honour. Both *Sundri* and *Bijai Singh* reference the success of Christian missionary efforts and suggest that the weakness of Sikh women facilitate this. As such the novels encourage Sikh women to summon up the strength of imaginary women to combat the influx of Christianity. Indeed, the narrator actually explains that books like *Sundri* are positive influences in assisting women to persevere in their Sikh *dharma* (moral order). However, the narrator is also clear that men must also honour these obligations.

Curiously, Sheel is a sahajdhari Sikh, perhaps a narrative trope intended to gloss the very serious Singh Sabha question as to where the Sahajdhari should be located in the Khalsa panth.[11] By virtue of marriage the Sahajdhari Sheel is included conjugally in the Khalsa panth. The separate but not-quite equal status of Sheel Kaur, when compared to the *kirpan*-swinging amritdhari Sundri, is manifest in several ways. First, unlike Sundri, Sheel and Bijai do not immediately join the Khalsa Army in the forest because of her initial injury. Second, Sheel Kaur does not engage in active battle; rather, she is crafty and uses ruses to escape her various predicaments. Third, when Sheel Kaur is in Mir Mannu's prison, various female prisoners exhort her to be like Sundri. Hence, intertextually, our Sahajdhari heroine is told to take her amritdhari predecessor as a model by which she can save herself. Fourth, she dies not as a consequence of battle wounds; such a death befits a Khalsa Sikh like Sundri. Rather, Sheel the 'true sati' collapses upon her husband's death. Like Sundri, Sheel cannot return to the life of a householder; she too must die.

Satwant Kaur

Unlike the other protagonists, Satwant Kaur is born into a Gursikh ('orthodox') family. Satwant, like Sundri, is captured by a Muslim soldier she was assisting. The reader learns the details of her abduction by Vir Singh's use of flashback and Satwant's own recounting of her travails with other characters. Satwant is sold into servitude in Kabul and becomes the private servant of a Khan's wife, Fatima. The Khan is an abusive alcoholic for which his wife seeks recourse with the Amir of Kabul. Much to the Begum's dismay, the Amir orders his execution. The Begum relies excessively upon Satwant in all spheres of life. Satwant even attacks the Khan and wrestles him to the ground when he attempts to kill Fatima. Ultimately, it is Satwant who manoeuvres to save the Khan's life through a gender-bending, cross-dressing escapade. He returns to Fatima, a reformed and doting husband. The Amir, of course, is amazed by Satwant's strength and courageousness which puts the men in his court to shame. He decides that she will convert to Islam and become his wife. Ultimately, Satwant escapes and reaches Fatima, who hides her in a secret chamber and cares for her surreptitiously. Fatima, in the course of Satwant's self-imposed captivity, comes to be exceedingly dependent on Satwant, who has become Fatima's protector and instructor in Sikhism.

Finally, dressed as Jaswant Singh, Satwant joins a caravan heading to the Punjab; to escape inspection, Jaswant must take on the dress of a Muslim man. In the caravan, she meets a soldier, Agha Khan, who is drawn to Jaswant because s/he is reciting Gurbani. Trusting Jaswant, Agha Khan entrusts her/him with the safety of his nanny, Saeen, who is also dressed as a Muslim man. Saeen reveals that she is a Punjabi Hindu woman who is sympathetic to the Sikh cause. She later reveals that Agha Khan is none other than a Sikh, the son of a famous Sikh ruler whose wife was captured. Khan's mother was killed, as she refused to convert, and he was raised by the cruel and ruthless Pathan, Hasan Khan. Saeen, the faithful servant of Agha Khan's mother, was charged with raising Agha Khan to, one day, rejoin the service of the Khalsa. Saeen is now endangered as Hasan Khan is worried that she will tell Agha of his past.

Upon learning that he was a Sikh, Agha Khan enthusiastically takes to serving the panth which he does vigorously. When they arrive in Amritsar, Jaswant tells Saeen and Agha Khan (now an amritdhari Sikh named Alamba Singh) that she is really Satwant Kaur. They are obviously shocked and express amazement that there was never even a hint of her girlhood. Back in Amritsar, people are amazed that Alamba Singh is alive and is a courageous Sikh, though he was raised as a Muslim all of his life. It is proposed that Alamba and Satwant marry, but Alamba, horribly embarrassed, insists upon the brotherly-sisterly affection between them. Satwant dedicates herself to a life of celibacy and community servitude. All are reunited with their families and everyone lives happily ever after.

Like Sundri, as Jaswant Singh, Satwant challenges men to master the virtues that she embodies. As Satwant, she is a role model for women, the appropriate companion for the 'new' Sikh man. Like Sundri, she does not become the marital companion and re-producer of new Sikhs. Rather, she refuses to return to the fold of the householder and pursues her life as a *sewakar* (one who performs *sewa* or service to the Panth).

SUMMARIZING THE FIRST LIVES OF THESE TEXTS

All of these heroines are radically uprooted from a stable familial structure: Sundri and Satwant Kaur are taken from their parental homes and Sheel Kaur is taken from her husband's realm. Nikky Singh alleges that Sundri, and perhaps by extension we can include the other heroines in the trilogy, defiantly rides in the forest alongside men. Nikky Singh argues that Vir Singh contrasts Sundri's rebellious freedom to the tortured women held under Mughal captivity. But does she ride *equally* beside men? Even though, when necessary, she does kill, she is still the domestic locus of the Sikhs in the forest. Clearly, these non-householding women are not the reproducers of Vir Singh's vision of Sikh culture. Moreover, the heroic deeds of these heroines are manifest only as the result of their continual response to the lustful pursuits of various Muslim men. Ultimately, having left the realm of 'patriarchal civilization' for the liminality of the 'uncultivated world' of the forest, they can never return. Their options are death/martyrdom or to become sewa-performing ascetics. Perhaps it could be that their deaths, or, choices to remain sewakar constitute resistance to 'patriarchal civilization'. However, they never leave that realm by choice, but by abduction. Therefore, it does not seem to me that the authorial disposal of these liminal heroines is a productive site upon which we may posit heroic agency.

This trilogy does much to distinguish boundaries between Sikhs, Hindus, and Muslims and to characterize them by behaviours. However, while Muslims are rapists and killers and Hindus are effeminate, these designations are not necessarily static. A Hindu can always take amrit and become a Singh like Surasti/Sundri, Ram Lal/Bijai Singh, and Agha Khan/Alamba Singh. However, it is interesting that the only nominal Muslim, converted via amrit, was by birth a Sikh. This trilogy contributes to establishing Khalsa hegemony within the panth, by narrating the persecution and martyrdom of the Khalsa panth. In *Bijai Singh*, Sahajdharis are brought in the Khalsa fold, but feminized and subjected to the masculine field of the Khalsa. All three texts address the lack of solidarity in the panth and the forsaking of Singh dharam among the author's contemporaries. The state of women is posited as the root of this rot, which must be apprehended. The 'Singhly' behaviour of women is to be established as the source of the panth, while it is the bravery and heroism of men that is to protect the panth. Moreover, men are saddled with the obligation to designate themselves as Khalsa by wearing the five Ks generally, but the turban specifically. Though women are also supposed to wear the five Ks, few wear the turban. In all three of these texts, the Punjab is posited as the *desh* (homeland/Punjab) of the Singhs. In *Satwant Kaur*, desh is meaningfully understood in terms of its counterpart, *pardesh* (Kabul).

THE SECOND LIVES OF THE TEXT: A NEW SIKH WORLD AND NEW SIKH NATIONALISMS

While highly speculative, this section contends that these novels, translated into English and circulating throughout a globalized Sikh world, in some measure had utility in the re-imagining of a transnational diasporic Sikh world. Translated into English and circulating in the 1980s during the most intense phase of Khalistan agitation, these novels helped to redefine the boundaries of the Sikh community at a time when boundaries were increasingly being challenged. It may be said that these novels by themselves are an insignificant artifact of Sikh reproduction of their community in English-speaking countries. *In situ*, however, these novels can be seen as one conveyance of Sikh identity production that works in conjunction with several others, similarly intended, imaginative instruments at the conjuncture of mediascapes and ideoscapes (Appadurai 1996). For this reason, it is useful to contextualize these English translations in their contemporary social and political ecologies. Note that *Sundri* and *Bijai Singh* were published in English in 1983 and again in 1988. Ujagar Singh Bawa first published his English *Satwant Kaur* in 1987 and 1988. The first two were issued in the midst of pre-operation Blue Star Khalistan agitations. *Satwant Kaur* was translated after Operation Bluestar and the subsequent anti-Sikh riots in November of 1984. Sikhs all over the world were jolted by this event, even those Sikhs who were not previously supporters of the Khalistan movement. Hence, these novels emerged at a critical time in the recent history of the Sikhs. Many of the themes of these novels lend themselves easily to being re-deployed in this particular environment.

The retooling of these novels for a new Sikh world are explicit objectives in the efforts of at least two of the translators of these novels. *Sundri* was translated by Gobind Singh Mansukhani and *Bijai Singh* by Devinder Singh Duggal; both were published as a set, courtesy of the Sri Guru Nanak Satsang Sabha Gurdwara Katong of Singapore. *Satwant Kaur*'s translation was entirely a 'diasporic' enterprise. Whereas the translators of the other texts seem to be working in India under the auspices of the Vir Singh Sahitya Sadan in Delhi, Ujagar Singh Bawa translated *Satwant Kaur* from Washington DC. Bawa, a professor of economics in Pennsylvania by profession, is highly involved and structurally important in the Washington Sikh Center, under whose organizational auspices the book was first published.

I asked Bawa in an interview why he translated this text. He told me that 'we were running out of books on Sikhism in English'.[12] Of course, these texts are not books on Sikhism, they are fiction. But Bawa has made, obliquely, an important note on the genre of these texts and the format in which Vir Singh wrote them. As historical fiction, they are footnoted. Though the exact footnotes are not retained in the English text, the translators still retained the footnoted format, though their exact notes differ. Given that the narrative landscapes are populated with legions of historical characters that are readily locatable in *The New Cambridge History of India: The Sikhs of the Punjab*, it is easy to question the fictional-ness of the protagonists. These footnoted novels appear to present an interesting case of 'genre-bending'. We can only assume that the translators of the texts had a similar opinion of the footnoted originals, as they retained the same structure in their own texts.[13]

What intentions underlie these translated texts? All three texts are armed with explanatory prefaces. For instance, Harbans Singh wrote in *Sundri*'s 'Foreword' that the Singapore Gurdwara 'have [*sic*] taken up a programme to get Bhai Vir Singh's works translated into English and other languages, publish them and make the [*sic*] available to the people in foreign lands' (Mansukhani 1983).[14] Devinder Singh Duggal writes in his 'Introduction' to *Bijai Singh* that he was motivated to translate the volume by many of the same passions with which Vir Singh wrote the novel, in the hope that it would contribute the 'moral regeneration of the Sikh Youth' (Translator's Note, unnumbered). Similarly Sat Jiwan Singh Khalsa, an Attorney at Law in New York, opined in Bawa's 'Foreword' that

the paucity of historic information about the Sikh way of life heightens the import of Bhai Vir Singh's works in terms of both their inherent value as historical accounts and as educational sources for all. As Sikhs increasingly become an international community and the ability of succeeding generations to be literate in Punjabi wanes, at least in present times, the importance of Dr. Bawa's translation of this classical work of Vir Singh is obvious (Bawa 1988: vii).

Bawa writes of his own work that:

Besides, selfishly, there is a dire dirth [*sic*] of English books for our children in *America, Canada, United Kingdom, and elsewhere in the western hemisphere* where Sikh children, for no fault of theirs, lack adequate preparation and facility in learning to read and write Punjabi....It is paramount for the Sikh children to be treated with religious and political episodes of our past, fictional or real, so that they are able to structure a perspective of their own. With these aims and constraints, *Satwant Kaur*, by Dr. Vir Singh has been translated (Bawa: ix).

It seems reasonably evident that these texts were translated with many of the same intentions as Bhai Vir Singh's in writing the novels. Of course, the scope and dispersion of the panth had radically changed by the time these translations came into existence. The language contention is no longer whether Sikhs should learn Punjabi at the expense of Hindi or Urdu, but how should children be taught in the Sikh world—be that American, Canadian, in the United Kingdom, or elsewhere in the western

hemisphere? Should they be taught Punjabi at all? How can they
know their history if they don't know their language? In these
texts, the Punjabi language and retention of the Khalsa five Ks
are the markers by which the Sikh identity is gauged to be self-
replicating or disintegrating.

These texts, apparently aimed at young teens, with some other
imaginative tools, provide a means to link second generation
Sikhs to the Punjab, a land that they may or may not have seen.
The Punjab, as all of these translators maintain, is the source
of Sikh identity, yet Punjab is far removed from most of these
children's lives. These novels are one of the means to bring
children into the world of the Punjab. Hence, these novels may
help to imagine a Sikh world both vertically through time, trans-
historically, and laterally through distance, transnationally. Sikh
pre-teens, and teens while reading these novels, are exhorted to
compare their lives with both the protagonists and the audiences
posited by Bhai Vir Singh. While imagining themselves as a part
of the historical panth, they are also drawn into the geographical
imagination of the panth. Sikhs in New York giving their speech
on Satwant Kaur are invited to move through Kabul with her
to get 'home' to the Punjab. It seems, therefore, that the 1980s
is a moment of redeployment of these texts during which time
the textualization of the 'homeland' and 'nation' becomes
particularly salient.

These novels also seem to have particular utility in defining
a Sikh homeland (that is, the Punjab) as well as particular
notions of Sikh nationhood. The translations are replete with
references to the Punjab as 'my country' (desh) and fellow
Sikhs (qaum) as 'countrymen'.[15] In many ways, these Punjabi
words are translated through the language of nationalism in
ways that are not entirely faithful to the original Punjabi. This
is consistent with Dusenbery's observation that a subtle means
of reconfiguring the Sikhs as an ethno-territorial community
is through the 'increasing substitution in Sikh discourse of the
Persian loan word qaum (literally, people who stand together)
or the English word 'nation' in reference to the Sikh collectivity'
(Dusenbery 1995: 26).[16]

In translation, these novels create a discursive homeland for
the Sikhs. *Satwant Kaur* in this regard is the most powerful as the
protagonist is held in Kabul, far away from the Punjab. Satwant

laments that she does not know the language there, though over time she does learn. For her survival, and for her family's survival, she must return to her *ghar* (home/house), desh, *watan* (homeland). These novels replicate a common theme that resonated throughout much of the 1980s that the Punjab must be the source of identity of the Sikh world—even if it is not in actual practice.

In the context of Khalistani aspirations, an exceedingly important feature of these texts is that the narratives are situated between the death of Guru Gobind Singh and the establishment of the Khalsa Raj, during which time the physically marked Khalsa Sikhs were subject to murderous assaults. The attack on Khalsa identifiers and the struggle to retain them in the face of martyrdom resonates on multiple fronts in the contemporary Sikh World. Operation Bluestar and the massacre of Sikhs that ensued have ruptured the imagination of the Sikh world and its connections with the Central Government in Delhi. While this is not a chapter about the Khalistan movement, it needs to be noted that these novels are exceedingly suitable for imagining the creation of such a Khalistan.

The depiction of the persecution of Khalsa Sikhs and horrific martyrdom in the eighteenth century under Aurangzeb and subsequent rulers invites young Sikhs to superimpose their own situations upon these narratives. The struggle of young men to wear their turban may resonate with their Khalsa forefathers who *died and killed* to keep these markers of faith and identity.[17] Readers of Bhai Vir Singh's trilogy likely know that in the texts' narratives, Maharaja Ranjit Singh will follow with the establishment of Khalsa Raj. Once the Khalsa Raj is established, the Khalsa can flourish without persecution. Hence, the readers are invited to desire such a sovereign Khalsa Raj, Khalistan, or Sikhistan, in which they are free from persecution. I think it is not unreasonable to suggest, as many Sikhs have, the parallels between Zion, the homeland of the Jews in post-Holocaust nationalist discourse, and Khalistan, the homeland of the Sikhs in post-1984 Sikh Nationalist discourse.[18]

In translation and for diaspora, the heroine cluster also serves potentially important purposes that Vir Singh could not have imagined. Young female Sikhs reading these texts are invited to make several identifications. The first is comparing herself and her contemporaries to those women that Vir Singh ostensibly addresses. Similarly, young Sikh girls are also invited to ask themselves whether they are the source of their panth's strength or decline. That is, are they more like Sundri or Bhai Vir Singh's female contemporaries? The pressures of the dominant culture include dating and intimate knowledge of partners prior to marriage. Hence, according to Bawa, the issue of dating is one which is addressed during the Sikh Youth Camps.

The heroines of these English texts are conveyances by which female sexuality is checked and subordinated to the needs of the panth. All three female protagonists would rather die than submit to sexual defilement or renounce their dharam. In chapter 15 of *Satwant Kaur*, in all three versions, Satwant's father and mother express that their 'greatest worry is that she should be able to retain her honor and Sikh faith. If she could retain these, it is immaterial whether she is dead or alive, it is all right' (Bawa 1988: 71). Needless to say, the entire narrative is compelled by the various protagonists endeavouring to protect their virtue and dharam. These heroines are interpreted as feminist models for Sikh women and girls, notably by Nikky Singh. Sikh women are trying to reconcile the scriptural equality between men and women, articulated by Guru Nanak, and the gross social inequality that persists. In fact, Nikky Singh's book is an attempt at reclaiming Sikhism for feminists of all persuasions. Sundri *et al.* provide young Sikh women and girls with apparent evidence that once, in the days of the Khalsa, men and women were equals. Moreover, Sundri *et al.*, when taken in moderation, are characters by which second generation Sikhs can have their feminism and their chastity too.

NOTES TOWARDS CONCLUSIONS

Placing these novels in the historical period of the Singh Sabha demonstrates how these texts contributed to early boundaries between Sikhs, Hindus, and Muslims and propagated specific notions of the Sikh community. That is, the primary identity of the Sikhs should be the Khalsa. The Khalsa, gendered specifically as masculine in its physical designators, subsumes and subordinates alternative Sikh identities such as the Sahajdhari. In translation, these novels provide an imaginative process by which young Sikhs visualize the Punjab as the homeland of the Sikhs. I have suggested that in the particular contexts of the Khalistan movement(s), these texts have a particular salience due to their historical situation and the ways in which they narrate Sikh resistance to persecution and renunciation of their physical markers in the face of adversity.

NOTES

1. By transnational nationalisms I specifically mean the various forms of Sikh nationalism (with or without Khalistani demands) that span several nation states. That is to say, Sikh nationalisms are not confined to one nation-state. Yet, these various internationally based nationalist organizations may be connected tentatively by their affiliation with such organizations as the SGPC or various Akali Dal organizations that have positioned themselves as global representatives of the Panth.

2. The Khalsa Sikh, either male or female, is initiated into the Khalsa by taking *amrit* in a ceremony called *khande di pahul*. Having undergone khande di pahul, a Khalsa Sikh is obligated to keep the five Ks, *panch khakar*, and follow numerous behavioural proscriptions and prescriptions. Sikhs who have taken amrit are called Amritdharis. Keshdharis are Sikhs who keep their hair and very likely maintain the other Ks as well, however they have not taken amrit. Sahajdharis Sikhs, in the current use of the term, are Sikhs who cut their hair but uphold the Khalsa as their ideal. However, Sahajdhari may not have always meant this. See Oberoi, 1994.

3. The CKD was the impetus and organizational base for numerous other Sikh political bodies, such as the Shiromani Gurdwara Parbandhak Committee (SGPC) and the Akali Dal.

4. S.S. Dulai indicates that 1899 was the publication date of *Sundari* (Dulai 1975). G.S. Khosla indicates that the publication date is 1898 (Khosla 1984). [Editor's note: There are variances in the spelling of Sundri/Sundari].

5. It is not clear whether or not *Bijai Singh* or *Satwant Kaur* were printed in serialized form.

6. Many scholars have noted this feature (see Oberoi 1994; Dulai 1975; N. Singh 1993). Most scholars agree that these texts constitute a trilogy (See Sekhon and Duggal 1992; Duggal 1983; Das 1991; and N. Singh 1993).

7. Dulai translated this from the Punjabi text; see the Introduction to the English version of *Bijai Singh* in Duggal.

8. At Surasti and Balwant's planned conversion, two sepoys are chatting about the might of a Sikh and the outright resistance of a Sikh to convert. The first sepoy says to the second: 'They [Sikhs] are very obstinate. Hindus are soft like butter, but the Sikhs are hard as stone. Heaven knows from where they have got the strength of their conviction' (Mansukhani 1983: 13).

9. For an alternative—but in my view, incorrect, interpretation of Vir Singh's use of the heroines, see Nikky Singh 1993: 189. Singh takes the mere use of female heroines in these novels as probative of Vir Singh's proto-feminist credentials.

10. For example, the women's children are dismembered alive and the subsequent body parts are thrown into their laps. This is one of the eighteen 'canonized' means of martyrdom that are recalled of the Mughal era.

11. The basic innovation of the Singh Sabha was to re-incorporate the Sahajdhari Sikh into the Khalsa Panth by rendering the Sahajdhari a 'slow adapter' to the Khalsa ideals. Though Sahajdharis are not, and may never become Khalsa Sikhs; they nevertheless, in Singh Sabha logic, hold the Khalsa to be the ideal to which they aspire. This semantic manoeuvring of the Singh Sabha erased the resistance to the Khalsa implied in the various histories of the term and inscribed the Sahajdhari into the Khalsa (McLeod 1989: 71).

12. Interview with Professor Bawa, February 1995.

13. Nikky Singh notes that this same criticism was lodged against Bhai Vir Singh. She quotes Harbans Singh, 'Bhai Vir Singh's most devoted admirer', who said: 'The footnotes added to later editions of the book to document some of the statements and events further weaken the illusion of the story' (N. Singh 1993: 203).

14. Harbans Singh, Honorary General Secretary, Bhai Vir Singh Sahitya Sadan wrote the 'Foreward' to Mansukhani's translation of *Sundri*.

15. See for example, 'O' Parmeshwar! What has gone wrong with my country? Why can't it take care of itself? What have my countryman [sic] to go through after they are brought here...My country has the strength but is unable to defend itself...She was bewildered at these surprises and contemplated deep thoughts about the impact of the truthfulness of her country' (Bawa 1988: 128).

16. Dusenbery also notes (based apparently upon Oberoi 1994) that the claim of intimate ties between the Sikhs and the Punjab is quite recent. If this is the case, Bhai Vir Singh was a pioneer in making this connection between Sikhs and the Punjab.

17. Again, we must keep in mind that the tradition of (male) martyrs is always in the foreground. Sikh Gurdwaras often have graphic pictures representing the eighteen ways to be martyred. A new addition to Gurdwara art is the depiction of the destroyed Akal Takht and a portrait of Jarnail Singh Bhindranwale.

18. In these texts, there seems to be a deliberate linking of events of Sikh history with the language of other aspects of Jewish history. For instance in *Sundri*, there is an account of the 'Small Holocaust' and in *Bijai Singh*, we find an account of the 'Big Holocaust'. Apparently *ghallughara* (massacre) was translated as Holocaust. This is not an innocent translation. Moreover, J.S. Grewal (1994: 229) makes the important point that the Delhi riots were a reminder of the ghallugharas of the eighteenth century. Attempts to frame murderous assaults on Sikhs within the language of the Holocaust, for a wide English-reading audience, seems to represent attempts to situate the Punjab crisis in a well-known idiom of hatred, genocide, and the need for protection in a sovereign state, Khalistan. The obvious implication of positing Khalistan as Zion, is that eventually Khalistan will materialize as a political, sovereign entity.

REFERENCES

Appadurai, Arjun (1996). *Modernity at Large: Cultural Dimensions of Globalization*, Minneapolis: University of Minnesota Press.

Bawa, Ujagar Singh (tr.) (1988). *Satwant Kaur*, New Delhi: Bhai Vir Singh Sahitya Sadan.

Das, S.K. (1991). *A History of Indian Literature: (Volume VIII): 1800–1910 Western Impact: Indian Response*, New Delhi: Sahitya Akademi.

Duggal, D.S. (tr.) (1983). *Bijai Singh*, New Delhi: Bhai Vir Singh Sahitya Sadan.

Dulai, Surjit Singh (1975). 'The Political Novel in Panjabi', *Contributions to Asian Studies*, Vol. VI, pp. 43–75.

Dusenbery, V.A. (1995). 'A Sikh Diaspora? Contested Identities and Constructed Realities', in Peter van der Veer (ed.), *Nation and Migration: The Politics of Space in the South Asian Diaspora*, Philadelphia: University of Pennsylvania Press.

Fox, Richard Gabriel (1985). *Lions of Punjab: Culture in the Making*, Berkeley: University of California Press.

Grewal, J.S. (1994). *The Sikhs of the Punjab*, The New Cambridge History of India II.3, Cambridge: Cambridge University Press.

Kapur, Rajiv A. (1986). *Sikh Separatism: The Politics of Faith*, London: Allen and Unwin.

Khosla, G.S. (1984). *Bhai Vir Singh: An Analytical Study*, New Delhi: Heritage Publisher.

Mansukhani, G.S. (tr.) (1983). *Sundari*, New Delhi: Bhai Vir Singh Sahitya Sadan.

McLeod, W.H. (1989). *Who is a Sikh? The Problem of Sikh Identity*, Oxford: Clarendon Press.

Oberoi, Harjot S. (1988). 'From Ritual to Counter Ritual: Rethinking the Hindu–Sikh Question', in J.T. O'Connell (eds), *Sikh History and Religion in the Twentieth Century*, Toronto: Centre for South Asian Studies, pp. 136–58.

—— (1994). *Construction of Religious Boundaries: Culture Identity and Diversity in the Sikh Tradition*, Delhi: Oxford University Press.

Sekhon, Sant Singh and Kartar Singh Duggal (1992). *A History of Punjabi Literature*, New Delhi: Sahitya Akademi.

Singh, Nikky-Guninder Kaur (1993). *The Feminine Principle in the Sikh Vision of the Transcendent*, Cambridge: Cambridge University Press.

Phulkaris

The Crafting of Rural Women's Roles in Sikh Heritage

Michelle Maskiell

> Heritage ... is a mode of cultural production in the present that has recourse to the past.
>
> —B. Kirshenblatt-Gimblett, *Theorizing Heritage*

Phulkaris, beautiful textiles stitched and worn by Sikh women in the late nineteenth and early twentieth centuries, are pre-eminent signs of Sikh heritage today. They are now as precious as gold in a much popular culture, at least if we are to judge from the top prizes awarded in The Miss World Punjaban pageant. The 2007 Miss World Punjaban is Japji Kaur Khaira from Australia, who won not only because of her beauty, but also because of her fluency in Punjabi, her performance of Gidha (a 'folk' dance), and her superior modelling of a Punjabi bride's clothes. According to the pageant's founder, Sardar Jasmer Singh Dhatt, the contest promotes awareness of Punjabi heritage. Japji Kaur won 'a Pure Gold Saggiphul (traditional ornament)' and a phulkari. While both the 'traditional' gold jewellery and the phulkari embodied Punjabi heritage, Jasmer Singh identified the phulkari rather than the jewellery as 'the pride of the Punjabans'.[1]

The word 'phulkaris' in this essay refers to the embroidered textiles that nineteenth- and early-twentieth-century Punjabi women commonly draped over their heads and wrapped around their bodies. Phulkaris could be worn expressively as shawls (*chadar*), scarves (*odhini*), or 'veils' (*ghungat*). They could also be gifted purposefully, or displayed meaningfully. 'Phulkari', literally 'flower-work', is the term for the embroidery style itself. Women used it to embellish tailored garments and scarves as well as these larger textiles. The Punjab Government Handicraft Emporium in Chandigarh today is named 'Phulkari', suggesting that these textiles are the most well-known Punjabi handicrafts and/or the most desirable among them. This essay will examine Punjabi women's agency in creating phulkaris from roughly 1850 to the 1940s, as well as the recent narratives that position phulkaris as embodiments of the positive values of Sikh rural heritage.

Since the Guru period, Sikh women and men have been crafting and re-crafting their own gender roles. The British annexation of Punjab in the mid nineteenth century led to what historian Doris R. Jakobsh called a 'pivotal' period for Sikh identity formation, one in which gender ideals of the Sikhs, the British, and other Indian communities were used by rival social reformers, officials and politicians alike to establish each community's unique claims for political and social loyalty. Punjabi women's social practices in the nineteenth century were not clearly demarcated among the province's three major religious traditions, a situation that was intolerable to many male leaders of competing colonial communities. Jakobsh delineated the work of the Singh Sabha movement in defining 'that which represented 'Sikh' and that which constituted 'un-Sikh,' or corrupted, tradition' (Jakobsh 2003: 2–3, 5). Of course, gender expectations were a critical part of this work. Processes of Sikh community self-definition that preceded 1947 continued afterwards as well. Leaders of Sikh political movements in independent India and the men who chronicled them constantly reiterated the rhetoric of a distinctive Sikh masculinity (Mann 2000). Sikh women have had to fashion their own roles both in daily life and within the ongoing processes of defining Sikh heritage in these gendered contexts.

Sikh, Hindu, and Muslim women all stitched, wore, and exchanged phulkaris in nineteenth-century Punjab. While members of the Sikh Sabha movement engaged in distinguishing what was or was not properly Sikh, so too leaders of Hindu and Muslim social reform groups actively sought to distinguish their groups' behaviours. No issue was more contentious among them all than purdah. Although the word literally means 'curtain', it referred to a system of social practices that could seclude women within a domestic space, require them to wear clothing that displayed modesty and deference, and teach them about an associated 'code of shame' (Malhotra 2002: 130). Sikh social reformers sometimes blamed Muslims for introducing purdah into the province, but there is no question that high-status Sikh women generally conformed to class- and age-specific purdah norms, just as Hindu and Muslim women did. Phulkaris belonged to the array of material culture that women used for purdah social practices in nineteenth- and early-twentieth-century Punjab.

The first section of this essay analyses pre-1947 narratives about phulkaris that positioned them within the material culture of the Punjabi 'folk'. On the one hand, some late-nineteenth-century British observers predicted that the introduction of industrial goods into the province would destroy the production of 'authentic' folk handicrafts and analyse the supposed 'degeneration' of phulkari embroidery 'tradition'. On the other hand, members of early-twentieth-century urban elites who celebrated the living 'traditions' of Punjabi rural life countered, consciously or unconsciously, imperial criticisms of their own 'mimicry' of European behavioural models (Bhabha 1994: 85–92). Historical depictions of phulkari making and gifting thus need to be considered as gendered lore supporting one or another of these standpoints rather than as 'objective' descriptions. The second section of the essay speculates about the agency of Sikh women, especially as embodied in their own phulkaris. It explores 'the parameters within which specific historical instances offer potential for and limits to women's power' (Nair 1994: 83), as expressed through Sikh women's material lives. Finally, some aspects of the transformation of phulkaris into Sikh heritage will be suggested.

PHULKARIS AS 'FOLK' HANDICRAFTS: IMPERIAL AND URBAN ELITE NARRATIVES

Phulkari embroidery motifs range widely from almost mono-chromatic golden tapestry-like, fabric-covering designs to embroideries using many bright colours to depict people and objects of rural Punjab. All of these textiles shared common construction techniques and a dominant embroidery stitch (the darning stitch). Extant phulkaris vary tremendously, most notably by design and colour but also by type of fabric, method of production, and size. Geographical location in western or eastern Punjab rather than the specific religious affiliation of the artisans appears to have been the primary factor determining details of colouring, design, and construction. Women in western Punjab created complicated geometrical patterns, chose distinctive colour combinations for their phulkaris, and embroidered their chosen motifs on narrow widths of cloth that they then attached together. Eastern Punjabi women stitched together narrow widths of cloth *before* embroidering their phulkaris. Their needlework incorporated figured designs like animals, plants, jewellery, and humans, generally traced in outline with black ink and then filled in with darning stitch. These *sainchi* phulkaris (considered further in the essay's next section) became especially popular among textile collectors after 1947 (Hitkari 1980: 33–4; Maskiell 1999: 361–99; Askari and Crill 1997; Frater 1993: 66–121; Grewal and Grewal 1988).

Women worked from the reverse of the background fabric, using soft untwisted silk floss (*pat*). The fabric was most often *khaddar*, a coarse cotton cloth with a narrow width; two or three lengths of cloth had to be sewn together to reach the average dimensions of a phulkari (about 2 1/2 yards or 2.30 metres, by about 1 1/2 yards or 1.40 metres). While embroidered motifs were discontinuous in an ordinary phulkari, the designs completely covered the ground cloth for a ceremonial *bagh* (literally a 'garden'). The time necessary to complete a phulkari varied dramatically, depending on the complexity of the design patterns and the skill of the embroiderer. On an average, women worked a month embroidering a phulkari, compared to the six-to-eight months required to complete a bagh.

The complexity and quantity of embroidery on particular phulkaris depended upon the generation and skill of the artisan. Ideally, before working their own first phulkaris with simple designs on an indigo ground, young girls started learning embroidery by imitating the stitches of their mothers or of other elder female relatives. Dalip Kaur Sanchu, born in the 1930s, recalled that she began embroidering phulkaris at the age of twelve, and crafted twenty-one phulkaris for her own trousseau. After marriage, she created six 'elaborate' phulkaris, one for each of her three daughters and three daughters-in-law (Gill 2000: 51–2).

Married women utilized their embroidery skills in their husbands' households, where they embellished phulkaris for their daughters' trousseau (dowries). Punjabi marriages included the exchange of many kinds of phulkaris. For their granddaughters' weddings, maternal grandmothers ideally embroidered the *chope*, which was 'made with a double running stitch, so that the [golden-yellow] design appears identical on both sides [of the deep red cloth]' (Dhamija 1964: 16). A senior woman in a groom's family might spend years embroidering a *vari da bagh*, which had a complicated golden-coloured silk pattern, as a present for his bride. The *vari* was the clothing and jewellery gifted by the groom's family to both the bride and the groom (Dhamija 1964: 16; Irwin and Hall 1973).

Today, the English word 'folk' has two primary meanings: first, 'a people; tribe; nation; ethnic group', that is, an entire collectivity; and second, 'of or existing among the common people', which refers to only a part of that larger collectivity. Nationalist writers have tended to use the broadest definition of the term 'folk'. However, colonial apologists emphasized the most narrow, often classifying common people into innumerable subsections, including the castes and 'tribes' identified by land revenue records, censuses, and other official registries. Clearly, each Punjabi linguistic tradition also had its own rich vocabulary identifying these social distinctions.

The rhetorics of gender and religion have been critical for the ways in which the concept of 'the folk' has been revisioned in India and in diasporic communities since 1947. Phulkaris were chosen as an evocative sign of an idealized village life in which gender roles were clearly delineated and the handicraft mode of production was not reduced to its post-Independence colonial euphemism of 'cottage industry'.

Several groups of people wrote about rural women's handicrafts in late-nineteenth- and early-twentieth-century Punjab: those associated with British imperial control of the province, and members of urban elites. Of course, each group had its own standpoint, although one English woman's short article published in the late 1880s has become the touchstone of a narrative of phulkari handicraft degeneration. Using her text as a source, I will compare and contrast her standpoint to that of slightly later Punjabi authors who positioned women and their handicrafts as unchanging emblems of the rural 'folk'. In both cases, gender played a critical role in attempts to portray the Punjabi folk through the depiction and appropriation of their material culture.

Flora Annie Steel (1847–1929) was married to a minor Raj official stationed in Punjab. Deeply influenced by the contemporary Arts and Crafts movement in Britain, she asserted that Punjabi phulkaris and other folk handicrafts were the antitheses of modern industrial productions characteristic of European capitalism and commerce. For Steel, the introduction of machine-made cloth into the late-nineteenth-century Punjab was inevitably leading to the destruction of 'authentic' phulkaris, which she closely associated with the Jat 'tribe'. Steel taught herself about embroidery in the 1870s and 1880s, when she used her time to collect phulkaris along with oral tales and tidbits of women's folk culture.[2] She established herself as a connoisseur of phulkaris and a judge of their authenticity through her knowledge of local languages and access to women in purdah, thereby basing her claims of authority quite literally on the extensively theorized colonial 'gaze'. Rural women stitched phulkaris as 'the work of leisure', Steel claimed. 'After doing yeoman's service with father or husband in the fields, [women] sit down in the cool of the evening to watch their threshing floors, and leaning, as I have often seen them, against the heaps of golden grain, darn away with patient, clumsy fingers at the roll of ruddy cloth upon their lap' (Steel 1888: 71–2). Steel's romanticized Jatni (female Jat), portrayed as stitching her own wedding clothes, personified the Victorian ideals both of morally superior rural handicraft production and of women's proper domestic work within a male-dominated lineage structure.

Steel linked authenticity to a gendered, non-commercial mode of folk production. When a Punjabi woman from a landed village family embroidered a phulkari, Steel considered her activity to be a leisured pastime firmly located in domesticity, the antithesis of (waged) work. Within Steel's representation of village life, a 'stalwart young Jatni of twenty, still unmarried, [walked] home from her father's field with a swing of russet and gold draperies matching the millet sheaf on her head', the woman and her phulkari blending seamlessly with the agricultural produce (Steel 1888: 71–2). The authentic phulkari was *simultaneously* a mark of the traditional—and thus of the fragmented, highly particularized tribal structure of Punjabi society—*and* of the universal feminine domestic space provided for by patriarchy. Steel wove phulkaris into an 'ethnographic pastorale' (Clifford 1986: 114), a timeless space from which phulkari 'tradition' would be subsequently appropriated.

Colonial apologists like Steel exercised no monopoly over use of the 'colonial archive' of regional folklore. Punjabi artists and writers mined it for their own purposes as well. Cultural nationalists exploited colonial-era essentialized folk identities, as demonstrated by the poetry of Puran Singh and his literary cohort in the 1920s and 1930s. Denis Matringe has analysed their 'lyrical evocation of the Punjabi countryside' by using a 'folkloristic prism' derived from the 'folkloristic approach of colonial perception'. This 'allow[ed] the poets a new reading of the myths and legends of popular Punjabi culture', according to Matringe, and provided a hero for the new poetry: 'the humble Punjabi peasant' who lived in a village characterized by sanity and authenticity. There, women were 'Sisters of the Spinning Wheel'.[3]

Neither Flora Annie Steel nor Puran Singh exhausted the possibilities for representing rural women and their phulkaris. Educated urban women in early-twentieth-century Punjab sometimes used phulkari imagery to evoke rural women. For example, in Punjabi novelist Dalip Kaur Tiwana's compelling autobiographical account of her 'journey on bare feet' to craft a personal identity as a writer, phulkaris appear within the household of her childhood village home as women's work, as trousseau items, and as wraps readily available to throw spontaneously around one's shoulders (Tiwana 1990: 61, 69, 84, 97). Amrita Sher-Gil (1913–1941), a Hungarian-Punjabi painter trained in Paris, draped phulkaris around the shoulders and under the sleeping bodies of peasant women she depicted in the late 1930s (Anand 1989).

If educated urban women used phulkaris to identify rural women and their surroundings, did any rural women use phulkari embroidery to express themselves with needle and thread? Some Sikh intellectuals in the 1970s and 1980s 'read' phulkaris as texts, treating them as metaphorical story-telling cloths. According to Harjeet Singh Gill of Punjabi University in Patiala, a country girl 'embroidered the semiological patterns of the discourse of her cultural destiny' onto her phulkari. Gill's narrative recounted 'the story of the Phulkari [as] the story of the happiness and the hazards' of one girl's life. 'Every stitch and every colour of this phulkari is culturally significant. The forms of sparrows, pigeons, peacocks, [etc.]...are semiological forms and present a conceptual network of metaphysical beliefs and precautions that are necessary for her to plod through the vicissitudes of social intercourse'. The phulkari is 'not a simple head-cover to be worn on certain auspicious occasions' but, with appropriate expert interpretation, a record of rural Sikh life and its timeless patterns in Bhatinda (Gill 1977: 5, 45). Still, it seems likely that Gill's focus on phulkaris reveal more about him and his own standpoint than about the women who created them.

Neelam and Amarjeet Grewal, both of Punjab Agricultural University in Ludhiana, also construed sainchi phulkaris as 'a means of communication'. Through 'the stitches, colours and motifs' of phulkari embroidery, 'a Punjabi woman...pours out her soul, her emotions, dreams and aspirations'. Phulkaris were 'true-to-life representations of the rural life of Punjab', the Grewals asserted, 'as interpreted by the embroiderer'. Thus, for example, '[t]he embroiderer's views on adultery have been made amply clear by the design showing an adulterous couple being bitten by snakes from all sides' (Grewal and Grewal 1988: 36, 48). Once again, though, scholars need to take care in unravelling the work of craftspeople who left few descriptions of their own intentions and meanings.

THE QUESTION OF AGENCY

While it is tempting to 'read' phulkaris as transparent evidence of Punjabi embroiderers' own voices, Emma Tarlo demonstrated convincingly that the interpretation of embroidery motifs examined in her field research differed significantly for 'lovers of folk art' and for the local women who stitched them (Tarlo 1996: 237). Deciphering motifs embroidered in the past is fraught with the strong likelihood that phulkaris become mirrors reflecting the interpreter's concerns rather than windows for historical investigation. Thus, I will not 'read' phulkari designs to evoke a 'lost female world' of cultural history, nor will I claim to explicate how Punjabi women 'really' thought about making and wearing phulkaris (Nair 1994: 88).

A more fruitful approach is to study phulkari practices as a way to demonstrate that women stitched and wore these textiles for as long as they served their own desires. We may not be able to understand completely their intentions from the phulkaris themselves, but we can discern something of their own purposes.[4] While there are many romanticized accounts of maternal emotions supposedly motivating women to make phulkaris for their daughters and granddaughters, two mundane aspects of this work need to be emphasized. First, women had to have some claim on family financial resources to assemble the materials required to stitch a phulkari. Second, creating phulkaris required real work, contrary to the claims that women stitched them in their 'leisure'.

For a Sikh woman to create a phulkari, she needed cotton cloth, embroidery silk for the design, a needle, and sufficient time to accomplish the work. Raw cotton was readily available in much of the Punjab, since it was one of the cash crops that farmers increasingly grew under the British Raj (Darling 1978: 151–3). Rural women often picked cotton, and then spun it into thread that could be woven into the background cloth for phulkaris.[5] Urban women similarly spun cotton into thread. Unmarried girls of more affluent rural and city families commonly used the thread they produced to fashion items for their own trousseau. These young women often worked together. Punjabi-language oral and written literature celebrated spinning bees (*trinyan*), with their accompanying gossip, stories, and folk songs. Indeed the *charkha*, or spinning wheel, rivals the phulkari in its ability to evoke women's work (Bedi 1971: 92–3; Nanda 1950).

Having spun the cotton into thread, women could pay a portion of it to a weaver to make khaddar, a coarse fabric of a narrow width. Women sewed together two or three widths of khaddar to produce a typical phulkari. As Tom Kessinger's account of handloom weavers in one Jalandhar-District Sikh village demonstrated, rural women could obtain hand-woven cloth without a cash transaction until well after Independence; alternatively, they might sell homespun thread for cash to purchase other items (Kessinger 1974: 57–8, 156–9). Women's skill at spinning fine yarn of uniform quality determined the quality of the khaddar woven for the background cloth of a phulkari.

First-hand accounts from the artisans who made phulkaris are rare. In the late 1970s, phulkari collector S.S. Hitkari interviewed Krishen Kaur Kohli (b.1907) about her embroidery work. Krishen Kaur was born into a 'very well off' landowning family of Rawalpindi District. She attended a village primary school for girls, where she learned basic literacy and received religious instruction. She reported learning some 'embroidery stitches', including 'a few Phulkari designs' at school, but learned the most about embroidering from her elder sister, who was a 'real expert' in stitching phulkaris. She remembered 'ordinarily' completing a bagh in three to four months, working after school for four-to-five hours a day while there was enough light (Hitkari 1980: 48, 49).

Krishen Kaur recalled that since her mother was 'an expert plier of Charkha', she insisted that the local weaver use her high-quality thread to make 'a better quality "Chaunsa" Khaddar... [which had] a very smooth texture and a finer feel' compared to ordinary khaddar. The women in this wealthy family could also choose to embroider on a 'finer and lighter cloth [known as] "Halwan",' which they could purchase in their local market. Before the introduction of chemical dyes, Krishen Kaur's mother or elder sister used vegetable dyes to colour the khaddar madder-red, chocolate-brown, indigo-blue, or black before they started their embroidery. Chemical dyes, when they became available, did not necessarily eliminate older dying technologies because 'one was not very certain about' the fastness of 'bazar or aniline dyes' (Hitkari 1980: 49).

In addition to cloth, women also required silk embroidery thread and needles when they stitched phulkaris. The untwisted silk thread they used (pat) was part of long-distance trade linking Punjab to Afghanistan, Kashmir, Bengal, and China.

Bright colours were the norm for embroidery floss, with golden yellow, crimson, orange, green, and white predominating. Specific embroidery colours were matched to appropriate fabric colours, and artisans embroidered the overwhelming majority of textiles in predictable colour combinations (Grewal and Grewal 1988: 38–9; Hitkari 1980: 19–21). Women could purchase embroidery thread in very small amounts, allowing them considerable flexibility for obtaining it through barter or cash transactions. Many women apparently bought thread for a single phulkari at different times, as evident in the varying thread colours (produced by different dye lots) in extant textiles. Female peddlers sometimes supplied needles and embroidery thread to those who could not obtain them at a local market. In the second decade of the twentieth century, 'fine needles' from Germany, China, and Japan as well as embroidery silk 'were easily available' from the 'village shopkeeper' in Rawalpindi District.[6]

Phulkari production, exchange, and consumption were all linked to changing fashions of both dress and behaviour of Punjabi women, and their study can help demystify the hypercultural discourses of colonial-era purdah practice. The particulars of Punjab purdah practices varied greatly for women according to their age and social position. Women in the poorest families nearly always worked outside of their own houses and, regardless of their desires, could not afford to follow the purdah practices of higher status groups. Indeed, some poorer women participated in phulkari production precisely to earn a wage. Krishen Kaur Kohli recollected that her mother purchased a few of the twenty-one phulkaris in her trousseau from 'some Sikh and Brahmin women in the village who belonged to poor families and who used to embroider Phulkaris and Baghs for others' (Hitkari 1980: 50; Steel 1988: 71–2; Kipling 1888).

As many recent studies have established, social groups in British India used cloth and clothing to claim and to symbolize social, political, and religious status during the nineteenth and twentieth centuries (Bayly 1989; Cohn 1989; Tarlo 1996). Modest dress that completely covered the body expressed respectability, status, and family honour for both Punjabi genders. It was, of course, not just the amount but the kind and style of the cloth, in other words fashion, that mattered. Sikh men's turbans immediately come to mind as an example. Purdah norms

may have been especially stringent for women at the top of
Punjabi status hierarchies, but customs of gender segregation
and respect for modest dress were quotidian realities for the vast
majority of Punjab men and women. If modest and status-ap-
propriate attire was also fashionable, so much the better.

There were explicit links between regional purdah behaviour
and some kinds of phulkaris. The 'Ghungat Bagh' of west Punjab,
with a narrow border and no embroidery in the middle, had
'in the centre of each side of the cloth, the portion that covers
the head while wearing it, large triangular motifs...embroidered
[which] would cover the face whenever [the] veil was drawn
over it'. Women wore analogous phulkaris in east Punjab, called
'Sar-Pallu', with 'bigger Pallus on both the ends', edges 'fully
embroidered in the Bagh fashion', and a narrow middle section
with figurative motifs (Hitkari 1980: 25; Pal 1955: 16). Still,
all phulkaris could be used to display modesty and deference
regardless of their specific decorative patterns.

Punjabi women from affluent families might contribute to what
Hanna Papanek termed 'family status production' through their
purdah practices (including, but not limited to what they wore),
as well as through displaying phulkaris. Stitching phulkaris for
the public display of trousseau in the nineteenth century would
have been especially important for the social position of families
at weddings. Patrilineages benefited from the non-waged work
of women in many culturally valued ceremonies (Papanek 1979:
778; Pal 1955: 19). Similarly, other scholars have analysed
purdah and its associated clothing as a system that constrained
women's behavioural choices and buttressed male lineages of
patriarchal economic, cultural, and social authority (Chowdhry
1994; Malhotra 2002; compare Agarwal 1994). However, how
can we understand Punjabi women spending so much time and
energy embroidering phulkaris if these wraps served primarily as
symbols of restrictions on their conduct?

Women living in social situations where strict purdah norms
were in effect could subvert them as well as conform to them.
Punjabi women might have used phulkaris to convey female
diffidence in conforming to expected deferential behaviour or
equally might have used them to articulate their own desires
and individuality. Focusing on Rajasthan, anthropologist Ann
Grodzins Gold argued that while wraps 'epitomized female

modesty', they could also seduce and display: 'from the women's perspective, poses of sexual modesty and reticence [could] readily flow into allurement, involvement, and manipulation'.[7] Her conclusions suggest that even though Punjabi women's desires, their wishes about their personal adornment, and other possible motivations have been lost to historians, they still should be considered in studying phulkari practices. Krishen Kaur Kohli, for example, remembered embroidering 'for the love of it', competing with 'friends, and cousin sisters as to who can embroider best...we would feel happy and proud with the sense of achievement' (Hitkari 1980: 52). No matter how coloured by nostalgia, Krishen Kaur's testimony of personal pleasure still seems undeniable, and it is consistent with other suggestions of women's pleasures in their needlework.

Sikh women could utilize phulkaris to express their agency through enriching their own social relationships—both at the intersection of women's negotiations and incorporations within their natal and conjugal households, and within their individualized lives among friends.[8] Women bargained for control over their own labour (and the time to do embroidery) and the financial resources to obtain the raw materials for a phulkari (cloth, silk embroidery thread, and needles). Women used their phulkaris to celebrate their bonds with one other, connections that required negotiation within and around the patriarchal girders of their family lives. Phulkaris and baghs were treasured and passed from mother to daughter. Phulkaris also embodied friendship ties, as shown in Amrita Pritam's autobiography when she mentions the practice of women exchanging shawls to demonstrate their affection (Pritam 1989: 37). Women who produced phulkaris for their own use participated in 'the sociability of female work and exchange' as well as exercising a socially valued set of skills (Ulrich 1998: 35).

Wearing phulkaris also shaped women's bodily experiences. When fabricated of khaddar, phulkaris were both thick and concealing. They required considerable skill for a woman to keep on her head, and wearing them moulded women's bodies by modifying their gait and overall movement. Yet, women did not necessarily perceive these as negative qualities that outweighed the advantages of the apparel. The embroidered cloths were 'texturally rich' and 'could provide a sensual experience, not only for the hands but also for the entire body'. Phulkaris were worn at the 'perceived body boundary', at a 'zone of comforting and protecting' (Gordon 1997: 245). The thickness of phulkaris, not inherently a negative quality of the textiles, could be construed negatively, however, if women started a fashion for thin cloth.

Clothing possibilities for women and men ranged along a sliding sartorial scale of thickness to thinness, from locally woven khaddar to the various kinds of thinner cloth produced regionally or outside the Punjab or imported from Britain. In 1888, Steel claimed that 'native women' preferred 'lighter wraps' that could be made from imported cloth; she believed the cheap price of foreign cloth rather than women's own wishes created this preference. She mocked 'Manchester baghs'—phulkaris stitched on thin, imported cloth—partially because her focus on rescuing 'authentic' phulkaris (as she defined them) blinded her to the positive appeal that imported textiles could have for Punjabis who could afford them (Steel 1888: 71–2). Still, neither the immoral connotations of machine-made cloth brought to Punjab by British supporters of the Victorian Arts and Crafts movement like Steel, nor the subsequent demonization of imported fabrics by Gandhi were widespread perceptions among rural Punjabis even after local nationalists organized urban demonstrations for *swadeshi* in the first decade of the twentieth century (Sohal 1992: 129–33).

The general direction of sartorial practices in early-twentieth-century Punjab was a shift away from wearing khaddar, a transformation that started decades earlier. According to Darling in 1921, 'the rise of the standard of living' since the British annexed Punjab meant that it was no longer 'a mark of extravagance and pride' to buy clothes. 'Machine-made cloth' had replaced 'country homespun', except in the poorer districts. As part of the 'growing refinement in dress', change 'has gone furthest of all in the zenana [the women's portion of a house]. The short economical *choli* [cotton blouse] is being replaced by the longer, well-cut *kurta*; the voluminous *gaggra* [cotton skirt] by the lighter pyjama or the muslin *salwar* [voluminous cotton trouser]'. Comparing the use of khaddar to industrially produced (but not necessarily imported) cloth, Darling cited an 'old peasant' who 'said with a sigh: Women's clothes are now so thin that sometimes you can see their bodies through' (Darling 1978: 139).

The availability of a wider range of fabrics and sartorial possibilities coincided with the Sikh Sabhas' social reform activities. As part of their efforts to distinguish respectable Hindus and Sikhs from one other and both groups from Muslims, their spokesmen (and occasionally spokeswomen) tried to dictate what reformed Sikh clothing practices should be.

Few social reform projects received more attention than the issue of Punjabi women's purdah practices, and few voices were more strident on women's proper public garb than those of the reformers. Male members of the Sikh Sabhas maintained contradictory positions on the subject of purdah, according to Anshu Malhotra. Reformers 'hardly wished to abrogate the sense of honour they accumulated by dressing women in a particular way, or indeed by veiling them. The concern for unveiling, uncovering certain parts of women, was paralleled with a desire to re-attire them' (Malhotra 2002: 127–31). Reformers consistently rejected women's wearing thin cloth (such as a *malmal bhochan*, a light, thin scarf). One Khalsa Tract Society pamphlet took an extreme position by praising a man who beat up and sent to her natal home the [Sikh] wife who dared to get a garment stitched of a thin cloth' (ibid.: 129). Not only did such literature criticize Sikh women for wearing thin cloth rather than respectable thick wraps, but it also condemned the use of imported cloth as an unacceptable financial extravagance by women (ibid.: 138). Disciplining Punjabi women and controlling their desires were prominent motifs of the reform rhetoric that sought to re-assert patriarchal rights over all of women's behaviour. Thin imported cloth thus seemed to become equally fashionable for women and objectionable for social reformers at the same time.

Within this milieu between the 1880s and the early twentieth century, the fashion for wearing phulkaris changed. While women had invested their time and resources in phulkaris earlier, largely through the desire to wear and to gift them, the number who did so in the twentieth century decreased significantly. When Punjabis had relatively modest clothing choices, many women could participate in the fashion for phulkaris by using few family resources other than their own labour. Discarding phulkaris as clothing was no doubt a gradual process; they could be altered somewhat to suit the styles of various times (Maskiell 1999: 382, Figure 5). Women in Lahore and Amritsar, where cloth and clothing choices would have been the widest, probably led the move to stop wearing them. Even when phulkaris were no longer consumed as clothing, they continued to be exchanged and valued as ceremonial textiles and family heirlooms, although the timing of this change in consumption behaviour must have varied throughout the region. Phulkaris continued to be exchanged through Punjabi trousseau through the 1940s and even after Independence.[9] The Punjabi women who stopped embroidering phulkaris rejected material objects that no longer served their own purposes. They had used their phulkaris in crafting their own lives for a while, but later generations would choose which of their foremothers' activities and material objects they would craft into Sikh heritage.

PHULKARIS AS SIKH HERITAGE

Much of the writing about phulkaris in the late-nineteenth and early-twentieth centuries rhetorically sequestered their production from commercial exchange by positioning them as regional handicrafts of an idealized 'folk' or, subsequently, as regional folk art. An associated rhetoric of revival and reclamation, of conservation and preservation, became the basis for transforming the phulkaris themselves into Sikh heritage, neatly abstracting them from the women's phulkari practices detailed above. The continuing appeal of colonial-era ethnographical writing about folk handicrafts is demonstrated by their selective appropriation for an aestheticized narrative of Sikh women transmitting tradition (which is equated with heritage) through their embroidery work.

Arjun Appadurai has suggested that 'things', like phulkaris, can be usefully studied through the concept of their having 'social lives' (Appadurai 1986). Once a woman stitched a phulkari, that same textile could morph from a newly made status marker for a trousseau, to a woman's daily head-cover, to part of an older woman's treasured savings to pass to younger female kin, to a conventionally defined commodity sold for cash during hard times. Alternatively, a Sikh woman might have worn a similar phulkari as a chadar until it was tattered and the fibres recycled. Worn phulkaris could be used by poor people to carry loads, and heavy 'good ones [were] made into Jhools or bullock wraps with Khadder or jute lining' to be used at 'a Cattle Fair or Mela' (Pal 1955: 47). Many extant phulkaris assumed new lives, if they passed unscathed through the fires of 1947, by being displayed on the wall of a middle-class Punjabi family's living room or in a museum, like the Home of Folk Art in Gurgaon. More mundanely, some women also recycled phulkaris into pillow covers, bedspreads, quilt tops, and gave them away as non-ceremonial gifts. The discourses of heritage have erased all of these possible social lives except for one, that of a cherished family heirloom.

One significant Sikh refocusing of phulkari lore in the late-twentieth and twenty-first centuries is setting the textiles apart as belonging to Sikh *religious* heritage. Krishen Kaur Kohli, stressing her own Sikh upbringing, reported that she never made any purposeful imperfections in her work, called '"Nazar-Buta" to avoid the evil eye', because she 'did not believe in superstitions', implicitly criticizing those Punjabi women who did embroider a 'Nazar-Buta'. Instead, she remembered embroidering the first words of the *Guru Granth Sahib* 'as an auspicious sign invoking God's blessings before starting a bagh' (Hitkari 1980: 51). Some nineteenth- and twentieth-century Sikh artisans clearly expressed their religious convictions through designing and embroidering specific types of baghs for gifting to gurudwaras.

More recently, Inni Kaur Dhingra recounted family lore about her great-grandmother's 'very large' phulkari, which her mother framed and hung in her living room. In commenting on a 2006 exhibit entitled *Early Sikh Art and Devotion* at the Rubin Museum in New York City, Dhingra claimed that 'Every stitch in this [family phulkari] was done reciting the Sukhmani Sahib'. Here, Dhingra linked the story of her great-grandmother's piety to the textile's symbolic role as a blessing for the household and family ('*Sadhie ghar di barkat*'). Dhingra thus removed phulkari making from a narrative of women's multifaceted desires, such as offered above, and positioned the work primarily as a religious matter of prayers and blessings (Dhingra 2007).

Contemporary girls and women have certainly played an important part in transforming phulkaris into Sikh heritage through valuing and displaying them when inherited from family members. However, the sharply gendered contours of idealized folk life that seem to be a mainstay of twentieth-century Sikh heritage, owe as much to the lingering influences of colonial-era ethnographic writing as to the power of 'traditions' among families. Nicola Mooney writes of a 'rural imaginary' that helps explain 'how Jat Sikhs maintain [their] identity as Jats despite living urban and even transnational lives' (Mooney 2007). Phulkari lore, likewise, is a conduit for conservative, nostalgic evocations of women's work in the timeless rural patriarchal household. It is, in short, a discourse of heritage, which occurs in the present despite its 'recourse to the past' (Kirshenblatt-Gimblett 1995: 370). This same discourse provides a frame for marketing the many innovative products, from soft household furnishings to shirts and scarves, which needy women have been embroidering with phulkari-like embroidery since 1947.

In her comments on the major exhibition of early Sikh art mounted in New York City at the end of 2006, Inni Kaur Dhingra restated the connections among folk culture, phulkaris, and Sikh heritage. While listening to some Punjabi folk songs she heard: '*Mera naa dha phulk na painie tu apni phulkari tey* [don't embroider my name on your phulkari]', which implies 'don't expect me to marry you'. Moved by these lyrics, Dhingra 'was transported into a world where young hearts connected via the phulkari. I look at [exhibited phulkaris] and I am reminded of what we lost in 1947. We lost our land, our roots and we also lost a way of life' (Dhingra 2007). The organizers and devotees of popular events like the Miss World Punjaban pageant, in which phulkaris are so nostalgically displayed, might well feel the same way.

NOTES

1. Information about the Miss-World-Punjaban pageant comes from three websites. The pageant rules explicitly state that, in the final round, contestants must field questions from a 'heritage quiz'. The details of the pageant's selection process are at http://www.missworldpunjaban.com/instructions.php, accessed 15 February 2007. For information about Japji Kaur Khaira, Miss World Punjaban 2007, see M.K. Singh (2007). The quotation from pageant founder Mr. Jasmer Singh Dhatt that phulkari is 'the pride of the Punjabans' can be found in 'Miss World Punjaban pageant this year' (2004).

2. Many of Steel's tidbits were published in *Panjab Notes & Queries* in the early 1880s or in *North Indian Notes & Queries* a little later. Richard Carnac

Temple, a British administrator assigned to various posts in northern India and an ardent member of the English Folk-lore Society, edited these publications. Steel went on to become a well-known novelist who set many of her romantic stories in British India.

3. See Matringe (1995). The enduring appeal of Puran Singh's poetry, particularly his famed 'The Sisters of the Spinning Wheel' is illustrated by a very recent set of excerpts. See P. Singh (2007).

4. The most frustrating problem for historicizing phulkari practice is that the extant textiles are notoriously difficult to date, and museum records necessarily tell when the textiles were collected rather than when they were made. Textile historians, collectors, and craft revivalists have analysed extant phulkaris in the subcontinent and abroad for details of construction and design, but, as art history is not a sub-discipline of history nor bound by historians' commitments to dating change, there has been little attempt to fix phulkari lore in time.

5. For Punjabi women's agricultural work, including picking cotton, see Maskiell (1990).

6. Appendix A, 'Biography, A Skilled Embroiderer of Phulkari', Mrs. Krishen Kaur, wife of Late Sardar Kartar Singh Kohli, in Hitkari (1980: 50). However, the predictability of these details is overemphasized in all sources. Krishen Kaur Kohli recalled stitching two phulkaris, and for both she used white cotton cloth and purple embroidery silk. See Hitkari (1980: 51–2).

7. Gold (1994: 47–52). Compare Gold's conclusions with the following lines excerpted from Puran Singh's *The Secret Kiss*, first published in 1921: 'She waved her veil to uncover her graces/She flaunted a braid aimlessly/ As a bird ruffles the surface of a lake and arranges its plume./She played with her robe...' Here, the English words 'veil' or even 'robe' could be interpreted as references to a phulkari. Of course, this poem provides no evidence whatsoever concerning women's actual social practices. See P. Singh (2007).

8. Inderpal Grewal develops the concepts of 'negotiations' and 'incorporations' in her analysis of Sara Suleri's *Meatless Days*. Suleri's text, according to Grewal, presents 'the contradictions resulting from the encounter between modernist and postmodernist subjectivities' (Grewal 1994: 236). I wish to steer between the construct of the Punjabi 'woman' that was 'part of the colonial and nationalist discourse of modernity', and the 'recuperati[on of] the also problematic discourse of 'role' within the patriarchal family [of wife, mother, sister] and consequently "tradition"' (Grewal 1994: 244).

9. Tiwana (1990: 97), for pre-1947 Punjab, and Gill (2000: 51), referring to 'a number of phulkaris' gifted at a 1965 wedding in Pune.

REFERENCES

Agarwal, Bina (1994). *A Field of One's Own: Gender and Land Rights in South Asia,* Cambridge: Cambridge University Press.

Anand, Mulk Raj (1989). *Amrita Sher-Gil,* New Delhi: National Gallery of Art.

Appadurai, Arjun (ed.) (1986). *The Social Life of Things: Commodities in Cultural Perspective,* Cambridge: Cambridge University Press.

Askari, Nasreen and Rosemary Crill (1997). *Colours of the Indus: Costume and Textiles of Pakistan,* London: Merrell Holbertson in association with the Victoria and Albert Museum.

Bayly, C.A. (1986). 'The Origins of Swadeshi (home industry): Cloth and Indian Society, 1700–1930', in Arjun Appadurai (ed.), *The Social Life of Things,* Cambridge: Cambridge University Press.

Bedi, Sohinder Singh (1971). *Folklore of the Punjab,* New Delhi: National Book Trust.

Bhabha, Homi K. (1994). 'Of Mimicry and Man: The Ambivalence of Colonial Discourse', in Homi K. Bhabha, *The Location of Culture,* London: Routledge.

Chowdhry, Prem (1994). *The Veiled Women: Shifting Gender Equations in Rural Haryana,* Delhi: Oxford University Press.

Clifford, James (1986). 'On Ethnographic Allegory', in James Clifford and George E. Marcus, (eds), *Writing Culture: The Poetics and Politics of Ethnography,* Berkeley: University of California Press.

Cohn, Bernard S. (1989). 'Cloth, Clothes and Colonialism: India in the Nineteenth Century', in Annette Weiner and Jane Schneider (eds), *Cloth and Human Experience,* Washington, DC: Smithsonian Institution Press.

Darling, Malcolm (1978 reprint; original 1925). *The Punjab Peasant in Prosperity and Debt,* Columbia, MO: South Asia Books.

Dhamija, Jasleen (1964). 'Bagh and Phulkari of Punjab', *Marg,* pp. 15–24.

Dhingra, Inni Kaur (2007). 'Comments' on *I see no Stranger—Early Sikh Art and Devotion,* at the Rubin Museum in New York City, 10 January 2007, http://sikhnet.com/sikhnet/news.nsf/newsarchive, accessed 25 January 2007.

Frater, Judy (1993). 'Elements of Style: The Artisan Reflected in Embroideries of Western India', in Nora Fischer (ed.), *Mud, Mirror and Thread: Folk Traditions of Rural India,* Ahmedabad: Mapin Publishing in association with Museum of New Mexico Press.

Gill, Brinda (2000). 'Phulkari and Bagh: Labor of Love', *Piecework,* Vol. VIII, pp. 51–2.

Gill, Harjeet Singh (1977). *A Phulkari from Bhatinda,* New Delhi: Department of Anthropological Linguistics.

Gold, Ann Grodzins (1994). 'Sexuality, Fertility, and Erotic Imagination in Rajasthani Women's Songs', in Gloria Godwin Raheja and Ann Grodzins Gold (eds), *Listen to the Heron's Words,* Berkeley: University of California Press.

Gordon, Beverly (1997). 'Intimacy and Objects: A Proxemic Analysis of Gender-Based Responses to the Material World', in Katherine Martinez and Kenneth L. Ames (eds), *The Material Culture of Gender: the Gender of the Material World,* Winterthur, Delaware: Henry Francis du Pont Winterthur Museum.

Grewal, Inderpal (1994). 'Autobiographic Subjects and Diasporic Locations: Meatless Days and Borderlands', in Inderpal Grewal and Caren Kaplan (eds), *Scattered Hegemonies: Post-Modernity and Transnational Feminist Practices,* Minneapolis: University of Minnesota Press.

Grewal, Neelam and Amarjit Grewal (1988). *The Needle Lore*, Delhi: Ajanta Publications.

Hitkari, S.S. (1980). *Phulkari: The Folk Art of the Punjab*, New Delhi: Phulkari Publications.

Irwin, John and Margaret Hall (1973) *Indian Embroideries. Historic Textiles of India at the Calico Museum*, Vol. 2, Ahmedabad: S.R. Bastikar.

Jakobsh, Doris R. (2003). *Relocating Gender in Sikh History: Transformation, Meaning and Identity*, New Delhi: Oxford University Press.

Kessinger, Tom G. (1974). *Vilyatpur, 1848–1968: Social and Economic Change in a North Indian Village*, Berkeley: University of California Press.

Kipling, John Lockwood (1888). 'Industries of the Punjab', *Journal of Indian Art and Industry*, Vol. 2, No. 20, pp. 34–66.

Kirshenblatt-Gimblett, Barbara (1995). 'Theorizing Heritage', *Ethnomusicology*, Vol. 39, pp. 367–80.

Malhotra, Anshu (2002). *Gender, Caste, and Religious Identities: Restructuring Class in Colonial Punjab*, New Delhi: Oxford University Press.

Mann, Harveen Sachdeva (2000). 'Religious Fundamentalism and the Twice-Fragmented Narrative of Gender in Contemporary Punjab', *Jouvert: A Journal of Postcolonial Studies*, Vol. 4, No. 2, http://social.chass.ncsu.edu/Jouvert/v4i2/con42.htm, accessed 25 January 2007.

Maskiell, Michelle (1990). 'Gender, Kinship and Rural Work in Colonial Punjab', *Journal of Women's History*, Vol. 2, pp. 35–72.

—— (1999). 'Embroidering the Past: Phulkari Textiles and Gendered Work as "Tradition" and "Heritage" in Colonial and Contemporary Punjab', *Journal of Asian Studies*, Vol. 58, No. 2, pp. 361–99.

Matringe, Denis (1995). 'The Panjab and its Popular Culture in the Modern Panjabi Poetry of the 1920s and Early 1930s', *South Asia Research*, Vol. 15, pp. 189–220.

'Miss World Punjaban pageant this year' (2004). *Tribune*, online edition, Ludhiana, 21 January, at http://www.tribuneindia.com/2004/20040122/ldh2.htm, accessed 15 February.

Mooney, Nicola (2007). 'Re: Your Forthcoming Book', email to the author, 7 February.

—— (2008) *Rural Nostalgias and Transnational Dreams: Identity and Modernity among Jat Sikhs*, Toronto: University of Toronto Press.

Nair, Janaki (1994). 'On the Question of Agency in Indian Feminist Historiography', *Gender and History*, Vol. 6, pp. 82–100.

Nanda, Savitri Devi (1950). *The City of Two Gateways*, London: George Allen and Unwin.

Pal, Rampa (1955). *The Phulkari: A Lost Craft*, Delhi: National Printing Press.

Papanek, Hanna (1979). 'Family Status Production: The "Work" and "Non-Work" of Women', *Journal of Women in Culture and Society*, Vol. 4, pp. 775–87.

Pritam, Amrita (1989 [1976]). *Life and Times* [*The Revenue Stamp*], New Delhi: Vikas.

Singh, Manpreet kaur (2007). 'The Punjaban from Down Under', at http://sikhchic.com/article-detial.php?id=59&cat=6, accessed 15 February.

Singh, Puran (2007). *The Sisters of the Spinning Wheel,* 1 February, http://www.sikhnet.com/sikhnet/news.nsf/recentnewsHTML, accessed 8 February 2007.

Sohal, Sukhdev Singh (1992). 'The Swadeshi Movement in the Punjab (1904–1907)', *The Punjab Past and Present,* Vol. XXVI, No. I, pp. 129–33.

Steel, Flora Annie (1888). 'Phulkari Work in the Punjab', *Journal of Indian Art and Industry,* Vol. 2, pp. 71–2 [with 28 examples of phulkari embroidery on unnumbered pages].

Tarlo, Emma (1996). *Clothing Matters: Dress and Identity in India,* Chicago: University of Chicago Press.

Tiwana, Dalip Kaur (1990). *A Journey on Bare Feet,* tr. by Jai Ratan, New Delhi: Orient Longman.

Ulrich, Laurel Thatcher (1998). 'Wheels, Looms, and the Gender Division of Labor in Eighteenth-Century New England', *The William and Mary Quarterly,* Third Series, Vol. 55, No. 1, pp. 3–38.

Lowly Shoes on Lowly Feet

Some Jat Sikh Women's Views on Gender and Equality

Nicola Mooney

Don't feel proud of us daughters, father, we belong to others.
Put the dolls in the cupboard, throw their clothes out the window.
Father your loving daughter has climbed on the palanquin and is leaving.
Don't have pride in your daughters, father, your daughters are 'foreigners'.
Daughters are the wealth of others, who will keep them at home?
All who bid her farewell sigh with grief and cry with bitterness.
Don't feel proud of us daughters, father, we belong to others.[*]

This song, sung at the Ladies *Sangeet*[1] held the day before Dimple Deol's[2] marriage in the Punjabi city of Moga in the spring of 1999, movingly narrates some of the cultural sources of gender disparity for Jat Sikh women. Although colourfully celebrated, marriage for Jat Sikh women such as Dimple can frequently mean the end of an enjoyable and carefree life, the severing of relationships with natal kin, the demand to adjust to ongoing daily life among affines, and the lived recognition of women's disempowered and disempowering social position as outsiders in both birth and conjugal families. Like many other South Asian women, Jat Sikh women's inequal-ity is typically located in marriage and kinship practices, including hypergamy, dowry, patrilocal residence, and son preference. Many of the women who movingly performed this ritual song before Dimple's marriage had married into conjugal families with significantly more social status in this transaction than their own natal kin, had brought considerable dowries of clothing, gold, consumer goods, and even cars, from their parents to their in-laws' homes, and were under pressure from family and society to bear sons rather than daughters so that the potential costs of future dowries might be allayed; they had themselves left their families and homes distraught and awash in tears.

Jat Sikhs[3]—hereafter referred to simply as Jats when their affiliation to the Sikh religion is not essential to my analysis—are members of an agrarian caste of farmers and landlords which in both socio-economic and demographic terms is the dominant caste (Srinivas 1966) of rural Punjab, although many Jats now live in urban and transnational contexts. Many of the inequities that Jat Sikh women suffer are features of their being Jat, Punjabi, and even north Indian, rather than their being Sikh. Indeed, for many Sikhs, socio-cultural notions of gender are often at rather profound odds with religious ideals. As a religious tradition, Sikhism advocates equality among both castes and genders (Mahmood 1996; Mahmood and Brady 2000; Singh 2005), and egalitarianism as a Sikh ideal is frequently noted by Sikhs in their commentaries on and interpretations of the religion, yet gender inequality—as well as the continued implications of caste difference—prevail in the everyday lives of many Sikh women. Thus, while Sikhism as an 'intellectual tradition' (Malhotra 2002) declares that women are the equals of men, many Jat women believe that this is a theoretical declaration rather than a statement of social fact, distinguishing between what Clarence McMullen (1989) has called normative and operative beliefs. There is some debate as to whether such distinctions might have been encoded in Sikh doctrine from its outset: while according to Nikky Singh, Guru Nanak utilized the feminine voice in his writings, which themselves honoured 'the feminine principle' (1993), and Guru Gobind Singh might be interpreted as a maternal figure who gave birth to the Khalsa (2005), Doris R. Jakobsh (2003) posits that while Nanak's view of women may have been in some ways positive to the extent that they—like members of the lower castes—could attain enlightenment, it nevertheless firmly and primarily associated women's comparative social worth with procreation. Today, the issue of Sikh egalitarianism is further complicated by the fact that certain Sikhs lay claim to being, and are often publicly recognized as, 'first among equals'. Brian Keith Axel (2001) has argued that Sikh orthodoxy, as uniquely expressed through the male *amritdhari* (orthodox Sikh, or, a member of the Khalsa who has undergone the *amrit* initiation rite and observes the five Ks[4]), body and masculinist discourse has become hegemonic among Sikh nationalists and has had great influence on diaspora Sikh communities; however, the influence of this position is by no means universally apparent among Sikhs and is indeed vigorously contested. Sikh egalitarianism is thus a highly problematic notion, and it must be noted that the differentiation of religious and cultural notions of gender (and caste) equality is nowhere as neat as the remainder of this paper may imply.

This essay explores some Jat Sikh women's experiences and understandings of their gender, and relatedly, their social and religious place. In particular, I focus on the differential understandings and experiences of gender between older and younger Jat women: I examine some of the changes in women's social position expressed by elderly Jat Sikh women, and contrast this with the ongoing gender inequalities—particularly to do with marriage and education—experienced, articulated by, and struggled against by younger Jat Sikh women. I suggest that as Jat women themselves do not recognize the same sources of gender inequity, establishing gender equality is problematic. My argument, and the narratives from which I craft it, are based on interviews undertaken during a year-and-a-half of ethnographic fieldwork in north India during 1998 and 1999 among urban, middle-class Punjabi women (and men), a majority of whom were Jat Sikh. My understanding of gender among Jat Sikhs is also informed by my own marriage into a Jat Sikh family, and my ongoing participation within an extended family and the Sikh and Punjabi communities in which it is embedded.

JAT KINSHIP, MARRIAGE, AND GENDER

I think women have more difficulties than men, especially because she has to face them all herself. She has to leave her parents' house and go to a *biganna ghar* (a stranger's home). She has to form relationships with all these *biganne aadmi* (unrelated men, people) and adjust to them. She has to face everything, all problems, herself (Mandeep Kaur aged 61).

For me, among the most daunting problems I faced as a Jat *bahu* (daughter-in-law) living among my affines in India was the process of what Jats like Mandeep call 'adjusting' to life with my in-laws. While I was not Punjabi, had had a love marriage into an urban, well-educated, and quite liberal Jat family several years before travelling to India, and was visiting as an ethnographer, my western feminist self nevertheless was assaulted at times by Jat traditions of marriage and gender (as well as occasionally insulted on behalf of the women I met). But slowly, a sort of paradigm shift occurred when I began to consider—as well as try to approximate—the notion of adjustment from the Jat perspective. The poetics of adjustment describe Jat daughters as foreigners in their own homes, while their destined in-laws are described as strangers; little wonder then that many unmarried Jat women fear marriage. However, as they mature in Jat families and are encultured into Jat family values, Jat women might be expected to settle into marital homes and families with comparative ease. Nonetheless, the challenges that they face at marriage are uniformly perceived as abrupt, daunting, and profound, and the metaphors of marital adjustment articulate women's inequalities in multiple ways. The very notion of adjustment is based on women's subjugation to collective ideals of a moral and honourable family good, and Jat women too face difficulties in accepting their own inequality.

For Jats, gender practices are deeply connected to being Jat, and thus to the expression and continuity of Jat culture. Indeed any ethnographic examination of gender must recognize the close links that exist between gender and ethnic identity. Bounded identities are constructed from gender practices: notions of social relationship (Eriksen 1993), ancestry and kinship (Greene 1996) are both gendered and ethnicized, such that women come to express boundaries about cultural identity and difference (Kandiyoti 1991). In India, as elsewhere, women embody notions of cultural tradition and boundaries of identity, including those of religion and caste (Chatterjee 1993; Sarkar and Butalia 1995; Sarkar 1998). Women's bodies become sites for the representation, contestation and control of identity, invested as they are with notions of collective loyalty, purity, and nurturance. Yet they typically have little control over or choice in the ways in which they represent and embody collectivities; not only do women mother communities and nations, but in appalling corollary are sexually brutalized when the collectivities that they embody come under attack (Appadurai 1999; Ranchod-Nilsson and Tétrault 2000). These forms of embodied identity, cast in moral tones of purity, were horrifically assaulted among Punjabis during Partition (Menon and Bhasin 1998; Butalia 2000). For Punjabi women, 'belonging' to both family and community is a matter uniquely 'linked to sexuality, honour, chastity; family, community, and country must agree on both their acceptability and legitimacy, and their membership within the fold' (Menon and Bhasin 1998: 251). Not only are women's bodies and bodily practices representative of ethnic or national difference, but women also reproduce the boundaries of ethnic or national communities by reproducing the community itself, while their deeds as mothers contribute to the ideological reproduction of these same communities (Yuval-Davis and Anthias 1989). Gender difference is thus based in kinship roles and organization (cf. Dube 1997) and within kin relationships, South Asian women construct group identity through their bodies, social roles, and womanly deportment. These constructions are essential to the organization of kinship, caste, religion, and culture in South Asia, but also are constitutive of gender difference and women's inequality. Not insignificantly, Guru Nanak's iteration of women's equality emphasized women's bodily importance to kinship and social reproduction: women give birth to men, as well as to the future mothers of men, and for this reason men should be bound to them as equals (cf. Jakobsh 2003).

Gender intersects and overlaps ethnic identities in Punjab, and to some extent also establishes a separate and unified category of South Asian women subjects beyond the pale of all other social inequities in the sense that they are, as argued by Anjali Bagwe (1995), 'of woman caste'. Like much of India, Punjab is a patriarchal and patrilineal region, where gender relations are infused with, oriented against, and expressed through discourses of men's *izzat* and women's *sharam*. Izzat means, variously, honour, respect(-ability), or reputation, while sharam, literally translated as shame, more accurately refers to modesty, humility, and propriety. These dual concepts, their meanings inter-penetrating and informing each other, are guided by male interest. Izzat marks the reputation of both the individual Jat male and his family, and is constructed through the deportment of his wife, sisters, and daughters, who attend to sharam in their modesty and humility; for Jats, 'a man's izzat is his women's sharam'. Sherry Ortner and Harriet Whitehead's feminist anthropological dictum 'that the sphere of social activity predominantly associated with males encompasses the sphere predominantly associated with females and is, for that reason, culturally accorded higher value' (Ortner and Whitehead 1981: 7–8) is clearly evident in this gender formulation. The epistemological containment of sharam, the concern of women, within the realm of izzat, the purview of men as a factor of gender difference, also suggests men are women's social superiors. Steve Derné remarks that Indian men 'have constructed a focus on honor that advances their own interests as men'; he found that 'men claim that the threat of dishonor is only a modest restriction on their own actions, while it tightly limits women's freedom' (Derné 1995: 30). As we might expect, men's lives are noticeably more public than women's, whose movement is limited following the customary dictates of *purdah*, or *ghund* as it is more commonly known in Punjabi, terms which literally refer to veiling, but in fact signify any practice which maintains social distance between particular classes of males and females. As Sharma (1978) has suggested, the veil reminds women of those relations with whom passive or submissive behaviours are appropriate, while according to Prem Chowdhry, the veil 'sustains the balance of hierarchy... reaffirm[ing] a social hierarchy corresponding to the social world outside' (Chowdhry 1994: 284). Although purdah practices are noticeably on the wane, there remains a gendered distinction between public and household spaces and activities, and it is still believed that women should spend as little time as possible in public, especially if they are unaccompanied (cf. Flueckiger 1996; Harlan 1992). For Jats, the moral universe of izzat-sharam, as expressed in ghund, is ongoing. Jat women continue to honour their in-laws with ritualized demonstrations of respect: prostrating to touch the feet of their elders, keeping ghund with affinal male relatives, and adjusting as best they can to their affinal homes.[5]

Compounding the structural inequalities of izzat-sharam are other social limitations on Jat women. Gender inequity and women's subordination, salient features of north Indian society, are encapsulated in regional kinship and marriage practices. Those few social roles which are sanctioned for women in north India are domestic and kin-based. Moreover, women's roles are always constructed in relation to men: women are socially bound in the primary kinship categories of daughter and sister in their paternal homes, and in the roles of wife, daughter-in-law, mother—and eventually mother-in-law—in their marital homes. As Mandeep Kaur observed in the quotation that opens this section, Jat women's ongoing gender difficulties are clearly connected to marriage. Women's natal relationships are supposedly severed when they are married, when their allegiances and interests are joined with the patrilineages of their affines. This is why daughters are described as belonging to others in the song that opens this essay; other women's songs lament that daughters are the 'the wealth of others' (*paraayaa dhan*, cf. '*bighana dhan*', Gill 1998). Resultantly, daughters experience fewer physical and psychological comforts and investments than do sons; increasingly dissociated from their birth families as they grow up, daughters may receive differential treatment in terms of diet, education, and discipline in comparison to their brothers. Discussing South Asian women's gender status, Leela Dube has observed that 'the cultural emphasis is on marriage as the destiny of a girl. A daughter's transfer to another home upon marriage is seen as inevitable' (Dube 1997: 34). Daughters are also transferred between lineages: they become part of their husband's patriline at marriage, but have property and inheritance rights in neither their natal nor affinal patrilineages[6] (cf. Maynes *et al.* 1996). Dowry (*dahej*) thus becomes especially problematic, as it is conceptualized as a woman's share of her natal inheritance (cf. Goody 1976 [1993]); but most often the majority of the dowry is presented as various gifts to the husband's family. Postmarital residency is another significant element in north Indian women's subordination: patrilocal residence expresses women's inferior social position (cf. Sax 1990) and is frequently the location of both adjustment and oppression. For each of these reasons, marriages in north India are described as hypergamous: the bride and her family are of markedly lower status than the groom and his family within the marriage transaction. Within marriage, a woman is able to gain some status if she gives birth to sons. Indeed her maximum status and power might be achieved when she herself is a mother-in-law of socially precarious new daughters-in-law. Here, women's oppressions come full circle, and the hegemonic nature of this cultural system of gender inequities is most apparent. Mothers-in-law are often a key force of gender subordination. Thoroughly incorporated into protecting the interests of their marital patriline by the time their sons marry, they are renowned to then dominate their daughters-in-law. In this way, unequal power relations, notions of gender hierarchy and women's subordinate social place are reproduced. These hierarchies and hegemonies of power are further complicated by the gendering of intimate relations. As Mary Hegland has noted, women share 'family ties, love, sexual relationships, economic and political interests, religious beliefs and affiliation, residence and long years of personal history with those who most directly dominate them' (Hegland 1998: 250).

Marriage, as both an everyday social practice and a ritual event, is of central importance in understanding gender inequality in Punjab, as well as for comprehending the possibilities for gender equality within Sikhism. While a wide system of male favour predicated on marriage exists for Jats—hypergamous marriage, dowry, patrililocal residence, ghund, son preference, and patrilineal inheritance, all set within the honour-shame paradigm, and all contributing to hierarchical and unequal gender relations, as well as to continued distinctions of caste—marriage also sets out some of the possibilities for gender equality in Sikhism. Significantly, although arranged marriage might be expected to factor into Jat women's subordination, this is perhaps the one feature of marriage in which the bride and groom are comparative equals. In my observation, younger Jat Sikh men voiced as many uncertainties over this process as Jat Sikh women; in Jasleen Singh's words, marriage demanded submission to 'that natural process of [family] life' in which the individual whether female or male has little choice. Although younger Jats today may claim marital veto over their parents' choice of partner—and they frequently see photos of their intended partners, and may even meet briefly before agreeing to a match—marriage is viewed by both women and men as a process in which individual hopes and aspirations must be sublimated to the family good. In this regard, it is interesting that both bride and groom begin the marriage rite of *anand karaj* in a veiled state, the bride's face covered with her *dupatta* (head and shoulder scarf)[7] and the groom's with a *sehra* (groom's head-dress).[8]

Ritually, the Sikh wedding rite meditates on women's equality to men in their relationships with God even as it physically symbolizes women's subordination. The four hymns (*laavan*) of the Sikh marriage rite (anand karaj), sung by *raagi*s (Sikh musicians) as the bride and groom circumambulate the Guru Granth Sahib, address bride and groom as equals. The duties of married life are laid out in an exposition on humility, moral living, and devoted love for both spouse and God within the householding 'path' of Guru Nanak in which married life becomes a means of religious devotion and spiritual realization. Marriage becomes a metaphor for divine union, both a reflection of this tenet and a step towards its realization, and bride and groom are partners in this process.

Meanwhile, the bride is symbolically 'tied' to her groom with a dupatta.[9] While he holds the end of the dupatta in his hands, it is slung over his shoulder, and clasped a few feet behind by his bride; she then follows him through the four laavan (circumambulations) of the Guru Granth Sahib while the moral and spiritual interpretations of gender equality in Sikh marriage are performed. The performance of this rite in the gurdwara in front of the Guru Granth Sahib lends it religious sanction, but for many young Sikh women, these rites seem to express a subordinate position for the bride, who physically walks several paces behind her husband, typically with her eyes downcast both to meet the convention of purdah and so that she does not trip on her heavily-embroidered bridal *lehnga* (full, floor-length skirt).[10] Recently, some Sikh couples have tried to match the equality of the laavan to its physical counterpart by having the bride lead the groom in two of the four laavan; however, a recent marriage at Gurdwara Rakab Ganj in Delhi, in which the bride took the lead in the last two of the four laavan, resulted not only in 'chaos' at the marriage, but also the suspension of the *granthi* for violating the *Maryada* (Sikh code) relating to anand karaj.[11]

Despite their supposed spiritual and doctrinal equality, in attending to gendered notions of social propriety and participating in the ritual and everyday contexts of marriage, Jat Sikh women are implicated in the construction and reproduction of relations of power in which they are clearly constituted as inferior. It has long been noted that Indian 'women are generally expected to be more strict than men are about domestic ritual observances and niceties of domestic status' (Mandelbaum 1970: 236); this reflects their comparative disempowerment. Differential relations of power in marital dynamics and gendered discourse were obvious among the Jat women that I lived among and spoke with in India. Indeed, it is a measure of the persistent hegemony of these relations that most women denied that their own lives were restricted in any way in almost the same breath as noting that women's inequality was still prevalent in various forms within their communities. As well, resistances and subversions were practised and reported infrequently. While the past century has registered profound and gendered social change in Punjab,[12] only the differential treatment of daughters within their natal homes seems to have become a thing entirely of the past for Jat women. I continue this analysis of gender among contemporary Jats by turning now to some elderly Jat women's narrations of gendered social change.

AURAT PAERH DI JUTTI HAI: 'WOMEN ARE LOWLY SHOES ON LOWLY FEET'

Every now and then, [the men] would swear at the women, 'this *paerh di jutti*, who cares much for it? The old one wears off, you wear a new one. We can leave her and get another wife' (Gurmeet Kaur aged 65).

Jat Sikh women born prior to Partition are far more likely than younger women to note profound changes in gender hierarchies, statuses, and possibilities. Many such women noted that while they were growing up, women were described as 'paerh di jutti', a term which implied women were base and menial, but such insults were said to be a thing of the past. While it was not uncommon for elderly Jat women to admit that they had lived limited lives as women, they asserted nonetheless that women are men's equals. For instance, Harpreet Kaur, an elderly housewife, told me:

In our Jat Sikh *samaj* (society), the position of men and women is equal.
{How?} Among us, in good 'families', or the 'families' which are doing well,
those men don't trouble the women that much. Among the rest, in certain
places one sees that the women are kept down. [But] in our Sikh society,
there's not that many problems.

While this can perhaps be attributed to elderly women having
become comparatively empowered in their positions as mothers
and mother-in-law, and being further removed from the ongoing
gender struggles of their younger counterparts—entrenched as
these are around kinship, marriage, and reproduction—it is also
true that elderly Jat women have indeed experienced significant
transformations in their gender role and status with urbanization
and, particularly, education.

An interview with Gurmeet Kaur, an elderly Jat Sikh woman
who provided the epigraph for this section, revealed a number of
changes in Jat women's everyday lives. A housewife married to a
retired army worker, Gurmeet and her husband lived in a small
city home with a large courtyard in a joint extended family with
their sons, daughters-in-law, and grandchildren. My research
assistant, Simran, and I asked her if she had felt any limitations
in her life because she was a woman. At first she was nonplussed
by the question, perhaps because it is obvious to women of her
generation that their lives have been limited; we rephrased the
question for her:

[Any dreams you had that you couldn't fulfil because you are a woman? …
Maybe you have some thought, 'if I were a man', I would have done this
or that?]

To this, Gurmeet replied with great enthusiasm:

Yes, that is a big dream! If I were a man, then I would have done a lot of
things by going outside, going to the courts, going to the *tehsil*, here and
there, everywhere… I would have done a lot of things. Yes. [But]. Being a
woman, I am sitting at home.

Gurmeet's answer emphasized that ghund is not only about
women's moral propriety but also about physical limitations on
their public movement. It also envisioned the possibility of a
professional career as a lawyer or civil servant, despite Gurmeet
being married, like a majority of Jat women of her generation,
before she could complete high school. When we asked her if
she thought that women elsewhere had different sorts of lives,

Gurmeet read into this question her opinion on women's lives abroad, and answered:

Well, of course there are differences outside. The women earn the same as men, they have no restrictions, they can come here and there whenever they please, nobody suspects them and their motives; such things are here in our Hindustan.

Her careful choices of phrase, that women abroad can go 'here and there whenever they please' unquestioned in their actions, 'motives', or selves, suggests that Indian women do not enjoy such freedoms. But while she clearly expressed concerns with Jat women's social position within families and communities in India, Gurmeet also observed that a number of changes in women's status had happened within her lifetime. She said, that compared to earlier times, life for a Jat woman was

Very different! In all things. Previously the girls were not educated, now they are. Previously, the girls wouldn't be allowed to do 'service', now they are equal to men. Previously they used to do *ghund* (veil themselves), now, even the older women have stopped doing so. Everyone has left this, yeah, truly everyone, at such old age even. Earlier, the women used to work all day in the house, they wouldn't dare go out. Men used to work in the fields, and if the woman took the *roti* too late to the fields, they would beat her with a stick right there in the fields, that why did you delay bringing the *roti*? The stick they used was called *paraani*, with which they would drive the bullocks. And every now and then, they would swear at the women, and say that '*aurat paerh di jutti hai*'. You know, 'this *paerh di jutti*, who cares much for it? The old one wears off, you wear a new one. We can leave her and get another wife'. This type of attitude was prevalent towards women in olden times. And now, it's not there.[13]

Gurmeet's narrative catalogues a number of oppressions suffered by Jat women in earlier times. Women were uneducated, prohibited from careers, and forced to live within the circumscription of ghund; a Jat woman's lot was domestic labour, and she was threatened with punishments reserved for livestock—thus equating her with beasts—were she to falter in her tasks. Gurmeet herself had veiled from all of her elder male affines, but stopped doing so when her eldest son was married in the 1980s. Thus, becoming a mother-in-law, as the literature on women's subordination in India might lead us to expect, had a liberating effect on Gurmeet. Kiran, Gurmeet's daughter-in-law, veiled in only a modified way among her in-laws', simply wearing her *chunni* over her head and tucked behind her ears—as one might witness women doing at the gurdwara—to signal respect. When we asked Gurmeet how she thought these changes had come about, she replied simply:

> Through education, [women] are more knowledgeable (*dimaag wadh gaie*, literally, their brains have become bigger).

We will return to the importance of education to Jat women's empowerment shortly, but first we must discuss the notion of women as 'paerh di jutti'.

Perhaps the most striking image in Gurmeet's narrative is that of women as lowly shoes on lowly feet. Among elderly Jat women like Gurmeet, the phrase paerh di jutti is widely used to describe women's former oppressions. In my interviews, the notion that women were paerh di jutti, lowly in status, and entirely replaceable, was common in Jat women's narrations of their traditional family life, and I learned that this phrase was an epithet frequently used against women. This phraseology reflects the contact that juttis have with sources of dirt and pollution on the ground, as well as the generalized bodily hierarchy of north India, in which feet are unclean and inauspicious parts of the body, perhaps because they are often in contact with polluting leather shoes.[14] Similarly, threats of assault with a jutti (or *chappal*), because of the polluted and subordinate connotations of shoes and feet, are more insulting than mere threats of violence. The colloquial Punjabi phrase '*tu jutti khaani hai?*', which threatens the person to whom it is directed with a beating, literally means 'do you want to eat a shoe?', thus exemplifying the connections among shoes, bodies, pollution, power, and submission. The symbolism of shoes in India is one denoting complicated intersections of inequality and power. Although shoes themselves are lowly objects, they are also objects of everyday comfort, and essential accessories to effective (and painless) agricultural labour. Ann Gold and Bhoju Ram Gujar (2002) have observed that in colonial Rajasthan, both lower castes and women were not entitled to wear them: the shoe is an important symbol of power, and discourses on shoes and power intersect discourses of honour.[15] Significantly, my mother-in-law related to me that women of her generation were told 'at the time of marriage' that 'their shoes would pinch them'. The shoe here articulates the—both physically and emotionally—restrictive and painful processes of a daughter-in-law's adjustment to life in her affinal home. In these gendered associations, shoes signal both women's real and symbolic subjugation, as well as their powers, reproductive and otherwise, which are essential to the nurturing and furtherance of family and society.

Despite their lowly social status, Jat women are well aware of the equality that exists for women within the Sikh tradition. Mandeep Kaur, a sixty-one-year-old housewife—although a *giani*, having done the baccalaureate in Punjabi—married to a retired schoolteacher, and with two sons living in Canada with their wives and children, told me that:

Women and men should be equal, if one really thinks about it, equality exists. In the guru granth sahib *de ghar* (the home of the Guru Granth Sahib, i.e., the gurdwara or temple), there's no high and low, no restriction that women can't go and worship (*matha tekna*, to bow one's head). They are the same in *guru sahib's ghar*. Only society has made the differences. Women are not physically so strong as men, and they are kept in *purdah*; they are not given the opportunities to be nurtured, to progress, and grow. They always keep the girls within the four walls of the house. Girls are not given a chance to have dreams and aspirations, they are always suppressed. Parents make these differences.

The equal position of Sikh women is confirmed in the egalitarian doctrines of the Guru Granth Sahib, but a clear majority of the Jat Sikh women with whom I spoke confirmed that this remains a matter of theory rather than practice. Although she begins by stating 'if one really thinks about it, equality exists', Mandeep uses the present tense to describe the gender inequalities she observes in Jat society, including purdah and the disempowering neglect of girls in terms of their own aspirations. Significantly, Mandeep recognizes that the differences between men and women are social constructs, created by parents and an ambiguous but presumably Jat 'society'. In this sense, Mandeep's account voices a quiet critique of a society that ignores Sikh doctrine to create gender difference, inequality, and the subjugation of women in its everyday culture.

Jats set aside Sikh doctrine in other gendered ways. Among urban middle-class Sikhs in India, religion is reinterpreted in relation to urban and middle-class social values. Mona Kaur, a forty-year old middle-aged housewife raising three children

while her husband worked at the district courts, told me how she
felt the Sikh religion should be observed in progressive middle-
class houses such as her own:

Regarding the religious code of conduct, of course, we can't take amrit
(rite of becoming an orthodox Sikh). According to our society, we don't
consider ourselves ready to take it. But the other basic rules that we can
follow, we should. Some of the principles that we can't follow, some of the
more rigid, difficult rules, then we can't do them, but the others, that we
can, then we should.

Mona expanded on her understanding of amrit as a ritual and
spiritual identity in which Sikh women and men were equals:

The real amrit, it's valid only if both [men and women] take it. Then it
is complete. The *jatha*s say, only if both husband and wife take it, then it
is meaningful. But, if a man says, I'm not going to take amrit at all in my
whole life, then the woman can take it alone. ... Of course, they beg that
both husband and wife should take it together, and of course, it will make
a difference if both take it together, or one or the other will be following a
different form. That's why they say both should take it.[16]

In her exegesis, women and men are essential to each other's
religious identity and spiritual progress. When asked to describe
the difficulty with taking amrit, Mona had responded:

There are some conditions, such as not even dying your hair. But of course
in our social setting, they are difficult, so we don't [do them].

This is a key line, 'in our social setting, they are difficult':
modern middle-class lifestyles and aspirations are to some
extent incompatible with the proscriptions of amrit. Very few of
the Jat Sikh women I met in India were amritdhari (orthodox,
having undergone the rite of *amrit sanskar*), and among these,
none wore turbans. The turban is largely interpreted by Jats as
a masculine symbol of Sikh identity. Although some diasporan
gursikh women wear turbans as a means of overcoming the
strictly masculinist symbology of the *dastaar* (turban) and thus
proclaiming gender equality (Mahmood and Brady 2000), Jat
women in India, at least in the late 1990s, were more concerned
with national public debates over the legislative ability of the
state to force them to cover their heads—sites, after all, of Sikh
identity—with helmets while riding on motorcycles. Feminine
identities remain more important than turbans to many Sikh

women. Although most Sikh women maintain the religious proscription on cutting their hair, they routinely wax their arms and have their eyebrows threaded, frequently visiting local beauty parlours with their friends and neighbours for these treatments. Similarly, many Sikh men drink in the company of their colleagues and friends, keeping and offering alcohol in their homes. These behaviours are widely featured in middle-class accounts of female and male social life, which may include daily visiting, weekly dinner parties, monthly 'kitties'[17] and frequent attendance at weddings; but in order to take part in their social significations of middle-class status, the strict codes of religion must be set aside. At the time of this interview, I assumed that Mona's lifestyle as a middle-class woman was more important to her than the pursuit of a fuller Sikh identity, but noting the amount of time she spent on the issue of amrit as I read and re-read the transcription of her interview later, I wondered whether Mona offered this gendered interpretation of amrit sanskar as a means of obliquely expressing her husband's failure to realize the importance of this ceremonial status to Mona's own Sikhism. After all, she was among the few Jat women I met that did not visit beauty parlours, while her husband's professional status made it likely that he shared a drink with colleagues; moreover, Mona told me that she prayed daily and visited the gurdwara regularly with a group of her women neighbours. Thus, in a Jat woman's interpretation of the equalities that might be found in Sikhism, we may find new iterations of gender inequality.

Indeed, Mona, like other comparatively younger Jat women were far more likely to remark upon the inequities of their lives. Mona commented:

In our society, equality is not there. In the whole country, there is no equality! Women should have equality, every person to be equal, to enjoy the same things as men. The conveniences that men enjoy should be provided to and expected by the women also. ... But in the Arora[18] community, there is a little more equality. They have some freedom. In our [Jat] society, men say women should not go out of their house, but they have some [of this] freedom. This is the difference, they say, you can go anywhere you like, you can take the children and go walking, you can enjoy your life, do everything, they have this freedom. But in our society, there are some restrictions. ... If we go, our people will criticize and restrict us. Their men give them some freedom, but our men criticize us.

Mona's words make clear that the physical restrictions of ghund still dominate Jat women's lives. Jat women, responsible for the izzat of their families and fearing the criticisms of their husbands, fathers-in-law, and brothers, do not have the freedom to 'enjoy' their lives. Moreover, they may be 'burdened' by the double duties they must perform if they have careers. This is precisely the term that Preet Kaur, a forty-five-year old teacher used when she told me that she awoke at five o'clock each morning to do the household chores required in caring for her husband and three children, although she did not have to be at work until nine o'clock, and then did several hours more housework each evening. Although she loved her family, Preet resented not having time for the literary pursuits that her education had taught her to cherish, and which she herself encouraged her pupils to enjoy. Still younger, unmarried Jat women—such as Dimple, a year before her marriage—told me they feared marriage as an inevitable 'prison'. Still, many Jat women would exert practical and moral limitations on themselves. Mona herself remarked that

Some jobs are not suitable for girls, if they have to go away for business, or if they have to go out at night, such as police work. We don't consider these good jobs for girls. [And, when girls and boys study in the same colleges together,] they can talk about their subjects, their studies, but they should not take wrong steps. They should stick to talking about their studies and not go beyond this.

Despite the equal position afforded Sikh women within Sikhism, and indeed despite a number of examples of Sikh women's bravery and valour,[19] Mona herself here seems to suggest that women are 'the weaker sex'. At the same time, Mona touches upon some of the key fears regarding women's education, to which we will now turn.

Now Their Brains Have Become Bigger: Jat Women's Education

I didn't want to be a housewife. I wanted education and I wanted to be in service. Financially one is strong if one earns something. Coming home, I would still do all the housework, I did not waste time in social life, going here and there (laughs). I did something positive for the house, for the family (Kuljeet Kaur aged 68).

Many elderly Jat women attributed the positive social changes they had experienced within their lifetimes to their education, and older women who felt under-educated often lamented this lack. We have already heard that Gurmeet was unable to have a professional career. Similarly, Harpreet told me that:

Lack of 'education' is a very big deficiency for a person. ...One thing I think is that if I were reborn, that I study, get educated, (laughs), but not necessarily that I have to be a man.

For many elderly Jat women, the limited availability of local schools, in conjunction with assertive grandfathers (*daada*, father's father) who did not wish their granddaughters to travel at large were typically noted to contribute to this lack. Indeed, Kuljeet Kaur, a retired girl's high school teacher, with whose words this section opens, completed parts of her matriculation and subsequent teaching degree through correspondence courses as her grandfather restricted her to the village while her father worked away in the army. Kuljeet firmly believed that her commitment to education and a career had benefited her affinal family, and that her affines themselves believed this:

My in-laws wanted me to be in service because at that time the position of the family was that they had come from Pakistan [after Partition], they did not have good earnings, and my husband also wanted to study further, so then they wanted an educated girl so she could help the family, she could work in some school. They were not against my service, they wanted me to serve. So I served for the whole of my life, as long as I could. They were also broad minded, they did not want that I should not go to this place and this place.

Kuljeet reminisced fondly about her career and her contributions to her marital family, despite the potential burdens of her multiple roles as teacher, housewife, mother, and daughter-in-law, and the apparently self-imposed limitations on her freedom of mobility and free time to which she admitted in the quote at the outset of this section. Like many Sikhs, and perhaps particularly teachers, Kuljeet used the term 'service' to describe her employment and work life; her usage of this term suggests a potentially religious meaning of moral work selflessly done. It is certainly possible to interpret a career in women's education this way, and perhaps the notion of *sewa* sustained Kuljeet through the double duties of home and work.

The apparent elimination of gendered distinctions and inequalities in Jat society noted by many elderly Jat women is attributed to the benefits of education. When asked whether there was any difference in the general social position of women in comparison to that of men, Mandeep gave a lengthy reply which emphasized the positive social change and gender equity that could result from women's education:

It depends on their education. In the families which are educated (*parhi-likhi*, literally, reading and writing, but locally meaning well-educated), there's no difference there between the two. In the villages, there are still differences...like, in the newspapers, there are many stories about bride-burning and problems of dowry. These things still happen. It all depends upon education, the educated families are doing alright, they are equal. But the ones which are not [educated], which are backward, they still consider the woman as 'paerh di jutti' and force her to work, work, work... You can see today, in studies, girls are surpassing boys. In 'service' also, they are advancing in their jobs, some girls have become 'officers'. The difference is only in the way they are brought up. They say, you are a girl, you should not go outside, you should not talk to anybody; they also give them less education as compared to boys. When I was growing up, girls were given very little education. I mean hardly up to the fifth-sixth grade was considered good enough for them. So that they could write letters, *bas* (that's all). And they were not going to do any service, right? ... In my life, I feel that I should have studied more. My mother appreciated the value of education, but my *dadaji* wouldn't send me.

This response encapsulates many of the recent issues of women's social position, and relatedly, their education. As Mandeep observed earlier, gender differences are social constructs, which can be transformed through education. In this sense, although women's education is typically undertaken with marriage in mind—as a well-educated bride will attract a better groom—and not as an empowering end in itself, it also has a recognizably positive social affect, giving women greater agency to get jobs and become 'officers'. As well, education might relieve women from problems of dowry and bride-burning. In Mandeep's narrative, dowry is not an issue for educated women like herself, but the problem of other apparently uneducated women who remain 'paerh di jutti', although in my interviews with less-educated women than Mandeep, still other women were said to be 'paerh di jutti' and the victims of dowry demands. Nevertheless, in closing her narrative, Mandeep hints at the challenges she—and her mother—faced in gaining an education in the 1950s. Gender oppression is thus a shifting object in Jat women's narratives on education, and Jat women's pride in their educated modernity remains dependant on status behaviour and ideals of family honour.

This is perhaps best witnessed when we examine Gurmeet's assessment that women are now more knowledgeable—*dimaag wadh gaie*, their brains have become bigger—in light of younger Jat women's experiences of education. For if women's brains have grown bigger with their education, perhaps they are now more able to recognize and question the gendered inequalities in which they remain culturally enmeshed. Many of these have to do with education, hopes for a career, and the 'cultural mandate' (Puri 1999: 16) of marriage amid Jat concerns over honour and shame. Although most of the women I spoke with said that there should not be any limits on the level to which a woman studies, the majority of women are married after their Bachelor's degree. Indeed, marriage arrangements are often made while the woman is still at school: in deference to the social expectation that 'girls' should be married by the age of 'twenty–twenty-one', occasionally the final year of college is jeopardized or lost. I was told that 'it doesn't look nice' for older 'girls' to be unmarried, nor for any to come and go to schools often far distant from their homes. Moreover, advanced age at marriage and 'too much education' are said to prevent 'girls' from properly adjusting to their marital homes. It is also a matter of status in middle-class families that the women of the household do not have to work outside the home; thus women's education does not have to be advanced or even complete, but just enough to impress potential grooms and their families.

A problem thus arises for Jat women who aspire to ends beyond those intended by their education. The limitations on a woman's education and professional possibilities are difficult experiences for women with academic or career interests, and a few younger Jat women suggested to me that these may be formulated with such women in mind. Education creates possibilities of agency for Jat women that their marriage is intended to contain through gendered notions of women's propriety; appropriate social roles are reinforced in marriage despite a woman's education and career aspirations. Simranjit Kaur, 26, who had an MA and was a lecturer at a local college while she waited for her visa and admission in an overseas graduate programme, told me that

I think it's really stupid how the system here works for women. I mean, there is all this money and effort put into getting us the best kinds of education, English language convent schools and good BAs, and then get married, bas, just like that. They don't expect us to use what we've learned. Especially if you do something like Home Science at school, they think you just learn how to wash clothes and stitch and cook, but it's about far more than just running a house—why would anyone go to college just for that? Now I am struggling to pursue my career. I don't want to have my studies wasted on just getting married.

Women's education is undertaken with an emphasis on improving marital prospects. Not only must a bride's education be carefully calibrated so as to be adequate to, but not in excess of her groom's, but girls are often encouraged towards particular kinds of study, such as teaching, medicine and, in Simranjit's case, home science. This particular discipline is replete with notions of domesticity deemed suitable to modern middle-class womanhood, and although it includes disciplinary study of family sociology and psychology, as well as arts and crafts, it was initially explained to me—by Simranjit's *mama* (mother's brother)—as 'how to cook, stitch, do laundry, and so forth'. Patricia Caplan has noted: 'by maintaining such an ideology [of female domesticity] and inculcating it into their own children women perpetuate their own subordination' (Caplan 1985: 19). Jat women like Simranjit today actively question the expectation of marriage, but given the entrenched weight of social sanctions inherent in izzat and purdah, sanctions enacted against the perceived shamelessness of unmarried women, they may have little recourse. Simranjit dreaded being married to someone she had not chosen for herself, but knew that this was likely to happen were she to remain in her hometown and thus within her father's sphere of social contact and influence.

Education among Jats is thus meant to encourage rather than alleviate the necessity of a woman's marriage. The potential scope of modern ideas inculcated in education which are viewed as having positive social impacts among elderly Jat women are limited for many younger women by the continuation of customary gender ideals. Even women with very promising careers are subject to their parents' and in-law's ideas about marital propriety. Amardeep, a thirty-three-year-old housewife, had begun work on her doctorate in Chandigarh when her marriage was arranged. Her parents had been particularly well-educated—her mother was herself a lecturer—and they had always supported her career aspirations. But her father had become ill, and, as is frequently the case when a Jat parent falls sick, her marriage became an immediate family priority. Although now apparently happily married, she told me of her disappointment at having had to discontinue her studies, and her further dismay at not having been able to work after her marriage.

There are no suitable jobs here. I was working in research, but here there are no facilities, no labs and all. I loved my college and my work. I had lots of friends over there, I was sorry to leave it. Here, I could teach at one of the colleges, but Mummy-Daddy don't think that I should.[20] Of course, I am the only one not working, so there would be no-one else to look after the house and the kids. Dhindsa uncleji, he has asked me to work in his college, there is a lectureship free there that I could take. But the commute is too long, and it's difficult for a woman to do it. Even lecturing is difficult in that way, I suppose. Research would be more suitable, and I really would like to work. The housework is boring. Really boring. But here, now, there is nothing like that for me to do. ... If I can't do research, then it is my dream to have a business. I often think that I should do some business. I really want to be doing something. My friend Radha and I, we think of opening a shop together. But her situation is more restricted even than mine, so she would only be a silent partner at least when her mother-in-law is here. I can't even do anything yet, until the kids are both in school. But I plan it out in my head, and think about it a lot. It will probably be children's clothes: what I will sell there, where I will get the things to sell, will we make them? But whether or not I can do it in the end is another matter.

Like Simranjit, Amardeep's narrative suggests that she too thinks it wasteful to educate women but then prevent them from fulfilling their potential to work. Aware of her position as a daughter-in-law, wife, and mother, however, she is less assertive regarding her desire for a career. The issues of education and career are more complexly gendered in Amardeep's case: not only is her own propriety, and inherently, the izzat of her natal and affinal families at stake in her choice of where to work, how to work, and how to modestly travel to and fro, but her position is also complicated by her maternal and domestic duties, and her own desire to meet them. Most Jat women see their roles in the

domestic realm as natural and necessary, if not always fulfilling.
I was never privy to any overt deviation from this position on
Amardeep's behalf, but I often suspected that her own adjustment to this situation must have been difficult, and indeed it
was occasionally hinted that she had a reputation as a sometimes
difficult daughter-in-law.[21]

Amardeep's mother-in-law, Dilpreet Kaur, had mixed feelings
on women's education towards professional careers. Dilpreet
in many ways is the archetypal older Jat woman advantaged by
education. She had worked as a teacher, and had encouraged
her own daughter, Pinkie, to attend medical school. But she told
me that she worried whether this had been a good decision

> Of course I wanted that my daughter should get a good education, I wanted
> her to work, and enjoy life like I had. But I see now how hard she has to
> work, with a baby, and she is the only bahu (daughter-in-law) at her in-
> laws, and getting ready for her qualifying exams, and I worry whether I
> have done the right thing in suggesting this to her, whether it isn't too
> much to expect. Even without work, life would be hard enough for her.

In Dilpreet's present analysis, in the struggle between a woman's
domestic work and that outside of the home, her domestic labours should be prioritized. This perspective does not necessarily
endorse traditional roles for Jat women, as it is informed by personal knowledge of the difficulties of combining domestic and
professional labours. Indeed, Dilpreet may remain uncomfortable with the return to traditional gender roles that her account
otherwise suggests. At another time, she told me

> It is not that we don't think our girls should work, it is just that there are
> not enough jobs for our boys as it is. And there are only certain jobs which
> girls can do: teaching, medicine, telephone exchange. Most of the work is
> not appropriate for them, *matlab* (that is), work outside.

She resorts to notions of societal obligation to support her position: women can more readily fulfil themselves with their homes
and families, so they should leave the work for men. In this sense,
women leaving their careers that men might work do a social
good. But Dilpreet's narrative is not without traditional gender
expectations. 'Work outside' refers not to all work beyond the
domestic realm, but only to those jobs in which women might
come into morally-compromised contact with non-related men.
The work that Dilpreet suggests as suitable is either subject to

fairly rigid spatial segregation, in the case of teaching and tel-ephone exchange work, where moreover, a woman's co-workers would be overwhelmingly female, or to another fairly rigid seg-regation in terms of social and educational power, if the woman is to work as a doctor.

Clearly education has not brought about an unproblematic or uncontested notion of women's progress and social equality to the Jat community. Women's education remains directed at their marriage, rather than at their opportunities for fulfilment through careers, even though some Jat women articulate such goals. But the understanding that education is a means to gendered social progress prevails nonetheless. The benefits of women's education are also evident with regard to some of the problems of Jat marriage. For instance, there is an observable correlation between increased levels of education and decreased dowry demands. The education of the bride in some sense allays requests for dowry because the bride herself is considered to be more valuable in terms of her likely compatibility with an educated groom, and with regard to her earning potential, even if she is rarely employed, and the amount of parental invest-ment made in her.[22] But dowry has by no means disappeared as a problem of Jat marriage; Jats ubiquitously blame excessive dowry demands for the horrific and growing incidence of female foeticide in the region.

Indeed, the prohibitive cost of dowry is the most commonly cited reason for killing girl fetuses among Punjabis as a whole and the state's record in this area is quite abysmal, especially given its comparative socio-economic development. As of 2001, Punjab recorded the most imbalanced sex ratio in India, with the census documenting only 793 girls per 1,000 boys, while *Outlook India Magazine* reported in 2006 that this figure had fallen to 776:1,000 (Dogra 2006). Social and economic issues are also at the crux of sex-selective abortion in India; socio-economic prosperity in encouraging women's education has altered their comparative value in marriage, but has not kept pace with the impulse to profit from dowry that accompanies the impulse of Punjabi modernity towards conspicuous consumption. This is complicated by women's seclusion in the home, which diminishes both their social status and their economic capital, and their low work force participation encourages the perception of their bodies as reproductive commodities and thus reinforces the likelihood of foeticide (cf. Kaur 2003: 51). As well, while most Punjabi parents oblige the state in keeping their families small, they also assert that the two-children ideal family should be comprised of a boy and a girl. In the absence of biological guarantees, sex-selection tests and foeticide become the means of accomplishing state-scripted reproductive goals, as well as ensuring what Veena Oldenburg refers to as 'the precise mix of sons and daughters that Punjabi families considered right for their existential rather than spiritual or cultural needs' (Oldenburg 2002: 69). Dowry and foeticide practices are enmeshed within the subjectification and commodification of Punjabi women's bodies and are thus perhaps 'logical' outcomes of izzat, purdah, and hypergamy, although few middle-class women will discuss their impacts in any way but indirectly, carefully constructed families aside.

GENDER AND GENERATION: SOME CONCLUSIONS

I have demonstrated some of the pervasive ways in which Jat culture, whether rural and historical or urban, middle-class, and contemporary takes precedence over the gender-egalitarian virtues and values of *Sikhi*, and given some indication as to how women's social difference and inequity are constructed and maintained by Jats. Jat women are fully cognizant of and well able to articulate the gap between gender equality as advocated within Sikhism and their everyday experiences of gender. At the same time, a discourse of historical and lived improvements in women's social position is prevalent, particularly among elderly Jat women. Indeed, a belief in the reality of gender-positive social change renders older and younger Jat women at some odds in their understanding of women's social place and the need for further transformations in gender equity. These generational differences among Jat women likely have much to do with their comparative social places: finally ensconced in the role of mother-in-law and at the pinnacle of women's status according to traditional gender ideals, or, struggling as young daughters-in-law, would-be professionals, or in pursuit of more education than is socially valuable for women. Tellingly, Harpreet Kaur, who earlier told us that 'in our Jat Sikh society, the position of men and women is equal', also remarked that:

in earlier times, my *sas-saurah* (mother- and father-in-law) didn't give 'respect' to me, but now my kids are giving it to me, my 'husband' is giving it to me, and I am living as an elder in my house (*vaddi ban ke reh rahi haan mere ghar vich*), as far as I am concerned. ... A woman will be okay if she takes good care of her household.

Certainly an acceleration of the gendered impacts of modernization is recently apparent, and we would expect to find generational differences in the ways that Jat women perceive their social position. However, the social changes and related social pressures on older and younger Jat women are very different. Almost all of the older Jat women with whom I spoke had experienced urbanization with their education and marriage, and Jat women uniformly appreciate urban life as less exacting and more enjoyable. Younger women, perhaps taking the benefits of their urban locations for granted, nevertheless experience newly-dispiriting oppressions amid a social atmosphere in which are made the uncomfortable suggestions that they not become too educated and that they leave jobs for men, as is the abhorrent demand to not only have sons but to kill unborn daughters.

Gender intersects other features of Jat Sikh society—kinship and marriage, religion, class, urbanization, and educated aspirations to modernity—in complex and unexpected ways. Some Jat women, particularly elderly women, believe that they face few gender inequities in their contemporary lives. Both Sikhism, and the social progress that has come with education, contribute to the equality they perceive themselves to enjoy. Women's lives have changed for the better around practices of ghund and discourses of paerh di jutti, but younger Jat women, frequently impatient of their lives and the equalities they are yet to see, lament their limited educational and career options. At the same time, there is little overt questioning, in a manner that we might describe as feminist, of the obligations of marriage and family life. As well, Jats continue to practise other forms of inequality, not only privileging men and masculinity but also marking if not celebrating caste differences. And when women themselves do not recognize the same experiences and sources of their inequality, the ability to establish gender equity, despite Sikhism's expression of egalitarianism, remains elusive. It remains to be seen if the younger Jat women I spoke with will feel a greater sense of equality as they age, and while this is my profound hope, it is my sad suspicion that they will not.

NOTES

* My sincere thanks to both Kulwinder and Dildeep for their assistance with translations.

1. The ladies song gathering corresponds to the ceremony traditionally known as the *mehndi*, in which decorative henna is applied to a bride's hands and feet on the eve of her marriage.

2. All names are pseudonyms.

3. For a fuller ethnographic description of this agricultural caste, see Leaf (1972, 1984) and Pettigrew (1975); Chowdhry (1994) and Datta (1999) have written more recently about Hindu Jats in Haryana. Mooney (forthcoming) analyses Jat Sikh identities amid the urban and transnational transitions of modernity.

4. The 'five Ks' (*panj kakke*) are the five physical markers of Sikh belief articulated by Guru Gobind Singh, whose Punjabi names all begin with the letter 'K'. Uberoi (1996) explains that *kesh*, (uncut hair) was ordered to make Sikhs visible and force them to represent their faith, that the *kirpan*, (sword/dagger) was prescribed so that Sikhs might defend their faith and fight injustice, and that a *kara*, (steel bangle) was worn to remind Sikhs of their integrity, honour, and duties; while the *kanga*, (small comb worn in the hair) symbolized order and cleanliness, and *kachha* (briefs or shorts worn beneath the *pyjama*, *salwar*, or *lunghi*) represented both sexual engagement and moral restraint, following the injunction that Sikhs be householders and not renounce sexual relations within marriage.

5. Many women also pointed out that they used the Sikh greeting, 'Sat Sri Akal', to afford respect.

6. Legally speaking, Indian women are entitled to inherit land (and other property); Jat women, however, almost ubiquitously defer these rights to their brothers.

7. Although today, the more 'modern' the bride and her family, the higher and more revealing the position of her veil.

8. The sehra, which is ceremonially tied over the groom's turban by his female relatives prior to the departure of the *baraat* (wedding procession), and is said to symbolize his 'exalted status' (Mina Singh 2005: 42), is comprised of a long fringe of tinsel strands which obscure his face; the sehra is ceremoniously removed by the bride's father before the anand karaj (Sikh wedding rite) begins. It is notable that no such rituals attend to the routines with which brides, and wives, must veil their heads and faces (cf. Nikky Singh 2005); and, while the groom is unveiled by his in-laws, and accepted in this state, the bride is veiled in her affinal associations.

9. Worn with a salwar-kameez, the dupatta or chunni joins these garments in marking a woman as Punjabi and Sikh (although unmarried girls and 'mod' Hindus, as well as Muslims, frequently also wear these clothes).

10. Some Sikh brides are assisted in the *chaar* laavan by four of their brothers (real or classificatory) who stand at the four corners of the dais on which the Guru Granth Sahib rests (*manji sahib*), each walking with his hands on the shoulders of the bride in a protective stance, for the length of the dais and then handing the bride off to a waiting brother.

11. *The Tribune* (Chandigarh), 12 September 2006. http://www.tribuneindia.com/2006/20060912/punjab1.htm#4

12. For instance, the colonial-era writings of Malcolm Darling (1925, 1930, 1934) describe a number of positive impacts of education on women's social position in Punjab.

13. Portions of Gurmeet's narrative, along with several others, are utilized in a different context in Mooney (forthcoming).

14. Taking off one's shoes before entering a gurdwara and ensuring that one does not turn the bottom of one's feet to face the Guru Granth Sahib once inside illustrate the currency of pollution practices among Sikhs, although in popular discourse these practices are construed as marking respect.

15. 'A shoe-beating, if administered, would destroy honour. But to resist a shoe-beating is to sustain honour, and hence to rise in others' estimation' (Gold and Gujar 2002: 106).

16. Interestingly, one of Mahmood and Brady's informants (2000: 56) told them that she compared amrit and the special spiritual vows it entails to getting married.

17. Kitty parties are an important form of sociality for some Jat women. Bi-weekly or monthly meetings of women which may be organized around either *paath* (prayers) or a game of tombola (a game akin to bingo), the kitty refers to the fact that women contribute a fixed amount to a group fund that is presented to one member at each meeting so that all of the women receive a lump sum of money periodically. While husbands must agree to release funds for the kitty, they almost ubiquitously give their wives control over the kitty monies received, thus providing a small amount of discretionary income or a useful means of saving for these women.

18. The Arora (or Khatri) caste is comprised of traders. Jat women frequently comment on the freedoms and autonomies enjoyed by Arora women, which I interpret as a result of the Arora community's greater experience with and ease in urban life (Mooney forthcoming).

19. Mai Bhago is one frequently cited example of a legendary woman warrior; as well, Rani Jindan, the wife of Maharaja Ranjit Singh and mother of Duleep Singh is sometimes described as a freedom fighter.

20. Amardeep here refers to her parents-in-law; it is customary for both women and men to refer to their in-laws in parental terms.

21. This made our association potentially problematic for her, for as an outsider, I was already so-reputed.

22. If dowry is to be understood as a woman's inheritance, as is commonly argued by Jats, then the value of an education can scarcely be compared to the consumer goods which are frequently given in dowry.

REFERENCES

Appadurai, Arjun (1999). 'Dead Certainty: Ethnic Violence in the Era of Globalization,' in Birgit Meyer and Peter Geschiere (eds), *Globalization and Identity: Dialectics of Flow and Closure*, Oxford: Blackwell Publishers, pp. 305–24.

Axel, Brian Keith (2001). *The Nation's Tortured Body: Violence, Representation and the Formation of a Sikh 'Diaspora'*, Durham, NC: Duke University Press.

Bagwe, Anjali (1995). *Of Woman Caste: The Experience of Gender in Rural India*, London: Zed Books.

Butalia, Urvashi (2000). *The Other Side of Silence: Voices from the Partition of India*, London: Hurst & Company.

Caplan, Patricia (1985). *Class and Gender in India: Women and their Organizations in a South Indian City*, London: Tavistock Publications.

Chatterjee, Partha (1993). *The Nation and Its Fragments*, Princeton, NJ: Princeton University Press.

Chowdhry, Prem (1994). *The Veiled Women: Shifting Gender Equations in Rural Haryana 1880–1990*, New Delhi: Oxford University Press.

Darling, Malcolm Lyall (1925). *The Punjab Peasant in Prosperity and Debt*, London: Humphrey Milford Oxford University Press.

—— (1930). *Rusticus Loquitur, or, The Old Light and the New in the Punjab Village*, London: Humphrey Milford Oxford University Press.

—— (1934). *Wisdom and Waste in the Punjab Village*, London: Humphrey Milford, Oxford University Press.

Datta, Nonica (1999). *Forming an Identity: A Social History of the Jats*, New Delhi: Oxford University Press.

Derné, Steve (1995). *Culture in Action: Family Life, Emotion and Male Dominance in Banares, India*, Albany, NY: SUNY Press.

Dogra, Chander Suta (2006). 'Death Becomes Her', *Outlook India*, February 27.

Dube, Leela (1997). *Women and Kinship: Comparative Perspectives on Gender in South and South East Asia*, New York: The United Nations University Press.

Eriksen, Thomas Hyland (1993). *Ethnicity and Nationalism: Anthropological Perspectives*, London: Pluto Press.

Flueckiger, Joyce Burkhalter (1996). *Gender and Genre in the Folklore of Middle India*, Ithaca, NY: Cornell University Press.

Gill, Gurjeet K. (1998). 'Female Foeticide as a Contemporary Cultural Practice in the Punjab,' *Dialectical Anthropology*, Vol. 23, pp. 203–13.

Gold, Ann Grodzins and Bhoju Ram Gujar (2002). *In the Time of Trees and Sorrows: Nature, Power and Memory in Rajasthan*, Durham, NC: Duke University Press.

Goody, Jack (1976) [1993]. *Production and Reproduction: A Comparative Study of the Domestic Domain*, Cambridge: Cambridge University Press.

Greene, Sandra E. (1996). *Gender, Ethnicity, and Social Change on the Upper Slave Coast: A History of the Anlo-Ewe*, London: James Currey Ltd.

Harlan, Lindsay (1992). *Religion and Rajput Women: The Ethic of Protection in Contemporary Narratives*, Berkeley: UCLA Press.

Hegland, Mary Elaine (1998). 'Flagellation and Fundamentalism: (Trans)Forming Meaning, Identity, and Gender Through Pakistani Women's Rituals of Mourning,' *American Ethnologist,* Vol. 25, No. 2, pp. 240–66.

Jakobsh, Doris R. (2003). *Relocating Gender in Sikh History: Transformation, Meaning and Identity*, New Delhi: Oxford University Press.

Kandiyoti, Deniz (1991). 'Identity and Its Discontents: Women and the Nation,' *Millenium,* Vol. 20, No. 3, pp. 429–43.

Kaur, Malkit (2003). 'Socio-Cultural Correlates of Low Sex Ratio in Punjab', in M.S. Gill. (ed.), *Punjab Society: Perspectives and Challenges*, New Delhi: Concept Publishing Company, pp. 43–55.

Leaf, Murray J. (1972). *Information and Behaviour in a Sikh Village: Social Organization Reconsidered*, Berkeley: UCLA Press.

—— (1984). *Song of Hope: The Green Revolution in a Punjab Village*, New Brunswick, NJ: Rutgers University Press.

Mahmood, Cynthia Keppley (1996). *Fighting for Faith and Nation: Dialogues with Sikh Militants*, Philadephia: University of Pennsylvania Press.

Mahmood, Cynthia and Stacy Brady (2000). *The Guru's Gift: An Ethnography Exploring Gender Equality with North American Sikh Women*, Toronto: Mayfield Publishing Company.

Malhotra, Anshu (2002). *Gender, Caste, and Religious Identities: Restructuring Class in Colonial Punjab*, New Delhi: Oxford University Press.

Mandelbaum, David Goodman (1970). *Society in India*, Berkeley: UCLA Press.

Maynes, Mary Jo, Ann Waltner, Birgitte Soland, and Ulrike Strasser (eds) (1996). *Gender, Kinship, Power: A Comparative and Interdisciplinary History*, London: Routledge.

McMullen, Clarence Osmond (1989). *Religious Beliefs and Practices of the Sikhs in Rural Punjab*, New Delhi: Manohar.

Menon, Ritu and Kamla Bhasin (1998). *Borders and Boundaries: Women in India's Partition*, New Delhi: Kali for Women.

Mooney, Nicola (Forthcoming). *Rural Nostalgias and Transnational Dreams: Identity and Modernity among Jat Sikhs*, Toronto: University of Toronto Press.

Oldenburg, Veena Talwar (2002). *Dowry Murder: The Imperial Origins of a Cultural Crime*, New York: Oxford University Press.

Ortner, Sherry B. and Harriet Whitehead (1981). *Sexual Meanings: The Cultural Construction of Gender and Sexuality*, Cambridge: Cambridge University Press.

Pettigrew, Joyce (1975). *Robber Noblemen: A Study of the Political System of the Sikh Jats*, London: Routledge & Kegan Paul.

Puri, Jyoti (1999). *Women, Body, Desire in Post-Colonial India: Narratives of Gender and Sexuality*, London: Routledge.

Ranchod-Nilsson, Sita and Mary Ann Tétrault (2000). *Women, States and Nationalism: At Home in the Nation?* London: Routledge.

Sarkar, Tanika (1998). 'Orthodoxy, Cultural Nationalism and Hindutva Violence: An Overview of the Gender Ideology of the Hindu Right', in Ruth Roach Pierson and Nupur Chaudhuri (eds), *Nation, Empire, Colony: Historicizing Gender and Race*, Bloomington: Indiana University Press, pp. 166–81.

Sarkar, Tanika and Urvashi Butalia (1995). *Women and the Hindu Right: A Collection of Essays*, New Delhi: Kali for Women.

Sax, William S. (1990). 'Village Daughter, Village Goddess: Residence, Gender and Politics in a Himalayan Pilgrimage,' *American Ethnologist*, Vol. 17, No. 3, pp. 491–512.

Sharma, Ursula (1978). 'Women and their Affines: The Veil as a Symbol of Separation,' *Man*, Vol. 13, pp. 218–33.

Singh, Mina (2005). *Ceremonies of the Sikh Wedding*, New Delhi: Rupa and Co.

Singh, Nikky-Guninder Kaur (1993). *The Feminine Principle in the Sikh Vision of the Transcendent*, Cambridge: Cambridge University Press.

—— (2005). *The Birth of the Khalsa: A Feminist Re-Memory of Sikh Identity*, Albany, NY: SUNY Press.

Srinivas, M.N. (1966). *Social Change in Modern India*, Berkeley: UCLA Press.

Uberoi, J.P.S. (1996). *Religion, Civil Society and the State: A Study of Sikhism*, New Delhi: Oxford University Press.

Yuval-Davis, Nira and Floya Anthias (1989). *Woman-Nation-State*, London: Macmillan.

Changing Identities and Fixed Roles
The Experiences of Sikh Women

Preeti Kapur and Girishwar Misra

Gender constructs are necessarily introduced by social structures in a given cultural setting for the process of differentiation between the categories of man and woman. This paper describes an important aspect of the construction of gender and gender relations in the case of the Sikh community. It must be noted that the influence of globalization has brought in winds of change, particularly impacting Indian lifestyles; yet one finds that the notion of arranged marriages are still the norm. It is still expected that it is the solemn duty of the elders in the family to select a spouse for the young. Thus, through analysis of matrimonial advertisements as reported in daily newspapers, this essay attempts to make sense of the current patterns of identity issues for both Sikh men and women within the context of arranged marriages. Matrimonial advertisements provide a window that not only looks into the basic components of the identity of the person concerned, but also come to serve as another medium that conveys a representation of, 'who am I?', 'what traits/qualities do I have', and 'what aspects do I (read community) value in my mate', meaning, what are the negotiable and relatively un-negotiable aspects of identity in the selection of a marriage partner? Significantly, both men and women are

mainly bound by religion, ethnicity, caste, and, kinship issues.
The configuration or use of certain words and phrases in
matrimonial advertisements for Sikh men and women reflect tacit
gender construction at work. The Sikh woman is expected to have
a host of desirable qualities, ranging from physical attributes—
light skin colour, slimness and beauty to psychological traits,
sweet-natured, sober, cooperative, and pleasing personality to
homely, domesticated, smart, educated, and capably qualified.
In current times, the Sikh woman is educated and professionally
qualified, thereby creating another additional/expanded space
and hence another facet of identity for her. But matrimonial
advertisements and in-depth interviews of Sikh women indicate
that she still continues to operate within the fixed role of
perpetuator of tradition and continuity as she is expected to be
'traditional' within the modern context.

Social relations in everyday lives are essential for the making
of social beings. Of significance are gender relations, which are
comprised of elements impacting nearly every aspect of human
experience. Since gender identity is acquired and moulded
through interaction with others (Kimmel 2000; Menon 2004),
understanding gender and its facets become crucial to human
relationships. Each child, growing in his/her environment
must have the necessary instructional manual, the norms and
expectations as defined by its cultural group, for developing into
a suitable and acceptable man/woman in his/her community.
The queries that come to the fore then focus on the qualities/
traits that must be present in man but not in a woman, what
markers or rituals are deemed suitable for males so they can
be characterized as truly male or, on the other hand, what is
prescribed for women, which ultimately contributes to women's
'becoming'?

The paper presents gender formation in the Sikh community
through the lens of matrimonial advertisements; it argues that
gender constructs are necessary for the process of differentiation between the categories of a Sikh man and a Sikh woman, as
reflected in terms of masculinity–femininity. By drawing upon
matrimonial advertisements as appearing in newspapers, it emphasizes that for an authentic understanding of gender building/
creation we need to relocate the concept of gender, beyond a
taken-for-granted biologically determined understanding of

gender (equal to sex) to a construct that is fluid, constantly changing, and constructed (Axel 2001; Geetha 2002; Jakobsh 2003; Menon 2004; Nandy 1988). These perspectives have contributed significantly to our understanding of gender formation. An attempt is made to appreciate the wide-ranging facets that flow into determining gender identity in the Sikh community. It addresses contextual factors such as, class, religion, status, and ethnicity that reveal the interplay of factors determining the 'right', 'acceptable' identity required, within the context of matrimonial advertisements. By and large, many of the roles played by women were, and still are, fixed and unchanging. The nucleus of a woman's role revolves around marriage, preservation and conservation of the domestic sphere within the realm of nurturer—as a daughter, sister, wife, and mother.

THE CONTEXT

Punjab state is ranked second in India in terms of the Human Development Index, it has the highest per capita income, but the Census 2001 report accords the second lowest rank in the nation regarding sex ratio. The 2001 child sex ratio in Punjab was 793 girls per 1,000 boys, in comparison to 1961 when it was 894:1,000. Snehi (2003) reports that this is not a recent phenomenon, the same situation prevailed during the British imperial rule. Innumerable factors are responsible for the continuation of this condition where the birth of a daughter leads to anxiety and financial worries, 'in a society where subsistence takes precedence over existence and the challenges of educating and marrying off a girl are getting stiffer...' (Kodkani 2004: 14). Age-old traditions of *stridhan* (literally, women's wealth or property),[1] *pativrata* (fasts kept by wives for the well being of their husbands),[2] class, caste, and status differentiation have also contributed towards organizing women's lives. Contrasting attitudes are evident with the birth of a girl child—there are no celebrations when girls are born, and, different role and expectations are assigned to boys and girls. Within Sikhism, these attitudes persist even though the *Sikh Rahit Maryada*, the Sikh Code of Conduct grants equal rights to both men and women who are prepared to accept the rules governing the Sikh community (Singh 2004).

These issues reflect salient contextual aspects related to the construction of gender. Clearly, the spectrum of gender construction is wide; the components of each aspect are varied, intertwined and complex. Historical context emerges central to gender relations. It maps the patterns and trends of the Sikh community from the time of its founder, Guru Nanak, to current times. It helps in our understanding of gender relations from another perspective, for it reveals the framework of social organization in shaping the identities of a given community. The various factors—cultural, religious, political, and psychosocial—are intermingled in an active, complex, and continuous negotiation of identity for Sikh men and women. Such an endeavour is essential because gender construction is an ongoing process that acquires new meaning in any given social or cultural context. It is thus that this present study, focusing on contemporary matrimonial advertisements, offers important insights into the process of gender construction for both Sikh men and women within their contemporary milieu.

Aspired Images: A Study of Matrimonial Advertisements

This study was conducted in two waves; the first comprises a collection of matrimonial advertisements for brides and grooms as reported in English and Punjabi newspapers; this was followed by in-depth interviews of Sikh women to study their responses to marriage and related issues and reinforce the findings of the advertisements.

Matrimonial advertisements are a conscious effort on the part of the person/advertiser to communicate his/her/their identity and an attempt is made to include into the family-fold only those people who can be identified having the necessary qualities/distinctive characteristics that they also have, or would like to have. Thus, matrimonial advertisements become the channel through which people of a given community convey their identities and look for like-minded families who also value similar characteristics. Matrimonial advertisements as reported in regional/local newspapers, namely, *The Tribune*, published from Chandigarh, and *Ajit* published from Jullunder, were selected for a period of five months. The time frame is from June 2003 through October

2003. The current analysis is based on advertisements that are reported under the heading 'Sikh'. *The Tribune* is available, both in English and Punjabi, whereas *Ajit* is published in the Punjabi language.

The selection of matrimonial advertisements as a source of information has not yet been explored in current research. Such advertisements work as a potential model of meaning transfer by bringing the advertiser and a representation of the culturally constituted world together within the frame of a message that is socially shared and shareable. The advantage of analysing matrimonial advertisements is twofold; the advertiser conveys, without being aware that s/he would be subject to analysis. Second, while locating a mate, two basic processes are working simultaneously; the family looking for a groom/bride advertises one's status with the mention of various indicators such as educational level, income, property held, caste, physical appearance, and other attributes, all significant markers of one's identity. Secondly it also conveys the culturally desirable traits required in the mate. Thus, the images and representation of gender become central to them.

Analysis of the data was conducted in two steps—the matrimonial advertisements as published on Saturday and Sunday were content-analysed from the period June–October 2003. These helped in determining the major issues of import in selection of a mate, and were converted into categories that are presented in this paper. In the second step, one set of advertisements, October 2003, percentages were calculated for the generated categories identified in step one (131 matrimonials for grooms and 206 for brides).

This matrimonial advertisement analysis is further supported by in-depth interviews of Sikh married and unmarried women in the age range of twenty to seventy-five years. The inclusion of the two generations of women helps span the gender discourse in the recent past as well as current times. Attempts were made to include daughters and daughters-in-law, mothers and mothers-in-law so as to tap into the varied roles of women. The interviews were carried out in Delhi. The salient characteristics of these women are as follows—the women came from a middle-class background, the sample consisted of both working and non-working women who were professionally qualified or had received education up to class four, were living in a joint family or a nuclear family, and the older generation reported having strong links to their village in Punjab. The interviews were initiated through individual matrimonial advertisements and discussions revolved around the central features of marriage. Attempts were made to get the women to talk about the feelings and experiences they underwent during the process of marriage settlement and the contemporary as well as historical gender perspectives.

Results and Discussion

Analyses of matrimonial advertisements reveal an interplay of gender roles and identities. Caste, kinship, ethnicity, and class emerge as significant predetermined constraints for both brides and grooms, in the election of marriage partners. These issues become the route to regulate, control, organize, and discipline its community. Physical attributes of both Sikh men and women are of relevance, but can be linked to totally different reasons.

THE OUTER, FIXED BOUNDARY OF IDENTITY—RELIGION, ETHNICITY, CASTE, CLASS, AND KINSHIP

Importance of Ethnicity: The GurSikh

The matrimonial advertisements, for both brides and grooms, when compared to other advertisement categories (Hindu, Jain, Tamil, Christian) show a clear distinction in classification of the Sikh community as a separate category of advertisers for a mate. However, Sikh advertisements (in *The Tribune*) have two distinct sections, one for 'Sikhs' followed by 'Jat Sikhs', and for 'Ramgarhia/Dhiman' indicating separate classifications within the community. The predominance of the term 'Sikh' is clearly the established means of identifying the followers of Guru Nanak and his nine successors. Yet, matrimonial advertisements, for both brides and grooms, have indicated an additional way to identify a Sikh; he or she can also be denoted as 'GurSikh'. Interestingly, the emphasis on being 'GurSikh' is clearly gendered—the data indicates percentages of 16–21 for males and 1–10 for females. It would appear that being a Gursikh is more important for male Sikhs.

The term can be divided into two elements, 'Guru' and 'Sikh', historically, a commonly used phrase, 'Guru ka Sikh', GurSikh being a shortened version thereof. It is used mainly by Sikhs themselves to distinguish and ascertain the 'true' Sikh, or, 'one who is a loyal Sikh'. In the Sikh community it is the highly visible Sikh male who stands out physically and figuratively. Due to unshorn hair (one of the five Ks) and turban the Sikh male prominently stands out in comparison to other non-Sikh or non-initiated Sikh males. Of the five Ks the unshorn and turbaned male have become the predominant symbol for Sikhism. On the other hand, many Sikh women also keep their hair uncut and combed neatly downwards, yet most do not stand out from other non-Sikh women. Thus, while both Sikh men and women may observe the unshorn hair, it is the Sikh male who has come to be closely associated as being the Gursikh. In other words, the male body has become the site for signification (Axel 2001).

One internet site for matrimonial advertisements for the Sikh community clearly indicates that *only* Sikhs who don't cut hair or consider caste, or take intoxicants, are considered to be practising Sikhs as defined in the *Sikh Rahit Maryada* and able to advertise on this specific site ('Gursikh Matrimonials').

Advertisements by the groom's family state physical features of the potential groom. Mention of the physical characteristics (95 per cent mention any one or combinations thereof) in terms of physique—tall, fair, very/handsome, well built, athletic, and healthy. Of greater importance are the distinctive physical features (31 per cent indicate concern about any one or more aspects) regarding whether the male is 'turbaned or clean-shaven, whether he 'trims his hair or is a 'non-trimmer', and, whether he is a vegetarian and/or a teetotaler. It is to be noted that *Rahit Maryada*, the Sikh code of conduct, is clear about four prohibitions (*char kurahit*) for Sikhs, namely, hair cutting, use of tobacco, adultery, and eating the meat of an animal that has not been killed with a single blow. This concern for the above mentioned physical attributes are of significance as outer symbols that distinguish between outsiders and insiders by erecting religious boundaries, but also conveys a distinctive image of what it means to be a Sikh: the heroic image '...of bravery, courage, fortitude, pride, fearlessness, obedience and justice' (Kapur and Misra 2003: 107) have been and still are characteristics of Sikh males, and in particular of Sikh soldiers. Through Guru Gobind Singh's introduction of a new Sikh ideal—that of a military brotherhood, or as it commonly is referred to, the warrior-saint ideal—the community was radically changed, the effects of which are still relevant today.

Caste, Kinship, and Marriage

Matrimonial advertisements, for both brides and grooms, clearly indicate (99.9 per cent) that Punjabi Sikhs continue to espouse and practise caste and class bias/preference in their selection of marriage partners. In fact, 95 per cent of the matrimonial advertisements, either for grooms or brides start with, 'Suitable match/alliance for—"Ramgarhia Sikh...", "Arora Sikh...", "Khatri Gursikh..."'.

The prime concern is of caste and ethnicity. Some advertisements (11.4 per cent) have also indicated their region of origin, Doaba, for example. Clearly, the Sikh community upholds its traditional social networks through family ties and kinship obligations, marriage ceremonies, and other ritual activities. The family has been, and still is, the basis of social organization, providing its members with both identity and protection.

This aspect is evident in the repeated use of the word *khandani* and the usage of its synonyms in English. *Khandani* is an Urdu word, comprised of two parts: '*Khan*' referring to a person of status, power, influence, has a say in society, respectable, of high status, and, one who provides a model image for others to emulate. '*Dan*' refers to a collection, a group, for example, a family. Thus '*khandan*' refers to a collectivity, namely, a family and kin that has the above-mentioned qualities. The role of the family and kinship is further indicated in the following ways: In the advertisements for grooms, a characteristic feature is the predominant role played by the family in a woman's life. The background of the family is often described using the following terms: respectable, established, educated, having status, cultured, well-settled, or as having a family of high repute. Further, the advertisement includes the profession (as it reflects status) of the father (88.6 per cent), 'Father, Chief Manager, SBI', 'father Class 1, gazetted officer', and 'father in government job'. At times the profession of both the mother and father is stated, 'parents in government jobs', 'father Class 1 officer, mother teacher'. In quite a few cases (45.7 per cent), the profession of the brother and/or uncle (maternal and/or paternal) is stated as bonus feature, thereby indicating the worth of the girl. Further, in some cases (15.3 per cent) the professional standing of the brother/sister/ brother-in-law/sister-in-law is stated as, 'brother doctor, *bhabi* (brother's wife) teacher', 'brother, uncle doctor, settled abroad', 'brother IAS officer', 'father, brother army officer', providing additional worth to the image of the girl. It also indicates the significance of family standing, class, and status in marriage matters.

It is the family that provides both man and woman with their identity. But the advertisements for brides have a higher percentage (94.6 per cent in comparison to 82.3 per cent for grooms) of family details description. The family 'protects' the woman from all dangers, real and imagined, which go on to impact her personal sense of value. The woman's self-worth arises from the family, and in this way, merit, importance, and meaning of identity are also derived.

Marriage is an important institution among Sikhs in sustaining ethnic bonds. One of its important roles is to create positive self-image through arranged marriages in which region, class, religion, and caste identities are maintained and promoted. These aspects provide the outer predetermined/preset/fixed boundaries within which the Sikh community has to regulate and manage itself. Issues related to personal attributes provide the second layer.

The 'Real' Woman

'Suitable match, fair, slim beautiful, educated, religious, adjustable girl for Gursikh boy....' (*The Tribune*, 11 October 2003)

'... smart, sweet natured, talented girl, professional...' (*The Tribune*, 21 September 2003)

'... homely, well mannered, sincere and adjustable girl, working preferred...' (*The Tribune*, 22 June 2003)

'...beautiful, talented, sober, soft spoken...government teacher preferred (*The Tribune*, 22 June 2003)

'...cultured, cooperative, pleasing personality ...' (*The Tribune*, 21 June 2003)

The 'real woman' is expected to have a plethora of attributes, ranging from the physical features—tall, fair complexioned, slim, beautiful; to psychological traits—sweet natured, sincere, sober, cooperative, pleasing personality; from being homely (read, domestically inclined), sober, (*susheel*) or 'good' and 'pleasant' in terms of behaviour, (*gheralu*) to being smart and economically independent, with a partiality for working girls, preferably in government service and teachers. These characteristics thus include being educated and professionally qualified as well as being well-versed in domestic aspects.

Fair Complexion

The high demand for light colored brides is an aesthetic orientation, with positive social value associated with light skin colour and West Asian or central Asian physical features of women. Pandian notes that '[i]n many Indian languages the words fair and beautiful are often used synonymously'. Folk literature, songs sung at marriages places a high value on fair skin colour. Béteille reported in 1968 that marriage through advertisements in newspapers (*The Hindu, The Hindustan Times, Hindustan Standard*) indicate that 'virginity and a light skin color are among the most desirable qualities in a bride' (Pandian 1995, citing Andre Béteille 1968: 73–4). The preference for fair brides continues even today. There is some mention of virgin girls, though current Sikh marriage advertisements term the latter as never married or unmarried.

Balwinder who is a sixty-eight year old explains that emphasis upon physical attributes is because, 'During our times it was easy to determine the bride's/groom's caste, class, status, ...whether they came from a well established khandan. This was very important. But it was very difficult to find out about the character (*subhav*) of the girl. What could be determined were her physical qualities, so it was sort of assumed that if she has good physical attributes, the girl was likely to have good personality also'. The association between physical and psychological attributes is well established.

Susheel and Gheralu

A predominant word used for description of brides is 'susheel'. Its literal and connotative meaning is difficult to elucidate since it incorporates a host of qualities. The word susheel is made up of two words, '*su*' + '*sheel*'. The former is a prefix meaning good, nice, and pleasant. The latter refers to character, behaviour (subhav). Taken together it refers to a complex combination of attributes—soft, gentle, respectful, having good thoughts, non-aggressive, humble, and honourable. These aspects connote a person of pliable nature. A pliant wife, one who adjusts to varied situations, is an asset, for she will quietly conform to the rules of the marriage game. A woman having a malleable personality is expected to be a good wife. She is expected and required to tailor her wants and needs according to the husband and his family. She is to be happy and cheerful at all times, and be dynamic enough to handle any eventuality and circumstance. The second commonly used word is 'gheralu', literally meaning 'homely'. The connotations of this word are equally complex. The respondents explained this term to mean belonging to home, bound to home, to show interest in domestic work and chores (cooking, cleaning, decoration of home, well-versed in cooking), to look after, maintain and organize family matters, to maintain the routine of the house, caring for family members (children, in-laws, husband, relatives), in essence, to fulfil the needs of family.

Fifty-three-year old Charandeep explains that after marriage she knew she had to be 'a good wife'. She was expected to forget her upbringing, her desires and feelings, and alter her wants and needs according to the husband and his family.

Women are adjusting to the rapid changes but marriage is still the most important event in Indian social life; it is considered to be the satisfactory and customary means to establish and create a socially acceptable space. Men have been the bread earners and this aspect is important in shaping their sense of self, manhood, and gender. Male success is to be determined

by his earning capacity, his job and his profession. Within the
contemporary milieu, in addition to these well-known aspects
of gender identity for males, women's education and profession
have also become central to gendered Sikh identity.

Professional Identity: A New Location of Self

Matrimonial advertisements clearly indicate that being educated and professional is highly desirable and preferred by the
prospective grooms' families. The occupation of professional
spaces indicates a general acceptance of women in public
spheres, a realm that has historically been reserved for men. It
must, however, be noted that rural Sikh working women have
historically contributed significantly to the economy of the
family and society.[3] Related literature has portrayed women
as mothers of the nation, playing the role of tradition bearers
of the communities and the nation (Puri 1999). No doubt
this perspective still holds true, but there are other issues that
need to be considered. Sikh reform movements provided an
impetus for the education of Sikh women. It was an accepted
and desirable norm that both, boys and girls, should be sent to
educational institutions. As one seventy-year-old mother states,
'During our time we were allowed to attend school, even though
my father rarely remembered the class in which I studied. Once
the marriage proposal came in, no choice was given to me, it
was clear that I would have to stop attending school. My father
told me, "You have studied enough. We are not educating you
so that you can work".' This informant continued, 'I went to
the Khalsa schools for girls and studied till class six. During
my time education for girls was essential, it prepared us for
facing life and its difficulties… but [did not] prepare us for any
occupation. It was unheard of…it was a slur on any family that
made its daughters work in the public sphere. The women were
to be educated but they were to remain within the four walls
of the house and learn domestic chores'. (Significantly, the
Punjabi saying, 'The woman who stays within the four walls is
worth lakhs, whereas one who moves about is worthless' is an
adage still utilized today). While education was considered to
be essential for Sikh women, the construction of private and
public spheres was clearly demarcated. She had an identity of

her own in the public sphere but her role as nurturer was fixed and unchanging.

Education and Work: Forging an Identity

Education did however unlock doors for women, although in a restricted sense. But once the door was set ajar it brought the necessary thrust and gathered momentum to allow women some achievements in other spheres of life. Women were still to remain and operate within the cultural boundaries of their acceptable, conventional, and customary roles. They were not to give up their traditional roles and identities of daughter, wife, or mother. Yet, while women's roles remained the same, education did allow them to forge another identity that was now permitted by the Sikh cultural system. The slow, yet gradual change has manifested itself in women gaining a sense of identity beyond the conventional realms of ethnicity, gender, class, and religion.

The interviews with Sikh women indicate two salient issues. Elder women were educated, but the amount of freedom allowed to control their lives was restricted. Daughters, a few decades later, were able to gain more freedom from conventional and customary expectations. Thus, an added income allowed her to set up an independent family unit; it gave her the opportunity to find another facet of herself. Further, she was able to 'shift' her identity, or smoothly switch from one identity to another—as an urban working woman to a 'good daughter-in-law'. However, a young twenty-two-year old notes, 'When it came to marriage, my mother had made it clear to me that I would have to marry within my own caste and community, the boy had to be from a "respectable family", it really meant he had to be from a well-to-do family. I had no problem with this aspect, as long as I was able to continue to work. In fact, I am proud to be a member of the Sikh community'. In the gender discourse, caste and ethnicity are the primary constraints, followed by personal attributes playing an important role. But, education and professional training have added on another layer of identity approved by the community. Matrimonial advertisements have clearly indicated that families of grooms certainly prefer educated and working/professional girls, but the additional aspects of physical attributes and personality qualities and traits (as sacrificer, nurturer, mediator) state the boundaries with which the women are expected to shape and mould themselves as and live in. Also a woman's income is still considered as 'supplementary/additional'.

Contemporary Identities: Internet Marriages

The traditional routes of finding a life partner with the help of '*nais*' (barbers), has given way to marriage bureaus and classifieds as important means for arranging suitable marriages. These now face competition from internet-based marriages. Marriages are being arranged by the click of a mouse. The internet marriage industry has started changing the way marriages are arranged in India and abroad. It seems that the days of chaperoned meetings are over; males and females of marriageable age now interact through e-mail, which is considered to be an acceptable means of communication by parents. Websites cater specifically to the needs of the Sikh community, and hence the options for finding a suitable match are wider than ever before. The content of such websites indicate the concern of the Sikh community in maintaining their identity, yet it reveals changes in the marriage patterns. Vasudev has put forward a new pairing equation,

The Internet is the most successful *pandit,* there is an increasing participation of girls fixing their own marriages, 'working, broad minded' girls are sought, instead of 'homely' 'God fearing ones'. Good looks are still a consideration, but not the only one, of salience is the demand/requirement to be 'well educated' and a 'working girl, preferably a teacher or lecturer'. These reflect changing contours of women's identity; the requirements in a woman of today are certainly different from the yester years, indicating value shifts in a society. Match making has started shedding its rigidity, its notions of tradition and is on its way to becoming practical, personal and adaptable (Vasudev 2004: 46).

The above discussion indicates that the relations between the sexes are strongly influenced by social organization. The socio-historical context within which the Sikhs as a group developed and grew to become a distinct community reveal how and why categories of Sikh male and female were constructed, whereas the matrimonial advertisements disclose the continuing and changing patterns of valued aspects in a marriage partner.

Education and her earning capacity has become another way of defining her personal and social identity, although, she continues with her role of a daughter, wife, and mother.

Matrimonial advertisement analysis reveals the outer and most important layer to revolve around religion, ethnicity, caste, and, kinship. Regarding Sikh religious and ethnic boundaries, these two aspects bind both men and women, but it is the Sikh man who plays a predominant role in the maintenance of these boundaries. Ethnic and religious affiliations are important because they are strategies of social control. In this respect the woman's identity emerges not 'in terms of herself but how she fits into the pattern of relationships' (Thapar 2004: 24).

The interplay of gender and religious identities is not just a focus on religious identities, but relevant social and political categories (Leslie and McGee 2000). At times these social and political processes, beyond the domestic sphere, impede the lives of women, specifically here, Sikh women. Gender identities are entwined with, and even influenced by, other social identities as those of religion, class, caste, and ethnicity. Historical circumstances often draw the allegiance of one dimension of one's identity to the foreground; at other times these loyalties are even in conflict with other personal allegiances one holds dear (Jeffery 2000, cited in Leslie and McGee 2000:). Under such circumstances, gender identities and related concerns are often compromised or take a back seat to religious and communal identities. Times of crisis force groups to close rank and place control over those categories that are easiest to manipulate, control, and discipline. 'Women' are and have historically been sites upon which such management takes place. The Sikh reform movements of the early twentieth century turned to women to project the true 'Sikh' image. Codes of conduct, written and implied, were laid down in an endeavour to define the 'true/real' Sikh man and Sikh woman as different from men and women belonging to other religious groups. The Sikh man was portrayed as one who followed the teachings of the Guru, placed service and duties before self, was a picture of bravery and courage, and hence was the 'protector'. The cultural values that were to be inculcated by the Sikh woman were modesty, a strong work ethic, piety and devotion, and education that was to provide for her moral and religious upliftment. Above all, women were the keepers of *izzat* (honour) of themselves, their family and of the community (Jakobsh 2003).

Even in current times, during the time period of 1980s to 1990s (particularly post-Operation Blue Star) the followers of Jarnail Singh Bhindranwale organized themselves under 'Panthic committees'. They defined a social reform programme that indicated acceptable and unacceptable behaviour, at individual, social, and institutional level (Judge 2004). Sikh girls were expected to attend only Sikh management schools, wear white *salwar-kameez* and always keep their head covered with the veil.

Even now at the beginning of the twenty-first-century Sikh women are contesting for the equal rights that their Constitution and faith has endowed them with. Sikh scholars often highlight the exemplary place accorded to Sikh women, of having the same status and equality of Sikh men. Yet women, even *amritdhari* Sikhs, those who have been initiated into the Khalsa order, are not allowed to serve, clean, or sing the liturgy inside the Darbar Sahib (Golden Temple). Traditional attitudes and practices have excluded Sikh women from such activities. Moreover, as noted earlier, the state of Punjab has a high ranking in India in terms of the Human Development Index, it also has the highest per capita income, yet the Census report of 2001 accords the second lowest rank in the nation regarding male to female sex ratio. Interestingly, in terms of education, there is little difference between girls and boys. Clearly, gender construction has worked on the contradictory principles of inclusion and exclusion. Marriage and motherhood are still the primary gender roles of women. 'Motherhood is the essence of womanhood, and marriage the context within which the woman bears children' (Puri 1999: 49). As most respondents stated, marriage and motherhood give women the 'good girl' status in society. These roles continue to be deeply ingrained and persistent in establishing social expectation for Indian women at large, and Sikh women in particular, cultural indicators, per se, that metamorphose the girl into an acceptable, suitable woman.

Women today are educated and many have options, but has the female consciousness really changed, has it registered a change, has it percolated to change the lives of everyday women? As one commentator notes, 'Young women should wisely combine traditional and modern roles for a harmonious relationship at home' ('Letter to the Editor' 2004). The success/ failure of marriage rests upon the woman. Hence, it becomes very important to select a bride who is educated and works, like a man, but must also be, '....fair, slim beautiful, educated, religious, adjustable girl...' or, '...beautiful, talented, sober, soft spoken...'

Ahmed, questioning the issue of woman's image for the twenty first century, ponders whether women will 'ever really have the right to choose how they portray themselves. Will it ever really be acceptable for powerful women to be seen as both authoritative and attractive at the same time' (Ahmed 2004: 11)? The matrimonial advertisements indicate the pattern of expectations: the predominant focus is on professional, educated Sikh women who can work 'like a man', but who must play a different role at home—of a keeper and preserver of tradition and convention. Balancing between the two worlds is her new identity.

NOTES

1. The term 'stridhan' literally means 'property of wife' and is in the nature of inheritance for the daughter. As per the Hindu customary marriage practice, it is that portion of wealth which is exclusively the property of the woman, and passes from mother to daughter.

2. Pativrata literally refers to a 'fast kept for the husband's well-being', while it connotes 'to follow a husband's wishes/desires without any doubt or query'. It was a virtue much sought after in the earlier times and is still of import for contemporary Indian women. The woman is expected to be a devoted and chaste wife to her husband and is to regard him as God himself. The ideal place of the woman is within the four walls of the home. Hence, she is expected to embody the virtues of self-sacrifice, patience, docile, and submissiveness.

3. In Punjab, the agricultural sector has traditionally contributed to the economy at large. The lifestyle patterns of urban and rural Sikh women vary and are beyond the scope of this paper. The present paper focuses upon urban Sikh womanhood mainly because the confluence of modernity and tradition are most prominent within this sector.

REFERENCES

Ahmed, R.Z. (2004). 'Why should a woman always be like a man?', *The Times of India*, 22 August, p. 11.

Axel, B.K. (2001). *The Nation's Tortured Body: Violence, Representation and the Formation of a Sikh 'Diaspora'*, Durham: Duke University Press.

Béteille, A. (1968). 'Race and Descent as Social Categories in India', in J.H. Franklin (ed.), *Colour and Race*, Boston: Hougton Misslin, pp. 166–85.

Geetha, V. (2002). *Gender: Theorizing Feminism*, Calcutta: Bhatkal & Sen.

'Gursikh Matrimonials', http://gurmat.com/mission.html, accessed 1 May 2008.

Jakobsh, D.R. (2003). *Relocating Gender in Sikh History: Transformation, Meaning and Identity*, New Delhi: Oxford University Press.

Jeffery, P. (2000). 'Identifying differences: gender politics and religious community in rural Uttar Pradesh', in J. Leslie and M. McGee (eds), *Invented Identities: The Interplay of Gender, Religion and Politics in India*, New Delhi: Oxford University Press.

Judge, P.S. (2004). 'Politics of Sikh identity and its fundamentalist assertion', *Economic and Political Weekly*, August, pp. 3947–54.

Kapur, P. and G. Misra (2003). 'Images of self in the Sikh community: Continuity of the core and global presence', *Psychology and Developing Societies*, Vol. 15, No. 1, pp. 103–16.

Kimmel, M.S. (2000). *The Gendered Society*, New York: Oxford University Press.

Kodkani, J. (2004). 'When will she be free?', *The Times of India*, 15 August.

Leslie, J. and M. McGee (2000). *The Interplay of Gender, Religion and Politics in India*, New Delhi: Oxford University Press.

'Letter to the Editor' (2004). *The Tribune*, 21 August.

Menon, L. (2004). *Female Exploitation and Women's Emancipation*, New Delhi: Kaniska Publishers.

Nandy, A. (1988). 'Woman versus womanliness in India: an essay in social and political psychology', in Rehana Ghadially (ed.), *Women in Indian Society: A Reader*, New Delhi: Sage Publications, pp. 69–80, reprinted from his *At the Edge of Psychology*, New York: Oxford University Press, 1980.

Pandian, J. (1995). *The Making of India and Indian Traditions*, New Jersey: Prentice Hall.

Puri, J. (1999). *Woman, Body, Desire in Post-colonial India: Narratives of Gender and Sexuality*, New York: Routledge.

Singh, Nikky-Guninder Kaur (2004). 'Mythic inheritance and the historic drink of the Khalsa', in P. Singh and N.G. Barrier (eds), *Sikhism and History*, New Delhi: Oxford University Press, pp. 51–76.

Snehi, Y. (2003). 'In Punjab daughter means disgrace', *The Tribune*, The Sunday Tribune, 3 July, p. 20.

Thapar, K. (2004). 'When man is the problem', *Hindustan Times*, Sunday Magazine. 1 Feburary, p. 24.

Vasudev, S. (2004). 'Rearranging marriage', *India Today*, 18 October, pp. 41–8.

Why did I not Light the Fire?*
The Refeminization of Ritual in Sikhism

Nikky-Guninder Kaur Singh

The most moving ritual I have participated in was my mother's funeral. My mother died suddenly five years ago. I had just finished teaching for the day when the phone rang and my father's secretary in India told me that my mother was no longer alive. From Waterville, Maine, I rushed to Boston and took a flight to Delhi. Throughout the journey I cried aloud, trying to convince myself that I was going home to attend my mother's funeral. I reached the bustling city of Patiala just in time for the ceremony.

When I finally reached our house, I was taken into the drawing room, where my mother's body had been placed on ice in the not-too-hot November. I hugged my mother as she lay there peacefully, as beautiful as ever. But she did not move. Her ever-nurturing hands did not caress me this time. Female family members and friends who were waiting for my arrival resumed their wailing with extra vigour. Together we began to undress my mother and bathe her body with milk and water. I shuttled between dressing mother in a pink dress and consoling my fragile father, who was in his room crying like a baby, all the males gathered around him. Some were decorating the truck outside with flowers.

Mother's pink dress was further complemented by pink lipstick, a red dot on her forehead, and red powder in the part of her hair. Punjabi society maintains a distinction between a widow (*duhagan*, a woman who is unlucky because her husband is dead, and grieves in white or black) and a wife (*suhagan*, who is lucky because her husband is alive, and rejoices in bright colours). Mother was dressed in hues of red and pink, just like the way in which the traditional Indian bride arrives in her new home. Now that her sojourn was completed on earth, she was once again a bride, ready to enter her everlasting home. People sang her praises, for mother was a *pativrata* (a wife devoted to her husband). Such a woman accrues merit on earth. She had died before her husband and would be waiting patiently for him in heaven.

Mother was carried outside on a bier. All the men and women gathered together and recited passages from the Guru Granth Sahib, the Sikh scripture. She was covered with white sheets, except for her lovely face, which was encircled by her pink scarf (*dupatta*) and bright flower garlands. She looked beautiful in her eternal sleep. Before she was placed in the decorated truck, fresh flowers and numerous shawls were draped over her. It is customary for relatives and friends to offer shawls at the funeral of a woman and turbans at that of a man. After the funeral, these shawls and turbans are distributed among the needy. *Ardas,* the prayer with which every Sikh ceremony begins and ends, was recited. Mother was leaving home, never to return. Before we reached the cremation grounds, my mother paid her last homage on her bier at the *gurdwara,* the Sikh shrine located in the outskirts of Patiala. More friends and members of the community joined the procession at the cremation grounds. The closest male relatives and friends carried the bier. As the cortege moved, scriptural recitations by the entire gathering filled the air. Even during the Sikh's last journey on earth, one is called upon to recognize and praise the eternal Reality:

Jag lehu re mana jag lehu kaha gafal soia
Jo tanu upajia sang hi so bhi sangi na hoia...
nanak hari gun gai lai sabh sufan samano.

Wake up my mind, wake up from the oblivion of sleep.
The body that came with you will soon bid you goodbye . . .
Says Nanak, sing the praise of the Ultimate One
For all else is an ephemeral dream.

(Guru Granth Sahib [GGS] 726–27.
All translations from the GGS are my own).

The procession culminated at a platform of wood upon which mother was placed. The shawls were taken off and given to the poor, with the exception of the one that had been offered by my father. More wood was placed on and around my mother's body. Men close to our family generously poured the oil. The evening prayer, *kirtan sohila,* was recited. Ardas was offered again as observers sought blessings for her final departure. Then the time came for the pyre to be lighted.

Who was going to light it? Since time immemorial, Indian society has depended on the eldest son to ignite the pyre of his mother and father. In fact, the first Vedic hymn is addressed to Agni (the God of Fire), soliciting the birth of 'heroic sons'. Elizabeth Bumiller has aptly recorded an Indian woman's most auspicious blessing: 'May you be the mother of a hundred sons!' In my family, there was only one son. My brother was in the United States. He could not make it to our mother's funeral. Who could be entrusted to perform his profound duty? A surrogate had to be found. From among all the men surrounding mother's body, my father asked his former secretary, who had been like a son to my parents, to light the pyre. I did not even question his choice. In the male-defined and male-controlled web of action, I was not even aware of being eliminated. The flames began to lap mother's body while the recitations from the Guru Granth Sahib sonorously engulfed her.

When we returned to the house, *karah prashad,* the Sikh sacrament made of flour, sugar, butter, and water was distributed to everyone. Taking karah prashad, normally a very joyous event, seemed incongruous to me at first. But I realized it was a symbolic declaration that grief must end and normal life must return once more. The traditional forty-eight-hour continuous reading of the Guru Granth Sahib began in the drawing room, which now enshrined the holy book. Family members and friends, both men and women, took turns assisting the official *bhaijis* ('brothers', the men in charge of a gurdwara) in the continuous reading of the Guru Granth Sahib. Auntie Manmohan Singh read for many hours. She was a close friend and neighbour of my mother's for years, and the two had even started a weekly reading of Sikh hymns with other friends and neighbours. Mother loved Auntie Manmohan Singh's melodious voice, which was now bidding her eternal goodbye.

Outside, in one tiny corner of the garden, our old Brahmin cook had sown a plant. For centuries, Hindus and Sikhs have remained very close in the Punjab, freely entering each other's sacred places and participating in each other's rituals. Panditji, as we endearingly call him, is a family member, for he has lived with my parents ever since their marriage. He dedicated this plant to my mother. He sat reading Vedic mantras, watering and feeding the young green sapling. When I visited him later in the day, he asked me to place a *chapati* (Indian flatbread) beside it before beginning any meal. These food offerings were left for the hungry animals and birds. I think Panditji was making a larger connection: he did not want my mother's *atman* (spirit) hovering hungrily anywhere.

The following morning we went to the cremation grounds to gather the remains. A lipstick container, a perfume bottle, a steel bracelet (*kara*), and bones and ashes—these were my mother and all her possessions! I wanted to gather them up, but female relatives gently forbade me. While we stood aside, my uncles and other men collected the bones, washed them in milk and water, and put them in a bag; the warm ashes were also collected by male hands and put in a larger bag. The cremation spot was clean, but before we left it we placed a few sweets on the spot for the hungry animals and birds, just as Panditji had done in the garden back at home.

The body, made up of the four elements, was to make its ultimate return. Fire to fire, air to air, dust to dust. The union with water remained: we still had to immerse the ashes in the river. My mother's younger brother carried the bag of 'flowers' (the bones are called *phul,* or 'flowers' in Punjabi) as we all went to make our homage at the local gurdwara. Mother and I had visited this shrine many times together. Before departing to immerse the 'flowers' in the river at Kiratpur, my uncle placed the bag on my father's lap. Father took the bones out and cried as he kissed each one goodbye. Then Uncle took them back again and joined me in another car.

We were coming to the finale of funeral rites. This was my last chance to touch the physical part of my mother. I wanted to hold the bag that Uncle, her younger brother, possessed. I asked for it; he refused. I asked again, and this time he reluctantly gave in. As I held my mother's relics close to my body, I felt wonderfully comforted. In this 'impassioned experience' (Turner and Turner 1982: 218) the tumult of the preceding days was soothed. All the agony and frenzy of those days was transformed into peace and harmony.

A year later, I had a baby daughter. Was this my mother returned to me? Since my mother's death, I have had a recurring dream that she has come back to me, but she will not tell me where she has been during the interval. This dream is telling me that her love is continuously returning to me through my daughter. As I look back upon that moment when I held my mother's ashes close in my arms, I wonder if the daughter in my arms is in some way the mother I lost. The holding of mother's physical remains became a psychological process; the without converted to the within, her tragic loss into an invaluable gain, her death into an ever-living presence.

As I began to reflect on the significance of rituals, mother's funeral came back to me again and again. What if I had also asked to light her funeral pyre? I may have been refused initially, but it is possible that I could have secured my claim. Was I not my mother's daughter, her own blood? Why was my right usurped from me? Why did I remain in the background? Why, why did I remain silent?

My understanding of the 'feminization of ritual' derives from the pain of not being able to participate more fully in my mother's funeral simply because I was a daughter and not a son. This personal pain extends to other women (and men) who are excluded and oppressed in our patriarchal society. But it also entails an awareness of the profound power of ritual and an optimism that if we become courageous and voice our wishes and claims, we will be heard. After all, Uncle did give in to me. The feminization of ritual is a vision of how our traditional ways—forms of worship, rites of passage, celebrations, and commemorations—could be means of personal and social renewal and change. Ritual itself is a transformative process. The feminization of ritual entails a double transformation through which we will be active subjects, not passive objects; we will confidently lead, not timidly follow; we will be whole, not fragmented; we will be powerful, not weak; we will be liberated, not oppressed. I agree with David Kertzer that ritual can be even stronger than transformation, for it can be used as a revolutionary strategy: 'Rituals help revolutionary political stances and organizations through providing legitimacy, creating solidarity, and leading people to understand their political universe in certain ways' (cited in Caron 1993: 144). Through feminization of ritual we can begin, as Mary Daly would say, 'to dream again of a time and space in which Mother and Daughter look with pride into each other's faces and know that they both have been victims and now are sisters and comrades' (Daly 1973: 150).

It is on this positive note that I turn to the theme of feminization of ritual in the Sikh tradition. In a way, I see this process at the very heart of Sikhism. Guru Nanak (1469–1539), the founder of the religion and first Sikh Guru, denounced external actions and rituals that were empty and oppressive (Goa and Coward 1986: 13). Guru Nanak's close association with his mother Tripta, wife Sulakhani, and sister Nanaki must have raised his awareness about the tragic situation of women in his cultural milieu. His older sister Nanaki, after whom he was named, must have been especially significant because he spent many of his formative years with her, and even went to live with her in her new home when she married. There are many instances in Sikh art depicting the closeness between brother and sister. In a painting by Phulan Rani, a popular twentieth-century artist, we find Nanaki with her arm around her little brother, gently leading him toward the viewer. As an adult, Nanak rejected all austere and ascetic practices, elaborate forms of worship and rites and ceremonies that segregated society on the basis of religion, caste, race, class, or gender. He was deeply conscious of the victimization of women that was prevalent in his society. Customs like *sati* (a widow being burned on her husband's funeral pyre) and *purdah* (veiling), as well as such beliefs as menstrual pollution, which denigrated women in his milieu, were loudly denounced. His ontology led him toward a new praxis, a formulation of new possibilities for the weak and oppressed.

Women scholars like Upinder Jit Kaur praise Guru Nanak for his respect for women:

Guru Nanak, the founder of the Sikh faith, raised his voice for justice to women and provided the scriptural basis for equality which was not to be found in the scriptures of other India-born religions.... In an age when the inferiority of women was taken for granted and female infanticide and the customs of *purdah* and *sati* were commonly practiced, the Guru spoke out against them with a voice of reason and sanity. (Kaur 1990: 308)

During his lifetime, Guru Nanak travelled extensively, spreading his message of the singularity of the Ultimate Reality, and the consequent unity of humanity. At the end of his travels, he settled in Kartarpur, a Punjabi village he founded on the bank of the river Ravi. A community of disciples grew around him there. It was not a monastic order of any kind, but a fellowship of men and women engaged in the ordinary occupations of life. Men and women shared equally in the Sikh institutions of *sewa* (voluntary labour), *langar* (community meal), and *sangat* (congregation). Together they listened and recited the sacred hymns, cooked and ate langar, and formed a democratic congregation without priests or ordained ministers.

The pattern of inclusivity set up by Guru Nanak in Kartarpur continued on, and women were not excluded by any of the Sikh Gurus from any aspect of religious life. In fact, their vital participation in varied dimensions is deeply etched in Sikh memory. For example, Mata Khivi, wife of Guru Angad (Nanak II), is fondly remembered for her liberal direction of langar. With Mata Khivi's generous supervision and her plentiful supply of delicious *kheer* (rice pudding), langar became a real feast rather than just a symbolic meal. Guru Amar Das (Nanak III) assigned leadership roles to women. In order to consolidate the growing Sikh faith, he created a tightly knit ecclesiastical system and set up twenty-two *manji*s (dioceses or preaching districts) throughout India. Along with men, women served as supervisors of these communities.

Sikhs maintain that it was Bibi Amaro, the daughter of Guru Angad and Mata Khivi, who played an important role in Sikh history by serving as a liaison between the second and third Gurus. A popular narrative recounts a contemplative Amar Das being totally mesmerized by a verse of Guru Nanak's recited by Bibi Amaro. When he expressed his wish to meet the Guru who had been invested with such a rich legacy, Bibi Amaro enthusiastically escorted Amar Das to her father, Guru Angad, residing a few miles away in the village of Khadur. Amar Das immediately became Guru Angad's disciple, and eventually succeeded him to guruship, becoming Nanak III.

Women were actively and fully engaged in the history of Sikhism in a variety of ways, and with Guru Gobind Singh (Nanak X), we have the inspiring case of Mai Bhago. She was a courageous woman from the Amritsar district who rallied men to fight for the guru against the imperial forces. She herself fought on his behalf and was injured in the battle at Muktsar in December 1705. Thereafter, she accompanied Guru Gobind Singh as one of his personal bodyguards. Sikhs have built shrines in memory of her.

Mata Jitoji, wife of Guru Gobind Singh, is yet another wonderful example of women participating in important Sikh institutions. Sikhs celebrate her as an active co-partner in the creation of the Khalsa, the Order of the Pure. On Baisakhi Day 1699, Guru Gobind Singh's vision of the singular Divine Reality became effective as a vital social reality. The Khalsa was instituted when the first five initiates sipped *amrit*, the alchemical nectar, from the same bowl, discarding all divisions of caste and class. As Guru Gobind Singh stirred the water in a steel bowl with his double-edged sword to the accompaniment of scriptural recitations, Mata Jitoji added sugar puffs into the bowl, thereby combining their sweetness with the alchemy of steel. Through the drink the initiates were physically and psychologically nourished to fight against oppression and injustice. When Sikhs drink amrit, they enter the family of the Khalsa and declare themselves to be the direct descendants of Guru Gobind Singh and Mataji, their two equally important spiritual parents. Men receive the surname of Singh, meaning lion, and women Kaur, meaning princess. Their rebirth into the Order represents an annihilation of their family (caste) lineage, confinement to a heredity occupation, and stifling beliefs and rituals.

The guru period, extending from the birth of Guru Nanak in 1469 to the death of the Tenth Guru in 1708, is thus replete with excellent paradigms of women leading Sikh institutions of sangat and langar, reciting sacred poetry, fighting boldly against oppression and injustice, and generating liberating new rituals. But this feminizing process was not limited to the Gurus' family members, nor was it just for women closely associated with them or for women of the elite. Rather, the Sikh faith opened up a wide horizon for all women, irrespective of their caste, class, or marital status; married and single, wives and widows, all were equally validated. Women were no longer segregated: they did not have to observe *purdah* or stay home as in the Muslim tradition, but could now freely participate in sangat wherever it met. Women were no longer restricted from entering sacred space: unlike the lower caste Hindu women who could only enter a temple, if at all, from a specific entry, Sikh women could enter gurdwaras from any of their four doors. Unlike Hindu women who were barred from the *grihya garbha*, the innermost or 'womb' chamber of a deity, women in Sikhism could see, touch, and recite the most revered Sikh icon and image, their Guru Granth Sahib. There were no rules stating that they must eat apart from or after men; in langar they not only sat along with men, but also cooked, served, and ate with them. No longer were menstruation and childbirth stigmatized as pollution; they were in fact regarded by Guru Nanak as essential natural processes. No longer were women regarded as temptresses to be left behind, as in the case of Buddhist monks or Hindu celibates; rather, women were celebrated as vital partners in spiritual growth. The Hindu ideal of *pati yoga*, in which the yogic discipline of restraint, purification, concentration, equanimity, and desireless-ness is exercised by the woman for her husband (*pati*) and his family, was discarded; the sacred word opening a woman to the transcendent became the sole focus of her life. The institution of the Khalsa was open to both men and women: both were to wear the same five symbols[1] and fight against oppression. Women were not barred from any place or action, and there are no instances of their silence or exclusion in Sikh memory. Women spoke, saw, and acted, and they were heard, seen, and followed. They were active subjects in all spheres of the evolving Sikh tradition. Men and women were equal partners in the nascent community. Indeed, during the crucial years of the formulation and crystallization of Sikh practices and rituals, women were dynamically present.

And very importantly, women were also vibrantly present in the primal poetic and imaginative worldview. In fact, the Gurus regarded woman as physically, psychologically, and spiritually more refined, adopting a female voice and tone to express their love for the Divine. Their poetry, enshrined in the Guru Granth Sahib, prizes woman's body, activities, dressing up, emotional tenacity, and spiritual longing throughout the text. Woman is the model in forging a sensuous and palpable union with the

Transcendent. In both praxis and poetry, the Sikh Gurus created a window of opportunity for women, an opening through which women could achieve liberty, equality, and sorority.

But what happened to the course of feminization begun by the Gurus? Five centuries after Guru Nanak, a clear reversal has taken place. The rituals that exist now are rituals of patriarchy, which have created a false consciousness. Sikh women have come to lean on male figures in their communication with the divine and to depend on father figures for their strength, instead of searching within. They do not publicly question women's omission from Sikh rites of passage, nor do they celebrate women's affirmation in their sacred literature. I myself was equally silent. The Guru Granth Sahib is the sole religious icon and image of the Sikh religion and the focal point of all Sikh rituals and ceremonies. Tragically, Sikh women do not have full access even to this scripture; its inspiring meaning and ways of self-discovery are closed off to them. What I propose in this article is a 'refeminization of ritual' by which Sikh women can return to the Guru Granth Sahib—in other words, to the origins of the Sikh faith—and can match our current ways of worship and rites of passage with the word enshrined in the scripture.

How can we link our rituals with the text if we cannot even approach it? There are many obstacles along the way: the Guru Granth Sahib is physically *enclosed by* men; its meaning is not property *disclosed;* it is linguistically *closed off;* it is *closed up* in rites of passage; and it is *closed to* women by their social conditioning. Refeminization advances that we shatter each of these closures and establish an intimate relationship with the sacred book. It urges us to move not only toward the past to redeem our heritage and discover ourselves but also toward the future, for as we conform our actions to the text, we create new and invigorating rites and experiences. The following five interlinking themes explain how the Sikh tradition can refeminize ritual.

CHANGING WORSHIP

Refeminization calls for a change in formal and public worship. In gurdwaras, the Sikh places of worship, male *bhaiji*s are the ones in closest touch with the Guru Granth Sahib. Their male hands dress the venerated book, their male hands open the holy book at random, and their male voices read out the sacred verses from the book. Sikhism has no priesthood, and nowhere in the scripture are men delegated to be the sole caretakers of the holy book. So why are women missing? Even the musicians performing *kirtan* (the devotional singing of hymns from the Guru Granth Sahib) are generally men. Thus, in the formal mode of worship, men have taken away women's direct access to the revealed word. Women may be in the vicinity—cleaning the sacred precincts, cooking, doing the dishes—but they are kept at a distance from the Guru Granth Sahib.

Private worship involves a much more egalitarian practice. At home we kept the Guru Granth Sahib in a room next to mine. All members of the household could enter this room only with their heads covered and shoes off. There was something different and numinous about this space. In the morning mother would drape beautiful silk materials around the book, open it with great homage, and read the text in her melodious voice. In the evening my parents and I would gather in the prayer room—together with my brother when he was home from school—and we would ceremoniously close the book. The opening of the book in the morning (*prakash*) and the closing of the book in the evening (*sukhasan*) were part of the daily routine. Any of us could do prakash or sukhasan, signifying that the Guru Granth Sahib is open to all, men and women, old and young. Yet in public places where these morning and evening rituals are carried on daily, women are shut out.

It is imperative that we come out of our homes and gain entry into the outside world. We have to be full members of the Sikh community. When the fifth Sikh Guru, Guru Arjan, constructed the Harmandir, or Golden Temple, in the town of Amritsar, it was built with four doors. This was an architectural statement that welcomed men and women from each of the four castes. But although women freely enter gurdwaras, they do not lead worship. We should be conscious of the fact that sisters and daughters and mothers perform such rituals at home, and we should demand that they do so in public as well. Otherwise, we legitimize women's subordination to men and promote male dominance over women.

It continues to baffle me that even when I lived at home my grandmother would start a new month by having my uncle read the *barah mah*. This hymn from the Guru Granth Sahib has a woman as the protagonist; it artistically depicts her journey through the twelve months of the year. Yet it was considered efficacious only if male lips recited it! Like many Sikh women, my grandmother unconsciously transferred the authority of the male bhaijis to the men of her household and invested all men with this power in the social realm. We cannot allow such one-sided projections of power. We have to become subjects, take positions of authority, and become shapers of our tradition.

Initially, we may have difficulty retrieving our rights. But we cannot give up, for there is hope that we will ultimately succeed. For years women were not allowed entry into the Golden Temple during the early-morning service. When some years ago I addressed this issue to Gurcharan Singh Tohra, the then-president of the Shiromani Gurdwara Parbandhak Committee (SGPC)—which was established in 1920 to manage all Sikh shrines—he gave me a vague answer: 'It is a conventional practice and is hard to change.' But demands continued to be voiced, and I was delighted to find out that the administrators finally lifted the ban.

In recent years we have also begun to see women performing kirtan. There are some wonderful female musicians whose talent is finally being recognized. We now see them in gurdwaras both in India and abroad, and we hear them on radio, audiotape, and television. If we persist, women will soon be conducting services in gurdwaras. Their hands will open their holy book, and their lips will recite the commandment of the day (*vak*). They will lead the congregation in saying ardas. They will move in and around the congregation, distributing the Sikh sacrament, the karah prashad. (Although men and women together prepare the karah prashad in the kitchen, currently it is only men who distribute it in the congregation. Never in a public gathering have I received karah prashad from a female hand!)

The SGPC, basically a male organization, has come to wield immense political power in Sikh life. The committee sets up rules and regulations for Sikhs to follow throughout the world. The president of the SGPC is the Sikh equivalent of the pope. Although Sikh women were the first Indian women granted the right to vote by the Gurdwara Act of 1925, in the next seventy years only three women were elected as SGPC members (*Tribune*

News Service 1996).[2] More women need to be present on this executive body, as well as in Sikh worship. If they are involved in it politically, there will be more sensitivity to women's concerns. With women in charge along with men, changes in the religious, political, and social spheres of Sikhism will become easier to implement, and hence we will come much closer to our ideal of the refeminization of ritual.

READING OUR OWN TEXT

Refeminization includes the reading and understanding of our sacred text from our own perspective. The Guru Granth Sahib has not been properly disclosed. A one-sided, androcentric approach has dominated Sikh scholarship, which means that the exegetes and translators of the Guru Granth Sahib have elaborated the masculine dimension and that partial and false hermeneutic disclosures have concealed the feminine dimension. In gurdwaras, for the most part, congregations hear interpretations of the Guru Granth Sahib from *gyanijis* (Sikh intellectuals) who speak in a male voice and from a male point of view. It is their interpretation of Sikhism that is broadcast around the world through radio and television. Why is it that the transcendent Reality of the Sikhs, utterly formless and infinite, is addressed in exclusively masculine terms? In the gyanijis' elaborations, why are even some female symbols in the Guru Granth Sahib turned into male symbols?

As I have shown in my earlier work *The Feminine Principle in the Sikh Vision of the Transcendent,* the imagery of conception, gestation, giving birth, and lactation is unambiguously and powerfully present in the Guru Granth Sahib (N. Singh 1993a, see especially chapter 2). The Sikh holy book fully celebrates the female body and affirms the centrality of menstrual blood in the creative process: '*Ma ki raktu pita bindu dhar*' [From mother's blood and father's semen is created the human form] (Guru Granth Sahib 1022). Here priority is given to *ma ki raktu* (mother's blood). This is also the case in another passage: '*Raktu bindu kari nimia*' [From blood and semen is one created] (Guru Granth Sahib 706). *Raktu* (mother's blood) is mentioned first, and then *bindu* (semen). Modern feminists such as Penelope Washburn and Judy Grahn and psychologists such as Judith Bardwick have explored the degrading of menstruation in western culture to the point where it is considered a private, shameful process equated with being ill or weak (Washburn 1977; Grahn 1982; Bardwick 1971). The concern of these spokeswomen is that disdain for this natural feminine phenomenon in our society has led to the lowered status of women: 'The status and social control women have had has fallen with the fall of menstruation' (Grahn 1982: 275). Far from being disdained, menstrual bleeding is acknowledged in Sikh thought as an essential, natural process. Life itself begins with it. In fact, Guru Nanak reprimands those who stigmatize as polluted a garment stained with menstrual blood (Guru Granth Sahib 140).

The physical acts of gestation and giving birth, which constitute the basis of the model of God as Mother suggested by Sallie McFague (1987) find a vivid validation in the Sikh sacred text. Moreover, the feminine images rediscovered by contemporary Jewish scholars in their retranslating and reimaging of Hebrew words are explicitly present in Guru Nanak's literary repertoire as well. For example, to recover meaning, as Ellen Umansky notes, Lynn Gottiieb transforms the meaning of *Shaddai* from 'the Almighty' to 'my breasts' (Umansky 1989: 193).[3] The energizing female vitality retrieved by this contemporary rabbi finds an open expression in the Sikh sacred text (Singh 1993a: 55–9). Sadly, both Sikh adherents and scholars in the field of religion miss the Sikh scriptural validation of the female. In their paternal interpretations and elaborations, male scholars and commentators have pushed aside vital feminine images and symbols. Western feminists have explored Hindu literature and have insightfully encountered the Hindu Goddess, but they have not entered the Sikh literary world. Through seminars, conferences, and simple conversations, I have tried to open this world to my sisters. They have been surprised to discover their bodies, emotions, and actions—their very selves—*so* positively affirmed by the Guru Granth Sahib.

Sikh women themselves need to read the moral sensitivity, the ontological grounding, the words, and the ideals of the Guru Granth Sahib. Many of us pray every morning and recite hymns to our families daily, but how many of us rid ourselves of deceptive interpretations in order to understand our text from our own point of view? When the encounter between the individual and the Infinite is put forth as a direct experience in scripture, why should we allow it to be mediated by male figures and masculine interpretations? We need to think with our bodies, as Naomi Goldenberg says, and to approach the Guru Granth Sahib non-dualistically. We must find our own voice and pass on what is *ours* to our family and community.

Thus, refeminization of ritual in Sikhism advocates that we actually study our text so that we are more knowledgeable when we conduct or participate in rituals. Since all Sikh rituals have the Guru Granth Sahib as the focal point, we really do need to know its words. The language of the Granth is simple. In fact, Guru Nanak and his successors chose the vernacular over the scholarly and elitist Sanskrit and Persian languages precisely so that their words would be available to the masses. Nevertheless, several factors have made the text difficult for us today. The spoken language of the Punjab has, of course, changed over time, but this is not the real problem. What make the text more distant are patriarchal intervention and the colonial experience. Lack of education and the underhanded exclusion of women from approaching the Granth require immediate attention. We must obtain access to our text, learn the words, and extract their meaning for ourselves. The SGPC, from its end, should support the education of women. In a private meeting with Gurcharan Singh Tohra, I urged him to promote the education of women in traditional Sikh institutions such as Gurmat College and Khalsa College. He endorsed my point and has fulfilled his promise by granting scholarships to women in these institutions. Only when we are educated to understand the words do the rituals performed in their accompaniment become fully meaningful.

CREATING NEW TRANSLATIONS

Refeminization similarly entails creating new translations of the sacred verse. The text is linguistically closed off to many young women within India and abroad. The British legacy has spurred young Punjabi Sikhs to study English and western philosophies and literatures, drawing them away from their mother tongue and their own literary heritage. Indoctrinated in English-speaking schools that were founded by Victorian colonialists, many Sikhs do not possess even the basic linguistic tools to understand their own sacred text. Similarly, younger generations of Sikhs in Canada, England, and the United States are not familiar with the original verse. The Guru Granth Sahib may continually be seen, read, and heard in its original language at all important occasions and during all rites of passage, yet its import may be totally closed off from those who hear it. How can we connect our actions with our concepts when we don't know the very words of the text?

Existing translations are archaic. When I attempt to teach through translations in my seminars and classes at Colby College, I am always amazed at the way translators and exegetes in the English language have managed to make the rich and inclusive literature of the Sikhs so foreign and alien. Furthermore, the existing translations are androcentric, closing off women's experience. The Ultimate Reality of the Sikhs is beyond gender, yet invariably this metaphysical being is translated into a male deity. The feminine imagery in Sikh poetry presents a plurality of viewpoints and provides a host of options for self-discovery. But translators both from within the tradition (such as Gopal Singh, C.S. Talib, and Khushwant Singh) and from the west (such as Max Arthur Macauliffe and W.H. McLeod) have all been men, and they have translated the scripture through their own lenses.

I have recently published a translation of selections from Sikh sacred verse, a project that I regard as a refeminization (N. Singh 1995). But it was a difficult task. As I mention in the introduction to the book, I had no problem with translation as such. In fact, I felt that the original verse lent itself quite well to English, and I was surprised that translators in the past resorted so excessively to words laden with Jewish and Christian connotations. I also enjoyed moving between past and present, East and West, sacred and secular. My problem instead lay with the five editorial advisers who had been appointed by the International Sacred Literary Trust to oversee my translation. They were particularly unhappy with my omission of 'usual' terms like 'God' and 'Lord'. All the translators of Sikh scripture to date have used 'God' as the translation of the various divine names, and 'Lord' for *sahib*. The western term 'God', as Mary Daly explains, is a reified noun that takes away the dynamism of the verb 'Be-ing' (Daly 1973:

33). In such a conception the omnipotent Reality stands up and above humanity. In the Sikh conception, however, the supreme Reality is utterly transcendent and closely present 'within each and every heart' (*ghati, ghati*), as Sikh Gurus reiterate in their verses. Thus, using the term 'God' in translation is incongruous. For me, 'the One' is a more appropriate translation, because it expresses that singular Reality as being totally beyond and yet intimately present in each and every person.

Similarly, the use of the word 'Lord' to translate 'sahib' is inaccurate. I could almost hear loud sighs from my five readers. 'What a pity you are not using the beautiful term 'Lord', said one of them again and again. The word 'Lord' is masculine alone, an attribute that does not apply to the inclusive term 'Sovereign', which I used. Furthermore, a lord can designate anything from the master of a tiny estate to the ruler of a country to the male God of Judaism and Christianity, whereas the term 'Sovereign' emphasizes the supremacy of a completely independent ruler, male or female. By clinging to established translations, we put words into a mould that destroys their vitality and we end up freezing our ideas and congealing our emotions. Our rituals become merely repetitive actions, stagnant and obsessive.

CHANGING RITES OF PASSAGE

The Sikh rites of passage also need to be refeminized. Arnold van Gennep (1960) coined the term 'rites of passage' to denote rituals that mark the individual's journey through different stages in the life cycle. In her study of the nature and function of rites of passage, Barbara Myerhoff (1982) spans the works of numerous distinguished anthropologists and brings out many insightful perspectives. What I find most interesting is that all of us, in spite of our temporal and spatial distance, have tried to unite nature and culture, continuity and change, private psyche and social values. Rites of passage are very important phenomena that consciously and unconsciously perpetuate the dominant values of a tradition. Although they may take place for only a short time, the ideology behind them drafts us into the roles we take on throughout our lives. It is imperative that we re-see how Sikh rites are performed and that we quickly change actions that debilitate and victimize women.

The rites of passage in Sikhism are child naming, initiation into the Khalsa, marriage, and death (Singh 1993b). These rites are very simple, based on the sacred verse. The liberating and inclusive vision of the founder gave them a 'feminist' grounding. In refeminizing Sikh rites, we must understand the female presence and peel away patriarchal accretions and distortions. We might also think of incorporating new experiences and new expressions that would help us deal with the tensions of modernity. I will focus on the example of marriage, which involves the vital balance of power between man and woman.

The Sikh marriage ceremony is known as *anand karaj* (literally, 'blissful occasion', from *anand*—bliss and *karaj*—occasion). During anand karaj, no words or gestures are directly exchanged between the bride and groom, nor any legal formalities performed between their families. The ceremony takes place either in a Sikh shrine or in the home of the bride with everyone seated on the floor in front of the Guru Granth Sahib. It is a simple ceremony that begins with the father of the bride handing one end of a scarf to the groom, and the other end to his daughter. Through the auspiciously coloured (pink or red) scarf, the couple is tied together. Holding each end of the scarf, the bride and groom then walk around their holy book four times as someone reads Guru Ram Das' sublime hymn *lavan* (meaning 'circling' (GGS 773–4). This hymn in four verses describes marriage as a rite of passage into higher and higher circles of existence. Owen Cole is quite right in his comment that '*Lavan* presents a reversal of the *varnashramdharma* process (duty according to one's caste and stage in life) by affirming that the path to *moksha* (liberation) is one of deepening love, not increasing asceticism' (Owen 1985: 124). After each of the four circumambulations of the Guru Granth Sahib, the bride and groom touch their foreheads to the ground, and then rejoin the rest of the congregation by seating themselves on the floor. Their bowing together to the Guru Granth Sahib marks their acceptance of each other. They are solely—and equally—bound to the sacred word rather than to any legal or social authority. The rite concludes with Guru Amar Das' rapturous hymn anand (bliss)—the name of the wedding ceremony itself. With its focus on the bliss that results from the union of the individual with the Divine, this popular scriptural hymn by the third Guru is liturgically recited at the conclusion of all Sikh congregational services and joyful ceremonies. It is sung by a plurality of voices to the accompaniment of various musical instruments. The celebratory singing of anand is followed by ardas recited in solo by the leading member of the gathering, during which the entire congregation stands. After ardas, the congregation bows in unison to the Guru Granth Sahib and sits down. At this point, the Guru Granth Sahib is opened at random, and the first passage on the left-hand page is read out loud. It is regarded as the *hukm* (divine command) for the entire congregation, but is especially significant for the newly-wed couple. Anand karaj ends with the distribution of karah prashad to everyone.

Sadly, this unpretentious ritual has grown into an elaborate commercial racket. Weekly newspapers in India and the United States are full of advertisements offering daughters who are 'fair-complexioned', 'convent-school educated', and 'young, easily moulded in any way'. The women are products to be marketed for the 'tall', 'handsome', 'landowning', 'medico', and 'engineer' sons. Dowry demands for an educated Sikh groom, especially for a practicing physician in the United States or an administrative officer in India, are skyrocketing.

The financial burden of parents toward their daughters does not end with the dowry they give in a daughter's wedding. It continues until the day she dies and even beyond, for the community meal after a daughter's death is also the responsibility of her family. Even when a child is born to her, jewellery, gifts, clothes, fresh and dried fruit, as well as cash are given to her husband and his family. Throughout a daughter's life, her parents are pressured to pay for extravagant ceremonies and gifts. No wonder female fetuses are aborted. From day one, daughters are a liability, sons an asset. A daughter is a debit, a son a credit.

Thus, wedding gifts are bestowed not to help a daughter set up her new home but to assuage the greed of her in-laws and, indirectly, to enable them to marry off *their* daughters. The public sees Sikh marriages as lovely and vibrant rites, but what they don't see is the ugly financial wheeling and dealing that goes on behind the scenes. In her comprehensive study of the various opposites that come together in rites of passage, Barbara

Myerhoff overlooks the negative connection between religion and commerce. Refeminization of the marriage ritual demands an end to dowries.

In fact, dowry is specifically forbidden in the *Sikh Rahit Maryada*, the Sikh code of conduct (1950). This booklet of thirty-seven pages was published by the SGPC in 1950. It is accepted as an authoritative statement of Sikh conduct and is used by Sikhs as the standard guide for performing personal (*shakhsi*) and organizational (*panthak*) duties. It categorically states that neither a girl nor a boy should be married for money.

In its attempt to formalize the message of the Guru Granth Sahib, the SGPC developed several rules in the *Sikh Rahit Maryada* that would combat female oppression. Twice the code makes the point that Sikh women should not veil their faces (Sikh Rahit Maryada 1950: 12, 18). It prohibits infanticide, especially female infanticide, and even prohibits association with people who would prastice it. The *Sikh Rahit Maryada* allows for the remarriage of widows, and it underscores that such a ceremony must be the same as that for the first marriage—a marked difference from the old Punjabi custom, when a widow was shamefully wrapped in a sheet and carried away to a brother of her dead husband. In traditional Indian families, there is also a superstitious custom that people should not eat at the home of their married daughter—forgetting that Nanak himself lived with his married sister Nanaki and her husband! The *Sikh Rahit Maryada* denounces this custom, which treats a daughter like an object or a piece of property passed to her husband and his family.

Unfortunately, this important modern manual, developed after years of deliberation and consultation among eminent Sikhs both in India and abroad, has failed to change social practices. Dowry holds paramount importance in Sikh marriages, women are usually restricted to domestic activities, mothers are forced to abort female fetuses, the remarriage of widows is not very common, and parents seldom eat in the homes of their married daughters. Parents continue to be burdened by gifts for a daughter and her in-laws throughout their lives. How can devout Sikhs ignore their essential code of conduct? The code is clearly expressed in everyday language, so there is no problem understanding or interpreting it.

The problem lies with the thick 'lenses' and heavy 'earmuffs' that the macho Sikh culture wears. With the establishment of the Sikh empire under Maharaja Ranjit Singh (1780–1839), elaborate pomp and ceremony were introduced at the royal court, ushering formal ritual and ceremonial into the Sikh way of life. The open and egalitarian world envisioned by the Gurus gave way to social and political hierarchies. There was an urge in the upper echelons of Sikh society to emulate the traditional upper class Muslims whose women 'virtuously' remained veiled at home, and upper caste Hindus whose wives 'heroically' gave up their lives in the funeral pyres of their husbands. Instead of an equal partner, woman became a proud possession. That trend continued on, and in post-independence Punjab, the area became very prosperous, with the result that marriages have become extremely opulent, dowries extravagant, and gifts to the daughter and her in-laws for every rite, ritual and festival exorbitant. Simple ceremonies are transformed into elaborate affairs, and the quantity and quality of what is hosted for or given to the daughter reinforces the power and prestige of her father. Daughters are commodities whose marriages are arranged and conducted with a view to buildup the status and honor of their fathers. Those who are not so wealthy feel extreme pressure to spend their hard-earned money to keep up with cultural norms. So, while sons are wanted more and more in order to increase their fathers' assets, daughters are less and less desired for the depletion of assets they represent. The economic and social demands of contemporary culture are so strong and pervasive that all the Sikh teachings against elaborate rituals and the objectification of women fall on deaf ears. There is an immediate need for the Sikhs to take off their thick lenses and heavy earmuffs, so that they can read and hear the words of their ethical code and put them into practice.

It is in this vein that I propose a variation in the rite of anand karaj itself. I feel that both the father and the mother of the bride should participate in the joining of bride and groom. Commonly, the bride's father hands each end of a scarf to the couple; instead, both parents should perform this rite, together holding the scarf as they walk over to the couple. Such a gesture would be a more appropriate articulation of the fact that the bride is jointly their daughter, not a possession passing from the father to the husband, that is, from one man to another. The sequence of the gesture could also be changed. Instead of first handing an end of the scarf to the groom and then to the bride (as is the common practice now), would it not be more natural for the parents to start with their daughter? Symbolically such an action would erase the centuries-old image of women as mere followers. It would be a symbolic step toward deconstructing a daughter's dependence on her father before marriage, her husband after marriage, and her son after widowhood. The joint performance of the parents would also be a repetition and a celebration of their own union. In it they would relive their youth and their daughter's marriage would become another joyous reminiscence, connecting their own past with their child's future.

In keeping with the spirit of the Gurus, it would also be more egalitarian if both the groom and the bride took turns in leading the lavan (circle). Currently, the groom leads the four circles around the sacred book. In fact, to take turns would be to fulfil the intrinsic circularity of lavan, which is without beginning or end and thus transcends linear hierarchies.

We must remember that the tenth Guru tried to liberate both sexes from societal oppression. He ended a daughter's dependence on her father by giving her the last name of Kaur. Sikh women do not trace their lineage to their fathers, nor do they adopt the surname of their husbands. A Sikh woman retains her identity: she is Kaur before and after marriage. It is vital, then, that we discover our true identity.

We should also have pride in our physical form, as described by the tenth Guru. Members of the Khalsa are both men and women, and both are to maintain the five emblems, popularly known as the Five Ks. *Kesh*, or long hair, is for both men and women to keep. It is nature's gift. Whether married or unmarried, let us not allow *Vogue* and *Cosmopolitan* to dictate and mask our true selves. As Mary Daly says, 'The process of exorcism, of peeling off the layers of mindbindings and cosmetics, is movement past the patriarchally imposed sense of reality and identity' (Daly 1978: 6). Confidence in ourselves comes from within. Let us be radiant and not let Eurocentric models bury us.

And I repeat: We must understand our sacred text. In their poetic articulation, the male authors of the Guru Granth identify with the female and in her voice depict their longing for the Divine Groom. The Sikh holy text abounds with verses in which the psychologically and spiritually refined female shares proximity with the wholly Other. For example, she passionately and intimately proclaims:

Mere prabhu rangi ghanau ati rurau
din daialu pritam manmohanu
ati rasa lal sagurau.

[My Groom is utterly glorious, brilliantly crimson
Compassionate, beneficent, beloved, enticer of the hearts,
Overflowing with rasa, like the *lala* flower] (GGS 1331).

The backdrop of this scenario is nuptial consummation. The red (lala) flower, the enticing of hearts, the latent joy—all point to this union. The bride in this phenomenal world sees her metaphysical groom directly and physically. She is not a submissive or passive person but the one who charts out the way that will make the Transcendent accessible to human experience.

Unfortunately, patriarchal exegetes conveniently distort this dynamic metaphor, and the distortions keep accruing in north Indian society. The Divine Groom is nonchalantly interpreted as indicating the man sitting in front of the Guru Granth Sahib; the textual import of the female voice is totally neglected; male-female equality—even their collective identity in the human-divine relationship—is utterly deleted. Whereas scripture states that husband and wife unite to serve the transcendent One, the bride is held a slave to the man to whom she is wedded. This misinterpretation of the sacred verse has terrible consequences in the lives of women. It justifies their dehumanization, constant abuse, and battering. Instead of promoting a liberating and authentic existence, the poetic discourse binds bride and groom in a horribly stifling situation. If a woman resists her husband in any way, her mother and mother-in-law—indeed, her society at large—remind her of the scriptural verse '*Pati parameshara*' [Husband is the highest One]. Pati yoga is the pervasive norm.

The message of the Guru Granth Sahib is not the subjugation of the woman to the man, for her Groom is beyond gender; rather, it is the rising of the individual spirit toward the absolute. Since it establishes an intimate and passionate relationship with the infinite Beyond, this image of the transcendent Husband from the Guru Granth Sahib has great potential to liberate us finite humans. But what we observe in daily life is that its one-sided androcentric interpretation exploits women, making them objects of their husbands' demands and desires. The context of the metaphor has to be understood. We need to read the words correctly, and we need to practice them correctly.

RECOGNIZING REFEMINIZATION

Finally, the process of refeminization involves a recognition of what we are refeminizing. What was the feminist vision of Guru Nanak? How did he begin feminizing rituals? Why? How did his innovations differ from existing ways? How was his feminization of ritual developed and crystallized by succeeding Gurus?

This inquiry is important, because only when the unique contribution of Guru Nanak's vision is recognized will Sikhs be able to cast aside the cultural burdens piled upon them. Sikhism is a relatively young religion; moreover, it is a quantitatively small one. Originating in fifteenth-century northwest India, it is practised by only 2 per cent of the Indian population. The result is that Sikhs have perpetuated the centuries-old values that surround their religion historically and geographically. They are unable to change their attitudes and thinking because they do not remember the new and unique contribution of the guru-poets. They are quick and rigid about following the external code (wearing unshorn hair and beard, as well as turbans) but very slow and callous about the internal processes initiated by their Gurus. The weights and veils that the major traditions of Hinduism and Islam put on their women have easily slipped into Sikh ideas and practices. Since the culture around us closes us off, we have to recognize and recover the feminizing vision as it is embodied in the Guru Granth Sahib.

The feminizing process started by Guru Nanak is now forgotten. It remains buried under the norms and rites that prevailed in his day. Today during their menstrual period, women are not allowed to do prakash or sukhasan. Old habits and customs imposed on Sikh women prevent them from recognizing their own heritage. So encrusted are these false memories that Sikh women see themselves as polluted and perpetuate these fallacies through their own daughters and granddaughters. The sacred book exalts women, but the ardent devotees of that very book victimize them. Menstrual blood, which is celebrated as the source of life in the Sikh holy writ, is denigrated as the cause of pollution and evil in Sikh daily routine. The birth of a baby girl in Sikh society is often a painful and agonizing event. Some Sikh parents nonchalantly and often even proudly mention their usage of the latest western technology to predict the gender of their unborn children—so that they can abort girl fetuses. Women's psyche, their person, their notion of the self, are strangled by the age-old habits and customs of the Punjab.

It is urgent that we recognize the unique feminist contribution of Guru Nanak and his successor Gurus. Sikhism is viewed as an offshoot of Hinduism or as a synthesis and marriage, even a syncretism, of Hinduism and Islam. In every case, Sikhs and scholars of Sikhism overlook the originality of the Sikh tradition. Some male scholars assert that prior to the Singh Sabha (the renaissance movement begun in the nineteenth century), Sikhism did not exist as a separate religion; it was just a synthesis or syncretism of various worldviews at the popular level. They look back to the early centuries of Sikhism nostalgically, as a Weberian 'enchanted universe' (Oberoi 1994: especially chapter 3). The 'enchanted universe' is a one-sided perspective. Yes, rural Punjabi society (Hindu, Muslim, and Sikh) historically has collectively participated in popular worship, rituals, pilgrimages, and festivals, and shared one another's saints, spirits, stories, superstitions, sorcery, and sacred sites, but many times in fear and trembling. They have searched in desperation for the answer to a particular need, and despair has motivated them to go from mosque to temple to gurdwara. As a child, I remember going with my grandmother and her friends to pay homage to Hindu goddesses and Muslim saints, as well as to Sikh gurdwaras. What did grandmother and her friends fervently pray for? Sons for their daughters! I am not suggesting that we construct boundaries to divide us into Sikh or Hindu or Muslim; to the contrary, I ask that we grasp the full impact of Guru Nanak's vision of our unity and oneness and practise it in our own time. What was the conscience and consciousness of Guru Nanak that enabled him to reject 'isms' like casteism, classism, creedism, and sexism? A thesis like Oberoi's only distorts the liberating praxis and poetry of the Sikh Gurus, and diverts us from a close

study of their specific institutions and works. Until we understand the special way in which Sikh Gurus included women in
religious rites and practices, and the distinctive mode in which
they expressed the feminine in their literature, we will not experience the true enchantment and empowerment of their legacy.
By blurring the autonomous message of the Gurus, we only ignore the feminizing process initiated by them. Thus we block
any change in attitudes, and Sikh women will remain, as Mary
Daly would say, 'mutilated and muted' (Daly 1978: 5).

CONCLUSION

The identification of the individual with her sacred text underlies
my five points. Reading the Guru Granth Sahib in public worship,
studying it from our own point of view, translating it in our
voice, enacting it in our rites, and recognizing its unique feminist
import are some ways of directly experiencing the book. This
relationship corresponds with the existential character of canons
that Delwin Brown discusses in his excellent chapter 'Canon,
Chaos, and Order: A Theory of Tradition', in *Boundaries of Our
Habitations*: 'Canons are negotiating spaces or fields of play
within which, and in relation to which, personal and corporate
identity is both given and won. In conversing within and with
canons people work out who they are' (Brown 1994: 76).

Canons and texts are usually regarded as the kingdom of
males. For Mary Daly, texts belong to the realm of reified word,
of condensed spirit; they are seen in contrast with textiles: 'In
patriarchal tradition, sewing and spinning are for girls; books
are for boys' (Daly 1978: 5). The Guru Granth, the Sikh canon,
is not anti-woman. It was written by men, but its many poets
identify themselves with women and articulate their longing
for the Divine in a woman's voice. Male authors and poets in
the Guru Granth do not confront women but seek to merge
themselves with feminine feelings and thoughts. The distinction
between male and female is overcome, thus establishing the
significance of being human.

The Guru Granth is polyphonic; it is full of multivalent and
complex feminine symbols and imagery. The text presents the
ontological ground of all existence as *mata,* the Mother; the
divine spark within all creatures as *joti,* the feminine light; the

soul longing to unite with the transcendent One as suhagan, the beautiful young bride; the benevolent glance of the Divine as the feminine *nadar,* grace. This varied imagery presents us with a host of options through which we can see who we are and what we might become. Like mirrors, the images reveal our true selves, giving us wisdom and hope. They enable us to discern the divine spark within, to legitimate our bodies, and to fully validate ourselves. We begin to act and perform in accordance with our empowering literature as literary symbols are translated into social, political, and economic realities. When all the closures that divide us from our text are torn away, word and action, the ideal and the real, mythos and ethos, being and becoming, moral sensitivity and social praxis can be linked together.

When we do not merely hear and recite sacred verse or sit in its presence on certain occasions, but instead identify with it, we begin to participate in the varied and interlinking realms of family, society, nature, cosmos, and the Transcendent all the time. We live life not in fragmentation and either/or divisions, but as a dynamic and flowing continuum. Ultimately, then, the refeminization of ritual directs us toward the integration of rituals and daily routine. It draws the Infinite into our temporary activities. Every day, every moment, every nook, every cranny is imbued with the sacred; our finite selves, with the Infinite; our cleansing showers, with the holy rivers; our daily dressing, with spirituality. The hymn recited by Sikhs before they go to sleep every night is also the hymn recited during funeral rites, as they go to sleep forever. I cannot put into words what I experience each night when my little daughter and I say *waheguru* (*wahe*— wonderful and guru—enlightener, a popular Sikh exclamation which recalls and shows appreciation for the divine beauty around us) for a few seconds in the corner of the bedroom where we keep the Guru Granth Sahib. It is the most sensuous and transcendent moment of the day for me. In this 'impassioned experience', mother and child, past and present, life and death, Patiala and Waterville, become one. Is it ritual? Is it routine? I do not know.

Hasandian khelandian painandia khavandian
vice hove mukti.

[While laughing, playing, dressing up, and eating,
We attain liberation] (GGS 522).

NOTES

*This paper was first published in the *Journal of Feminist Studies in Religion*. The research for this study was carried out through the help of the Humanities Grants Committee at Colby College in 1996. I also thank my colleague Michelle Chilcoat for her valuable suggestions.

1. These five symbols, known as the Five Ks, are the emblems of the Khalsa, to be maintained by both Sikh men and women. They are uncut hair (*kes*), *a* comb to keep the hair neat (*kangha*), a steel bracelet (*kara*), breeches (*kaccha*), and a sword (*kirpan*). They were instituted by Guru Gobind Singh during his inauguration of the Khalsa in 1699.

2. They were Jagdish Kaur, Jagir Kaur Faguwalia, and Nirlep Kaur.

3. Umansky explains that *Shaddai* is 'a literal translation of *Shad* (breast) and the possessive plural for 'my' (Umansky 1989: 193).

REFERENCES

Bardwick. Judith (1971). *Psychology of Women: A Study of Bio-cultural Conflicts*, New York: Harper & Row.

Brown, Delwin (1994). *Boundaries of Our Habitations: Tradition and Theological Construction*, Albany: State of New York Press.

Bumiller, Elizabeth (1990). *May You be the Mother of a Hundred Sons: A Journey among the Women of India*, New York: Random House.

Caron, Charlotte (1993). *To Make and Make Again: Feminist Ritual Thealogy*, New York: Crossroad.

Cole, W. Owen (1985). *The Sikhs: Their Religious Beliefs and Practices*, 2nd rev. edn, Brighton, England: Sussex Academic Press.

Daly, Mary (1973). *Beyond God the Father: Toward a Philosophy of Women's Liberation*, Boston: Beacon.

—— (1978). *Gyn-Ecology: The Metaethics of Bodied Feminism*, Boston: Beacon.

Goa, David and Harold Coward (1986). 'Ritual, Word and Meaning in Sikh Religious Life: A Canadian Field Study', *Journal of Sikh Studies*, Vol. 13, pp. 13–32.

Naomi, Goldenberg (1990). *Returning Words to Flesh: Feminism, Psychoanalysis and the Resurrection of the Body*, Boston: Beacon Press.

Grahn, Judy (1982). 'From Sacred Blood to the Curse Beyond', in Charlene Spretnak (ed.), *The Politics of Women's Spirituality*, New York: Anchor-Doubleday, pp. 265–79.

Kaur, Upinder Jit (1990). *Sikh Religion and Economic Development*, New Delhi: National Book Organisation.

McFague, Sallie (1987). *Models of God: Theology far an Ecological, Nuclear Age*, Philadelphia: Fortress Press.

Myerhoff, Barbara (1982). 'Rites of Passage: Process and Paradox', in Victor Turner (ed.), *Celebrations: Studies in Festivity and Ritual*, Washington, DC: Smithsonian Institution Press, pp. 109–35.

Oberoi, Harjot (1994). *The Construction of Religious Boundaries: Culture, Identity, and Diversity in the Sikh Tradition*, Chicago: University of Chicago Press.

Sikh Rahit Maryada (1950). Amritsar, India: Shiromani Gurdwara Parbandhak Committee.

Singh, Nikky-Guninder Kaur (1993a). *The Feminine Principle in the Sikh Vision of the Transcendent*, Cambridge: Cambridge University Press.

—— (1993b). 'Religious Life and Rites of Passage', in *Sikhism*, New York: Facts on File, pp. 64–85.

—— (1995). *The Name of My Beloved: Verses of the Sikh Gurus*, San Francisco: HarperCollins.

Tribune News Service (1996). 3 September.

Turner, Victor and Edith Turner (1982). 'Religious Celebrations', in Victor Turner (ed.), *Celebrations: Studies in Festivity and Ritual*, Washington, DC: Smithsonian Institution Press, pp. 201–19.

Umansky, Ellen (1989). 'Creating a Jewish Feminist Theology: Possibilities and Problems', in Judith Plaskow and Carol P. Christ (eds), *Weaving the Visions: New Patterns in Feminist Spirituality*, San Francisco: Harper & Row, pp. 187–98.

van Gennep, Arnold (1960). *Rites of Passage*, tr. Monika B. Vizedom and Gabrielle L. Caffee, Chicago: University of Chicago Press.

Washburn, Penelope (1977). 'Becoming Woman: Menstruation as Spiritual Challenge', in *Becoming Woman*, New York: Harper & Row, pp. 1–19.

The Role of Sikh Women in their Religious Institutions

A Contemporary Account

Jagbir Jhutti-Johal

Most scholars of Sikhism agree that the Sikh Gurus attempted to raise the status of women. By acknowledging their oppression and rejecting the concept of pollution the Gurus took a stand against established ideas and practices and set the foundation for the advancement of women. It has also been argued that Sikhism advocates gender equality. However, this remains an ideal rather than a reality.

The origins of Sikhism can be traced back to the fifteenth century when Nanak, the first guru and founder of Sikhism, was born. Sikhism now boasts a worldwide population of around twenty three million followers. The central message of Sikhism is contained within the Guru Granth Sahib, the holy book of the Sikhs, a voluminous body of work containing the collected works of the Sikh Gurus and sacred writings of other Indian (Muslim and Hindu) saints. It is the embodiment of the Sikh Gurus and is regarded as the eternal Guru, a title conferred to it by the tenth and final living guru of the Sikhs, Guru Gobind Singh. It is perhaps unique amongst major world religions in that its authorship can be directly attributed to its founders and its authority is beyond question for Sikhs who view it as the repository of God's word transmitted through His messengers, the Gurus. Sikhs do not accept the authority of holy books from any other religion. It is with this scripture therefore that we begin our study of attitudes towards women in Sikhism.

The Guru Granth Sahib focuses on humanity's search for answers about God. It is an attempt by its contributors to explain the mystery, beauty, and omnipotence of the one universal creator and how to break the shackles of *humai* (self-centredness, ego) to achieve enlightenment and oneness with God. It also warns of the dangers of not living a God-centred life and traipsing the endless cycle of birth and rebirth. It is not written as a moral code or as a document recording history, and hence cannot be judged as such. The paucity of references within the Guru Granth Sahib describing contemporary historical events or moral dilemmas is an indication that the Gurus wished it to transcend these issues and focus on, what for them was infinitely more important, a relationship with the timeless and eternal creator (Jhutti-Johal 2005). What is clear from the Guru Granth Sahib is that both men and women are enjoined to search and submerge themselves in the essence of God and that enlightenment was open to all irrespective of gender, creed, or caste. And hence, there is little argument that the Gurus preached equality on a spiritual level. For example, women have an equal right to participate in the congregation:

Come my sisters and dear comrades!
Clasp me in thine embrace.
Meeting together, let us tell the tales of our Omnipotent spouse.
In the True Lord are all merits, in us all demerits (Guru Granth Sahib: 17).

On an empirical and practical level, there are references in the Guru Granth Sahib which aim to elevate the status of women:

Of woman are we born, of woman conceived
To woman engaged, to woman married.
Woman we befriend, by woman do civilisations continue.
When a woman dies, a woman is sought for.
It is through woman that order is maintained.
Then why call her inferior from whom all great ones are born?
Woman is born of woman;
None is born but of woman.

The one, who is eternal, alone is unborn.
Says Nanak, that tongue alone is blessed that others the praise of the one.
Such alone will be acceptable at the court of the True One (Guru Granth Sahib: 73).

One must be careful about judging quotes like these from a twenty-first-century feminist perspective on gender equality. The surrounding society during the Gurus' lives was undoubtedly patriarchal; power structures, whether religious or political were exclusively occupied by males and generally males dominated all walks of life. Hence, the references in the Guru Granth Sahib to women should be considered within this context and are generally aimed at the level of uplifting women's status in society, quite often being a direct appeal to men to better their treatment of women. Whether this was a stepping stone for advocating total gender equality on a practical level in the future is a matter for argument and conjecture but advocating a message of total gender equality in an age where women were seen as 'unclean', a hindrance to spiritual progress and on a lower stratum of humanity may have been lost on its audience.

Further, the concept of 'pollution' surrounding women during childbirth and menstruation is firmly rejected in the Guru Granth Sahib and the Gurus took a stand against established practices including *sati*, dowry, and female infanticide, although the effectiveness of these teachings amongst Sikhs throughout history and today is questionable (Takhar 2005). Finally, it has also been argued that the abundant use of feminine symbols in the Guru Granth Sahib supports the Gurus' ethos of equality (Singh 1993).

APPLICATION OF TEACHINGS IN CONTEMPORARY SOCIETY

Sikhs generally enjoy a prosperous position within India. The Green Revolution of the 1960s boosted the agricultural economy in the state and an influx of other industries has led to Punjab having the highest GDP per capita of all the states in India. Increased wealth in Punjab has led to an improved standard of living, better education, and opportunities to travel. Sikhs have also taken great advantage of opportunities to migrate to western nations and a sizeable Sikh community now resides in the west. This immigration amongst Sikhs worldwide has had implications for the development of the faith, particularly with reference to gender equality.

While much has been written on the status of women and their role in Sikh societies (Jakobsh 2003a, 2003b; Singh 1993; Rait 2005; Takhar 2005; Bhachu 1985b, 1987, 1993) there has been little attempt at a contemporary ethnographic account of women's perceptions of life, *sewa* (service)[1] and their roles in the gurdwara. This study aims to do this through an ethnographic and comparative study of the views of women in India and the UK.

AN ETHNOGRAPHIC STUDY

This study is an ethnographic account of how Sikh women view their role within their religious institutions. Research about minority communities by western academics is fraught with problems, and analysers have warned against outside researchers, especially those who are white, undertaking studies of race. As Lee writes 'more recently, minority communities, at least, have increasingly come to feel threatened by the attention of outside researchers' (Lee 1993: 140). Others have questioned the value of studies by outside researchers, 'how can white scholars contribute to our understanding of the experiences of racial groups? Can dominant groups comprehend the experiences of outsiders and, if so, under what conditions and with which methodological practices' (Andersen 1993: 40)? Anderson further asks, 'how can white scholars study those who have been historically subordinated without further producing sociological accounts distorted by the political economy of race, class and gender' (ibid.: 41)?

Thus, some argue that while a white female researcher might be universally united by biology, historically, culturally, and socially females are all very different. Diverse backgrounds and experiences inevitably lead to different ways of thinking and perceiving the world. This is why it is impossible to view women universally rather than specifically. Many western feminists can be viewed as being imperialistic with their views, both within their own countries and when looking at cases from other countries (Lazreg 1988; Anthias and Yuval Davies 1983).

It has been argued by many, especially the Sikhs themselves, that they have been affected by such thought processes. For example, in studies focusing on women from a particular ethnic background, it can be argued that researchers carry their own cultural nuances which are difficult for them to expunge before addressing the cultural context in which the ethnic population reside. As a result, a group's ethnicity is constructed by an outside group, for example, researchers trained in the west; the group studied is being spoken for rather than speaking for themselves. bell hooks eloquently sums this up, '[A]s subjects, people have the right to define their own reality, establish their own identities, name their history. As objects, one's reality is defined by others, one's identity created by others, one's history named only in ways that define one's relationship to those who are subjects' (hooks 1989: 42).

Such discussions and attitudes have made Indian women apprehensive about talking to western researchers. Being a Sikh, albeit one who has been brought up and educated in the west, my hope was that Sikh women would be more receptive to my line of questioning and hence be more frank with their answers. The objective of this ethnographic research was clear: to meet with a sample of Sikh women in the UK and in India, Punjab and objectively learn how they perceived themselves within the religion and within the Sikh society as a whole with particular reference to their roles in religious institutions like the gurdwara. The study was then to analyse their views on the basis of location, education, and age group. Views of respondents were garnered using a semi-structured interview-based questionnaire. The research was not trying to seek definitive answers, but come to a general understanding of Sikh women's perceptions.

THE STUDY

All the respondents were promised absolute confidentiality. It was essential that if respondents were to offer an accurate assessment of the situation as they understood it to be, then they would need to be assured that their details were confidential. Most importantly, it was understood that the study was not a critique of the Sikh religion but rather an exploration of attitudes among Sikh women. This latter point was paramount to many of the elderly respondents. However, it was explained that the results of the findings would be presented in an objective and unbiased manner.

To gain access to respondents, personal contacts were used, particularly in Punjab due to time limitations. A relative of mine was asked to locate women in various villages in the Punjab who would be willing to participate. The relative was sent a brief about the study, together with a sample of the questions in advance, so that she could relay this information to the women before they made up their minds about participating in the study. The final study questions were not made too academic or lengthy and the questionnaire was kept reasonably short (fifteen questions) to avoid respondent fatigue. Women of all age ranges were located in three different villages in the Punjab, India.

My own ethnic background and personal circumstances, a young and married Sikh woman, made access to respondents easier, both in India and the UK. Again, achieving consent for the questionnaire was relatively easy because I was viewed as one of 'them'.

A sample of twenty women in India consisted of eight women who were between the ages of fifty and eighty, and twelve women who were between the ages of eighteen and fifty. The women over the age of fifty had received no formal or very little education when they were young, and had not worked outside of the home. Out of the women between the ages of eighteen and fifty, eight were educated up to university level and four were educated up to secondary school level. All were married, with the exception of a thirty-year-old doctor and a twenty-five-year-old university graduate.

The sample of women in the UK consisted of thirty women: eleven women were between the ages of fifty and eighty; nineteen were between the ages of eighteen to fifty. All the elderly women had received little or no formal education when they were growing up. The women between the ages of eighteen and fifty had received some form of education. Most of the younger women had gone to university or had plans to attend, with the exception of two women who had married young.

The women were asked about their experiences and roles in the gurdwara, with reference to sewa, administration, religious duties, and interaction with male members of the Sikh congregation.

Since the respondents were women taken from different age groups, and, from a wide cross-section of the society in which they lived, it became clear from the responses that the aspirations of women within gurdwaras differed considerably with respect to their varied ages and social classes. For example, elderly Sikh women, who on the whole spend time in the gurdwaras cleaning or preparing food, were generally of the opinion what they did within the gurdwaras was fine for them and that they had no problems with their roles. However, it was the younger women in the UK who were of the opinion that women needed to be on the front lines and that there needed to be more prominent Sikh women in key positions such as on gurdwara committees, whether young or old, who could argue their case and fight for facilities and services such as nurseries, health care, and adult education facilities.

All interviews were on a one-to-one basis and lasted a minimum of one to two hours. Notes were taken and if the respondents consented, the interviews were recorded and then transcribed. Younger women were more receptive to having their views recorded than the elderly women.

In spite of certain shortcomings of this study, for example the small sample size, the research was able to identify what women felt about their position within religious institutions. The qualitative and descriptive nature of the research, while precluding any statistical analysis, was able to provide insights into what can sometimes translate into very sensitive issues.

As the responses are discussed it will become clear that even though there was some consensus with respect to certain answers given by the respondents, there was also a great divergence in others. As Bogdan and Taylor suggest, '[O]ne person may describe an experience in one way and another person may describe the same experience in quite another way. Yet both may be "telling the truth" according to their own perspectives: their own interpretations, rationalisations, fabrications, prejudices, and exaggerations' (Bogdan and Taylor 1975: 9).

Thus, because different respondents understood the same question in different ways, each respondent was taken to be a 'case study' in her own right. It was also clear that the responses varied according to a number of factors including age, location, economic and caste status, educational background, and degree of religious belief. For example, the age of the respondents indicated what generation they came from and it was clear that this influenced certain responses. The views of the elderly Sikh women sometimes varied considerably from the younger generation of women. In other instances it was clear that caste and the economic situation of the women influenced how they responded to certain questions. It was also apparent that women from the so called 'higher' castes had a different response to that of the women from the 'lower' castes and sometimes this was also evident across the age groups. The women in the UK and in the Punjab all viewed the religion differently and all had varying degrees of belief, and it was very evident that this influenced their responses. (Different levels of religious commitment caused respondents of the same religion to offer different answers.) However, it was also evident that while the responses of women from different towns and villages varied, varied answers were also received from respondents living in the same village. One can only speculate as to why this was the case; education and outside influences, such as the media, may have played a role in the different responses.

Respondents in India

Most of the respondents in India whose experiences had mainly been confined to their local gurdwaras, no matter what their age was, were generally in agreement that they did not feel discriminated against by the gurdwaras. Instead, they felt that women were the ones who made the decision about where they worked and what kind of sewa they did in the gurdwaras.

When asked about the women who were denied access perform sewa in the inner sanctum at the Golden Temple in 2003,[2] elderly women were in agreement that this was because that was how it has always been done. However, some of the younger women, especially the two who were university educated, were of the opinion that that was discriminatory. They did not agree with the elderly women that it was 'tradition'.

One woman, aged twenty-five, an unmarried law graduate commented:

Why is it tradition? How can we take it has truth that women in the past have never cleaned the inner sanctum of the Golden Temple. Women could have done it and the men in the hierarchy today are just propagating what they feel is correct. Is it written anywhere that women cannot clean inside the Golden Temple or sing or give parshad?

Another young woman, aged twenty-one, married for one year and educated up to secondary school level said:

We live in a society where the men feel that they have to look after women and uphold their honour. Many men feel that they have to keep us under their thumb so they make the rules, and the situation in the gurdwara was probably due to this. By keeping us out of the gurdwara politics we avoid contact with men and our honour is upheld.

I asked this young woman what made her feel like this and she told me that:

Throughout my life the men in my life have always controlled what I do and this is also true for my sisters and cousins. I was always told what I could do by my father and brothers. My uncles and male cousins also played a big role in what I could do and where I could go. The reason for this is that they have to uphold their honour/*izzat*. If we did what you women did in the west we would bringing dishonour to the family. It would also change the nature of our community.

When questioned what she meant when she claimed 'you women', she said, 'Women in the "West" are very open and outgoing. They are not like us in India. They do not listen to their elders and have a lot more freedom and they make their men do the work of women.'

These comments were surprising, in my opinion. When I put forth the view that girls in India seemed to have more freedom, she strongly denied this. She then did contradict herself by saying that 'girls in the towns have more freedom and do mix with the boys more'.

These quotes are representative of many of the young women I spoke to in India. There was some anger or resentment towards traditional male dominated power structures but this was overridden by the acceptance of tradition and the pressure to maintain izzat or honour within the community. Although there may have been a desire to challenge the status quo it would be unlikely that this would be carried out because other issues, such as education, raising a family, and job opportunities were deemed more important. There was also a sense that they were powerless as women to invoke any sort of change in a society dominated by males. In my opinion, the lack of positive Sikh female role models within this contemporary society may have contributed to this. The elderly women in India were from what could be called the 'old school of thought' and a common view, as expressed by one fifty-nine year old woman from a village was: 'The woman's place is in the home. Even our religion says that our duty is to obey our husband and raise our children to be good Sikhs.'

However, there was one sixty-two year old woman from a large town who had been married to an army officer who was completely against such thinking. In her opinion:

Sikh women should play more of an active role in society. They should be educated and go out to work. Most importantly they should take an active role in politics and even religious affairs. I am not religious, but I think I am correct in saying that it is women who attend gurdwaras more than men and it is for this reason that they should have a say in the running of the gurdwaras and should be allowed to participate in all activities in the gurdwara. I am aware that my views might seem too radical to most Sikh women in India but I do feel that we need to stand up for ourselves and have an equal right in all religious activities since the religion gives us equality.

This view was certainly not representative of the older generation, and it is interesting to note that that it came from someone who stated that she was not religious. Most elderly women were very religious and felt comfortable accepting their role as homemaker, wife, and childrearer.

Most elderly women and even some young women were resistant to change and felt that such thinking would serve only to disrupt society and create disharmony. There was also some resentment towards western attitudes on equality and its application to the Sikh community in Punjab.

It is this kind of talk that causes trouble and gives our girls the wrong ideas. Such ideas and views in my opinion lead to the breakdown of values and traditions (fifty-five-year-old woman who lived in a village and had no formal education).

Another woman, aged forty-five, was of the opinion that

[O]ur practices in the past have never caused us any trouble or problems. Why is it that all of a sudden they seem so wrong? Our religious activities and our participation have worked nicely to date. Why change a system that has worked so well? The young women are trying to be modern and copy women in the west but they don't realize that our system and values work for us and that by demanding these changes they are causing problems for themselves but also the women who accept the traditions and practices.

A common theme in the responses about sewa at gurdwaras or other types of sewa traditionally carried out by women was that they should be grateful for any form of sewa; quibbling over the type of sewa defeated the objective of sewa itself, leading instead to self-centredness. One woman told me how she had been to some of the major religious sites such as the Harmandir Sahib and Anandpur Sahib and how:

I go to the gurdwaras and I am grateful for any sewa that I can do. God will count whatever sewa you do. Don't think that by doing sewa where the Guru Granth Sahib is in the Harmandir Sahib that you will automatically receive liberation or that your sins will be removed quicker. You only receive liberation if you do sewa with a pure heart and if you concentrate on the name of God.

Another woman, aged thirty, married and educated to secondary school level reiterated this comment:

I am grateful for any sewa that I can do. I am not going to make a fuss if I am not allowed to do something. In my opinion if I was to make a fuss I would hurt the other person's feelings and cause distress, and in our religion we are not supposed to do this.

This may seem at odds with western feminist thinking in which women are exhorted to take on any roles that males do. However, an important element here within the perspective of Sikhism is the concept of humai (ego or self-centredness) and how sewa is an integral part in overcoming this. For Sikhs, the removal of humai is seen as the most crucial step in the path to enlightenment or liberation, and thus for many Sikhs this goal transcends other issues such as equality.

Another woman who was an *amritdhari* Sikh (initiated into the Khalsa order), aged thirty-nine, spoke about the tradition and did not accept there were any problems with current practices.

I know that I am an equal to man. Just because I am not allowed to clean within a particular area in the Harmandir Sahib does not mean that I am in any way inferior to man. The Gurus gave us our equality and we should not read too much into traditions and practices that have been passed down to us. What we should remember is that our Gurus have passed down our traditions and practices to us and that to date they have worked without any problems. So why are we creating problems when there are none?

When broached with the comment that some people would say that these traditions and practices do not sit well in today's society and hence they need to be changed to fit the expectations of today's society, she became very angry:

Yes, society and communities have changed in the last five hundred years. However, that does not mean that you have to abandon your practices and traditions. If they have worked for us up until now why change them. I believe that the Sikh community and the religion has some strong values and practices and I do not feel that we should change them just because they seem contradictory to people from the 'west'. Other religions have tried to change their traditions and practices to fit into today's people's way of thinking and I think they have caused themselves more problems.

When asked what she meant by other religions she did not expand. Such comments and the belief that one should be grateful for whatever sewa women could perform were indicative of the majority of women interviewed in India.

Respondents in the UK

For the respondents in the UK it was apparent that there was a clear dichotomy between their views and the views expressed by most of the women in India. In the survey, most argued in varying degrees that women should play an active role in all activities within the gurdwara and were prepared to challenge the status quo of male-dominated institutions. However, there were some dissenting voices. Two young women who were both amritdhari Sikhs in their twenties, and a few elderly women, one of whom was amritdhari, felt that such comments were inappropriate and amounted to stirring up trouble in the community. A twenty-nine year old woman who had been brought up in the UK, was a housewife, not very religious, and stemmed from what is considered a 'low' caste, made some surprising comments:

Women should do the sewa that is assigned to them, or do the sewa that is meant for women. In my opinion I feel that women can not demand more because they don't always have the capacity to fulfil their role due to obligations in the home. It is easy for men to stay in the gurdwaras for long periods of time, but not women. They have to go home and look after children. For example, when the Guru Granth Sahib is being put to sleep then most women will be at home putting their children to sleep. Our first responsibility is to our husband and children and then to such extra-curricular activities.

This comment highlights that the traditional role played by women in society still exists amongst the young, although comments like this were rare; they probably reflected the educational and social status of the respondent. The majority of the comments by younger women reflected their other priorities that stopped them from having a more active role in the gurdwara.

I think many young women would like to be on gurdwara committees and do all kinds of sewa but I think this is difficult for any women no matter what their age. We have too much to do already—work, raising children, housework, etc. We can not commit 100 per cent to sewa in the gurdwaras. I am grateful for whatever sewa that I can make time for. I will not argue that I want to do a particular form of sewa which is normally done by men because there is a normal explanation for this.

The majority of UK respondents wished for change. A young amritdhari woman in her thirties was of the view that women should have a lot more say in what they can and cannot do in gurdwaras; this was in consonance with most of the UK women. She commented:

I am an amritdhari Sikh and I have to say that until the issue [of sewa at the Harmandir Sahib] was raised by Mejinderpal Kaur and Lakhbir Kaur, I did not know that women could not do sewa within the temple itself. I do not understand why not. Yes, people have commented that this has always been the way, but where is it written that women can not do sewa within the Golden Temple. Which Guru said this? These two women were right to raise the issue. Where I live most gurdwaras allow women to do whatever sewa they want. Their might be some in the UK who do not allow women to do particular things but I think that has nothing to do with tradition but with a code of practice that has been established by them. In our gurdwara women can work in the kitchen, distribute food, and read the Guru Granth Sahib. The only place they do not seem to have a role is on the committee, and this is what I am concerned about. I don't want to make a generalization but I think most gurdwara committees are made up of men and even the SGPC is dominated by men.[3]

Most women, young and old, were of the opinion that while women did all sorts of sewa within the gurdwaras they were nearly always absent from gurdwara committees and that in some instances if an important official, for example, from a government body, was coming to visit the gurdwara, a 'token woman' was quite often placed on the committee or leadership team on the day of the visit.

One sixty year old woman who was an active participant in the gurdwara circle lamented that there was no proper representation of women's views and subsequently women's needs were not being met.

We can do whatever we want to do in the gurdwara in terms of sewa. However, we have no say in the day-to-day running or what should be done to benefit the community. This all seems to be decided by the men who are on the committees. However, these men do not always know what is best, particularly for the women. More women need to be appointed on committees so that our voice can be heard and our needs met. For example, it is only women who realize that we need nursery facilities to help many of the elderly women who look after grandchildren but who want to attend the gurdwara to be able to fulfil both duties. It is only women who know that we need to teach our young children how to sew and cook and that such classes should be held within the gurdwara. It is women who mainly look after the children and who attend the gurdwara so they should have more of an active role in the day to day running and in the organizing of events. This is what concerns me most, nothing else.

The above quote also reveals the divide between the views of older and younger Sikh women in the UK. Both groups wish for more rights and representation but in the case of older women, their concerns were generally focused on seeking more representation to then push for better facilities for women and children. The majority of the young women seemed to be of the opinion that they should have access and a say in all activities within gurdwaras and should not be sidelined from any particular activity. They were prepared, on record, to make a fuss and fight for equal rights but the extent to which they would actually carry this out in public remains unclear. Societal and traditional pressures still bear large on community affairs and there is a reluctance to challenge elders within the community.

CONCLUSIONS

This study has attempted to capture the views of a small number of Sikh women regarding their roles in religious institutions, as well as their interpretations of Sikh teachings on gender equality. In retrospect, the research should have attempted to interview more respondents in both India and the UK. Time however prohibited this. Further information may have been obtained if the views of Sikh men, particularly those in positions of power in Sikh institutions, had been ascertained with regard to the position of women in the Sikh religion and society as a whole. This will be the subject of future research. However, the study has provided a valuable insight into the attitudes and views of at least a small number of Sikh women in the Punjab and UK; it also highlights the disparity and parity of views across different nationalities, ages, social and educational backgrounds.

Sikh women in the UK, particularly the young, are wedged between two cultures, western and eastern (Punjabi), but have carved out amalgamated Anglo-Sikh culture for themselves in the UK. The level of influence of each culture on the individual will depend on family background, education, and social status, but in general, Sikh women in the UK have enjoyed a greater level of 'freedom' in the UK than their counterparts in the Punjab, in terms of education and job opportunities. This has inevitably led to a greater sense of confidence amongst them. Many now see gender equality in all walks of life as a fundamental right and a truer reflection of Sikh scripture. We therefore have Sikh teachings now being viewed, interpreted, and adapted for 'westernized' Sikh females who would argue this is the natural evolution of a progressive faith to meet the needs of its followers while remaining true to its fundamental beliefs.

While this notion of gender equality is now firmly embedded in the mindset of Sikh females in the UK and practised in employment and education there is still pressure on females (and males) to conform to traditional Punjabi practices when it comes to marriage, family, and the community affairs. Hence, there is still much resistance to a change in traditional power structures; gurdwara committees and religious bodies have a disproportionate number of males representing the community. This is also partly due to the fact that many younger women simply feel that they don't have the time to serve on gurdwara committees and that their priorities focus on raising their children and/or developing their careers. However, most of the younger respondents in the UK do think that the current system is unfair and that the male/female balance on gurdwara committees needs to be addressed.

The older women in the UK generally believe that the 'traditional' male and female roles work reasonably well, but that women's needs on matters such as childcare are being ignored because of lack of representation of women on gurdwara committees. Generally however, these women were happy to do the sewa they had always done, for example, cooking and washing utensils in the gurdwaras.

The Punjab focus of the study was comprised of Sikh women from a very wide range of social and economic classes as well as educational status. This diversity was certainly reflected by the views of the respondents. Amongst the elderly (generally of low educational status) and women of lower social status there was an acceptance of the status quo of gender roles. Most were certainly aware, and in a few cases slightly resentful of discrimination and male dominance in gurdwaras, but did not believe they had any power to change things. The majority were happy to perform any form of sewa open to them as women and were not concerned with encroaching on sewa traditionally performed by men. The responses of educated women interviewed in Punjab were more similar to those from the UK. Increasing 'westernization', economic liberation, and educational opportunities have inevitably led women to question their 'traditional' roles in society. However, even amongst this group, there was a sense of apathy on issues of gender inequality in gurdwaras; other issues, including marriage, career, and education were far more important to them. It is interesting to note that the issue of women not being permitted to perform certain types of sewa at the Harmandir Sahib was raised by Sikh women from the west.

None of the respondents, from the UK or Punjab, were critical of fundamental Sikh teachings and most believed that the Gurus of Sikhism advocated gender equality; others didn't raise this issue at all. This notion of equality was construed by Sikh women in different ways, depending on their backgrounds and their immediate needs. The Sikh religion, through its power structures, will have to adapt to meet the future needs of its female members. However, at this present time, this study did not find any sense of urgency amongst respondents to drastically change things, for three reasons. First, some women were generally happy with the current situation. Second, some women were generally apathetic to the whole issue of gender roles within the gurdwara. Third, this issue was simply not seen as a priority for other women. Nevertheless, there is evidence that Sikh women will increasingly demand a greater say in gurdwara affairs, but that this demand will be stronger in the UK (or the West) than in the Punjab in the short term.

NOTES

1. Sewa is the act of performing selfless service, without any thought of reward or personal benefit and is central to the spiritual life of a Sikh.

2. On 13 February 2003, two British Amritdhari (initiated) Sikh women, Mejinderpal Kaur and Lakhbir Kaur, were refused the right to participate in the Sukhasan procession (the laying to rest of the Guru Granth Sahib in the night) at the Harmandir Sahib in Amritsar (see Jakobsh 2003b).

3. An exception to this is Bibi Jagir Kaur, a female, who has twice been appointed as president of the SGPC, but whose tenures were marred by accusations of criminal activity and corruption.

REFERENCES

Amos, Valerie and Pratibha Parmar (1984). 'Challenging Imperial Feminism', *Feminist Review*, Vol. 17, pp. 3–19.

Anderson, Margaret (1993). 'Studying Across Difference—Race, Class, and Gender in Qualitative Research', in John H. Standfield II, and Dennis M. Rutledge (eds), *Race and Ethnicity in Research Methods*, Newbury Park, California: Sage Publications, pp. 39–52.

Anthias, F. and N.Y. Davies (1983). 'Contextualising Feminism: Gender, Ethnic and Class division', *Feminist Review*, Vol. 15, pp. 62–75.

Bhachu, Parminder (1985a). *Twice Migrants: East African Sikh Settlers in Britain*, London and New York: Tavistock.

—— (1985b). *Parental Education Strategies: The Case of Punjabi Sikhs in Britain* (Research Papers in Ethnic Relations), Centre for Research in Ethnic Relations: University of Warwick, pp. 1–26.

—— (1986). 'Work, Dowry and Marriage among East African Sikh Women in United Kingdom', in R.J. Simon and C.B. Brettell (eds), *International Migration: The Female Experience*, Totowa, New Jersey: Rowman and Allanheld Publishers, pp. 229–40.

—— (1987). 'Culture, Ethnicity and Class among Punjabi Sikh Women in Britain', *New Community*, Vol. 17, No. 3, pp. 401–12.

—— (1988). 'Apni Marji Kardhi. Home and Work: East African Sikh Women in Britain', in Sallie Westwood and Parminder Bhachu (eds), *Enterprising Women: Ethnicity, Economy, and Gender Relation*, London and New York: Routledge, pp. 76–102.

—— (1993). 'Identities Constructed and Reconstructed: Representations of Asian Women in Britain', in Gina Buijis (ed.), *Migrant Women: Crossing Boundaries and Changing Identities*, Oxford: Berg Publishers, pp. 99–117.

—— (2003). *Dangerous Designs: Fashion, Asian Women and Diaspora*, London: Routledge.

—— (2004). 'Twice and Direct Migrant Sikhs: Caste, Class and Identity in Pre- and Post-1984 Britain', in Ivan Light and Parminder Bhachu (eds), *Immigration and Entrepreseurship: Culture, Capital and Ethnic Networks*, Piscataway, New Jersey: Transaction Publishers, pp. 163–84.

Bogdan, R. and S.J. Taylor (1975). *Introduction to Qualitative Research Methods: A Phenomenological Approach to the Social Sciences*, New York: John Wiley & Sons.

Guru Granth Sahib, Vol. I–IV (1969). Amritsar: Shiromani Gurdwara Prabandhak Committee.

hooks, bell (1989). 'Feminist scholarship: Ethical Issues', in *Talking Back: Thinking Feminist*, Thinking Black, Boston: South End Press, pp. 42–8.

Jakobsh, Doris, R. (2003a). *Relocating Gender in Sikh History: Transformation, Meaning and Identity*, New Delhi: Oxford University Press.

—— (2003b). 'Sikhism, Interfaith Dialogue and Women: The Scenario', paper presented at a joint international conference at Birmingham University, *Sikhism and Inter-religious Dialogue Conference*, 25 and 26 October 2003.

Jhutti-Johal, J. and S.S. Johal (2005). 'The Sikh Grand Narrative', in A.R. Gatrad et al. (eds), *Palliative Care among South Asian*, London: Quay Books, pp. 83–94.

Lazreg, Marina (1988). 'Feminism and Difference: The Perils of Writing as a Woman on Women in Algeria', *Feminist Studies*, Vol. 14, No. 1, pp. 81–107.

Lee, R.M. (1993). *Doing Research on Sensitive Topics*, London: Sage Publications.

Rait, Satwant Kaur (2005). *Sikh Women in England: Their Religious and Cultural Beliefs and Social Practices*, Stoke-on-Trent: Trentham Books.

Singh, Nikky-Guninder Kaur (1993). *The Feminine Principle in the Sikh Vision of the Transcendent*, Cambridge: Cambridge University Press.

Takhar, Opinderjit Kaur (2005). *Sikh Identity: An Exploration of Groups Among Sikhs*, England: Ashgate Publishing.

Sikh Women in Vancouver

An Analysis of their Psychosocial Issues

Kamala Elizabeth Nayar

The Sikh community is one of the important immigrant groups in Canada during the post-war period, though its roots in Canada go back to the early decades of the twentieth century (Nayar 2004: 3, 17–18). The marked increase in migration of Sikhs into Canada occurred during the post-war period as a result of the establishment of the sponsorship system as part of Canadian immigration policy (Johnston 1988: 296–313). This system, not only allowed family members to migrate to Canada, but it also worked in favour of Sikh immigrants since most of the earlier East Indian immigrants had been Sikh (Nayar 2004: 15–18). In fact, the Sikh community is now the largest non-Christian group in the Vancouver Lower Mainland (Statistics Canada 2006).

The majority of Sikh immigrants came to western Canada during the 1950s and thereafter under the family sponsorship programme, although the change in immigration policy in the 1960s also opened the door to educated white-collar professionals from India (Basran and Bolaria 2003: 103–4, 150–2; Wood 1978: 547–67). The largest influx of East Indian immigrants occurred, however, during the era of Prime Minister Trudeau in the 1970s, especially after he initiated the policy of multiculturalism in 1971. During this time, many Sikhs migrated to Canada and found jobs as skilled or semi-skilled labourers (Chadney 1984; Nayar 2004: 18; Basran and Bolaria 2003: 104–7).

Most of the Sikh immigrants (mostly from the Jat caste) have come from an agricultural farming community background in India. And, before their arrival in Canada, they had been primarily rooted in the traditional and economically underdeveloped society of village Punjab. In other words, they came from a society that had not gone through a full-fledged period of industrialization and urbanization (Nayar 2004: 3–5). As a consequence, the majority of Sikh immigrants have had some formal education; then after coming to Canada, they have primarily worked as blue-collar labourers in lumber mills, fish canneries, construction, and on farms.

The Sikh community has, in a sense, been directly 'transplanted' into the western capitalist society of Canada without undergone having the experience of modernization. As it shifts from the traditional society of village Punjab to a modernized Canadian metropolis, the Sikh community encounters serious issues arising from the fact that its culture is rooted in traditional society. While most Sikhs certainly continue to have an identity derived from their cultural and religious heritage, an overwhelmingly modern society such as that of Canada nevertheless inevitably has a transformative impact on Sikh traditional cultural patterns of behaviour. The time lag in working things out for the smooth functioning of the community in its modern host society is indeed an intergenerational one.

Drawing on the premise that the Sikh community confronts considerable challenges in the process of its adaptation to modern society, this paper explores the impact that migration to western Canada is having specifically on Sikh women. In doing so, the paper delineates (1) the particular psychosocial issues women in each of the three generations (grandmother, mother, and granddaughter) are experiencing, (2) the tension between the traditional cultural and societal values that Sikh migrants have brought with them to Canada and the modern ideals associated with developed countries such as Canada, and lastly (3) the inner conflict related to the inherent, but not manifested during earlier times, contradiction between Punjabi culture and the Sikh religion. The analysis therefore not only brings to the fore the clash between the systems of tradition and modernity, but more significantly, it also sheds light on the often overlooked, if not completely ignored, inner conflict many Canadian-born Sikh women experience because of the intrinsic contradiction between Punjabi cultural values and Sikh religious beliefs.

METHODOLOGY

As an extension of the author's post-doctoral research, the analysis investigates the psychosocial issues of women belonging to the Sikh community in Vancouver. The research methodology consists of two main elements: (1) 'participatory observation' (Palys 1992: 210)[1] by the author within the Vancouver Sikh community in general; and (2) thirty-six semi-structured interviews using open-ended questions with Sikh women and social service personnel who work with them. The Sikh women surveyed for this article were found through the snowball sampling method (ibid.: 148–9). The present article is based on thirty-two semi-structured interviews conducted with women belonging to each of the three generations of the Punjabi-Sikh community in the Vancouver Lower Mainland: seven first-generation participants, ten second-generation participants, and fifteen third-generation participants.

The delineation of the three generations here is primarily based on the participant's stage in life: grandmothers, mothers, and daughters. The first generation consists of the elders who are 'grandmothers'. The women in this group are all Indian-born and spent their formative years in India. They came to Canada during their adult life, primarily through sponsorship by family members, most often by their adult children. The second generation consists of 'mothers' who are middle-aged, married and have families, and predominantly migrated to western Canada during the 1960s and 1970s. Although the women of this group may have been born in India, they came to Canada from India in their late teens or early twenties and have thus spent most of their adult life in Canada. The third generation consists of the 'daughters' of immigrant parents who were born and raised in Canada.

The participants volunteered to be interviewed to discuss the socio-cultural issues surrounding gender that the Sikh community finds pertinent in its experience in Canada. It was found that fewer interviewees from the first and second generations were necessary for the research because the information relayed by them in their responses quickly reached a saturation point. In contrast, in the case of the third generation, more interviews were conducted as there was more variation in their answers. When cited in this study, the interviewees are identified by a code in order to maintain confidentiality. The interviewees are labelled as Kaur; the three generations are marked by their particular generation (that is, 1, 2, or 3), which is then followed by a number given to the specific individual. For instance, Kaur 3.6 refers to interviewee number 6 from the third generation. Many of the interviews of the first generation were translated from Punjabi into English. Four social service providers were also interviewed regarding gender issues in the Punjabi community.

THE TRADITIONAL ROLE AND EXPECTATIONS OF THE FEMALE

The first generation consists of the grandmothers, who are all Indian-born and spent their formative years in India, and therefore carry with them a strong traditional orientation characteristic of an agricultural society. First-generation women, who for the most part are illiterate, maintain an oral or traditional mode of communication. Their communication style involves telling stories and narrating traditions, while their thoughts express a collectivity orientation often in a concrete form based on personal life experiences (orality) (see Appendix 10.1 and Nayar and Sandhu 2006: 139–52; Nayar 2004: 28–33). It is important to note that they are often unable to relate to an understanding of something that is foreign to their own life experience. And, since knowledge is based on wisdom that has been orally passed down through the ages, change for them is a very slow process (Nayar and Sandhu 2006; Nayar 2004: 28–33).

In the larger context of the cycle of rebirth (*sansar*), life events are often accepted as one's fate or destiny (*kismet*). The life of Sikh villagers revolves around the *gurdwara* (Sikh temple). Upon entering the gurdwara, they approach the scripture with great reverence, prostrate, and then circumambulate around it. Subsequently, the elders join the congregation and chant the Divine Name (*nam-simran*), participate in devotional singing (*kirtan*), listen to sermons (*katha*), and recite the scripture (*path*). Since the first-generation women are most often illiterate, the hymns or prayers are known by memory for the purposes of kirtan and path. Devotion is expressed through respect for the sacred space, regardless of whether it is a picture of a Guru or the scripture itself.

The hagiographies or sacred biographies about the Gurus are in actuality central to Sikh belief and practice. Hagiographies convey a supernatural message in concrete terms suitable for the orality mode of thought. There is greater familiarity with the hagiographies of the Gurus than Sikh theology. The hagiographies are a testimony of faith in that they are stories reflecting the spiritual stature of their Gurus. It is the traditional role of grandmothers to narrate these stories to their grandchildren. Even though reverence is given to the words of the Guru, it is not uncommon for first-generation Sikh women to continue to adhere to folk beliefs; some, in fact, resort to superstitious practices like wearing a black string or amulet containing a mantra to ward off evil spirits, as well as seeking comfort from a traditional healer (*baba*).

The elders often hold the worldview of religion as one that encompasses all facets of life, including the socio-economic aspects of the family and the socio-political dimensions of the community (Nayar 2004: 128–33, 165–9). Family is the centre of all social organization; kinship forms the basis of one's identity. The governing principles of social behaviour include *dharam* (duty) and *izzat* (honour). One is to fulfil one's duty according to one's stage of life in order to maintain family honour (ibid.: 47–52). Duty and honour are also gender-based. The female's role is determined by her stage in life within the family context. Notwithstanding the Sikh value of gender equality (*Sikh Rahit Maryada* 1982),[2] the pan-Indian socio-religious law-book known as the *Code of Manu* (*Manusmrti* 1979) is a collection of the rules of life compiled around 200 BCE (Klostermaier 1989: 46–7, 419) and has shaped the manner in which gender roles are defined in South Asian communities, regardless of their religious background. *Manusmrti* states: 'In childhood let her remain under the control of her father; under the control of her husband in youth; and under the control of her son after the demise of her husband in old age (*Manusmrti* 1979: Chapter 5, verses 148–60). *Manusmrti* justifies this constraint on a woman's autonomy with the belief that women are the essential medium through which the traditional culture can be passed on to the next generation (Naidoo 1984: 338–50).

A girl is therefore reared so that she can fulfil her roles as a wife, a mother, and a daughter-in-law. Note the response made by an eighty-year-old Sikh woman when she was asked about the level of her education:

I went to school. It was in the home [laughs]. Mother taught caring for the house to the kids. We learned how to cook, make clothing and the value of respect for the elders. ... There was no school in the village (Kaur 1.14, trans., July 17, 2000, Vancouver, British Columbia, from Nayar 2004: 89).

It is imperative for a young maturing girl to maintain her virginity in order to be marriageable even as she simultaneously acquires the skills necessary for married life. Since the household is an economically interdependent unit, the woman has a crucial role; women's role is home-based, orientated toward the smooth functioning of the household, including activities such as cooking, cleaning, washing clothes, sewing, as well as childbearing and rearing.

Although social status is mainly ascribed, based on the family or caste she is born into, a Sikh woman also traditionally acquires status and respect in the wealth she possesses through her material possessions like gold jewellery and the son(s) she bears. There is not only great pressure for the woman to produce a son for the family at large, but the son also is her social security in old age. Respect is based on social status and seniority. Therefore, upon becoming a mother-in-law, it is now her turn to enjoy the respect and decision-making power within the household.

Even after migration to western Canada, the traditional value system and customs predominate even as there may be some adjustment in a new environment with a completely different system of values. The major changes relate to the family dynamics within the household. These include the shrinking of the family size to a nuclear family with grandparents. There is also a shift in the power dynamic as a direct result of the economic independence that the second generation experiences from participating in the paid labour force. In effect, the first generation elderly (both female and male) often find themselves economically dependent on the son and/or daughter-in-law (Nayar 2004: 54–6, 58–60; Choudhry 2001: 388–9).

This alteration in the power structure of the family can be a source of tension between the first and the second generations (Nayar 2004: 54–6; Choudhry 2001: 386–90). Tension continues to exist between the mother-in-law and daughter-in-law; the elders remember all that they had to do for their mother-in-law and thus feel the daughter-in-law should do the same. That is, the elder women feel that they have paid their dues as daughters-in-law, and now it is their turn to experience the respect and service as a wise elder. However, since there is often more autonomy in Canada for the daughter-in-law because she participates in the workforce, she may not necessarily feel the obligation to follow tradition in this respect.

While the tension between the first- and second-generation women is related to the impact of economic independence on the household, the tension that the first-generation women experience with the third generation is related to the influence of western social values on the latter and the resulting loss of Punjabi/Sikh culture or language. Communication and cultural barriers exist, which result in the attitude among the first-generation women that the Canadian-born children are 'selfish' because of their adopting independence as a value instead of sacrificing oneself for the welfare or benefit of the collective (Nayar 2004: 56–8).

Despite the challenges within the household, the major acculturation stress for first-generation women after migration to Canada is associated with their interactions with the mainstream (out-group stress), including language barriers, culture clash, and discrimination (Abouguendia and Noels 2001: 163–73). Out-group stress can and often does result in the experience of loneliness, social isolation, and alienation (ibid.; Choudhry 2001: 383–6). Since first-generation women continue to identify with their kin, group or clan, they place primary importance on social interaction with people from their family, the village or region, and caste from which they themselves have come. Therefore, interaction with mainstream society in Canada or even with other non-Sikh South Asians is often very limited, if it exists at all. As a consequence of social isolation, there is the tendency toward ethnic insularity, whereby first-generation women engage mostly in religious or cultural activities within their tight-knit social network based on extended family and clan. The gurdwara can be a home base where they can speak Punjabi and function according to traditional mores. Senior groups and senior centres are places of recreation, where women gather together to talk about cooking, clothing, their physical ailments, and family life.

THE TRANSITIONAL EXPERIENCE OF ECONOMIC INDEPENDENCE

The second generation consists of mothers who migrated to western Canada predominantly during the 1960s and 1970s. In contrast to the first-generation women, the second-generation women are, for the most part, able to read and write. They tend to possess the *literacy* mode of thinking (see Appendix 10.1), which reflects a shift to differentiating the 'self' from the collective. Knowledge is no longer limited to personal life experiences alone, but also includes concrete facts that have been read or formally learnt. Furthermore, while thought continues to be expressed in a concrete form, interpretation is now likely done at the literal level (Nayar and Sandhu 2006; Nayar 2004: 33–8).

These women have a traditional orientation toward the role of religion while also being able to read about their religion (Nayar 2004: 133–41). Being literate, second-generation women can also read or study the scripture. However, comprehension of the scriptural teachings may remain at the literal level. Continuous with the first generation, second generation women also pay great reverence to the words of Guru (*gurbani*) even as they may simultaneously also adhere to folk beliefs and/or give importance to the words of a traditional religious healer (baba). The second generation's traditional approach to religion however often results in the mixing of culture and religion, which can become a source of tension with their Canadian-born children.

Since religion and culture are understood as an integrated whole, the governing principles of social behaviour—dharam and izzat—continue to be viewed as religious-driven. One is expected to fulfil one's duty according to one's stage of life in order to maintain family honour. The notion of respect has, however, become modified; while it continues to be based on seniority, it is also taken as deserved by second-generation parents who have worked hard to survive and establish the family in a foreign environment. Second-generation women often experience both internal and external pressure to maintain traditional norms of dharam and izzat while simultaneously helping establish the family in the host society.

Many second-generation mothers have entered the paid workforce even if only on a temporary or seasonal basis. Women who enter the workforce begin to experience a sense of economic independence or autonomy (Nayar 2004: 60–4). Naidoo and Davis asserts that South Asian women have successfully adapted to modernity through distinguishing the economic sphere from the social values of the local society, treating the former as modern and the latter as Western (Naidoo and Davis 1988: 311–27). However, the values that come with or follow economic independence—like self-orientation—can become a source of intra-psychic tension; they are likely to engender conflict between fulfilling the traditional role expectation as wife and daughter-in-law and the desire to exercise personal choice. The outcome of this tension is the experience of alienation from role-playing; second-generation women are likely to feel alienated from playing the role of the 'obedient' wife and/or 'dutiful' daughter-in-law even as they have not fully developed self-orientation (Nayar 2004: 67).

The growing desire to assert personal choice places strain on the relationship between husband and wife as well as between daughter-in-law and mother-in-law (Nayar 2004: 64–9). Note the comment of a forty-six-year-old Sikh woman, who eventually rejected her role as the obedient wife and daughter-in-law:

... I worked hard and then had to give the money to [my] husband. I used to have to give the money, and [then] ask for money from my husband when I wanted to buy something. It was like this at the beginning, but now it has changed. My mother told me before marriage that you have to listen to your husband and in-laws. I did not listen to my in-laws, which is why there were problems (Kaur 2.19, September 14, 2000, Surrey, British Columbia, from Nayar 2004: 63).

Along with the experience of economic self-reliance, second-generation women continue to place great importance on rearing their children. While second-generation women often wholeheartedly provide for their children, such care is often based on how they remember children were reared back in the homeland. They expect that, in turn, children will be respectful of, and dutiful toward, their elders. However, there is often growing tension in rearing children in a western environment. Second-generation women (and men) as parents attempt to provide everything for their children; this finds concrete form in the showering of food, shelter, clothing, and material possessions on the children. In attempting to overcome their fear of losing control over the children in a western environment, they often provide material goods increasingly as their children reach adolescence (Nayar 2004: 69–70, 97–9).

There is strong pressure on second-generation women to fulfil their traditional womanly role by first having to produce a son and then to have him remain in the home after marriage. It can become very difficult for second-generation women when their son moves out because they have not yet developed their self-orientation enough to feel comfortable living solely with the husband. The collectivity remains important for the women's sense of connectedness—especially in relation to children and grandchildren—for their smooth functioning in the household and community at large. Furthermore, such women often lack the skills required to build a social network in a western environment. Despite their economic independence, second-generation women still have a strong traditional orientation and a psychosocial need for living amongst the extended family.

As with first-generation women, the major acculturation stressor for second-generation women is interaction with the mainstream (Abouguendia and Noels 2001: 163–73). On the other hand, the Punjabi community provides a familiar home base within the 'host' country, where one can speak the Punjabi language and behave according to the cultural mores of the homeland. However, even with the Punjabi community as the home base for second-generation women, there can be much in-group stress in relation to requiring their Canadian-born children to adhere to the traditional culture. There is pressure on second-generation women to assure that their children preserve the culture, which has become a new standard for maintaining family izzat.

LIVING IN A PUNJABI HOUSEHOLD WITHIN CANADIAN SOCIETY

The third generation consists of the daughters of immigrant parents. Since third-generation women have been educated in a western milieu, they have for the most part acquired the *analytics* mode of thinking (see Appendix 10.1), wherein self-orientation and critical inquiry are manifest. Furthermore, these women also demonstrate a move toward a mode of communication that involves an explorative and inquisitive style, in that abstract concepts are utilized to go beyond personal life experiences or the physical world (Nayar and Sandhu 2006: 142–6; Nayar 2004: 38–41). The questioning communication style possessed by third-generation women, however, can become a potential source of conflict with regard to intergenerational relations, especially since the first and second generations have an orientation that is rooted in tradition.

A lot of intra-psychic tension arises from living in a Punjabi household while at the same time functioning in a modern society (see Appendix 10.1) (Nayar 2004: 114–16). The familial-cultural value system initially forms the core of a Sikh's identity, making the maintainance of good family relations an important aspect of being a Canadian-born Sikh. However, because of socialization to western values that occurs in schools and because of greater interaction with mainstream society (which adheres to a wholly different value system), conflict easily emerges. The culture clash experienced by Sikhs, or South Asians in general, begins early in life since there is a lack of congruence between the child's two primary socialization agents: the parents and the teachers (Bhattacharya 2000: 77–85). The parents, who hold a traditional or collectivity orientation to education, tend to view education as a mechanism through which their children will acquire values and patterns of behaviour that will help them achieve in accordance with the family's interests. Parents, therefore, expect their children to respect the teacher, just like their parents would have done in their former homeland. However, since teachers in the west manifest an individualistic orientation—as a result of which students are encouraged to develop personal autonomy and critical thinking—children of South Asian immigrant parents often endure a considerable amount of intra-psychic tension due to the lack of congruence between their two primary socialization agents (ibid.: 77–85; Nayar 2004: 114–16).

The critical thinking encouraged in western education is eventually applied to the many facets of the third-generation woman's personal life, including inquiry into and exploration about Sikhism (Nayar 2004: 141–53). While for the first- and second-generation women, raising questions about Sikhism is considered rude and disrespectful, for third-generation women (and men) it may be a necessity in their acquiring an understanding of the religion. The hagiographical stories often transmitted by grandmothers seem illogical to those possessing an analytics mode of thinking. Third-generation Sikhs are likely to raise questions concerning history and theology that would perhaps seem to be of little relevance to those possessing an orality mode of thinking.

The gurdwara has traditionally been the centre of community life. Although interested in learning about their heritage, many Canadian-born Sikhs have drifted away from gurdwaras because of the politics, culture clashes, and the lack of proper facilities to learn about the Sikh tradition according to the western model of education. Since many are reared in traditional households, third-generation Sikh women often confront the challenge of having to reconcile the two disparate social contexts, which entails grappling with their position as females in the family, the Punjabi community, and mainstream society in general. Thus, in some cases the analytics mode of thinking can lead women to re-evaluate their own belief system and socio-cultural practices. Take the comments of a twenty-two-year-old Canadian-born Sikh woman:

I went to—Gurdwara. There was a display about the Sikh tradition. When I asked the Sikh administrator about the status of women in Sikhism, he answered 'Read it in the *Sikh Rahit Maryada* (Code of Sikh Conduct and Conventions). It says it in there. In Sikhism there is gender equality. The discussion ended there. He was not willing to discuss the practices in the community or answer why there are never women *giani*s or female participants as a *panj piari* ('beloved five', the representatives of the five Khalsa Sikhs chosen by Guru Gobind Singh), (Kaur 3.9, March 20, 2000, Vancouver, British Columbia).

This is not only an example of conflict between the different styles of communication (the literacy and analytical modes of thinking), but it also reveals the culture barrier in discussing gender equality in the context of Sikh tradition. While the *Sikh Rahit Maryada* does put forth the proposition that Sikhism teaches gender equality, the issue is not adequately addressed or discussed. For third-generation Sikh women, the main point of inquiry and/or contention concerns gender equality both in terms of the Sikh tradition and their life situation in the Punjabi community. In fact, religion for them no longer encompasses all facets of life as it does for the first and second generations. Rather, the third generation increasingly makes a distinction between Punjabi culture and Sikhism.

While third-generation females are raised in the household to act according the traditional mores of Punjabi culture—to learn the skills necessary for married life—they are also exposed to the opportunities and choices found in western society. Many believe that respect should be based on being human and on one's own personal achievement. In being raised in a traditional Punjabi household in the midst of Canadian society, third-generation women experience a double standard to a large degree, especially when there are brothers and/or male cousins in the extended family. This situation further exacerbates tension because while having to grapple with parental expectations and the demands of mainstream culture, they see more freedom being given to their male siblings.

The double standard often manifests itself in terms of the freedom, or lack of it, surrounding social life with one's peers, especially after primary school, and secondly regarding career choice (Ghuman 1994: 229–43). While there may be a strong sentiment among parents for their children to become well educated, third-generation women face the pressure to remain in the home until marriage, thus making it difficult for them to study away from home. Furthermore, the pressure to marry by the age of twenty-five becomes an obstacle for them (Talbani and Hasanali 2000: 615–27; Nayar 2004: 101–3). At times, some third-generation women feel the pressure to quickly finish a diploma programme that will allow them to make money and to be marriageable during their early twenties. In some cases, women marry with the belief that 'it [marriage] will give them

With entrance into the Canadian labour force, second-generation women demonstrate some change in their cultural orientation even as they adhere to many traditional mores. With economic independence, many other values associated with it, like personal choice, soon follow. The experience of economic independence is the primary catalyst to the impact of modernity on the Sikh community; it entails the shift in the power dynamic within the household.

Third-generation women, who are not only born in western society but educated in, and socialized by, western institutions, are even more exposed to the value differences between the two systems. While in the home they are reared to conform to the traditional norms of dharam and izzat for the benefit of the collective whole, third-generation women are exposed to the modern ideals of developing self-orientation, individual choice and personal achievement. Thus, the clash between the value systems of tradition and modernity becomes a major source of intergenerational tensions.

The unintended intergenerational tension that exists is, of course, to be expected as the Sikh community shifts from an agricultural society that is 'transplanted' in a modernized western country such as Canada. There is necessarily a time lag in the adjustment to the value system of a wholly different society, and therefore in the smooth functioning of the community in its new modern setting. In the process of coping with the communication barriers and social contradiction of their existential situation, many Canadian-born Sikh women have also come to experience additional inner conflict resulting from the intrinsic contradiction between Punjabi cultural values and Sikh religious beliefs, the topic of the following section.

The Intrinsic Contradiction between Sikh Religion and Punjabi Culture

While women face tension between tradition and modernity, an often overlooked source of inner conflict for many Canadian-born Sikh women surrounds the intrinsic contradiction between their traditional Punjabi cultural values and Sikh religious beliefs (see Appendix 10.1). There is, indeed, a complex relationship between Punjabi culture and the Sikh religion. Historically, the culture preceded the religion. Punjabi culture, which is over two millennia old, has a stronghold over Punjabis, the people from the regional linguistic-cultural group from the region of the Punjab. In contrast, the Sikh religion emerged in the fifteenth century in reaction to the contemporaneous pan-Indian and Punjabi cultural values and practices. Although Sikh theology is universal, for the most part its adherents were limited to the Punjab. As a result, Sikhism as practised in the Punjab became imbued with Punjabi cultural values.

There is confusion surrounding the relationship between culture and religion in the Sikh diaspora (Nayar 2004: 141–4). The third generation experiences confusion between religion and culture as a result of the way in which the first and/or second generations have imparted religion to the third generation (ibid.: 144–9). Some third-generation women were able to clearly articulate their frustration about how Punjabi customs are passed down from their parents as religion when in fact there is a difference between the two. Note the passionate response, expressing frustration, offered by a twenty-three-year-old Sikh woman:

Kismet is not abuse. Guys do not put up with shit because of kismet. [Women] should fight abuse because they are in the right. Guru Granth Sahib is greater than cultural norms. What is understood as kismet is culturally defined. I am born in a religion, which states [establishes] equality. ... Kids are anti-religious until they hear that [there is a difference between culture and religion]. Kids are confused because their parents present religion as culture mixed with religion (Kaur 3.27, September 11, 2000, Richmond, British Columbia, in Nayar 2004: 144).

Indeed, the position of women in the Sikh community was the most common Punjabi custom that third-generation women saw as clashing with their scripture.

The confusion surrounding the relationship between culture and religion can, in part, be related to the different attitudes among the three generations toward the relationship between religion, culture, and society. Religion in traditional society encompasses all aspects of life. In contrast, modernity is more specialized and differentiated, as a consequence of which a distinction is made between culture and religion. For the first- and second-generation Sikh women, religion is the foundation of their culture and therefore it encompasses culture. However, more freedom, life will begin [anew], only to find themselves in the exact situation of their birth home' (Kaur 3.23, July 19, 2000, Vancouver, British Columbia).

Even though they may still experience out-group stress related to prejudice and discrimination (though less than their second-generation parents), the acculturation stressors for third-generation women predominantly lie within the Punjabi community (in-group stress) and the family (family stress). In-group and family stress often occurs as a result of the pressures to conform to or preserve one's culture, and to fulfil traditional roles for the sake of family honour. For example, college Sikh women may wear modest clothing and have their hair tied up in a bun when leaving the house, yet change their appearance with their peers at school or in a shopping mall. However, in-group stress also results from lack of support from one's own cultural group for becoming 'too Canadian' (Abouguendia and Noels 2001: 163–73). The in-group and family stress can often result in both the experience of playing the role of the 'dutiful' daughter and/or living a double life in order to be able to engage in western social activity (Nayar 2004: 103–5). While the playing of incongruent roles may be understood as a coping mechanism in their existential situation, such strategy can be a great source of feelings of anxiety, guilt, alienation, and confusion.

TENSION BETWEEN TRADITION AND MODERNITY

Most of the Sikh immigrants have come predominantly from an agricultural farming community. They have therefore brought with them the beliefs, values, and customs of their Punjabi culture and the mode of communication rooted in the traditional society of village Punjab. At the same time, they are subjected to the demands of living in Canadian society with its modern values. In effect, there results an unintended but inevitable clash between two different social systems—tradition and modernity.

The first-generation women reflect, for the most part, the traditional orientation of the role and status of women in a patriarchal society. Since religion encompasses all facets of social life, the female role is viewed as part of their Sikh worldview. Even after migration to a western environment, first-generation women usually hold a strong traditional orientation.

third-generation Sikh women view religion and culture
more discriminatingly and critically; they feel that there is a
considerable difference or even contradiction between Punjabi
culture and Sikh religion. Indeed, modernity has had an impact
on the third generation's approach to understanding religion.

While there is a radical difference between Punjabi culture
and the Sikh spiritual teachings, traditional Sikh mentality
approaches the two as an integrated whole despite the fact that
that *the customs are often in direct contradiction with the scriptural
teachings.* And, while Sikhism may speak against the many
traditional socio-cultural practices—like the position of women
and the caste system—as unjust, the highly 'masculinized' Sikh
tradition has been unable to get rid of these strongly ingrained
cultural norms (Singh 2005; Jakobsh 2003).[3]

Women, especially, reproach the mixing of Punjabi culture
and Sikh religion as a hindrance to their plea for social equality,
given the cultural norms that prevail in the community. Another
Sikh woman of twenty-three years noted:

There is confusion in the community, both young and old, regarding religion
and culture; while they interact they are not the same. Culture deals with
the day-to-day affairs whereas religion is an addition. The problems are
not with the religion, they are with the culture. If the cultural problems are
helped, then one would be free to prastice the religion (Kaur 3.23, July 19,
2000, Vancouver, British Columbia, in Nayar 2004: 144).

Along with the confusion between Punjabi cultural values
and Sikh spiritual teachings, hearing about the Sikh value of
gender equality in sermons (*katha*) offered at the gurdwara
or reading about it in texts including the *Sikh Rahit Maryada*
(1982), or even reciting the daily prayer composed by Guru
Nanak called *Asa di Var*, can also reinforce feelings of alienation
among Canadian-born Sikh women. The prayer called *Asa di
Var*, in a sense, uplifts the position of women at the time when
Guru Nanak composed it:

From the woman is our birth, in the womb we are shaped.
To the woman we are engaged, to the woman we are married.
The woman is our friend and from the woman is the family.
If one woman dies, we seek another;
Through the woman are the bonds of the world.
Why call a woman evil?
She gives birth to kings!

From the woman comes the woman;
Without the woman there is none (*Adi Sri Guru Granth Sahib*: 473).

However, verses like the one cited above can leave third-generation Sikh women disheartened because it is not reflected in the attitudes prevalent in the community. This experiential contradiction for many triggers feelings of alienation and/or confusion even as it may in some serve as a catalyst for some inquiry into the teachings of Sikhism.

In the primary Sikh scriptural text, known as the Adi Sri Guru Granth Sahib or Guru Granth Sahib, Guru Nanak critiques the prevailing socio-religious norms. Guru Nanak not only explicitly discounts the specific socio-religious goals—like begetting a son or acquiring izzat—but, in doing so, he also mocks the patriarchy of the traditional household. According to Guru Nanak, one ought to renounce the ego while 'living-in-the-world' through becoming a socially involved renunciate.[4] He expresses this through a poetic critique of the socio-cultural norms of his time. For Guru Nanak, the experience of honour (izzat), such as begetting a son or accumulating wealth, is attachment to illusion (*maya*). And, for him, it is this desire of acquiring worldly goals that brings suffering (Sandhu 2004: 33–46).[5] The dominance of the Punjabi cultural hold on the Sikh religion has, however, resulted in Sikh institutions being more reflective of Punjabi norms than of Sikh spiritual values (Nayar and Sandhu 2007).

The contradiction between many Sikh religious and Punjabi cultural values actually highlights the strategic means to empower women who find themselves caught between Punjabi households and mainstream Canadian society (Sandhu 2005: 40–51). Ironically, third-generation women eager to resolve cultural issues surrounding the role and status of women can, in fact, use the Sikh theological teachings about gender equality as an intellectual framework. In effect, they can seek validation for their cause from within their Sikh heritage. While there may be a major clash between Punjabi culture and Sikh religion, the actual Sikh religious value of gender equality can be used to assist in the erosion of patriarchy that is associated with modernity (Nayar 2004: 169–76). In some respects, the attempt to uplift the status of women and the value of universality found in Sikh scripture can be used as an intellectual framework by third-generation

Sikh women in their plea against the double standard and the traditional gender role expectations that exist in the Punjabi culture, and by extension in the B.C. Sikh community.

The Sikh religious teachings about gender equality can also, in turn, be used to modify traditional Punjabi cultural practices. Take, for example, the statement of a twenty-year-old Sikh woman:

There is confusion between the theology and customs of Sikhism/Punjab. There is equality [of human life] in terms of the theology. However, because of this confusion, people, both males and females, turn away from the religion. The issues of equality in terms of culture and custom need to change and will over time (Kaur 3.8, March 21, 2000, Vancouver, British Columbia, in Nayar 2004: 143–4).

Interestingly, recently the Canadian-born generations of Sikhs, who are starting new families, are spawning off change or at least modifying Punjabi customs. For instance, sweets are now offered to family and friends on the birth of a daughter (instead of only passing out *laddoo*s on the birth of a son). Likewise, there has also been some change over the last several years in the Punjabi festival called Lohri—which celebrates the birth of the first male child. While traditionally Lohri has been specifically oriented to the son, there has recently been an active attempt on the part of some Sikhs in the Vancouver Lower Mainland to include the celebration of the birth of daughters, which is now referred to as *kuri-munda lohri* (girl-boy Lohri).

CONCLUSIONS

The Sikh community, which hails from an agricultural society, has no doubt upon arrival in western Canada experienced the tensions that are natural to the clash between traditional society and modern society. Economic independence is having an inevitable impact on the Sikh community, causing for some change in traditional values and customs. In effect, the Canadian-born Sikh youth is facing challenges primarily related to grappling with the contradictory orientation of their Punjabi household and the modernized western educational institution, their two main socializing agents.

The issue of gender equality has emerged as a predominant issue for third-generation Sikh women. In their experience with parental expectations about fulfilling traditional female roles, third-generation Sikh women encounter the double standard in relation to the treatment of brothers or male cousins. In coping with the family stress of conforming to traditional expectations— albeit modified somewhat—and the desire to 'fit in' with western culture, third-generation Sikh women often resort to role-playing and living a double life. While such mechanisms are but a strategy to deal with their fears about alienating the family, which continues to form a strong aspect of their identity, they can often become a source of anxiety, guilt, and alienation.

Besides the tension between tradition and modernity, which is inevitable and predictable, there is another source of psychic tension for third-generation women that is often overlooked. That pertains to the intrinsic contradiction between their Punjabi culture and Sikh religion. Ironically, the scriptural teachings of the Sikh religion attempting to uplift the status of women, can serve as a tool for third-generation women to empower themselves in their situation of being caught between the conflicting values of tradition and modernity. Interestingly, some Canadian-born Sikhs are beginning to initiate change— or at the very least—modifying Punjabi customs according to intrinsic Sikh religious values.

NOTES

1. A participatory observer shows greater allegiance to the observer role even as he/she participates in order to blend in and cultivate a 'feel' for the subject matter (see Palys 1992: 210).

2. The Shiromani Gurdwara Parbandhak Committee was set up in 1925 by the Sikh electorate to administer the principal gurdwaras, and issued the *Sikh Rahit Maryada* (Sikh Code of Conduct) in order to delineate the rules and principles for Sikhs and to distinguish the Punjabi-Sikhs from the other Punjabis.

3. For a detailed discussion on the 'highly masculinized' evolution of the Sikh tradition (see Singh 2005 and Jakobsh 2003).

4. Guru Nanak denounces the traditional role of the householder, especially in regard to its ego-oriented goals of acquiring the 'fruits' of (1) wealth (*arth*), (2) sensual-pleasures (*kam*), and (3) religious merit (*dharam*). (*Sri Guru Granth Sahib*: 61.)

5. 'The desire for maya attaches one to one's son, relatives, household and wife. ... Attachment has robbed me, and the ego has destroyed the world.' (*Sri Guru Granth Sahib*: 61).

REFERENCES

Abouguendia, M. and K. Noels (2001). 'General and acculturation related daily hassles and psychological adjustment in first and second generation South Asian immigrants to Canada', *International Journal of Psychology*, Vol. 36, No. 3, pp. 163–73.

Adi Sri Guru Granth Sahib (Sri Damdami Bir). Amritsar: Sri Gurmat Press, standard pagination.

Basran, Gurcharan S. and Bolaria, B. Singh (2003). *The Sikhs in Canada: Migration, Race, Class, and Gender*, New Delhi: Oxford University Press.

Bhattacharya, G. (2000). 'The school adjustment of South Asian immigrant children in the United States', *Adolescence*, Vol. 35, No. 137, pp. 77–85.

Chadney, James (1984). *The Sikhs of Vancouver*, New York: AMS Press.

Choudhry, U.K. (2001). 'Uprooting and Resettling Experiences of South Asian Women', *Western Journal of Nursing Research*, Vol. 23, No. 4, pp. 376–93.

Ghuman, P.A.S. (1994). 'Canadian or Indo-Canadian: A Study of South Asian Adolescents', *International Journal of Adolescence and Youth*, Vol. 4, pp. 229–43.

Jakobsh, Doris R. (2003). *Relocating Gender in Sikh History: Transformation, Meaning, and Identity*, New Delhi: Oxford University Press.

Johnston, Hugh (1988). 'Patterns of Sikh Migration to Canada 1900–1960', in Joseph T. O'Connell, Milton Israel, and Willard Oxtoby (eds), *Sikh History and Religion in the 20th Century*, Toronto: Centre for South Asian Studies, University of Toronto, pp. 296–313.

Klostermaier, Klaus K. (1989). *A Survey of Hinduism*, Albany: State University of New York Press.

Manusmrti. (1979). tr., M.N. Dutt, Varanasi: Chowkhamba Press.

Naidoo, Josephine C. (1984). 'Contemporary South Asian Women in the Canadin Mosic', in P. Caplan et al. (eds), *Sex Roles II: Feminist Psychology in Transition*, Montreal: Eden Press, pp. 338–50.

Naidoo, Josephine C. and J. Campbell Davis (1988). 'Canadian South Asian Women in Transition: A Dualistic View of Life, *Journal of Comparative Family Studies*, Vol. 19, pp. 311–27.

Nayar, Kamala Elizabeth (2004). *The Sikh Diaspora in Vancouver: Three Generations amid Tradition, Modernity and Multiculturalism*, Toronto: University of Toronto Press.

Nayar, Kamala Elizabeth and Jaswinder S. Sandhu (2006). 'Intergenerational Communication in Immigrant Punjabi Families: Implications for Helping Professionals', *International Journal for the Advancement of Counseling*, Vol. 28, No. 2, pp. 139–52.

—— (2007). *The Socially Involved Renuuniate: Guru Nanak's 'Discourse to the Nath Yogis'*, Albany: State University of New York Press.

Palys, T. (1992). *Research Decisions: Quantitative and Qualitative Perspectives*, Toronto: Harcourt Brace Jovanovich.

Sandhu, Jaswinder S. (2004). 'The Sikh Model of the Person, Suffering, and Healing: Implications for Counselors', *International Journal for the Advancement of Counselling*, Vol. 26, No. 1, pp. 33–46.

—— (2005). 'A Sikh Perspective on Life-Stress: Implications for Counseling', *Canadian Journal of Counseling*, Vol. 39, No. 1, pp. 40–51.

Sikh Rahit Maryada (1982). Amritsar: Shiromani Gurdwara Parbandhak Committee.

Singh, Nikky-Guninder Kaur (2005). *The Birth of the Khalsa: A Feminist Re-memory of Sikh Identity*, Albany: State University of New York Press.

Sri Guru Granth Sahib (1993). Translated and annotated by Gopal Singh, 4 Vols, New Delhi: World Book Centre.

Statistics Canada (2006). 'Population by Religion by Province and Territory (2001 Census)', retrieved on-line at www.statcan.ca, 25 March 2006.

Talbani, Aziz and Parveen Hasanali (2000). 'Adolescent Females between Tradition and Modernity: Gender Role Socialization in South Asian Immigrant Culture', *Journal of Adolescence*, Vol. 23, No. 5, pp. 615–27.

Wood, John (1978). 'East Indians and Canada's New Immigration Policy', *Canadian Public Policy*, Vol. 4, No. 4, pp. 547–67.

Appendix 10.1

Religious and Social Elements according to Traditional Punjabi Values,
Sikh Spiritual Beliefs, and Modern Social Ideals

Religious and Social Elements	Traditional Punjabi Values	Sikh Spiritual Beliefs	Modern Social Ideals
Religious Elements: Worldview	Homogeneous; Religion encompasses all facets of life; One's fate or destiny (kismet); Cycle of rebirth (*sansar*)	Universality; *Sansar*; Ultimate Reality or the single underlying spiritual essence that exists within all (*EkOnkar*)	Heterogeneous; Religion weakens with the rise of science
Role of Religion	High priority given to religion as a form of social control; Accumulating good merit for a better rebirth	High priority given to liberation (*mukti*) from *sansar* and the betterment of humanity	Decline in religious institutions as an aspect of social control
Religious Belief	Folklore; Good and evil spirits; Concept of the evil eye	Inner five vices (attachment, greed, anger, lust, and ego) are the source of suffering; Following the will or teachings of the Guru is the only means toward liberation	Heterogeneous; Split between theology, and philosophy
Religious Practice	Evil spirits can be destroyed through magic; Wearing amulets or black string to ward off evil spirits	The five spheres of spiritual development (righteousness, knowledge, effort, grace and truth); Meditation on Guru's name (*namjapo*), hard work and honest living (*kirat karo*), sharing one's earnings with the needy (*vand ke chhako*)	Heterogeneous
Social Elements: Communication	Storytelling; Questioning is regarded as rude; Formal gossip (*gup shup*)	Inquiry and dialogue are encouraged	Critical and objective inquiry

Relationships	Collectivity-orientation; Connectedness to family, clan, and ethnic group; Little anonymity and privacy	Self-orientation; Connectedness to Ultimate Reality (*EkOnkar*); Rely on, or keep the company of, others on the path (*sadh sangat*)	Self-orientation; Considerable anonymity and privacy
Family	Interdependence; Extended family; Attachment to family members is encouraged; Central for socialization and production	Worldly attachment to family and others is regarded as a barrier to liberation or connectedness with *EkOnkar*	Nuclear family; Some socialization but more of a unit of consumption
Status	Predominantly ascribed; Also attained through power and wealth	The desire for permanence through status, wealth, and power is viewed as a disease	Both ascribed and achieved; Meritocracy
Gender Pattern	Patriarchal; Gender role expectation; Woman is dependent on father, husband, and sons	Soul transcends gender; Person strives for a balance between masculine and feminine qualities	Declining patriarchy; Increase in women entering the paid workforce
Stratification	Caste system; Rigid pattern of social inequality with little mobility	Against the caste system; All humans are equal regardless of caste, creed, and gender	Fluid patterns of social inequality with considerable mobility

Making Sikh Women Refugees in 1990's USA*

Inderpal Grewal

As human rights' advocates argued that the refugee asylum system of the late-twentieth century did not safeguard the human rights of refugees and that nation-states often evaded their responsibilities in providing safety and security to citizens (*Amnesty International Annual Report* 1997), they consolidated human rights as an effective tool for addressing the refugee crisis. Human rights instruments served as key mechanisms for management of refugees and for many at the risk of violence, especially with regard to asylum to the West, that is, to Europe and North America. On the one hand, these instruments were used to select a few refugees out of populations of tens of millions as appropriate for admission into the countries of the West, and on the other, they justified expansion of new kinds of criteria under which refugees could be identified. Such strategies of expansion were visible most clearly in the 1990s in the debates regarding asylum on the basis of gender. Yet what was clear was that the mechanisms for refugee asylum in the West worked through the production of knowledge generated not simply by the state, but also through a number of non-state transnational organizations and institutions that created transnational connectivities.[1]

In the case of persons seeking asylum on the basis of being persecuted as Sikh women in Punjab in the 1990s, it was also the local Sikh communities seeking to protect and help these asylees who utilized these discourses of human rights. This essay examines the ways in which Sikh female refugee subjects in the West were produced through gendered human rights discourses, and the ways in which some were able to become such subjects, while many others failed to do so. However, the process raises questions about the criteria and mechanisms used to provide asylum and the construction of the Sikh woman as refugee subject.

While feminists critiqued the representations of the refugee as a male subject and produced alternate representations of female refugee subjects, western states, such as the US, used these critiques to select out appropriately deserving female refugees who were allowed to settle in the US. Others were prevented from entering, either by denial of refugee status or by the refusal to prevent those fleeing violence to leave their countries (Dubernet 2001).[2] By instituting modes of adjudicating which refugees had truly suffered human rights abuses, the US was able to contain the numbers of persons from Asia, Africa, or Latin America while maintaining its nationalist discourse of being a country that supported freedom and humanitarian efforts. For instance, the Senate Report on the landmark 1980 Refugee Act stated that the Act 'reflects one of the oldest themes in America's history—welcoming homeless refugees to our shores. It gives statutory meaning to our national commitment to human rights and humanitarian concerns....' (United States Congress. Senate Judiciary Committee 1979). Yet this 'national commitment' relied on racialized and gendered regimes of knowledge based on human rights.

In this framework, then, of understanding how human rights discourse worked in refugee asylum and the ways in which dominant frameworks of a benevolent nation and state constructed unequal transnational subjects, I will focus on the production of Sikh women from Punjab as refugees in the US during the 1990s. By examining the construction of such gendered subjects as 'victims of violence' or 'victims of human rights violations' (Ervolina 1995), institutionalized through a globalized discourse of human rights and feminism that was taken up in some measure by the US state, I suggest the ways in which national and international regimes of knowledge production create transnational subjects. I argue that the mobilization by a nation-state such as the US of human rights within refugee asylum produced transnational subjects which were both cosmopolitan and national; the politics of humanitarian cosmopolitanism existed alongside the politics of religious nationalism and state nationalisms. The refugee in the US was both the subject of the state, but also of an internationalism and a cosmopolitanism constituted through humanist discourses of rights and liberal freedoms that moved sometimes powerfully and sometimes less so within transnational connectivities. Neo-colonial racial, gendered, and classed discourses operated within the networks of such connectivities through which individuals, communities, NGOs, and states communicated with each other. Thus, my approach examines refugees not in the terms of their belonging to diasporic communities, but as constructed within networks of human rights discourses that moved between states, communities, organizations, and individuals.

In order to explain how discourses moved within connectivities to produce transnational subjects who were also subjects of states, I will examine how a transnationally connected US cultural feminism's focus on sexual abuse as the dominant sign of the oppression of women became the paradigmatic experience constructing the female refugee. By critiquing the discourse of sexual exploitation within the production of the female refugee, I do not mean to disregard the pain and suffering of sexual abuse and violence. Rather, my goal is to understand how these discourses of pain and suffering produced new subjects of transnational governmentality as well as of American nationalism that was also raced and gendered.

However, while this essay is focused on the narratives that enabled Sikh women refugee applicants to obtain asylum, it is also an important reminder that there are many who are unable to cross borders. This inability may suggest a weak connectivity or cosmopolitanism in that these were subjects who failed to become the subjects of the US state. They are a reminder that discussions of cosmopolitans as border-crossers, or as internationalists, or as national and international subjects, or as part of transnational migrant networks are often based on those who are seen as strongly connected transnationally rather than on those who fail to connect or cannot cross boundaries. They are also a reminder that nationalisms, states, gender, class, and race interact in myriad ways to produce many different subjects, not all of whom are claimed by state or nation. At the very least, in the context of this chapter, attention to those who fail to make a successful claim of asylum tells us a great deal about the nature of migrant networks, and of the specificities of gendered, racialized, and classed subjectivities in relation to nation and state.

Since my focus is the advocacy for refugee asylum based on gender, and their debates and the ways in which these become connected to the narratives of Sikh women from Punjab seeking refugee asylum in the US, I use the term 'Sikh' as a religious subject (gendered male for the most part) which becomes identified through the 1980s by the Indian state as a figure of terror. Within Sikh nationalism, the 'Sikh' was a transnational subject created out of diaspora (Axel 2001) and homeland politics as well as state nationalism and religious nationalism. Human Rights discourses also participated in producing knowledge of Sikhs, as has the academic field known as Sikh Studies. The masculinity of this subject is the point at which all of these knowledges coincide and it is the problematic of what is left out of such a normative gendering that I end this essay.

In the context of transnational knowledge production and Indian nationalisms, it is important to examine the use of human rights discourses in India. While some groups in India through the 1990s used human rights to combat its violation by the 'law and order' machinery of the government in Punjab which regularly killed and tortured mostly poor people in jail,[3] other groups began to argue for the democratic rights of powerful Hindu fundamentalists ('Rights: Rethinking Theory and Practice' 1998). In addition, the Indian state began to assert its adherence to human rights doctrine by claiming, for instance, that such instruments were part of its training of police officers (Subramaniam 2000). In such a context, the denial of rights of those identified as minorities in the nation was also justified by a Hindu-majority state through representational practices in the media in which Sikhs and Muslims could be designated as 'militants' or 'terrorists'. At the same time, Sikh groups in the US, many of them collaborating as the World Sikh Council, organized against state violence by utilizing the discourse of human rights after the Indian state intensified its counter-insurgency efforts. They did so to bring their issues to the US Congress so that the US government could pressure the Indian government on its human rights record. Sikh community leaders, who were committed to fighting the Indian state's counter-insurgency operations, lobbied their legislators and were able to get a number of Congressmen, mostly Republicans, since Democrats were less critical of the Indian state, to put forward criticisms of India in terms of human rights violations. During the 1990s, when the state operations to clear Punjab of 'militants' allowed security forces to kill civilians and others with impunity,[4] many Sikh groups in the US organized to use human rights as a tool to fight against the Indian state practices of killing through 'encounters' and 'disappearances'. A number of articles in the newspaper of the World Sikh Council, *World Sikh News*, published out of Stockton, California, routinely reported on Amnesty International's findings or those of Physicians for Human Rights or other news reports on the topic. An example of this reporting was an article entitled 'Human Rights under Siege in India', which summarized a *Toronto Star* news report on anti-Muslim violence in Bombay, gang rapes and killings by security forces in Assam and Kashmir and police brutality in Punjab ('Human Rights Under siege in India' 1993: 4). One can see in virtually every issue of this newspaper through the 1990s there appeared one or two articles on the topic, along with reports on Canadian and US politicians supporting the condemnation of human rights violations by the Indian state.

Ultimately, while human rights discourses were not effective enough to prevent police terror or combat state discourses of 'security' or even to address the needs of many who were jailed for being militants, they were helpful in putting pressure on the Indian government to defend its human rights record. An additional benefit emerged as human rights discourses were used by Sikhs to get refugee asylum in the US if they could prove that they were targeted by the police and the Indian state.

Such utilizations of human rights were not confined to India. Rather, the knowledge of these utilizations moved through the transnational connectivities through which first Sikh men, and then, women, were able to claim human rights abuses by the Indian state and thus seek refugee asylum in the US. Transnational migrant networks have been vital for Sikh nationalisms through the twentieth century to constitute themselves as adherents of a 'world religion' and thus as a group with a distinctive religious identity (Dusenbery 1989). The *World Sikh News* constituted one set of networks through which information about refugee asylum cases as well as news about India and human rights violations, was disseminated in both English and Punjabi. In 1993, for instance, there were five separate articles regarding asylum gained by Sikhs especially by the efforts of one lawyer who was reported to have been successful in over thirty such cases. Most of those reported in the *World Sikh News* were cases of young men who had been part of the All India Sikh Students Federation (AISSF) and had been detained and tortured by security forces ('Five AISSF activists granted asylum'). One report, however, mentioned a young woman who had obtained asylum; she had been part of the AISSF as well, and the *World Sikh News* reported that she had been 'molested' and tortured in jail 'because of her political opinion and active participation by peaceful manners to achieve independence from India' ('Political Asylum for Sikh woman' 1993). The newspaper reported that her case was decided by an asylum officer in San Francisco rather than by the Board of Immigration Appeals which heard claims after asylum had been denied.

Under United States law there were two ways in which an asylum claim could be heard. There were 'affirmative' claims in which a person applied directly to the Immigration and Naturalization Service (INS) for asylum and these were claims heard by an asylum officer and believed to be 'non-adversarial' (Lynch and Scialabb 1997: 73–5).[5] There were also 'defensive' claims which arose when the INS had begun a deportation proceeding and the claimant had to seek relief from deportation. These hearings were conducted before an immigration judge and, if appealed, went before the Board of Immigration Appeals, which was a twelve-member panel whose decisions were binding on the INS (ibid.).

In order to indicate a 'well-founded fear of persecution', the evidence to be presented before the Asylum Officer could include US state department country reports, information from domestic or international human rights monitoring agencies, academic institutions, or other NGOs. Evidence included information from the asylum seeker which had to be credible and evidence from friends and relatives was accepted (Jackman

1992). The US Court of appeals recognized in 1984 that corrob-
orative evidence was not required if the claimant's testimony was
persuasive or credible (ibid.). Claims of human rights violations,
especially through torture or political detention, were often part
of narratives through which refugee asylum was granted.

In a practice that had continuities with early twentieth-
century Chinese immigration to the US, when immigrants were
detained on Angel Island and had to prove through examination
by authorities that their papers were legitimate, getting through
the INS remained a major hurdle in which the hearings were
like examinations that had to be passed or a claimant could be
deported. Asylum officers, even in supposedly 'non-adversarial'
situations, had to make determinations about the veracity of
claims and to show how claims fit legal and cultural standards.
The so-called 'non-adversarial' process simply meant that
lawyers were not involved in arguments on both sides, but did
not mean that the process involved equal parties. Since the INS
rejected many thousands of claims and deported a large number
of those who sought asylum, the Asylum Officer had a great deal
of power. Often the Asylum Officer was the only person before
whom a claimant could be heard; although recent changes in
refugee law has meant that officers at an airport can hear a claim
and make a judgement of deportation before the claim moves
through the DHS. While notions of credibility changed to allow
that 'credible' claimants could present contradictory information
because of fear or trauma, asylum officers regularly demanded
that claimants not depart from the legal and cultural conceptions
that the officers held, or, from the historical accounts presented
by 'experts' or by the State Department.

The credibility demanded by current US refugee asylum laws
required that human rights violations, as defined in the Geneva
Convention, became the measure of the necessity for rescue.
Thus, Asylum Officers task was to figure out whether human
rights violations had taken place. Questions of credibility were
important especially since the job of the Asylum Officers was to
judge who had really been persecuted. In such determinations,
cultural and political questions became key measures to assess
credibility regarding human rights abuses. By recuperating global
feminism's universal female subject through the guidelines for

gender-based asylum, US state practices frequently identified rape as a determining factor of human rights violations in these claims (Kelly 1993). Even in political asylum cases, the impact of US cultural feminism and its emphasis on rape as a primary determinant of violence against women meant that other forms of violence did not make such an impact at asylum hearings. The threat of rape became the most important determinant of persecution for women, and the raped woman was the paradigmatic female refugee. A woman's credibility thus often depended on her ability to convey the threat of rape or the experience or trauma of rape to the hearing officer. Although, as Eithne Lubhéid points out, only 'certain instances of rape are deemed to merit asylum' it is striking that rape became the paradigmatic way to establish persecution if the claimant was a woman (Lubhéid 2002: 113). Credibility regarding rape became one of the technologies for selecting the truly deserving refugee as the one who had suffered human rights abuses. Given the centrality of the figure of the raped woman in a great deal of nationalist discourse, and since Sikh nationalism was no exception to such representations, the use of rape as a determinant of human rights violations was central to seeking asylum for Sikh women.

While in the early 1990s many men from Punjab were applying for asylum because they presented claims that the Indian state persecuted them, by 1993 some women began applying for asylum. Here we are not talking about vast numbers, although it is difficult to obtain information on numbers of people already in the US who were given refugee asylum. One US State Department document from the Bureau of Democracy, Human Rights and Labor mentioned that as of 30 September 1995, there were 8,789 applications from Indian citizens pending before the INS Asylum officers, and that 3,209 applications were filed in FY 1994; out of these the report estimates that about 65 per cent of applicants were Sikhs ('United States Department of State' 1996). However, this report does not mention how many of these applicants obtained refugee asylum. These numbers suggest that refugees from South Asia may not be very large especially in comparison with other groups. From 1996–8, each year the ceiling for refugee admission from a category called

Near East/South Asia was approximately 4,000, with a majority coming from Iraq and Iran ('United States Department of State' 1998).

According to the INS and community workers in legal non-profits, claims by the Sikh women stated that they were being persecuted because of family vulnerability to the police for three main reasons. 1) Either the family was either *amritdhari*, that is, initiated Sikh, since formal initiation is not done to all Sikhs but must be done at the person's request. 2) They were believed to be or were supporters of the movement for Khalistan, that is, the movement for the creation of a separate Sikh nation. 3) Either they themselves, or more commonly, someone in the family was a members of AISSF, an organization which became more political as the Indian government began to target them as 'terrorists'.

It has been widely documented that in the 1980s and through the 1990s, security forces were deployed by the Indian government to put down a Sikh insurgent movement for autonomy, and there were severe violations of political and civil rights.[6] The Indian parliament in 1985 enacted the Terrorist and Disruptive Activities Act (TADA) to control what it called 'terrorism' in Punjab, in which the so-called 'security' forces (to combat the 'terrorist' threat to the state) could detain anyone (Kumar, Singh, Agarwal, and Kaur 2003). Especially under the police chief K.P.S. Gill, himself a Sikh, the police let loose a reign of terror that deprived everyone living in the state of any civil rights in the state. Police checkpoints manned by police with machine guns sprang up at city intersections, rural roads, and highways, and anyone could be harassed at random for a bribe or be thrown into jail. Police were given rewards if they killed the insurgents and this of course led to police becoming bounty hunters. In a regime of terror by the police, no one was safe unless they had some access to power. Anyone could be designated a terrorist and shot, and it was particularly the randomness of the police violence that was most effective at disciplining the population.[7] While in the postcolonial state, the rule of law is often no guarantee of rights, and many poor people and Dalits in India live under these conditions everyday, for many even those networks that often protect those with access to state power were rendered ineffective.

While the randomness of the application of power by the police which terrorized the population worked effectively to repress the insurgent movement, the US (and Geneva Convention defined) refugee asylum law did not allow for such occurrences, and demanded that political activity (only such as might be sanctioned by liberal democracy) exist for which persons might be persecuted by the police. Even if gender-based asylum was not being claimed, the premise that a woman could be persecuted if someone in her family was being targeted had impacted political asylum claims. Consequently some Sikh women applicants for refugee asylum to the INS narrated that they had been thrown into prison not for their own political activities, for the most part, but for the activities of fathers, brothers, or husbands, and were raped or threatened with rape while in custody. Most of the Sikh women seeking refugee asylum presented themselves as political workers in the AISSF, although these narratives were risky since the US State Department identified some groups within this organization as 'terrorist' groups. The Indian state used terms such as 'terrorist' and 'militants' to designate the enemies of the state, and the Indian media also utilized these terms. The widespread reach of the Punjab police in collaboration with the Indian government, made it impossible for these refugee applicants to flee to anywhere in Punjab or in India.

Some of the cases involving the operations of the Punjab police in faraway states as West Bengal were highly publicized. The highly publicized cases in which the Punjab police hunted and killed suspects in regions as far away as West Bengal state. Refugee applicants stated they were released after a bribe was paid to the police and with the help of an 'agent' put on a plane to the US, sometimes leaving behind children or elderly parents.

The suddenness and the number of these claims led INS and immigration lawyers to believe that some of the women were not 'credible'. US government reports corroborated this concern. Thus the US State Department report on Country Conditions in India stated, 'Close study of hundreds of applications filed by Sikhs indicate that many applications are identical or follow a well-established pattern. There would appear to be a high level of misrepresentation in many applications and many applications appear to be fabrications' ('United States Department of States' 1996). Both for the INS and for legal aid workers, the task then became to figure out who was telling the truth so that only those who they believed were really suffering human rights violations could be helped.

It is also because of geopolitics, that is, because of relations between India and the US and because of the production of the 'terrorist' as the post-Cold War threat to national security both in the US and India, that the refugee narrative became convoluted in some instances. Since the US State Department reports (ibid.) designated the brutal counter-insurgency campaign by Indian security forces as an 'anti-terrorist' campaign, it concluded that the articulations of Sikh nationalism were waged through 'terrorism' in the Punjab rather than through political struggle, and that this 'terrorism' was a long-standing problem within Punjab: 'Ethnic strife and separatist violence in the state of Punjab has been one of India's intractable problems...But fear of domination by India's Hindu majority and economic concerns have fuelled discontent and strife. A separatist movement using terrorist tactics but supported by only a minority of Sikhs exploited this tension of its own purposes' (ibid.). The use of terrorism here articulated this movement to the US' own geopolitical role in the struggle against 'terrorism' globally.

The issue of 'credibility' along with the impetus of proving that they were not terrorists created new narratives for refugee asylum. Consequently, the need to prove the link between political action and state persecution ignored the ways in which the randomness of police terror became the chief means to subjugate the population. Consequently, Sikh applicants for refugee asylum had to prove that they were persecuted by the Indian state for expressing political opinion but that they were not part of so-called 'terrorist groups'.[8] Thus, if they were in the AISSF, they had to be careful in saying what kinds of work they had performed and which groups of the AISSF they were working with, and that they were expressing political opinions in a way that the immigration officials would see as legitimate. The narratives of both men and women applying for asylum claimed only that they were persecuted by the state for working on voter registration, putting up posters, making speeches, participating in peaceful protests, and similar activities, since anything else was seen as suspect. It was not enough to state that the police could blackmail, kidnap or use extortion at will to demoralize a population. Furthermore, since the US state extradited some so-called 'terrorists' at the request of the Indian state, the slippage between 'political worker', 'nationalist', and 'terrorist' produced a great deal of anxiety for applicants since the distinctions were shifting and uncertain. The problem occurred because the claim of asylum effectively meant that the claimant must not have participated in any activity against the state he/she was fleeing from, although the refugee asylum was by definition escaping from what were conceded to be repressive practices by the state. So on the one hand, claimants had to be non-violent and the state they were fleeing must be deemed violent, but if that violent state demanded extradition, with documentation (and the credibility of this documentation was not often questioned) that claimant must be extradited. In this way, although refugee claims also problematize state practices, nation-state sovereignty was protected.

Given that the designation of what constituted a 'terrorist' group is a political and geopolitical act, since in post-Cold War geopolitics, 'terrorism' has emerged as the 'Other' of the international network of nations that participate in the UN, the designation of a 'refugee' distinguished from a 'terrorist' was reflective of a contingent and shifting political agenda that could not be seen as neutral or even humanitarian. Human rights violations by a repressive state were not acknowledged if an act against the state could be designated as a 'terrorist' act; again, the supranational claims of human rights discourses could not succeed against the maintenance of nation-state sovereignty.

For the Sikh women claimants, the particular logic of refugee asylum claims was a new discourse that they had to learn to become gendered subjects of the US state. In its Country Reports, the US State Department during this period represented Sikhs as normatively 'male' and political agency as 'male' as well. Without much of a historical representation of women's political agency, given the limited scholarly work in Sikh Studies on the topic, Sikh women were unable to claim refugee asylum on the basis of political activity, despite the complexity of their participation in the community. Although almost none of the Sikh women claimed asylum on the explicit basis of gender, yet, to a certain extent, the narratives they used were gender-specific since they were based on the threat of rape or rape by state police as the basis of their claims. Legal scholar Nancy Kelly argued that there could be gender considerations even without a claim of gender-based asylum: 'Even when the applicant's gender is not central to her persecution or her fear of persecution, however, there may be gender-related aspects to her case' (Kelly 1993: 813–28). Rape therefore became a central narrative in these cases, and was used to articulate sexual difference within the supposedly gender-neutral category of political asylum. Consequently, other ways in which women were gendered were erased by the simple binary of global, reified, and historical male/female subjects. In such a binary, the women had to negotiate between presenting themselves as political victims rather than as political actors.

Some INS Asylum Officers, especially those in San Francisco, wished to be helpful and unprejudiced. In order to do so, they used 'community experts' to gain the knowledge that they feared the State department reports had left out. They expressed concern that they needed to know more about the lives of Sikh women so that they could be able to find out when cases deserved or how to tell if a claimant had *truly* been persecuted. While the standard for 'credibility' allowed that claimants may not be wholly 'truthful' at certain times, given the circumstances of repression that they might have endured, it was still the case that Asylum officers were required to make judgements about credibility, and the Immigration judges could also deny relief from deportation if they did not find a claimant to be credible. In San Francisco, where many Sikh women applied for asylum, most asylum officers and legal practitioners believed that a majority of the claims were false and thus created their own narratives about what was credible and what was not. Since alongside the humanitarian impulse of some asylum officers and the legal community was both the INS' mandate to only give asylum to those who had really suffered human rights violation, and, to keep the number of refugees quite low, asylum officers had to turn down a majority of claims. However, the problems for the claimants went beyond the difficulty of establishing credibility at the hearings. Even obtaining legal services became difficult, since women had to prove credibility even to get past the paralegal at the front desk of an office of a lawyer or a legal aid organization.[9] For instance, if a women sought legal help from other members of the *gurdwara* (the Sikh temple), she was not thought of as credible since it was believed that contacts were available there that would help formulate spurious claims. This suspicion regarding community sources did not extend to legal sources, because going directly to a lawyer was believed to be a better indicator of credibility than seeking help within the community. One could, of course, conclude that going directly to a lawyer was class-specific behaviour since those with more resources would go to lawyers and those without such access would seek help wherever they could find it. The Sikh 'community' thus was represented as a site where fictional narratives were generated, rather than as a location where newly arrived migrants participated in transnational connectivities and learned how to 'access' the state and the narratives and the language they were required to speak in order to remain in the US.

The basis of these widespread doubts within the INS and legal community about the credibility of Sikh claimants was the charge that most of these narratives were too similar. While Asylum Officers seemed to be questioning why many of the claimants had the same narrative, believing that these were being generated within the community in the US for 'illegals' to remain in the US, the determination of asylum clearly necessitated telling the same story. Since this narrative was the hegemonic narrative of the Sikh woman refugee, to depart from it meant risking deportation. Claimants could not depart from the cultural or historical narratives given to asylum officers by the US State Department; if they did, they risked losing their 'credibility'. The 'information' that Asylum officers relied upon to judge credibility was generated by 'consultants' from the community that the INS used, as well as by Country Reports compiled by the State Department. Within all of these circulations of information, there were common assumptions about 'traditional' cultures of Sikhs as opposed to the 'modern' west. Such assumptions are also visible in the ways in which gender was created in *World Sikh News*, for instance, in which the category of women was relegated to being the bearers and transmitters of community values and religion to the younger generation, or, were represented by their human rights violations in Punjab with much less information regarding their political or economic participation. Even though many of these women were represented in the newspaper advertising pages as professionals and active in the workforce, there was very little about them in any other capacity other than mothers, and caregivers. Torn between showing that Sikhism was a 'modern' egalitarian religion, unlike other religions in India, and that Sikhs were 'modern', alongside a paternalistic approach to women which denied their multifarious contributions, community leaders, as represented by the contributors of the *World Sikh News*, displayed their gender biases and thus contributed to a dearth of knowledge about the lives of Sikh women both in India and in the diaspora.

In wider circulation than *World Sikh News*, however, was the common belief that Sikh patriarchy was homogeneously violent and the women were represented as victims of such patriarchy. Such beliefs were obvious in the questions that Asylum Officers asked me when I agreed to be an 'expert'. While these questions seem to be about obtaining the best kind of information to 'help' women, they assumed that patriarchy was not being negotiated by Sikh women but rather than Sikh women were helpless before Sikh patriarchy. This 'cultural' narrative that represented 'the Sikh woman' was created by human rights NGOs, global feminist constructions about 'traditional' cultures, and, the mostly male 'community consultants' brought in by the INS. Within these narratives, a victim of human rights violations was constructed, either as raped or threatened by rape, who could then be rescued by the US state if she represented her experiences in the 'proper' language of human rights and women's rights. In the case of Sikh women, agency had to be restrained to the proper modes of political protest, the proper 'culture' of Sikh women. Within these asylum claims, this figure of the 'Sikh woman' was narrated as being a victim, politically active only in putting up posters, for the most part, but also wholly identified in relation to family, obedient to the men folk, and one who remains within the household, veiled and shy. She was governed by 'shame' and 'honour', those anthropological constructs through which 'traditional' cultures are identified, was subservient, yet had to explain how she came to take flight to another country. She had to explain that she had a well-founded fear of persecution by the state, because of her political actions, or, because of the political actions of members of her family, but that she was quite uninvolved in more fierce forms of protest; she was either under threat of rape or had been raped. Whereas the male refugee had to show persecution because of political opinion, this gendered female refugee could simply be a victim, persecuted because of family connections rather than for her own beliefs or actions, and threatened by rape by the police. If she could not articulate this narrative within the asylum hearing and before the Immigration judge, she could easily be deported. Any departure from a narrative of the victim and she might be termed a 'militant', that is, a terrorist, a designation which was a constant danger for any Sikhs seeking asylum. The safest narrative thus minimized all kinds of agency, although the agency might have been found in the narratives of flight and migration—those aspects of the story that had little to do with human rights discourses, and which were unspeakable for many reasons.

Consequently, INS and State Department knowledges produced a raciology in which Sikh refugees were constructed as uniformly devout, all of one caste and class (that of rural small farmers), without differences of caste, class, sexuality, religious affiliation. Although there are many forms of belief that have been subsumed under Sikhism, the transnational discourse of Sikhs was as a homogenous collectivity. The only differences that have been produced was that between the initiated (that is, rigorously devout) and the uninitiated (that is, casually devout) Sikh, a binary in which the former could either be refugees or terrorists. Religious affiliations also became very clearly defined as religious stable identities rather than as shifting practices.

All of the questions posed by asylum officers during a consultation with a community 'consultant' revealed such ahistorical views. As a 'consultant', I was asked to respond to questions such as the following: the age of marriage for Sikh women, whether a single woman could relocate in India, the percentage of unmarried adult women in Punjab, the average age of marriage for Sikh females, or most centrally, information about 'sexual violations' by police or in custody.[10] All of these questions assumed a homogeneous, ahistorical Sikh 'culture' and an undifferentiated Sikh female subject. Another set of questions posed by another officer did assume that Sikh women could be political activists, but that within such activism, 'women's rights' struggles were opposed to and separated from struggles for 'Sikh rights'. Asylum officers seemed to have little knowledge about class and caste and gender issues in Punjab, how these altered with historical contexts, and had no knowledge about the many kinds of Sikh communities in the US. Thus, while this refugee process was part of a long history of transnational connectivities, Sikh women were seen as victims of static and unchanging cultures.

Although I have focused on representations produced within and by the US state, these representations came from a variety of sources which included NGOs, individual consultants and scholars, the state department, and a variety of media sources. In describing the counter-insurgency movements carried out by the state in the early 1990s in Punjab, Human Rights Watch/ Asia and the Physicians for Human Rights documented the torture of women detained along with family members by the police for extortion. Such NGOs continue to represent woman as victims of their state and, sometimes, their culture, or as innocents (that is, non-political). Yet these reports also revealed other forms of gendered agency and other representations of 'the Sikh woman'. An analysis of one such report on Punjab revealed subjects who were most interesting because they were not the 'objects' of concern of these global NGOs or global 'victims' or even 'innocent bystanders' of state violence, as most women refugees are deemed to be (Human Rights Watch/Asia and Physicians for Human Rights 1994). Gendered agency seems to be much more diverse and complex than these discourses of the transnational Sikh female subject would suggest. In one most revealing incident, the Human Rights groups obtained evidence from a female police officer who was married to an undercover agent and who told the group quite a few details about her husband's activities, which included many human rights violations. In another incident, the wife of a policeman told human rights advocates about police being rewarded monetarily for killing 'militants', telling them that 'My husband twice received Rs 3,000 for the people he killed (ibid.: 23–5). Thus while the human rights narrative about Sikh women represented them as tortured and raped, other forms of gendered agency, complex and problematic, slipped into the narrative, disrupting the representation of a normative female Sikh subject.

Human Rights NGOs in India produced a related but different subject from transnational human rights NGOs when they focused on Sikh women. Since Sikh males have been represented within British colonial and Indian nationalist discourse as hyper-masculine and aggressive, Sikh women are discursively produced within postcolonial India as aggressive, large, and physically active. Consequently, the report by the Citizens for Democracy group based in New Delhi depicted these women as courageous in the face of police terror, but courageous as mothers and as wives rather than as Sikhs: 'Lonely, overworked, harassed daily by the Army and the Police, dishonored, beaten up for not being able to produce the men who have been missing—they came to meet us out in the open regardless of the fear of the police' (Citizens for Democracy 1985: 41). These narratives do include reports of being raped, what we are told is translatable as being 'dishonoured' by the police. The section on the women concluded that 'the list (of requests for help) is endless—so is misery and so is fortitude and magnificent pride...' (ibid.). Here, instead of the passive 'Asian woman' of the US state narrative, we have a narrative of the women of Punjab as proud and stoic, a construction that came out of British notions of people of Punjab as masculinist and tough. But such representations have come to have a long existence within Punjabi and Sikh culture.

These are of course women from the same part of India that underwent the Partition in 1947, where women's bodies and their sexualities were most carefully and problematically disciplined by the emerging nation-states. The work of Ritu Menon, Kamla Bhasin, and Urvashi Butalia, as well as many others on the Partition have revealed the ways in which the sexuality and sexual agency of women from the region was recuperated by national/state narratives, as well as how the women's narratives often contradicted these state narratives; they reveal that women's narratives often subverted the narratives of the state that constructed religious, national and gender subjectivity as unchanging and static (Menon and Bhasin 1998; Butalia 1998). The Recovery Operation in which women kidnapped were to be returned to their 'proper families' was much more about consolidation of patriarchies of kin and nation-state, as Veena Das argues, rather than about the well-being of the women. The women themselves sometimes had developed relationships with their kidnappers or had formed new families and were resistant to being returned. Questions of a monolithic religious identity were irrelevant to them; what concerned them was how to create some kind of possible future when often their relatives were often the source of violence. The subjectivity of women was also, both in the narratives of Partition as well as in the representation of the event in postcolonial Punjab, defined by sexuality in terms of reproduction and as objects of violence.

The question of sexuality of women in Punjab remains to be examined and there is a dearth of work in this area. Historical and cultural evidence in Punjab has noted that many practices around marriage and/or sexuality did not conform to the notion of the brahmanical Hindu woman, especially in areas such as widow remarriage. Since widows could, under colonial rule, inherit property, women tried to keep their property and their sexual autonomy. Prem Chowdhry described this period as a time when 'dual control...of their rights of inheritance and their sexuality was openly contested by the widows (in colonial Punjab) resulting in prolonged legal battles and open confrontations' (Chowdhry 1996: 65). Women who became widows worked actively to retain their sexual and economic autonomy against the wishes of their families to perform 'levirate' marriage, a practice in which they could be remarried to one of their dead husband's brothers, and so lose control of property. So many women tried to be autonomous, and women's acceptance of their unchastity became such a common way to refuse remarriage that the colonial government had to take action against this practice.

While I don't wish to suggest that nineteenth century provided more sexual autonomy for women in Punjab, this narrative about other kinds of sexual subjects suggests that there are more negotiations that we can focus on in order to problematize the production of state subjects. Furthermore, historical information is important in revealing the ways in which narratives of the state and the nation have collaborated with human rights internationalism and with global feminism in order to consolidate the production of Sikh woman sexualized solely as a victim of violence.

If community and grass-roots organizing was based on this subject of violence, then we need attention to the various discourses of nation, community, and family within which conflicting and intersecting subject positions are produced. Thus these forms of agency that I have mentioned above, that may suggest the failure of the women to fully become the subjects of the US state, come to be important areas of feminist analysis for they indicate that agency may not be contained by one nation-state.

Refugee advocates and feminist and immigrant-rights NGOs in the US struggled to provide 'access' to the state for such subjects. In providing such resources, both internationalist and nationalist discourses represent the Sikh woman as a victim of violence. Often, it is when access cannot be provided that we see a glimpse of subjects beyond the state and nation; the 'failures' of an NGO working with women can also be illuminating. A major realm of failure for such NGOs in the US occurred when women were unable to explain their experiences to the INS officials or to the immigration judge in the language in which rape could be understood to be traumatic in US contexts, or even if her actions did not fit the representation of a proper female refugee as victim of violence. If, for instance, she left her children behind to seek asylum in the US; if she did not seem to US 'experts' to be traumatized by her experiences; if she refused psychological counselling or if the counsellor was unable to understand her experience of trauma; if she began to live with another man in the US to whom she was not legally married; if she tried to hedge her bets by having a child with the man she was living with in the US; if the middle-class experiences of the community worker failed to connect with the many negotiations that a woman needed to perform in order to survive. It is in these failures that the agency can also be attributed to the figure of the Sikh woman as transnational subject.

It is in these failures that we find the figure of the Sikh woman as escaping the state, evading the transnational subject of human rights, but remaining a mobile subject across many networks of communication and connectivity. Though an unnamed, stateless, displaced subject not claimed as a citizen anywhere, this failed human rights subject is also a result of transnational networks and their related mobilities, as well as of the Indian state, its communities and cultures that name it as 'Sikh woman'. If human rights instruments are critical to creating state subjects of what is called the 'global north', this subject, like many others who do live in this North but who are not captured by the state, is testimony to the displacements produced by many violent transnationalisms.

Notes

* This essay is a version of a longer chapter from my book, *Transnational America: Feminisms, Diasporas, Neoliberalisms*, 2005.

1. For/ more on this term, 'transnational connectivities', see Grewal (2005). I use this term to refer to the degree and variety of networks that constitute a transnational field, in which historical and spatial formations intersect.

2. See especially Dubernet on the 'international' reaction, in 'Internally Displaced People in Eastern Europe', (2001).

3. A quick reference is available at The Hindu, '7.4 68 Custodial Deaths in last five years', Aarti Dhar, Monday, 30 June 2008. http://www.hindu.com/2008/06/30/stories/2008063052390700.htm, 7 May 2009. See also Chandra Mohan Upadhyay, 'Human Rights in Pre-Trial Detention', New Delhi: A.P.H. Publishing Corporation, 1999, for account of 'normal' detention practices in India.

4. Human Rights Watch has been most assiduously tracking these abuses and in 2007 published a report on the 'policy of impunity in Punjab. Human Rigths watch, 'Protecting the Killers', 17 October 2007. http://www.hrw/org/en/reports/2007/10/17/protecting-killers, 9 May 2009.

5. From a Country Presentation on the USA by Paula Lynch, Department of State, and Lori Scialabba, Immigration and Naturalization Service, at the Symposium on Gender-Based Persecution, Geneva, February 1996.

6. A number of laws, past and present, were used in Punjab during this period. See for instance the section on 'black laws' in *Oppression in Punjab, Citizens for Democracy*, September 1985. U.S. Edition published by Columbus, Ohio, Sikh Religious and Educational Foundation, 1986. Asia Watch, *Punjab in Crisis: Human Rights in India*, New York, Human Rights Watch, 1991. Kirpal Dhillon, *Sikh Militancy in India 1978–93*, New Delhi: Penguin Books, 2003. An interesting footnote come from the memoir of a police officer, V.P. Kapur, *The Crumbling Edifice: Experiences and Thoughts of a Police Officer*, Delhi: Rupa and Co., 2003, pp. 9–10, in which Kapur mentions that he disagrees with those who put individual rights before national security.

7. The experience of living in Punjab during this period was striking and has not been recorded in any systematic way though it can be deduced from the records of police violence, extra-judicial killings and fake 'encounters' as well as the 'collateral' damage of the counter-insurgency. One indication is the numbers of paramilitary forces in Punjab during this period which are striking. According one account, there were 60,000 Punjab police, 15,000 military, 40,000 paramilitary, an increase of 230 per cent during the 1980s. Shinder Singh Thandi, 'Counterinsurgency and Political Violence in Punjab, 1980–94, in *Punjabi Identity: Continuity and Change*, Gurharpal Singh and Ian Talbot, eds, Delhi: Manohar, 1996. Also see Manoj Joshi, 'Combating Terrorism', in *Punjab: Indian Democracy in Crisis*, London: Research Institute for the Study of Conflict and Terrorism, no. 261, May 1993.

8. My thanks to Jagdeep Singh Sekhon for making this point.

9. This was my experience trying to get pro bono legal assistance from a supposedly progressive non-profit legal organization.

10. The information about the refugee applications is obtained from lawyers in San Francisco who shared with me the applications that they were filing. In addition, I also spoke to several INS officers who had worked on these applications. I served as a consultant to the INS since this was one way to learn about what Asylum Officers believed. The meeting in San Francisco in early 1998 was instructive. The list of questions sent to me for my comment were the following:

- If a woman is in custody, is it assumed that she has been sexually violated? If so, does this affect her chances of marriage?

- Can a single woman or widowed woman relocate in India?

- If a woman has been sexually violated in police custody, would she reveal this to her family and friends?

- Would the police target a woman merely because her husband is a political activist?

- What kinds of discrimination do women face in India?

- Are there differences between the ways Sikhism regards women's role in society and that of Hinduism?

- What percentage of women are never married in Punjab?

- What is the average age of women when they marry?

- Are 'dowry deaths' a problem in the Sikh community?

REFERENCES

Amnesty International Annual Report (1997). London: Amnesty International Publications.

Axel, Brian Keith (2001). *The Nation's Tortured Body: Violence, Representation, and the Formation of the Sikh 'Diaspora'*, Durham and London: Duke University Press.

Butalia, Urvashi (1998). *The Other Side of Silence: Voices from the Partition of India*, New Delhi: Penguin.

Chowdhry, Prem (1996). 'Contesting Claims and Counter Claims: Questions of Inheritance and Sexuality of Widows', in Patricia Uberoi (ed.), *Social Reform, Sexuality and the State*, New Delhi: Sage, pp. 65–82.

'Citizens for Democracy' (1985). *Report to the Nation: Oppression in Punjab*, September, US Edition, Columbus, Ohio: A Sikh Religious and Educational Trust Publication.

Das, Veena (1995). *Critical Events: An Anthropological Perspective on Contemporary India*, New Delhi: Oxford University Press.

Dubernet, Cecile (2001). *The International Containment of Displaced Persons: Humanitarian Spaces Without Exit*, Burlington: Ashgate Publishing.

Dusenbery, Verne A. (1989). 'Introduction: A Century of Sikhs Beyond Punjab', in N. Gerald Barrier and Verne Dusenbery (eds), *The Sikh Diaspora: Migration and Experience Beyond Punjab*, Delhi: Chanakya Publishers, pp. 1–28.

Ervolina, Anna J. (1995). 'Fatin v. INS: Gender-Based Persecution Under United States Asylum Law', *New York International Law Review*, Vol. 8, No. 1, pp. 61–83.

'Five AISSF Activists Granted Asylum', (1993). World Sikh News, 29 October, p. 16.

Grewal, Inderpal (2005). *Transnational America: Feminisms, Diasporas, Neo-liberalisms*, Durham: Duke University Press.

'Human Rights Watch/Asia and Physicians for Human Rights' (1994). *Dead Silence: The Legacy of Abuses in Punjab*, New York, Washington, Los Angeles, London: Human Rights Watch/Asia and Physicians for Human Rights.

'Human Rights Under Siege in India' (1993). *World Sikh News*, 12 February, p. 4.

Jackman, Barbara (1992). 'Well-Founded Fear of Persecution and Other Standards of Decision-Making: A North American Perspective', in Jacqueline Bhabha and Geoffrey Coll (eds), *Asylum Law and Pracice in Europe and North America*, Washington DC: Federal Publications Inc., pp. 37–70.

Kelly, Nancy (1993). 'Gender-Related Persecution: Assessing the Asylum Claims of Women', *Cornell International Law Journal*, Vol. 26, pp. 625–74.

—— (1994). 'Guidelines for Women's Asylum Claims', *Interpreter Releases*, Vol. 27, pp. 813–28.

Kumar, Ram Narayan, Amrik Singh, Ashok Agarwal, and Jaskaran Kaur (2003). *Reduced to Ashes: The Insurgency and Human Rights in Punjab*, South Asia Forum for Human Rights, Kathmandu, Nepal.

Lubhéid, Eithne (2002). *Entry Denied: Controlling Sexuality at the Border*, Minnesota: University of Minnesota Press.

Lynch, Paula and Lori Scialabb (1997). 'Symposium on Gender-Based Persecution', Geneva, February 1996, *International Journal of Refugee Law*, Special Issue Autumn, pp. 73–5.

Menon, Ritu, Kamla Bhasin (1998). *Borders and Boundaries: Women in India's Partition*, New Delhi: Kali for Women.

'Political Asylum for Sikh Woman' (1993). *World Sikh News*, 26 February, p. 14.

'Right: Rethinking Theory and Practice' (1998). Introduction to Special Section, *Economic and Political Weekly*, Vol. 33, No. 5, February 31, PE-2.

Subramaniam, S. (2000). *Human Rights Training*, New Delhi: Manas.

'United States Department of State' (1996). Bureau of Democracy, Human Rights and Labor, 'India: Comments on Country Conditions and Asylum Claims'.

—— (1998). US Refugee Admissions Program for Fiscal Year 1998, Department of State Publication 10559, Bureau of Population, Refugees and Migration, Office of Admissions, April.

'United States Congress. Senate Judiciary Committee' (1979). Refugee Act of 1980, S. Rep. No. 256, 96th Cong., 2nd Sess. 1, 23 July.

By an Indirect Route
Women in 3HO/Sikh Dharma

Constance Elsberg

In the 1970s, people living in a number of cities in the United States and Canada encountered young people wearing turbans and dressing entirely in white. These young men and women had been born into other religious traditions, but had adopted the Sikh faith. Ethnic Sikhs in the United States and Canada were particularly surprised to discover these '*gora* (white) Sikhs', whom they encountered with mixed reactions. They were impressed by the piety and discipline of the new Sikhs, but often dubious about their interest in yoga, which is not widely practised by Sikhs, and troubled by the intensity of their devotion to their teacher, Yogi Bhajan. Today, their teacher is gone and their numbers reduced, but many persist with unabated faith. This is a brief look at the women who became adherents of Sikh Dharma and a sister organization, the Healthy, Happy, Holy Organization (3HO). It is based on previous ethnographic research (Elsberg 2003), a review of websites (both official organization sites and sites used by ex-members) and an examination of books written by some of the women members. It looks at the unusual combination of yoga and Sikhism that Bhajan and members of 3HO/Sikh Dharma created, and at the appeal of 3HO/Sikh Dharma to women. It views the organization primarily in terms of the possible value of its syncretic form and in terms of benefits that women members may experience. But it is not intended to imply that all of its women members have been satisfied by 3HO's offerings. Female ex-members typically leave out of disillusionment with the way that 3HO is organized and administered, and a number report a haunting sense of years lost and of opportunities missed. 3HO/Sikh Dharma has its strengths and its weaknesses, but it clearly 'works' for many of its long-term women members.

To understand the beliefs and the roles of women in 3HO/Sikh Dharma it is necessary to understand that their organizations grew out of a distinctive spiritual milieu. This milieu was a somewhat eclectic compound of ingredients. These included the spiritual yearnings of many participants in the counterculture of the 1960s and 1970s, the influence of the New Age Movement, the birth of the second wave of the US women's movement, the ongoing appeal to Americans of a number of Hindu- and Buddhist-oriented spiritual groups, the spread of what came to be called 'New Religious Movements', and the changing nature of Sikh immigration to the US.

The founder of Sikh Dharma was Harbhajan Singh Puri, who came to be known by his students and followers as Yogi Bhajan. A Sikh, he was born in a village called Tehsil Wazirabad, which, at the time of Partition, became part of Pakistan. Propelled by Partition, he and his family migrated to India and settled in New Delhi. In India, according to the 3HO website, 'Yogi Bhajan studied comparative religion and Vedic philosophy in his undergraduate years, going on to receive his Masters in Economics with honours from Punjab University' (Healthy, Happy, Holy Organization). He married Inderjit Kaur with whom he had three children. Bhajan was employed as a customs and security officer, and official organizational biographies say that he began to study yoga when he was a youth and continued this interest throughout his life. In time, Bhajan decided to try teaching yoga in the west, moving first to Canada, and then to Los Angeles in 1969. In Los Angeles, he began to teach at a YMCA and then at another well-known institution, the East-West Cultural Center. Thus, his first contact with his American students was not as a purveyor of Sikhism, but as a yogi.

By the time he arrived in North America, various forms of both Hindu and Buddhist practices were well-entrenched and were growing increasingly popular with western spiritual seekers. Eastern religions have a long history of appeal to alternative cultural groupings in the US (Ellwood 1987; Harper 1972; Miller 1995), and counterculture youth were among those who were responsive to the growing appeal of their wares. The enthusiasm for things Eastern had not really included Sikhism, however, and Sikh-inspired movements were not common, although Sant Kirpal Singh who led a group called Ruhani Satasang, a breakaway from the Radhasoami movement, was active. The most readily available model for an Asian-born spiritual leader at the time was probably that of the charismatic male guru who taught yoga and/or meditation. The gurus who seemed to appeal particularly to a western audience emphasized the importance of finding the sacred within the self, of uniting modern science with spirituality, and of following prescribed rituals and practices (Ellwood 1987).

Bhajan originally fitted into this mould. As a teacher at the East-West Cultural Center he began to attract members of the local hippie community (Tobey 1976: 7). Bhajan's approach clearly appealed to his young audience, although directors of the Center were not necessarily pleased by the influx of young hippies or by Bhajan's influence over them. Soon, a number of his early students joined with him to open an independent ashram in Los Angeles. The organization they created in the process was incorporated as the Healthy, Happy, Holy Organization (3HO) in 1969. As the name implies, its mission was to teach classes and workshops in subjects such as yoga, meditation, and nutrition. Bhajan taught his version of Kundalini yoga, a vigorous form which includes a variety of postures, the use of rapid deep breathing ('breath of fire') and chanting. The intent of these techniques is to 'awaken' the Kundalini energy said to reside at the base of the spine. Over time, the adept can move that energy up through the energy centres, or chakras, of the 'subtle body' until it reaches the highest chakras. The long-term result is said to be enlightenment and oneness with God. Short-term results, which are often emphasized in 3HO yoga classes, may be more pragmatic and are said to include improvements in health, clarity of mind, and increased capacity to withstand stress.

As the 3HO website describes it:

Practicing *Kundalini Yoga* keeps the body in shape and trains the mind to be strong and flexible in the face of stress and change. It increases oxygen capacity, boosts blood flow, balances the glandular system, strengthens the nervous system, and reduces stress-induced toxins such as adrenaline and cortisol. The effect is a heightened self-awareness and vitality that allows you to harness mental and emotional energy. Individuals feel more in control of themselves, with enhanced peace of mind, concentration, and a deep inner calm and self-confidence (Healthy, Happy, Holy Organization).

Bhajan referred to himself as the Mahan Tantric, and taught classes in what he called White Tantric Yoga in addition to his Kundalini courses. White Tantric classes are particularly interesting for Bhajan's early approach to gender. These classes required that men and women sit in rows opposite one another and work with a partner of the opposite sex. Long and demanding yoga sets were intended to raise energy, to help the individual to overcome 'blocks' in the subconscious mind, and to 'balance' male and female energies (Shakti Parwha Kaur Khalsa 1983).

One of the early and influential woman members of 3HO, Shakti Parwha Kaur Khalsa, has written a book about Tantric and Kundalini yoga. (Kundalini is usually considered a form of Tantric practice, but 3HO members talk about Tantra and Kundalini classes as separate disciplines). 'White Tantric Yoga', she notes, 'is the guided (by the Mahan Tantric) use of tantric energy which serves to accelerate the psychological transformation of the individual, dissolving deep-rooted subconscious neuroses' (S.P.K. Khalsa 1996: 179). Following Yogi Bhajan, she makes a point of saying that this is not a form of tantric practice that includes any form of sexual activity: 'Although it is practised with a partner, White Tantric Yoga is not a "sexual" yoga. On the contrary, it transmutes the sex energy from the lower chakras... to the higher chakras'. She goes on to say that 'each person's experience of White Tantric Yoga is different. Each gets what he or she needs at that point in their journey along the path. It is a very deep and transformational cleansing process...' (ibid.: 180).[1]

The exact sources of Bhajan's Tantric teachings are unclear, as are some other sources of his philosophy and ideas about yoga. He at times claimed to have studied with a Sant Hazara Singh and to have inherited his title (Mahan Tantric) from him. At other times, he seems to have said that Hazara Singh passed the title to a Lama Lilan Po, who in turn passed the title to Bhajan. A respected writer and critic of Bhajan, Trilochan Singh dismissed the claim:

As Hazara Singh died decades ago, the time gap had to be filled by a fictitious Mahan Tantric from Tibet Lama Lilan Po. But Yogi Bhajan does not state whether it was before or after the Chinese occupation. Did Lilan Po come to Los Angeles – or he flew to Tibet with the special permission of the authorities (Trilochan Singh 1977: 108).

Ex-members have attempted to trace Bhajan's connections to these figures without success, but they are not expert researchers. It is probably best to assume that Bhajan's tantric lineage is unresolved.

In discussions with ex-members and with people interested in the Sanatan tradition,[2] I have encountered a number of other fairly convincing candidates for major influences on Bhajan's teachings. One ex-member,[3] suggests that as a Khatri, Bhajan's alliances were often with non-Jat Sikhs, such as Kirpal Singh of Ruhani Satasang (a Khatri) and with the Namdhari community, which has a high proportion of Ramgharia participants. A number of ex-members who were involved in the formative stages of 3HO also say that Bhajan spoke frequently of Baba Virsa Singh in those early years. Baba Virsa Singh has established a number of what his website calls 'farm-based communities' both in India and in the US (Baba Virsa Singh). There is one in Punjab in his village of Sarawan Bodla. Judging by the themes and views expressed, he could easily have influenced Bhajan's early thinking. For example, Virsa Singh is dismissive of differences between sects and religions. Bhajan's participation in interfaith activities, and his readiness to combine traditions, reflects this spirit. Virsa Singh is quoted as saying that 'religion is meant to be practical, not theoretical' (Baba Virsa Singh) which is a belief echoed throughout Bhajan's teachings and the expressions of his students. Virsa Singh insists that 'God's light and truth are within us all' (ibid.), a view echoed in one of Bhajan's sayings, 'if you can't see God in all, you can't see God at all'.[4] Virsa Singh claims to have had visions of Baba Siri Chand (a son of Guru Nanak and founder of the Udasi order, considered to be outside of the line of Guru succession by Khalsa Sikhs) and of Guru Gobind Singh. This might explain the presence of images of Baba Siri Chand at some 3HO/Sikh Dharma sites (although images of the Baba can also be found in Sikh gurdwaras in east Punjab, so this may just be an importation of this tradition). Virsa Singh urges his devotees to 'recite Nam...read Jaap Sahib....do seva...

and rise early in the morning to begin thanking God and look within yourself to battle your own evils' (ibid.). This is very close to Bhajan's prescriptions, as is the use of the meditation, 'Ik Ongkar Sat Nam Siri Wahe Guru', (this is the transliteration used on the Baba Virsa Singh website) although Virsa Singh suggests repeating it silently throughout the day. People in 3HO/Sikh Dharma instead speak this phrase aloud.

One ex-member of 3HO/Sikh Dharma describes Baba Virsa Singh, rather aptly, as a 'self-styled Udasi' and goes on to suggest that Udasi influence would explain the 3HO use of 'mantras, ayurved, emphasis on yoga, and dietary habits'. ('The Wacko World of Yogi Bhajan').[5] And an ex-member, who was present in the early years and later went on to study Vaishnava and other forms of worship in the Punjab, says that he encountered forms of meditation and visualization in the Punjab that were quite similar to those that Bhajan taught. He suggests that Bhajan probably borrowed freely from a variety of sources: Sikh, Hindu, and Sanatan. Another of Bhajan's teachers is said to have been Swami Dhirendra Acharya, Indira Gandhi's yoga teacher. Acharya's yoga manuals included some of the early yoga postures that were used in 3HO. The spiritual package created by Yogi Bhajan, in what was, perhaps, an ad hoc fashion, was clearly syncretic, and it is the distinctive mix of elements that appealed to many of his female students.

3HO and Sikh Dharma were founded during a time of political upheaval in the US. Social movements representing a variety of constituencies were seeking to transform the country. But, as the Vietnam War ground on, recession set in, and the counterculture imploded, a growing disillusionment with political action and hippie lifestyles began to spread. The alienated young, many distrustful of the major institutions, looked in new directions, among them Hindu and Buddhist oriented groups, alternative Christian groups, the Human Potential Movement, and New Age groups. Many of these youth apparently came to the conclusion that personal change had to precede cultural and political transformation and turned to these groups because they offered modes of personal transformation and empowerment (Kent 2001; Tipton 1982). Other young people simply looked for a way to return, at least halfway, to the mainstream, and sought out groups that could 'combine or synthesize countercultural values with traditional or mainstream orientations' (Robbins, Anthony, and Curtis 1975: 51).

Young alienated women had particular needs to meet, and some of the early teachings were especially appealing to these female yoga students. Because the women's movement was emerging when Bhajan began to teach, some of his students naturally expected him to address issues such as sex roles, female empowerment, and the nature of gender. In response, Bhajan drew on tantra and the associated concept of *shakti* (or *sakti*). To quote the 3HO website once again:

> According to the 3HO lifestyle, a woman is referred to as a 'Shakti' which means Primal Creative Power. As a woman you are fundamentally equipped with this creative principle of the Universe. When you relate to your true self then you tap into this well of unlimited resources. You experience your power; you begin to realize the depth of your own strength and wisdom; you witness the power of your prayer to manifest. (Healthy, Happy, Holy Organization: women's page).

While it is difficult to define tantra, and there are a number of different schools of tantric thought, a general assumption is that 'the Absolute, although singular in essence at the highest level, is understood to be essentially polarized into female and male aspects....The male aspect of God cannot act alone...only through his energy, his *sakti*, with whom he is inseparably united and who is hypostatized as a goddess' (Pintchman 1994: 110).

In Vaishnava and Shaiva forms, male deities are paired with female consorts. The male deities are conceived of as pure consciousness; it is the female of the pair whose shakti activates the male principle (Erndl 1997: 21). There is also another form, which 'views shakti as more than an ancillary power of *Brahman*: shakti is the Goddess, and the Goddess is *Brahman*' (Pechilis 2004: 24). My impression is that the 3HO approach is probably closer to the Vaishnava and Shaiva versions than to the idea of shakti as ultimate divinity, but 3HO teachings sometimes come close to viewing shakti as goddess.

Bhajan, and a number of women in 3HO, built on tantric ideas, arguing that women's innate spiritual power had been eclipsed by American culture and institutions. Modern America, Bhajan argued, demeaned women and alienated them from their spiritual core. He was particularly critical of the media: 'Woman is used as a tool of the advertising industry...the most graceful being on this planet is treated disgracefully as a playmate, a sexual toy...under no circumstances should woman become graceful, because if woman becomes graceful, who will sell their booze?' (Bhajan 1977: 191–2).

Beginning in 1970 Bhajan taught a mantra, 'I am Grace of God', ('the' is omitted, evidently because Bhajan did not use it) which he urged women to repeat. 3HO women, in turn, incorporated the mantra and the sentiment into the yoga classes and workshops they taught to other women. Bhajan referred to this repetition and spreading of the mantra as the 'Grace of God Movement for the Women of America'. One of the founding members of 3HO, Shakti Parwha Kaur Khalsa, provides an account of its origins:

On September 22, 1970, a group of women Kundalini Yoga students in San Francisco asked Yogi Bhajan how to control and channel their powerful, sometimes overwhelming emotions. They recognized that women do, indeed, have a lot to deal with! This was the day the GGM [Grace of God Meditation] was born (S.P.K. Khalsa 1996: 137).

3HO teaches that women are, by nature, changeable and emotional, so the idea behind the Grace of God meditation may simply have been the management of female affect, but it may well be that the emotions referred to include those unleashed by the women's movement. One devotee who was very active in women's issues wrote, quite optimistically:

The Grace of God mantra gives each woman the technology to look deep within her innermost being to heal herself, to regain the positive image of her infinite potential and to restore her rightful place in society....The fears, limitations and the debilitating concepts that an exploitive society has placed on her can then be lifted. The Grace of God mantra gives woman the hope of real liberation and the fulfillment of human life (Shanti Shanti Kaur Khalsa 1979: 42).

Another woman who was active in the Grace of God Movement told me that before her contact with 3HO, she had participated in women's consciousness-raising groups while she was in college. These discussions left her acutely aware of ways in which women have been exploited and under-valued, and they burdened her with a great deal of 'anger and grief'. Joining 3HO provided her with a way to ease the burden. She found it 'healing' to view herself as the grace of God. It 'healed the wounds, sorrow, betrayal'.[6]

This opportunity to 'heal' and move on was one of the benefits that were of particular value to the women students, whether they wanted to leave behind unsatisfying roles, relationships, or emotions. Such healing, it was assumed, could, in turn, free women's creative powers and thus alter society. Thus, this particular woman went on to say that Bhajan's 'single greatest gift to the West is elevating the consciousness of women', because, if women's self-esteem can be restored and her powers unlocked, this can 'affect everything' (ibid.).[7]

As his students progressed, Bhajan sent them out to establish ashrams around the US and in Canada. (The use of the term, 'ashram' is yet another example of the early thinking that fit into the model then being used by Indian gurus). The Santa Fe, Washington DC, Massachusetts, and San Francisco areas were among the first locations. Residents of the early ashrams lived communally, thus continuing a central counterculture value. From the point of view of the general public, the early ashrams probably looked like typical hippie communes, but in actuality residents were making major changes in their lifestyles. Members rose early to face challenging sessions of yoga and meditation. They were expected to give up meat, caffeine, alcohol, and drugs, to work in order to help support the ashram, and to learn the art of living closely with others in the community.

It is unclear if Bhajan originally had any intention of introducing Sikhism through his teachings, but some of Bhajan's yoga students began to study his religion. One of the early members said that a few of the Los Angeles students attended a Sikh study circle with Bhajan; they then found a gurdwara to attend. In 1970, a group of 3HO adherents joined Bhajan on a visit to India, and a few underwent the rite of Sikh initiation, *khande ki pahul*, at the Akal Takht. Bhajan met with officials of the Shiromani Gurdwara Parbandhak Committee (SGPC), the central gurdwara managing committee, and received recognition for his missionary efforts. He received honorific titles in both 1972 and 1974, after which his students referred to him as the Siri Singh Sahib.

This opened a new phase of organizational life. The group established its first gurdwara in Los Angeles in 1972. Copies of the Guru Granth Sahib were distributed to the existing centres, and students began to learn some Gurmukhi and Punjabi and to seriously pursue an understanding of Sikh principles. They were not required to become Sikhs, but there was considerable pressure to grow hair long, to wear a turban, or at least to explore these changes as a possibility.

At first, Bhajan explained Sikh principles in yogic and New Age terms, and this may have made the transition more palatable to countercultural youth, many of whom distrusted established formal religions. Thus, for example, students were told they should grow their hair and wear a turban because

The hair regulates the inflow of sun energy into the body system. To let the solar energy flow without obstruction, let the hair grow to its full natural length and take good care of it...If the hair is down, unkept or uncovered so that it is electrically imbalanced, this natural process of raising the kundalini energy will be impeded (Gurucharan Singh Khalsa 1978: 28–29).

Naam simran was sometimes adapted to the language of yoga. Bhajan called 'Sat Nam' the '*bij* or *mul* (original) mantra'. In her book, Shakti Parwha Kaur Khalsa claims that repeating the phrase 'instantly attunes us to our highest Self' (S.P.K. Khalsa 1996: 24). As previously mentioned '*Ek Ong Kar Sat Nam Siri Wahe Guru*' is frequently chanted, and Shakti Parwha Kaur Khalsa claims that it 'opens the chakras' (S.P.K. Khalsa 1996: 215).[8]

Such interpretations have troubled some ethnic Sikhs who have come into contact with 3HO. Some have argued that the 'Bhajan Sikhs' do the right things, but for the wrong reasons. The critics certainly have a point, but one could argue, as did one contributor to an ex-members' email list shortly after Bhajan's death, that Bhajan's approach was essentially Sikh: 'The essence of Yogi Bhajan's kundalini yoga is meditating on the name.... The vast majority of mantras Yogi Bhajan used were from the Sikh tradition, albeit the Sikh tradition including Nirmalas, Udasis, and his teacher Sant Hazara Singh' ('The Wacko World of Yogi Bhajan', October 2004).

Sikh practices were also presented as a 'structure' for the kundalini energy that the students had raised—as a way to channel and apply it. First, yoga would empower the devotees, then practising as a Sikh would encourage humility and appropriate application of that power. Sikhi and Tantra together would meet the spiritual requirements of Bhajan's young students. Thus, the belief systems were combined in the 'daily sadhana' which, after

1972, included yoga, meditation, *kirtan*, and readings from the Guru Granth Sahib.

In 1973, Bhajan incorporated the Sikh Dharma Brotherhood, an organization separate from 3HO. He established a governing unit, the Khalsa Council, and a ministry which included both men and women. Devotees began to adopt their version of Indian dress. Bhajan told them that white would provide a pure vibration that would attract people to the ideas and service that Sikh Dharma could offer. Soon they were dressing mostly in white, in *kurta*s (a long shirt worn by both men and women) and *chuddidar*s (fitted pants), with white turbans and *chunni*s (long, flowing scarves, usually worn around the neck in India, but draped over the turban in 3HO/Sikh Dharma). They also changed their names. Bhajan assigned first names, and ashram residents took the last name of Khalsa.

One observer described Maharaj, an early ashram in New Mexico:

In 1970 the members of Maharaj retained their English names and did not wear turbans or the other symbols of Sikh identity, but by 1973...the movement traced its lineage to Guru Nanak...and had by then adopted the Sikh ...ceremonies, texts, and life-style virtually in their entirety (Gardner 1978: 130).

These outward signs represented a move toward normative Sikh ideology. The Khalsa model of the saint-soldier rapidly became the ideal in Sikh Dharma, for both men and women. More members chose the formal Sikh initiation, becoming *amritdhari* (initiated into the Khalsa order), while others took Sikh Dharma vows, which included acceptance of the Guru Granth Sahib as sole guru (Dusenbery 1975; Bailey 1974). The newly minted Sikhs valued the poetry and music of the Guru Granth Sahib. They interpreted their adopted religion in ways that were congruent with their previous backgrounds and values. Thus they saw it as an egalitarian one in which all were spiritually equal, whatever their station in life. They tended to construe it as universalistic, independent of Punjabi culture, and as an experiential religion in which beliefs and creeds mattered less than a direct experience of God.

The women also came to their own interpretations of the saint-soldier tradition. When asked about the rather military Khalsa ideal and its relevance to women, 3HO women interviewed in the 1980s tended to say that it represented staunch defense of core values and a willingness to fight for the rights of all—an interpretation in keeping with counterculture thinking and many members' previous political values.

This ideal clearly has been internalized as a generalized sense of empowerment which still resonates today. Thus, in an official 3HO announcement of a 2007 workshop, Shanti Kaur Khalsa harks back to earlier days:

Khalsa Women's Training Camp in the summer of 1983 was a revolutionary time for women in Sikh Dharma. For the first time, SSS Harbhajan Singh Khalsa Yogiji set the roots of the Khalsa women of the west deep into the identity of Guru Gobind Singh and the path of the spiritual warrior. What we discovered that summer is that, unlike what most of our mothers had taught us, women are true warriors by nature. It is in our psyche (S.K. Khalsa 2007).

In a similar vein, but in an earlier posting, she writes that, 'We bow to no man...We bow to the Word, the Shabd, the sound current. As women we cannot underestimate the power of our own words and language' (S.K. Khalsa 2006).

The Khalsa Women's Training Camp, familiarly known as 'ladies' camp', was instituted in the mid 1970s by Yogi Bhajan and several women students (the camp is a Sikh Dharma invention, and does not arise from Punjabi roots). Originally women spent weeks there during the summer learning more about Sikhism, yoga, and Indian culture. Campers rose early (4:00 a.m.) for daily sadhana, took courses, and every afternoon assembled for a lecture by Yogi Bhajan. There were also entrepreneurial opportunities. The women could teach classes and ply their wares (recordings of songs and kirtan, clothing, artwork, and the like). They also enjoyed a respite from home and family. At first it was mostly women who were affiliated with 3HO and Sikh Dharma who attended. Later, the camp began to cater more to their yoga students. It was at the camp, during the early years, that many of the 3HO/Sikh Dharma ideas about the nature of women and women's experience were formulated.[9]

A content analysis of Bhajan's lectures during the years between 1976 and 1995 captures some of his major themes (Elsberg 2003).[10] A central idea is that women should 'control environments' rather than react to circumstances. According to

Bhajan, 'the basic quality of every woman is that she can change every negative thing around her to be positive' (Bhajan 1979: 211). By being graceful, calm, centred, and attuned to her higher Self, a woman can overcome any obstacle and alter conditions simply by the power of her spirit and 'radiance'. She does, however, have many obstacles to overcome because women have been so exploited in the US and because women need a certain level of 'security' which is not always readily available. Security implies self-esteem, acceptance, and freedom from high levels of competition and stress, and assurance that in a domestic relationship 'every facet of your life, your reproductive faculty and your delicacy is protected' (Bhajan 1976: 42).

Other themes include communication and self-presentation ('projection'). The listeners are told that choice of clothing, words, and tone are important, for if 3HO women are to help others, then they must project calm, grace, and respect for others' opinions and expectations. If they are to avoid unwanted advances and attention from men they should 'entertain no rude words...no words which do not have as their objective to sponsor you as a woman' (Bhajan 1979: 19). Moreover, by appearing graceful, centred, confident and able, a woman finds that she can actually obtain all of those qualities because 'you are what you project' (Bhajan 1981: 36). Women were urged to strive for excellence, to become 'like steel' and toughen themselves so as to be able to cope with coming hard times. Bhajan made many predictions of future hard times and 'insanity' which would call for the strength and 'spiritual technology' of his students (Bhajan 1974). This theme was softened over the years, though, so that there were fewer references to toughening the self and more allusions to women's artistic nature and to living with 'elegance'.

Bhajan often reminded women that they were shaktis and sometimes even equated his listeners with the goddess. But his comments suggest that their creative capacity must be used only in certain ways. Women should attract, influence, and mould others rather than stride aggressively into the world. Women should not compete with or act like men: 'Whenever you use male language or male technique you are absolutely a failure as a woman... what has gone wrong in America is that the American woman has become a male...' (Bhajan 1979: 157). A woman should be 'a living tranquility, peace, harmony, grace and sophistication' (Bhajan 1986: 30). And, 'kindness, compassion, forgiveness and beautiful behaviour are the basic gestures of the female' (ibid.: 10).

Women were also criticized for being manipulative, overly emotional, forgetting God, being too 'sexy and sensual', and for not supporting the men in their lives. Women were said to adopt such behaviour because they felt insecure, exploited, neglected, or abused and alienated from their spiritual core. When that happened they were lost, shallow, readily influenced by others, and caught up in identities that did not spring from their spiritual essence.

It is not difficult to understand how these ideas might have resonated with female converts who *were* feeling alienated, who indeed felt that they were objectified by the media and not respected or treated well by men, who had experienced role overload and uncertainties about their identities (Palmer 1994). However, in the area of what women did 'wrong', the lectures often seem excessively critical. Bhajan complained that the women were spoiled. He accused them of cheapening themselves, and even asked at one point, 'Why the hell are you always on sale' (Bhajan 1992: 53)? He told them that they were often 'obnoxious'. He suggested that women cause most of their own problems, and even said that arguments and abuse between spouses wouldn't occur if women just smiled more and agreed with their husbands. He justified such comments by describing himself as a hard teacher (a 'Cancer teacher') who criticized the student in order to break down her ego and change her entrenched patterns of behaviour. But, even allowing for this technique, his criticisms were perhaps not the best way to create the place of security and respect that he said women should inhabit.

Whatever their reactions to his lectures, women came up with their own interpretations of Bhajan's message; individual women have incorporated some of his teachings into their lives and left others to the side. Many have become yoga teachers, leaders of workshops for women seeking spiritual and personal growth, and recently have trained to become life coaches. As teachers, they appear to adjust Bhajan's ideas and their understanding of Sikhism to the needs and backgrounds of their audiences. Much of what Bhajan said about the nature of men and women runs counter to the expectations of the women who take classes from 3HO teachers. So when 3HO teachers encounter objections, they appropriately frame and soften their message.

Here, for example, Shakti Parwha Kaur Khalsa is trying to convey 3HO ideas about gender to her readers, knowing that her audience will not necessarily agree with her views. 'It's obvious that the current belief system of the "equality" of men and women has not brought us happiness and fulfilment. Discontent, depression, and frustration are common' (S.P.K. Khalsa 1996: 131). Difference, not equality, is the key, she argues. Thus, 'women were not created to compete with men...men and women were meant to complement and supplement each other' (ibid.: 137). Men are supposed to be steady, predictable, rational, focused on one thing at a time, out and about in the world. Women are more changeable and intuitive, better able to deal with many things at once and in need of some protection from the external world (ibid.: 135).

Not only did the young devotees adopt this gender ideology, they accepted what for American and Canadian youth had to have been a very difficult proposition: arranged marriages. Bhajan explained that Sikhs are householders and he encouraged marriage, often actually arranging the marriages himself. In some cases, he would just tell a man or woman that he had chosen an appropriate spouse for that person. In other cases, a student would go to Bhajan asking him to choose someone as a spouse. Then Bhajan, or his secretary, might ask if the person had someone in mind and would act as a go-between if such was the case, or would simply suggest someone if the student expressed no preference. Individuals who had already chosen mates simply asked their ashram director to approve a marriage. Bhajan claimed to choose mates on the basis of their 'auras'. He was critical of American marriages, based, in his view, on temporary emotions and likely to create discontent and high divorce rates. He encouraged his students to think of marriage as yoga, a yoking or 'amalgamation' of two individuals, a union that should last for a lifetime. It is interesting that their counterculture and New Age backgrounds may actually have made his students more likely to go along with these arrangements. Many were disillusioned with contemporary marriage and American culture. A completely different approach to marriage, one that turned it into a spiritual journey and a strike against the seeming superficiality of American culture and commitments, appealed to them, or at least seemed worth considering.

Most of the major features of 3HO/Sikh Dharma were put in place in the 1970s. People settled into their lives as householders, raised their children, attended the gurdwara on Sundays, tried to get up early for morning sadhana, and performed sewa (service) for their community. They travelled to large summer and winter solstice celebrations (solstice celebrations were another innovation adopted from the American counterculture), and sometimes to India. Things were new and exciting.

But as the 1970s ended, many of the ashram residents who lived in cities began to move to the suburbs in order to find enough space and safety to raise their children. Their lifestyle was less communal than it had previously been as each family unit made its way. But there were still communal aspects to everyday life. Families often found houses close together. Children ran in and out of those houses with all of the parents, particularly the mothers, sharing the burdens of childrearing. Parents chose Montessori schools for their young children, and when the children grew older they decided to send them to school in India. The idea was that this would protect the children from the attitudes and the 'sex and drugs' that permeated the American school system. 3HO/Sikh Dharma has used three different schools in India. The current school, the Miri Piri Academy outside Amritsar, includes some Sikh Dharma staff and seems to be more satisfactory than earlier choices.

Many ashram residents worked together in 'family businesses' such as landscaping, accountancy, shoe sales, jewellery sales or restaurants (a number of ashrams opened 'Golden Temple' vegetarian restaurants). Although Bhajan originally said that women should be homemakers, many families encountered the realities of the time—it took two earners to raise a family comfortably. Some men and women went back to school (a significant proportion had dropped out of college to be in 3HO) to improve their earning power. For his part, Bhajan, in time, accepted the reality of two-earner families in North America.

The 1970s and 1980s appear to have been a time of considerable conformity and discipline. People were praised for being devout and committed. Members talked about 'keeping up' and being tested. It was also a time when events in India changed the nature of Sikh immigration to the US and Canada. Immigrants who left India in the wake of the violence following Indira Gandhi's assassination brought painful stories, intense political feelings, and a tendency to adhere strictly to the outward symbols of Sikh identity. The gora Sikhs criticized some of these Sikhs for bringing politics into gurdwaras, for the importance they attached to caste, and, sometimes, for giving women secondary status. In general, they tended to stand apart from what they called 'Sikh politics' (Dusenbery 1990; Elsberg 2003; Fenton 1988; Gurudarm Singh Khalsa 1993; McLeod 1989).

For people who had been rebellious and hip and eager for alternative cultural perspectives not long before, the new serious lifestyle was, at times, too much. Many leaders at the centre in Espanola New Mexico left in 1984, 'complaining of the intense discipline and being cut off from the Sikh community as a whole and from American culture' (Lewis 1998: 113). Many also left the Washington ashram with questions about the leadership. In addition, there were troubling legal problems with some businesses and a suit brought by ex-women members against Yogi Bhajan (*S. Premka Kaur Khalsa* v. *Harbhajan Singh Khalsa Yogiji* et al., and *Katherine Felt* v. *Harbhajan Singh Khalsa Yogiji et al.* 1986).

The 1990s and the turn of the century brought a number of changes, generally leading in the direction of somewhat more open and conventional forms of organization and increased outreach. This created more leadership openings for women members. All ashram directors had been (and still are) male, but ashrams added elected councils to their leadership structure, and these included women. Women became much more active in running and administering 3HO-related businesses. For example, a woman runs Ancient Healing Ways, which sells products for 3HO. Four of the five directors of the Unto Infinity Board are women. This board essentially oversees all of the group's for-profit and non-profit enterprises (although it is currently at the centre of some controversy). 3HO increased its efforts to train yoga teachers, and most of the teachers and students are women. 3HO has created an organization for these teachers, the International Kundalini Yoga Teachers Association, which claims 2000 members. Sikh Dharma became increasingly active in interfaith and international affairs. 3HO is a non-governmental member of the United Nations, with Bibiji Inderjit Kaur, Bhajan's wife, serving as leader of NGO activities, a position she had assumed before his death. There was also a concerted effort to rationalize the businesses run by members of 3HO and Sikh Dharma, including Yogi Tea, Peace Cereal, and the remarkably profitable Akal Security.

After 11 September 2001, SikhNet, created by a member of Sikh Dharma, worked actively to address hate crimes and prejudice that ensued. Akal Security became even more successful. Akal now guards a number of military bases in the US, provides court security for the US Marshall Service, guards the Ronald Reagan Building in Washington DC and provides security services at Baltimore/Washington and El Paso international airports. The chief executive is Sat Nirmal Kaur Khalsa, and her husband, Daya Singh, is Senior Vice President. Another woman, Shanti Kaur, is a director as well.

Women like Shakti Parwha Kaur Khalsa have written instructional books on yoga and stress reduction techniques. An interesting case in point is Guru Rattana Khalsa. When she encountered 3HO/Sikh Dharma she already had a PhD in political science. She had taught for Dartmouth College, and had been a post-doctoral fellow at MIT. She had worked for the President's Council for Environmental Quality. She now publishes her own work and teaches yoga and self-empowerment.

One of her books is a series of what she calls 'essay-poems' about 'women of the twenty-first century'. It incorporates much of the 3HO view of women, and adds strains of eco-feminism. Guru Rattana Khalsa begins by telling her reader that 'the goal of this book is to lead you through a process which will help you know, understand, and accept yourself as a woman. My intent is to help you tap into your own inner knowing and begin to resonate with your divine feminine essence' (G.R. Khalsa 1996: 22). She introduces a 'vision' of a future where every woman

Experiences her essence as a woman/Knows who she is and why she is here/Acts from her inner strength and creativity/Discovers and claims her own unique identity/ Delivers her own individuality and gifts to the world (ibid.: 37).

The first pages echo the 3HO description of modern western society. 'There are no safe environments./There is no cozy home./In its place is junk food/ junk TV programmes/junk relationships'. And 'the average woman today is so mentally scared and insecure/that she has lost touch with her true essence./ Instead of being a peaceful beacon of light/she is a shadow of/ irritation/obnoxiousness/aggressiveness or/depression' (G.R. Khalsa 1996: 58).

But Guru Rattana Khalsa goes on to make a plea to women. They must save the environment, because only women understand mother earth and can truly 'welcome the counsel of the Divine Mother'. Women must stop being the enablers 'who allow men/to get away with half-truths'. They let 'men clutter the world with partial solutions and linear answers/that seldom deal with the real cause of the problem'. Why is this? 'The current patriarchal, hierarchical system does not/ acknowledge/understand/respect or/accept/women/the Earth or/the divine feminine' (ibid.: 128, 148). And women have allowed this to happen because they do not respect themselves: 'you are obsessed with external facades. /You ignore your essence as the Grace of God. /You cultivate appearances and not your radiance'. When women truly recognize themselves as 'the Grace of God' and 'emanate this', then '[f]or the first time men will be able/to respect/to honor/to cherish/women/the Earth/the divine feminine/their own feelings/the feminine within themselves'. Women should 'do what you have to do and want to do/for yourself/for the planet/for the children/for the women of the world/and see what happens' (ibid.: 150, 151, 153). Guru Rattana Khalsa's work is interesting as an example of an activist application of 3HO gender ideas. Her tone bears some similarity to that of Vandana Shiva and other Indian women ecologists and activists who, in their 'struggles to conserve forests, land and water' invoke goddess themes and the view of nature as the 'primordial energy' (Shiva 1988: xvii). But Rattana incorporates both the criticisms of women and the visionary hopes for women that one hears in 3HO/Sikh Dharma.

Will 3HO women play the part that Rattana imagines? It is interesting to contemplate the role that women will play in the future of Sikh Dharma and 3HO. Bhajan died on 6 October 2004 at the age of seventy-five. He did not appoint another Siri Singh

Sahib, instead leaving instructions that divided authority among a number of individuals and organizations. His instructions for the continuation of his institutions and enterprises were complex. According to a notice issued in 2004 by Guru Terath Singh Khalsa, Chancellor of Sikh Dharma, Bhajan bestowed 'Chief Administrative Authority' on the Unto Infinity Board created in 2003. The board is supposed to 'provide overall management and to maintain the mission and values for the non-profit and for-profit corporations'. Both the boards of directors and CEOs of the corporations were to continue in their positions. In the case of Sikh Dharma, Bhajan's wife already held the title of 'Bhai Sahiba for Sikh Dharma of the Western Hemisphere'. Upon her husband's death she was given the responsibility to advise Unto Infinity and the Khalsa Council on religious matters and 'she is responsible for the perpetuation and standardization of the teachings on the practice of Sikh Dharma as taught by the Siri Singh Sahib'. There is also a new position, 'Siri Sikhdar Sahiba' to be held by Guru Amrit Kaur Khalsa, previously Secretary General. The Siri Sikhdar Sahiba is responsible, along with the Bhai Sahiba, 'for creating and maintaining the quality of spiritual practice in the Sikh Dharma communities of the Western Hemisphere'. Additionally, she is to oversee the education of the children of Sikh Dharma and is tasked with 'overseeing the development and maintenance of Gurdwaras in the Western Hemisphere, and delivering a State of the Dharma address to the Khalsa Council every Baisakhi'. This seems to give her a pre-eminent position. On the 3HO side Bhajan created yet another position, 'Director of Spiritual Trust' and appointed another woman, Sopurkh Kaur Khalsa, to that position as well (Guru Terath Singh Khalsa 2004).

The proliferation of governing positions seems to have been intended to spread power widely, and it has, predictably, led to considerable testing of limits and jostling for authority. Whether these are simply growing pains or signs that the organization is in the process of fragmenting remains to be seen. As things stand now, the Unto Infinity Board has moved actively to control the boards of individual businesses and the affairs of a local *sangat*. To further complicate matters, the four members of the Unto Infinity board have evidently ceased to wear their turbans and to live as Khalsa Sikhs. They are being opposed by individual sangats and by Sikh Dharma International on the grounds that only individuals who adhere to the Sikh Dharma way of life can legitimately run the businesses. An additional source of friction concerns a trust Bhajan created before his death. Three women who have served on Bhajan's staff have sued his widow. They represent one half of the trust (their half is the Staff Trust and the other half, the Survivor's Trust, goes to Inderjit). They claim that Inderjit has received what she is due from Bhajan's estate and that she is 'making unsubstantiated claims for millions of dollars against a trust set up to benefit the late Sikh leader's assistants' (Sharpe 2007). Inderjit, in turn, maintains that gifts were made from the trust just prior to Bhajan's death and that these should not be taken out of the Survivor's share (Khalsa 2009). This matter is in court.

Melton has suggested that the corporate structure of contemporary religious movements mitigates intense rivalries and power struggles when a leader dies: 'Given the collective nature of the board leadership, it is not subject to the disturbances caused by the death of any single person' (Melton 1991: 10). But, where there are a number of boards and governing entities and a divided trust involved, this may not prove to be the case.

Bhajan surrounded himself with women to whom he gave supporting roles. They now seem to have stepped out of the background and into the foreground, and some are behaving like very tough businesswomen. The ideal 3HO woman has been empowered, but via spiritual practices. Her power is that of the shakti and is inherent in being a spiritual female rather than being lodged in material wealth or social roles. Wealth and significant positions may exist, but according to Bhajan's teachings they cannot constitute a woman's basic identity. Now that some women are positioned to control considerable wealth, they are defining power differently. It is unclear whether the future of 3HO belong to the women of Unto Infinity, to the more traditional women members, to the women appointed as Bhai Sahiba (Inderjit Kaur) and Siri Sikhdar Sahiba (Guru Amrit Kaur), or to the kinds of women that Guru Rattana Kaur wants to inspire.

Appointing a Bhai Sahiba and a Siri Sikhdar Sahiba is a long way from the anointing of a female replacement or guru, an arrangement that would have retained the central role of a charismatic leader, and would have clearly made a woman the dominant figure. While North America has welcomed a growing number of woman gurus (Pechilis 2004), the duties of these two women leaders of Sikh Dharma are clearly circumscribed. Inderjit is often the public face of 3HO and Sikh Dharma. She has received a number of awards, attends some meetings at the United Nations and she has been active in pushing the SGPC (the overseer of gurdwaras in Punjab) to give women more visibility in Sikh rites. The following is a quotation from a letter she wrote on 9 August 2005 which was posted on SikhNet:

I extend my congratulations to the SGPC and its President Bibi Jagir Kaur for the timely steps they are taking...I applaud the move by the SGPC yesterday to allow Sikh women to perform kirtan at Darbar Sahib and also to take part in carrying the Palki Sahib...In 1996, then-acting Jathedar of the Akal Takhat, Singh Sahib Bhai Manjit Singh issued a Hukamnama granting Sikh women the right to perform seva at Harimander Sahib. On March 10, 1996, with the full support and blessing of the Siri Singh Sahib, it was my blessing to lead a group of women to the Harimandir Sahib to perform seva. The group was comprised of Sikh women from around the world. Unfortunately, there was so much anger in the crowd and so much resistance to our presence that we could not come back again after that night...In February of 2003, I issued a letter calling for signatures to encourage the Jathedars to correct this situation. Over 8,000 people signed the petition, and the signatures were presented to the Sikh leadership. Although it has taken two years for SGPC to act, we are grateful to God and Guru that they are listening to the will of the Panth and supporting the rights of Sikh women ('Sikh Women to perform seva in the Golden Temple').

Perhaps 'the rights of Sikh women' will continue to be a concern, given the presence of more female leaders in 3HO/Sikh Dharma and the passing of a fairly conservative male spiritual leader.

Much of the literature on women and religion suggests that female-led and woman-centred religions have distinctive characteristics. While 3HO/Sikh Dharma has not become one of these religions, it is interesting to compare it to such organizations. Sered finds that 'female-dominated religions' have a 'rich ritual repertoire focused on concrete problems' (Sered 1994: 145). Adherents tend to assume the immanence of divinity. The human body is treated as sacred, rather than as a source of temptation, and teachings are often grounded in physical practices and bodily imagery. There is concern with health and physical activity. The women in these religions do not worship 'a single, all-powerful, male deity' (ibid.: 285). These characteristics clearly apply to the Tantric/yogic aspects of 3HO/Sikh Dharma and it is interesting that so many of the women have embraced these and have become yoga teachers and healers. The Sikh elements of the teachings are not so clearly consistent with the characteristics Sered lists. Certainly Bhajan tried to make the contributions of Sikhism concrete and practical. He often seemed to depict God as immanent, as in the case of the mantra, 'God and Me, Me and God are One'. (This was a meditation that Bhajan frequently used in his classes and meditation sessions). And one can certainly argue for immanence as a basic principle in Sikhism. But if divinity was sometimes immanent in Bhajan's teachings, it was also elusive. His primary emphasis seems to have been more on maintaining 'God-consciousness' and women members often spoke about feeling either 'connected' or 'disconnected' to God. In numerous interviews women spoke about 'forgetting' about the sacred and finding themselves mired in trivia and daily concerns. As for teachings about the sacred quality of the body, Bhajan dismissed ideas of original sin, and insisted that happiness, including the joys shared by a loving couple, is a birthright. But, as we have seen, he also scolded women for being flirtatious and sensuous and thought that women should be modest and covered. While covering does not necessarily imply a demeaning of women's bodies, it does seem to fit with a strain of his teachings and attitudes which harken back to purdah and notions of women as a source of temptation and dishonour.

Bednarowski (1993) finds similar themes in the work of women theologians. These are particularly interesting for considering the future of 3HO/Sikh Dharma. Alongside a focus on the immanence of the divine, she also notes that female theologians tend to emphasize an inward-looking spiritual journey, something certainly present in 3HO/Sikh Dharma in the form of meditation and in the emphasis on expansion of consciousness, and, in activities like Solstice celebrations and women's camps. Bednarowski also finds that the female theologians prefer community over individualism, a value shared by many in 3HO/Sikh Dharma, although the communal elements have waned over the years. She finds a preference for 'relationship as an organizational principle rather than hierarchy' (Bednarowski 1993: 229), a principle that is not so dominant in the history of 3HO/Sikh Dharma. It will be interesting to see if this changes at all under the new leadership.

In another context, Bednarowski notes that women's religious thought often turns to 'the revelatory power of the ordinary'. One critique women make of traditional theology, she says, concerns 'the assumption that any ordinary day requires tasks that must be carried out and endured so that more important things can be accomplished—often by more important people. Further, goes this line of thought, women have always had more than their share of responsibility for these daily tasks, and their religious significance has never been adequately articulated' (Bednarowski 1999: 90).

This is an area in which 3HO/Sikh Dharma has much to offer. There is, for example, the insistence that cosy homes are essential in order to revitalize American culture and raise generations of healthy, happy, holy children. Creating such a home is women's work. The idea of service (seva) is important in Sikh life—serving the community is a central value. There is also a host of daily practices that give added meaning to daily life. During meditation a practitioner tries to focus the mind for the day so that thoughts will not stray and she will remember God throughout the ordinary routines. There are numerous supporting reminders ingrained in the teachings and practices: wearing white, covering the head with a turban, answering the telephone with 'Sat nam', rather than a simple 'hello', for example. 3HO/Sikh Dharma even provides instructions for how to wake in the morning, how to shower, when to pray, and how to interpret everyday problems.

Holistic thinking was very important in counterculture movements (Tipton 1982), and many of the young devotees carried this mindset with them when they joined 3HO. A holistic approach to the world links different aspects of life: physical, spiritual, emotional, intellectual, and political. It is the opposite of the analytical, bureaucratic, and specialized way of thinking that many youth at the time saw as soul-destroying and unproductive. The holistic quality of 3HO/Sikh Dharma life probably holds a special appeal to women as it is a perspective that integrates the spiritual with the ordinary and is one that is probably associated particularly with women's thinking and experience.

As a Canadian Sikh woman put it, in Sikh Dharma 'Mind, body, and spirit are one. Everything affects everything else...all our values are behind every breath' (telephone interview, 2001). While some of the beliefs and practices of 3HO/Sikh Dharma may appear to be heterodox to many Sikhs, the distinctive combination of elements that Bhajan originally included had a particular appeal to women. Some of the yogic or 'Hinduized' elements may have made the organization appear less patriarchal than other religious traditions. Certainly this is true of the Tantric emphasis on empowerment and shakti which came at the same time that the women's movement was spreading, and in a sense, represented a spiritual version of that movement's message. The yogic idea that the body can be a site of spiritual awakening was attractive to counterculture women. Added to the above benefits are Sikh values. As Jakobsh says, 'Guru Nanak and the subsequent nine Sikh gurus were visionaries—their message of liberation extended to all, regardless of caste, religion, and gender' (Jakobsh 2003: 1). Nanak's teachings on the dignity of women, the egalitarian aspects of Sikhi, and the sense of community and service inherent in Sikhism were all important to women converts. And, perhaps most important, there was the Sikh expectation that people should live their beliefs and visibly express commitment. One woman told me that studying Sikhism when it was first introduced was 'the most inspiring thing I ever did in my life, to this day'. She embraced the idea of the warrior-saint, interpreting 'warrior' as 'someone who, when there's a problem, when there's pain or there's injustice, doesn't hesitate to take responsibility' (interview, April 1981). For women who wanted to see major changes in the world and its systems of power, who did not want to embrace traditional women's roles, but did not embrace feminism, who desperately wanted to find ways to unite meaning and action, it was Sikhism that provided the form and structure they needed. The beliefs and practices of their version of Kundalini yoga met needs for a bodily, engaged, practical, empowering form of spirituality. Sikhism introduced the inspiring words of the Gurus, the beauty of kirtan or hymn singing, the values of commitment and service, and affiliation with an international community.

Nonetheless, it must be said that many of the women who have left the organization view it in much the same terms as

Bhajan sometimes described women: 'manipulative', 'for sale', 'not what it should be'. They question some of the business practices of the organization. They also suggest that the talk of honouring women was more words than reality. Some feel that they are more empowered now, as participants in the wider world, than they were in the small world of 3HO.

It may well be that many of the teachings—that women are meant to be graceful, calm, supportive, poised, and appropriately dressed, for example—suited the leadership. Bhajan and other leaders must have wanted loyal women members who did not readily disagree with them. They benefited from the organizational stability that strong families with dedicated wives and mothers could provide, and from the services that women rendered. There is much in 3HO/Sikh Dharma that has been of use to women seeking a new reality, but it is one thing to participate in the construction of an alternative religion, which many women have done, and quite another to truly lead it and shape it, which few have done.

Whether that is the next chapter in the story remains to be seen.

NOTES

1. While the classes are definitely without sexual content, it is interesting that one 3HO writer compiled a book of Bhajan's teachings and yoga sets around the theme of *Sexuality and Spirituality* (Khalsa and Maxwell 1989). The authors introduce the subject with what seems to be a New Age approach to relationships and sexuality, saying that 'there is now abundant planetary love energy to support each of us going inside and finding our own purity, light, harmony and peace, and implementing the sharing of unconditional love with another human being without fear, restriction or withholding'. Yoga sets included are said to increase and maintain beauty and sexual potency, to raise and control subtle energies, to create emotional balance, to sustain 'healthy, satisfying and nurturing relationships', and to 'combine male and female polarities' (G.K. Khalsa and Maxwell 1989: 10).

2. The Sanatan tradition dates back to the nineteenth century, and draws upon Hindu as well as Sikh sources. Today, the term often refers to a variety of practices and beliefs, like Udasi, Namdhari, and Nirmali teachings, not all of which are recognized by Khalsa Sikhs.

3. Writing anonymously on a website for ex-members.

4. This is a phrase that Bhajan often used in public classes and talks. The author attended a number of Sikh Dharma activities and regularly heard this phrase and others cited in this paper.

5. This is a forum for ex-3HO members, and it offers anonymity to those who post on it. The individual who provided the information is very knowledgeable about the history and influence of Udasis, but did not give me permission to include his name.

6. Private interview with author (by telephone), 7 December 1984.

7. Private interview with author (by telephone), 7 December 1984.

8. A 3HO handout, 'Sadhana Mantras for the Aquarian Age' (n.d.), suggests that the beginning of *Jap-ji* is to be recited for seven minutes, and that it is 'the Mul (Root) Mantra [which] gives the capacity to retain rulership'. 'Sat Siri, Siri Akal'. which was also to be chanted for seven minutes, is described as 'the Mantra for the Aquarian Age'. Chanting of various *shabd*s (hymns) was said to bring particular results such as prosperity, improved communication skills, change in habits, or improved health.

9. The author attended the 1983 camp, interviewed 3HO women from the Washington DC and Los Angeles ashrams about their camp experience, and other subjects related to gender in 3HO/Sikh Dharma, and reviewed printed versions of Bhajan's lectures to the camp.

10. Bhajan's lectures have been transcribed and collected as the Women in Training Series, a volume for each year's lectures.

REFERENCES

Akal Security, Accessed 22 May 2007 at http://www.akalsecurity.com/

Bailey, Raleigh Eugene, Jr (1974). 'An Ethnographic Approach toward the Study of a Spiritually Oriented Communal Group in the USA: The Healthy, Happy, Holy Organization'. PhD dissertation, Hartford Seminary Foundation 1973, Ann Arbor: UMI, 7418679.

Bednarowski, Mary Farrell (1993). 'Widening the Banks of the Mainstream: Women Constructing Theologies', in Catherine Wessinger (ed.), *Women's Leadership in Marginal Religions*, Urbana: The University of Chicago Press, pp. 211–31.

—— (1999). *The Religious Imagination of American Women*, Bloomington: Indiana University Press.

Bhajan, Yogi (1974). *Beads of Truth*, Vol. 23.

—— (1976, 1977, 1979, 1981, 1986, 1992). 'Women in Training Series', 3HO Foundation, S.S. Sat Kirpal Kaur Khalsa (ed.). Transcriptions of lectures delivered by Yogi Bhajan at the Khalsa Women's Training Camp. Eugene, Ore.

Davidman, Lynn (1991). *Tradition in a Rootless World: Women Turn to Orthodox Judaism*, Berkeley and Los Angeles: University of California Press.

Dusenbery, Verne A. (1975). 'Straight Freak Yogi Sikh', Master's thesis, University of Chicago.

—— (1990). 'Punjabi Sikhs and Gora Sikhs: Conflicting Assertions of Sikh Identity in North America', in Joseph T. O'Connell, Milton Israel, and Willard G. Oxtoby (eds), *Sikh History and Religion in the Twentieth Century*, eds. and visiting editors W.H. McLeod and J.S. Grewal, New Delhi: Manohar Publications, 1990 South Asia Edition, pp. 334–55.

Elsberg, Constance Waeber (2003). *Graceful Women: Gender and Identity in an American Sikh Community*, Knoxville: University of Tennessee Press.

Ellwood, Robert S. (1987). 'Introduction', in Robert S. Ellwood (ed.), *Eastern Spirituality in America: Selected Writings*, New York and Mahwah: Paulist Press, pp. 5–43.

Erndl, Kathleen M. (1997). 'The Goddess and Women's Power: A Hindu Case Study', in Karen L. King (ed.), *Women and Goddess Traditions: In Antiquity and Today*, Minneapolis: Fortress Press, pp. 17–38.

Felt, Katherin v. *Harbhajan Singh Khalsa Yogiji* et al. (1986). Civil Action 86-0839, US District Court, Albuquerque, N.M.

Fenton, John Y. (1988). *Transplanting Religious Traditions: Asian Indians in America*, New York: Praeger.

Gardner, Hugh (1978). *The Children of Prosperity: Thirteen Modern American Communes*, New York: St Martin's Press.

Harper, Marvin Henry (1972). *Gurus, Swamis, and Avatars: Spiritual Masters and Their American Disciples*, Philadelphia: Westminster.

Healthy, Happy, Holy Organization website: Accessed 22 May 2007 at http://www.3ho.org/.

Healthy Happy, Holy Organization—women's page: Accessed 4 June 2006 at http://www.3ho.org/women/womens-new/women.htm

Jakobsh, Doris R. (2003). *Relocating Gender in Sikh History: Transformation, Meaning and Identity*, New Delhi: Oxford University Press.

Kaufman, Debra Renee (1991). *Rachel's Daughters: Newly Orthodox Jewish Women*, New Brunswick, NJ: Rutgers University Press.

Kent, Stephen A. (2001). *From Slogans to Mantras: Social Protest and Religious Conversion in the Late Vietnam War Era*, Syracuse: Syracuse University Press.

Khalsa, Amrit Kaur (2009). 'Update Regarding Lawsuit', 2 October 2009. http://www.khalsacommonwealth.org/zap_site/docs/update.htm. Accessed on 28 December 2009.

Khalsa, Bibi Inderjit Kaur (2005). 'Bhai Sahiba Congratulates SGPC on Moving Forward,' 9 August 2005. Accessed 4 June 2006 on SikhNet, http://www.sikhnet.com/ under 'Community'.

Khalsa, Gurucharan Singh (1978). 'Morning Sadhana, the Foundation of a Spiritual Life', in *Kundalini Yoga/Sadhana Guidelines*, Pomona, CA: KRI Publications.

Khalsa, Gurudarm Singh (1993). 'Disappearing Differences: Sikhs Becoming Americans, and Americans Becoming Sikhs'. Paper delivered at conference on 'The Sikh Diaspora', Columbia University, 3 April 1993.

Khalsa, Gurudain Singh (1979). *Beads of Truth*, Vol. II Nos. 1 and 2.

Khalsa, Gururattan Kaur and Ann Marie Maxwell (1989). *Sexuality and Spirituality: With the Kundalini Yoga Sets and Meditations of Yogi Bhajan*, Coronado: Yoga Technology Press.

Khalsa, Guru Rattana (1996). *The Destiny of Women Is the Destiny of the World*, Palo Alto: Heart Quest Press (Also see Khalsa, Gururattan Kaur).

Khalsa, Guru Terath Singh (2004). 'Leadership Structure for Sikh Dharma'. 14 October, Accessed 11 March 2005 on http://fateh.sikhnet.com/s/SDLeadership2

Khalsa, Premka Kaur (1971). *Peace Lagoon*, San Rafael: Spiritual Community Publications.

Khalsa, Shakta Kaur (2002). *Yoga for Women*, New York: DK Publishing.

Khalsa, Shakti Parwha Kaur (1983). Orientation Course, Khalsa Women's Training Camp.

—— (1996). *Kundalini Yoga: The Flow of Eternal Power*, Los Angeles: Time Capsule Books.

Khalsa, Shanti Kaur (2006). 'Spiritual Strength of Women', part 6, March 2006, Accessed 22 May 2007 on http://www.sikhwomen.com/Sexuality/BeautifulWomen/spiritualstrength/ss6.htm.

—— (2007). 'Bowing Jap Sahib', Accessed 22 May 2007 on http://www.mrsikhnet.com/?/s+shanti+kaur. Mr. SikhNet 1007 Picks, 17 May 2007.

Khalsa, Shanti Shanti Kaur (1979). 'From Mantra, to Meditation, to Movement', *Beads of Truth* 2, Nos 1–2, April, pp. 42–4.

Khalsa, S. Premka Kaur v. *Harbhajan Singh Khalsa Yogiji* et al. (1986). Civil Action No.86-0838. US District Court, Albuquerque, N.M.

Lewis, James R. (1998). *Cults in America*, Santa Barbara: ABC-CLIO.

McLeod, W.H. (1989). *Who Is a Sikh: The Problem of Sikh Identity*, Oxford: Clarendon Press.

Melton, J. Gordon (1991). 'Introduction: When Prophets Die, The Succession Crisis in New Religions', in Timothy Miller (ed.), *When Prophets Die: The Postcharismatic Fate of New Religious Movements*, Albany: State University of New York Press, pp. 1–12.

Miller, Timothy, ed. (1995). *America's Alternative Religions*, Albany: State University of New York Press.

Palmer, Susan J. (1994). *Moon Sisters, Krishna Mothers, Rajneesh Lovers: Women's Roles in New Religions*, Syracus, NY: Syracus University Press.

Pechilis, Karen (2004). 'Introduction: Hindu Female Gurus in Historical and Philosophical Context', in Karen Pechilis (ed.), *The Graceful Guru: Hindu Female Gurus in India and the United States*, New York: Oxford University Press', pp. 3–49.

Pintchman, Tracy (1994). *The Rise of the Goddess in the Hindu Tradition*, Albany: State University of New York Press.

Pond, Toni Kaur (1972). 'Sikh Dharma', *Beads of Truth* (16), p. 7.

Robbins, Thomas, Anthony Dick, and Thomas Curtis (1975). 'Youth Culture Religious Movements: Evaluating the Integrative Hypothesis', *Sociological Quarterly*, Vol. 16, No. 1, pp. 48–64.

'Sadhana Mantras for the Aquarian Age', n.d., 3HO handout.

Sanatan sources: See http://www.sarbloh.info/, accessed 8 March 2005. Also see http://www.udasi.org/, Accessed 30 January 2005.

Sered, Susan Starr (1994). *Priestess, Mother, Sacred Sister: Religions Dominated by Women*, New York: Oxford University Press.

Sharpe, Tom (2007). 'Late Sikh Leader's Trustees, Widow at Odds Over Estate'. *The Santa Fe New Mexican*, 9 October 2007. at: http://www.santafenewmexican.com/ Accessed on 28 December 2009.

Shiva, Vandana (1988). *Staying Alive: Women, Ecology and Survival in India*, New Delhi: Kali for Women.

Sikhnet, Accessed 22 May 2007 at http://www.sikhnet.com/.

'Sikh Women to perform seva in the Golden Temple', Accessed 4 June 2006 on
    http://www.petitiononline.com/kaurseva/petition.html.

Singh, Shamser (1979). 'The Fruits of Inner Searching', in Premka Kaur
    Khalsa and Sat Kirpal Kaur Khalsa (eds), *A Man Called the Siri Singh
    Sahib*, Los Angeles: Sikh Dharma, pp. 44–6.

Singh, Trilochan (1977). *Sikhism and Tantric Yoga*, Model Town, Ludhiana,
    India: Privately printed.

Singh, Baba Virsa, Accessed 16 June 2006 on http://www.gobindsadan.org/

Stacey, Judith (1991). *Brave New Families*, New York: Basic Books.

Thursby, Gene R. (1995). 'Hindu Movements Since Mid-Century: Yogis in
    the States', in *America's Alternative Religions*, ed. Timothy Miller, Albany:
    SUNY Press, pp. 191–213.

Tipton, Steven M. (1982). *Getting Saved from the Sixties: Moral Meaning in
    Conversion and Cultural Change*, Berkeley and Los Angeles: University
    of California Press.

Yogananda, Paramahansa (1946, 1983). *Autobiography of a Yogi*, Los Angeles:
    Self-Realization Fellowship.

Tobey, Alan (1976). 'The Summer Solstice of the Healthy-Happy-Holy
    Organization', in Charles Y. Glock and Robert N. Bellah (eds), *The New
    Religious Consciousness*, Berkeley and Los Angeles: University of California
    Press, pp. 5–30, Reprinted in abbreviated form, (1979) '3HO's Summer
    Solstice' in *Beads of Truth* 2 (1, 2), pp. 10–23, 1979.

'Wacko World of Yogi Bhajan'. (2005). Delphi Forums. January. Described
    by the moderator as 'an online book and salon for ex-Yogi-Bhajanites',
    accessed on 30 January 2005.

Transnational Migration Theory in Population Geography[*]

Gendered Practices in Networks Linking Canada and India

Margaret Walton-Roberts

Geographers have commented on the absence of dialogue between population geography and social theory (White and Jackson 1995; Graham 1999; Graham and Boyle 2001). More recently Bailey has suggested that transnational migration theory can contribute to the development of a 'critical population geography framework' (Bailey 2001: 424). What might such a critical population geography look like? In this paper I consider this issue in three ways. First I consider why geographers, and in particular population geographers, have been late to engage with transnational concepts, and second, I highlight how gender has been underplayed in the transnationalism literature. Third, I draw upon examples from my research on immigrant networks between Canada and India to highlight how processes of marriage are informed by the presence of extensive transnational influences that maintain and reinforce gendered hierarchies of power. I suggest that attention to a gendered transnational migration theory can contribute to the development of a critical population geography.

BRINGING A TRANSNATIONAL FOCUS TO HUMAN GEOGRAPHY: OVERCOMING SUBDISCIPLINARY BOUNDARIES

Since the early 1990s several scholars, particularly anthropologists, have found the concept of transnationalism useful for understanding the socio-spatial structure and role of immigrant networks (Rouse 1991; Basch *et al.* 1994). This approach replaces the traditional binary focus on linear movement from pre- to post-migratory location, and replaces it with a model that highlights the recursive nature of movement associated with international human mobility. Geographers possess a strong tradition of migration research that can both benefit from and contribute to this transnational approach; but until recently geographers, especially population geographers, have not embraced transnationalism methodologically or theoretically (for some exceptions see Mountz and Wright 1996; Hyndman and Walton-Roberts 2000; Wong 2000). I contend that one explanation for geography's limited adoption of a transnational migration approach is due to the discipline's fragmented nature. Multiple sub-disciplinary divisions, whose boundaries are vigorously defended and re-inscribed, increasingly define geography, this fragmentation leads to the intellectual separation and isolation of issues relevant to international migration under conditions of globalization. Distinctive topics of interest within geography such as population geography, area studies, and development provide important fields related to a transnational approach, yet demarcation of these approaches has resulted in a spatial and conceptual division when it comes to understanding how migrant communities operate across a globally extensive range. To further this argument, I briefly consider each of these sub-disciplines in turn.

The argument that population geography can be strengthened through an engagement with transnational approaches needs to be seen alongside recent debates in the sub-discipline. White and Jackson (1995) argue that population geography has tended to separate itself from wider changes in geography through its reluctance to engage with social theory. Findlay and Graham (1991) and Graham (1999) echo this call by encouraging population geographers to consider using mixed methods and to think more seriously about how the type and availability of data shape their research questions. Though there has been a long tradition of using mixed methods in developing contexts due to the paucity of reliable numerical data (Skeldon 1995), the models and frameworks developed traditionally tended to be limited to the narrow concerns of individualized migrant decision-making, without forging stronger links with wider structural processes such as capitalism and patriarchy. Certainly transnationalism overcomes this conceptual narrowness by encouraging connection between these wider processes. The demands for the employment of diversified methods in population geography intersects well with a transnational approach, since the diversity of the transnational field (spanning as it does multiple political and administrative units), necessarily present limited and/or inconsistent 'official' data sources to rely upon.

While population geography can be critiqued for its conceptual narrowness, other branches of geography, such as area studies and development geography, have traditionally limited our recognition of the presence of transnational migrant networks due to practices of spatial containment. For example, compared to anthropologists, geography's sluggish recognition of the importance of transnational migrant networks can be interpreted as one of the consequences of the bounded spatialization, or 'regionalizing ritual' (Livingstone 1992: 33), that geographers traditionally bring to the study of place. Area studies provide a pertinent example of the way in which perceptions of spatial interconnectedness have been hindered in recent years. Emerging during the Cold War within the political context of an ideological mindset of spatial containment and alignment driven especially the USA (Cumings 1998), area studies was predicated upon isolating particular countries or regions in order to define them as subjects of special research attention. Escobar (1995) has advanced a similar critique at development discourse, arguing the idea of the 'third world' emerged during the Cold War when powerful political interests controlled the debate, and reinforced agreement on where the 'problem' areas were, and why they were deemed to be problematic. Even when the ideological imperative for the 'creation' of these regions withered, their spatially contained representations endured.

In place of spatial separation scholars from across the social sciences are now stressing the linkages between places through a focus on process:

'areas' need to be thought about as the results of processes, including research processes, rather than as objective clusters of cartographic, material or cultural facts. Emphasizing 'process' geographies suggest new ways to approach both space and time in relation to 'areas', with space becoming more flexible and porous and time less sequential and cumulative (Ford Foundation 1999: 8).

Such integrative thinking can pose a serious challenge to the powerful spatial binaries of developed/undeveloped and rural/ urban that tend to delimit geography's sub-disciplinary interests. The incorporation of research approaches that focus on transnational immigrant practices can contribute to a critical population geography framework that challenges traditional methodological, political, and conceptual stances, and in so doing offers more complex and process-driven explanations for current social, political, and economic transformations.

GENDER AND TRANSNATIONAL MIGRATION

A focus on transnational migration involves dealing with diverse forms of data, not only numerical, and it requires an adept negotiation of scale, since the intersection of state and migrant are central elements of a transnational approach. Basch *et al.* (1994) stress that a transnational approach to migration must be grounded in issues of power, class, gender, the state, and political economy. Certainly much of the work that has emerged since the early 1990s has argued that more emphasis needs to be directed to the ways that global capitalism (Ong 1999) and the state (Bailey *et al.* 2002) are implicated in transnational migrant practices. But we must add to this the need to be cognizant of the powerful structuring tendencies of gender, not as a mere variable, but as an ideological power structure that is mobile and malleable. Global migration tends to be examined as a component of the sphere of production, concerned with the experiences of the predominantly single male migrant worker (for example, see Stalker 2000), rather than as an aspect of social reproduction involving the family, the spouse, and the community. Increasingly this bias has been altered through attempts to explicitly highlight how gender exerts a powerful influence over the migration process (Willis and Yeoh 2000), and population geographers have been active in calling attention to and addressing these issues (Hugo 1996; Ford and Kittisuksathit 1996; Brown *et al.* 1998; Boyle and Halfacree 1999). However, despite this corrective in the field of migration studies generally, Mahler and Pessar (2001) maintain that transnational research still inadequately considers the structuring effects of gender, and they argue that recognizing how gender 'becomes embedded in institutions, lays the foundation...for analyzing the structural factors that condition gender relations in addition to ideological factors' (Mahler and Pessar 2001: 442). To examine this in more detail they advocated that we pay greater attention to how 'gendered geographies of power' operate through transnational migrant spaces.

A focus on gender and transnational migration is particularly useful for considering contexts where marriage processes connect countries of pre- and post-migration. For population geographers this type of marriage migration provides an important indicator of future population trends. Smith and Bailey (2001) focus on this dimension of transnational migration by inserting a focus on the 'lifecourse' to understand the spatial and social articulations exercised by migrants. Lievens (1999) argues that this type of family forming migration for first and second-generation Turkish and Moroccan immigrants in Belgium in some cases permits women to challenge patriarchal pressures from family and co-ethnics in Belgium. But such social pressures in marriage practices may be increased in specific cases where the demand for a partner of the same ethnic or religious group creates tight boundaries of acceptability in partner selection. Aligned to the strength of social norms, the degree of global dispersal of the population from which a suitable match can be drawn creates spatially extensive transnational circulations, while simultaneously exhibiting intense social connection. With over twenty million people of Indian origin residing overseas, the potential for such social practices to occur are certainly evident within the global Indian Diaspora (High Level Committee Report on the Indian Diaspora 2002). While recent work on Indian immigration considers the intersection of migration with the presence of marital violence (Abraham 2000) the complex intersections of race, class and gender (Nager 1998) and the racist and sexist tendencies of immigration policy (Bhabha and Shutter 1994; Hall 2002), less work has explored specific transnational migratory networks from an explicit gender perspective. I turn to consider this phenomenon in the context of India–Canada links, and I consider how social practices marked by strong patriarchal norms migrate and mutate alongside this human movement.

India–Canada Immigrant Networks

Indian women overwhelming enter Canada as dependent immigrants, with 87 per cent of Indian female landings in 2000 entering as spouses, parents/grandparents and dependents, or dependents of skilled workers. Of the 25,936 Indian immigrants to Canada in 2000, almost one quarter were spousal applicants, and 60 per cent of these were female (Citizenship and Immigration Canada 2001). This highly gendered dependency provides a context for the transmission and reinforcement of patriarchal assumptions about female behaviour across both Indian and Canadian space (Bal 1997). Traditionally, immigration from India to Canada has comprised Sikh migrants from the Doaba region of Punjab (Johnston 1984), and Sikh matrimonial practices create the potential for extensive transnational networks because marriages are traditionally required to be socially endogamous, but spatially exogamous (Ballard 1990). Before considering this transnational context, I offer a brief overview of customs and norms related to marriage in northern India, particularly Punjab. Typically such detail is provided by geographers involved in development and population geography fields, but is rarely envisioned as active beyond the spatial confines of the subcontinent. In this paper, I reveal some linkages between the cultural norms of north Indian and wider transnational marriage practices as they pertain to immigrant groups overseas.

Women and Marriage Norms in Northern India

It is important to understand that marriage norms cannot be seen in isolation from the wider position of women within Indian society (Hershman 1981; Uberoi 1993). Female inequality begins with male preference, a strong social force particularly in northern India (Arokiasamy 2002). While India's sex ratio in the 2001 Census was 107.8 males to 100 females, Punjab is one of the most skewed of all Indian states at 126.1 males, up from 114.3 in 1991 (India Census 2001; Arnold et al. 2002). Numerous studies have shown that at all ages female mortality in Punjab is higher than male mortality, and this is explained through the preferential allocation of nutrition and medical care to male children (Gupta 1986; Das Gupta 1987). Female infanticide has also historically been practised in northern India, especially by Jats and other higher castes who would normally face difficulty finding an appropriate high caste match for their daughters (Bhat and Halli 1999). Arnold et al. (2002) argue that the practice of sex selection through abortion is rampant in Haryana and Punjab, and though the actual termination of a foetus due to male preference is illegal, the practice is a social reality (Shah 1993). In the fieldwork I conducted in Punjab during the winter of 1999/2000, private ultrasound clinics were a common sight in most large towns in Doaba, a wealthy region that is the site of significant international out migration.

The cultural preference for male children is a potent force with systemic socio-economic 'rationales' reinforced through a number of cultural practices that overlap to strengthen the desire for few, if any, daughters. Traditional marriage practices explain some of these systemic biases against the female child. While living in her father's house the girl is *amanat* ('held in trust') until such time as she departs to join her husband's family; having a daughter is seen as akin to 'watering your neighbour's tree' (Tee 1996: 115). When a daughter becomes sexually mature, her family, especially her mother, become vigilant in monitoring her behaviour, and protecting her sexuality (Das 1993). Her brother, or *bhai*, also closely guards the girl's honour, and it is the brother's job to defend his sister from malicious gossip. Even after her marriage the brother is still considered the protector of his sister and her children, especially against her husband, should the situation arise. This relationship is symbolized through the ceremony of *rakhri*, where the sister ties a bracelet to her brother's wrist to demonstrate her material dependence on him, and his responsibility for maintaining his sister's honour (Gillespie 1995). Though the woman's honour will be protected by her brother and father, in cases where she brings shame to the family, for example through sexual relations prior to marriage, these same patriarchs often avenge the family honour by punishing the woman and the offending male, in some cases through violent means (Hershman 1981). In this way a woman's body becomes the repository of the family honour or *izzat,* and her rights are subsumed, sometimes violently, to those of the patriarchal family.

The female child, once she reaches marriageable age, will leave her natal family to join her husband's family. Sikh marriage practices are caste endogamous, but are strictly exogamous in that women cannot marry into their parent's and grandparent's *got* (descent group). Within a village most members of the same caste are also of the same got, so the woman usually marries into another village where she has no prior kinship ties (Ballard 1990).

Marriages are usually arranged in some manner, but the nature of the process varies depending upon several factors, including religion, geography, and class position (Jyoti 1983; Puri 1999). Without suggesting that there are rigid rules regarding marriage, generally in rural Punjab today marriages are commonly arranged, in that the female may never have met the male before. However, in urban areas and for middle-class families the couple may have been introduced and the woman may have some influence over the final decision (Schurmer-Smith 2000). In marriage matches, friends, family, work colleagues, newspapers, professional marriage brokers, and increasingly the internet, act as matchmakers. The occupational status of the potential groom is of central importance, and middle-class Indian families have an acute knowledge of the different levels and incomes of Indian civil servants, with Indian Police Service (IPS) and Indian Administrative Service (IAS) at the upper end of the spectrum and Railways and Post Office departments at the lower. The woman's educational background is also important, but this has not reduced the expectation for a dowry to accompany the bride. In fact, dowry is playing a larger part in marriage matches, especially for upper- and middle-class families in general and in northern India in particular (Menski 1998). While the 1961

Dowry Prohibition Act officially outlaws dowry, the practice is widespread.

Dowry in its widest sense refers to many things (Menski 1998). First, it includes the cost of wedding celebrations, and the gifts given by guests to the bride and groom. Second, it refers to the things a woman takes with her into her husband's house and in normal circumstances these goods are seen to belong to the woman and contribute to her status in her husband's family. For some, this aspect of dowry is seen as representing the daughter's inheritance, but Sharma (1993) argues that dowry does not represent a fixed share of the bride's father's property because it is the outcome of current marriage market negotiations. It is also wealth transferred to the son-in-law. Therefore 'dowry property' is not women's wealth, but wealth that goes with women. Women are the vehicles by which it is transmitted rather than its owners' (Sharma 1993: 352). Third, dowry now refers to property or cash demands made by the groom's family, for things such as cars, appliances, and so on. This 'new dowry' (Srinivas 1989) is seen to be the major contributor to the modern problems of dowry, especially for middle-class families. Normally the amount of dowry would be controlled through internal community-based norms, but over time these have been undermined as processes of modernization and upward social mobility increase access to expensive and desirable consumer goods. The increase in dowries is also internally reinforced by families who offer a match with their son, while demanding dowries equal or greater to the costs they incurred in marrying off their daughters. The 'evils of dowry' present in Indian society tend to be connected to this new dowry and occur when the groom's family—in some cases led by the mother—continue to demand gifts or cast aspersions on the quality of gifts given, thereby demeaning the bride and her family. The izzat of the bride's family is damaged by such claims, and so families may place themselves in severe debt to meet dowry demands. In extreme cases the groom and members of his family have murdered the bride, in order that the groom may remarry. These 'dowry deaths'—often due to burning or poisoning—have been receiving increased media attention in India. In 1999, there were eleven dowry deaths reported in Punjab, and fifty-three cases of harassment (Talwar 2000). In addition to murder, suicide linked to harassment from in-laws and dowry demands accounted for 80 per cent of female suicides in Punjab during the first half of 2000 (Singh 2000). The problems of dowry death and wife harassment have been of major concern to feminist organizations in India, but there has been no general agreement as to what might be the solution; education certainly will not displace the practice because if anything dowry has been on the increase for middle-class educated families (Bramham 1996). Sweeping assumptions suggesting that this practice is directly responsible for the lower status of women in India are simplistic and divert attention away from other forms of discrimination that undermine the position of women more generally. Many feminists recognize the deep complexity of the problem, in that women and men can both benefit and suffer through the practice of dowry (Leslie 1998). The failure of the 1961 Dowry Prohibition Act to be enforced has encouraged some feminists to argue that rather than outlawing dowry, women's inheritance rights should be promoted (Kishwar 1989; Leslie 1998). This approach can arguably assist in improving the status of women, while directing attention to processes of domestic violence and discrimination against Indian women more generally.

Transnational Patriarchies

This extended discussion about patriarchal practices in northern India is relevant to my argument about the need for a trans-national approach in population geography because as Mahler and Pessar ask '[A]re gender relations and ideologies reaffirmed, reconfigured, or both across transnational spaces?' (Mahler and Pessar 2001: 441). Rather than the simple assumption that im-migrants 'assimilate' to the host society, in the case of gender relations, boundaries are far more porous; social norms as well as people often migrate across space. In these cases we need to draw upon research that is seen as a component of population studies in development contexts, in this case India, and intro-duce it into a more extensive landscape of immigrant settlement in western contexts. Here we see the importance of developing an integrative approach that calls upon the work of numerous subsections of geography.

One example that reveals how social practices in post-migratory contexts are marked by the resilience of patriarchal norms in pre-migration sites, is in the case of male preference. Fair (1996) has investigated a situation where a US-based clinic was advertising prenatal sex selective procedures in the Indo-Canadian media in an effort to target Vancouver's Sikh community. The marketing of prenatal sex determination and selection testing is a growing issue in the USA, where clinics offering such services have been advertising to the Indian immigrant community through outlets such as *India Abroad* and the North American issue of *The Indian Express* (Times of India 2001). In some cases the pressure to have a male child has been considered as intense for immigrant women overseas as it is in India, and the possibility of domestic violence emerging as a response to having too many female children is seen as on one of the pressures forcing immigrant women to turn to such services (Sachs 2001). Migration does not therefore necessarily erase traditional gender norms and relations, though they can be transformed and reshaped. Such transformation is evident when we consider the practice of arranged marriage.

As with my consideration of marriage practices in northern India, it is impossible to suggest there is a fixed essentialized set of processes in place for Indian immigrants overseas. Nonetheless, it is possible to say that the concept of arranged marriage for the children of immigrants in Canada while still present, often exhibits tensions as the balance of control between parents and children adjusts. Karen Ai-Lyn Tee's (1996) research on first- and second-generation South Asian Canadian women suggests that second-generation women more openly debate the issues, and she notes that the norm tends to reflect a move from arranged marriages to arranged introductions; parents may present options, but their children are not necessarily pressured into accepting them. Despite the cultural changes occurring in the precise mode of marital arrangements, the geography of marriage markets extends to include not only the original migrant source area, but also other sites of immigrant settlement such as the United Kingdom and the United States, where Non Resident Indians (NRIs) reside (Divakaruni 2000).[1] This transnational marriage practice has an effect on women not just in

India, but also within the Indian immigrant communities present
in these places. In both Canada and Britain South Asian origin
women have commented on foreign-born South Asian men's
preference to select a wife from India, which has an effect on
their marriage options:

> Guys my age who are born and raised in Canada—when it comes to get
> married, they go to India, to the villages, to find a wife. They want a woman
> who will cook and clean. I'm just a misfit (Howard 1999: 90).

A similar observation is provided in the British case:

> The truth is, Asian men are also disillusioned, faced with women motivated
> solely by the promise of financial security. The men, in turn, are fighting
> back, seeking out nubile Indian village girls in favour of their British Asian
> counterparts (Joshi 2000: 135).

Such matches between NRIs and young women in Punjab are
subject to a number of pressures emerging from family needs,
status, and the desire for suitability in matrimony. The normal desire of parents to secure a suitable and promising match
for their daughter may often be eclipsed by the overpowering
attraction of the international migration option following an international marriage. In the following section I review a selection
of interviews and field observations to illustrate some examples
of how such matches are undertaken, and how they act to channel characteristic male biases between India and overseas sites of
settlement.[2] Again, this focus requires that we overwrite the research division between developed and developing sites through
a combination of relevant material that allows us to illustrate
the mobility of cultural practices within a wider context of immigrant settlement, and the effects they have on the populations
concerned across a transnational field.

Transnational Marriages

Marriage Networks and NRIs

While conducting fieldwork in the Doaba region of Punjab, I was
invited to the wedding of a young Indo-Canadian male, Jassi[3]
from Vancouver, and a young Punjabi woman, Amar. The wedding was arranged through Raj, Jassi's employer in Canada and
a friend of his father. The bride was Raj's cousin, the daughter

of his mother's sister. Such marital matches provide a cultural connection to pre-migratory sites, but they also offer the opportunity for the continued reunion of the extended family to a single location. In this case, local community members speculated that Amar and Jassi's wedding match was arranged so that once Amar was in Canada she could sponsor her mother's immigration, and thereby allow Raj's mother and her sister to be reunited. Obviously finding and securing such complex social and familial arrangements that meet both the legal immigration requirements of the Canadian state and Sikh cultural norms—caste endogamy but village exogamy—can create intense pressure. The search for a suitable match can mean that some people wait years without ever successfully finding a partner. Understandably, this context adds urgency to the need to locate a suitable NRI match in a timely manner; those who can broker a linkage between a family in India and an NRI, engender great respect. On the other hand, the importance of the broker can be seriously undermined if they cannot deliver on promises made.

In Punjab I met Harjeet, an Indo-Canadian from Surrey/ Delta in British Columbia, Canada, and his story reveals how these tensions can manifest themselves.[4] Harjeet had been asked by an acquaintance in Vancouver to consider marriage to a woman from a family in Punjab. Harjeet refused and instead married the sister of a prominent industrialist from Punjab. The man who had initially proposed the first union was so furious that he informed the Canadian High Commission in Delhi and the local police that Harjeet was a terrorist. Since this accusation was made at the height of the Khalistani separatist movement in Punjab the situation created huge problems for Harjeet's relatives in Punjab. Eventually Harjeet's name was cleared, but only with the assistance of his wife's influential brother. These two illustrations indicate how possible marriage matches are produced through of the operation of social networks within spatially extensive immigrant communities that possess similar regional and cultural backgrounds. But such dense social groupings can also provide the context for intense negative social pressures. Individuals involved in matchmaking put their status on the line, and coercion to oblige these matches can be directed at men as well as women.

Gender and Power: Transformations in the Marital Selection Process

In the rural village of Palahi near Phagwara in Kapurthala Punjab, I attended a wedding involving a young couple from Punjab.[5] The host, Jaswant, was the maternal uncle of the bride, the person traditionally responsible for finding an appropriate match for his nieces. In the case of this marriage, the couple had never met before. In the conversation following the ceremony Jaswant commented that this traditional marriage practice (admittedly more prevalent in the villages than in urban areas), where the bride and groom first meet at the wedding, was being transformed because NRIs wanted to meet the prospective bride before any marriage agreement could be made. He argued that many rural families had abided by this change in social custom because they were keen to secure a match with an NRI because it permitted subsequent family migration. His displeasure with this process was obvious as he stated: 'marrying a girl to an NRI in order to get the rest of the family overseas was not marrying the girl, but *selling* the girl'. As the uncle to his sister's daughters he took his responsibility in judging potential suitors and their families seriously. The long process of discussion and negotiation between families, not the potential bride and groom, allowed the families to ascertain each other's character and status. He argued that the families do the work and make the decisions, since the elders are seen to possess the wisdom necessary to making this important decision. He felt this process was being undermined by the presence of NRIs who inserted a power imbalance into the traditional marriage process, and demanded a much shorter time frame to formulate marriage arrangements. This transnational marriage process overwhelmingly favours the mobile male NRI, and reveals how intersections of uneven development, inserted into culturally-specific contexts such as Sikh wedding customs, can produce new gendered imbalances in power, since it is typically the male who seeks the partner overseas. These concerns were amply demonstrated to me in a subsequent matchmaking process I observed.

While visiting one of the larger urban settlements of Punjab I met Hari, a wealthy Indo-Canadian in his fifties who was twice divorced. Hari had been visiting Punjab annually since his second marriage ended in order to locate a third wife who would be intellectually stimulating, but also take on the chores of keeping his large house in good condition. He had placed an advertisement in the matrimonial section of the *Punjab Tribune* stipulating that he wanted a woman no older than thirty-five with a good figure, and had received over one hundred responses. After selecting the most promising options he arranged to meet the families and their daughters, and in one day, accompanied by his friend Preet, Hari visited six families. Preet later expressed concern over how desperate these families were to marry their daughters off to Hari, immediately if need be, despite the fact that during negotiations he stressed that he wanted a pre-nuptial agreement because he was already paying maintenance to his previous wives in Canada. Despite the ample choice Hari was offered, he was growing tired of the process, and in place of seeking a bride in Punjab he speculated that perhaps he should try to find a Cuban or Mexican wife instead. What is striking about this case is the commodified nature of these transactions, and how underdeveloped regions of the world are envisioned as sites receptive to western male wealth status. The fact that he was older and twice divorced seemed to have no bearing on his 'quality', which stemmed from his accumulated wealth and citizenship, whereas the women he 'viewed' had to be carefully sorted and selected through their bodily attributes of age and perceived qualities of purity and domesticity. And yet, despite the imbalances present in this particular match, plenty of families were willing to offer their daughters to him, providing evidence of the widespread desire for marriage to an NRI, even if it meant that the bride would be entering a relationship offering less compatibility in terms of age and marital background. With the impact of a pre-nuptial agreement, it would also potentially offer less security. This case demonstrates that cultural traditions and norms will be altered in response to the presence of NRIs who offer immense rewards, if not to the woman directly, then potentially to her family through subsequent immigration opportunities. Just as with the 'new' dowry, western influences are rarely adopted in their entirety, but intersect with current cultural practices in various complex and contradictory ways, but can result in outcomes marked by similar, perhaps even stronger, elements of gender inequity.

Cultivation and Protection of the 'Global' Marriage Pool in Punjab

The desire many rural families and their daughters have to marry NRIs was made most obvious to me through a visit to Guru Nanak Khalsa Girls College, in Sang Dhesian, District Jalandhar. The college is a well-respected vocational institution providing a broad arts education to 1,300 to 1,400 women between the ages of fifteen and twenty-four.[6] NRI respect for this institution is displayed in the donations made for new buildings, and in the fact that some NRIs have sent their daughters back to Punjab to be educated at this college. The school therefore provides a well-educated and morally 'protected' pool of potential marital matches. Though all students have to be unmarried at the time of admission, the headmistress estimated that 60–70 per cent of the students marry NRIs while at the college, and the majority of these, about 70 per cent, married Canadian NRIs. In fact, she told me that in one area in Surrey, British Columbia, Canada, there are so many students from the College that they jokingly refer to a street in the area as Sang Dhesian Street. Many girls who become married or engaged to NRIs stay and complete their studies at the college while their visas are processed, a system that accommodates the six months to a year visa processing time that can accompany such international marriages. The headmistress felt that in her experience, 80 per cent of NRI marriages were successful, and the majority of women led happy lives overseas, often visiting the school years later with their children. She did, however, acknowledge that problems can arise, especially when if there is a 'mismatch' between the age or marriage background of the partners. She mentioned a few cases where young women had been deceived, even by their own families, and how often the reality of the situation only becomes apparent when the woman is overseas, isolated, and with little access to support. This reflects an important component of marriage as a transnational practice, since despite the intricacies of immigrant networks between these physically distant sites, local social familial support for women once transplanted to Canada becomes more complicated.[7]

In the production and maintenance of these international marriage networks, the extent of information sharing between sites of Punjabi immigrant settlement overseas and communities in Punjab was related to me in a series of discussions with teachers from Guru Nanak Dev College in Nagoda, District Jalandhar.[8] The Vice-principal estimated that though many of the students are interested in travelling overseas, only about 30 per cent actually do migrate internationally, mostly through family and spousal migration routes. When I asked about the success of overseas marriages, the Vice-principal stated that in her opinion divorce was more common in overseas marriages because the husbands had developed bad habits such as drinking and smoking. She also commented on stories of deception, where NRI husbands had abandoned young women once their families had handed over the dowry. In a discussion with one of the college's teachers, when I commented that the large number of girls desiring to go overseas must make them keen English students, she replied 'they don't work hard at English because they know they will pick it up overseas. Also they know they will be doing jobs that need little English'. The range of detailed information relayed between the site of out migration and destination is testament to the dense social interactions occurring across this transnational space. Similar sentiments about international marriages were mentioned at a half a dozen colleges and schools I visited in the Doaba region, and the estimate of about 25–30 per cent of students migrating overseas was reiterated by other Vice-principals I spoke with. For example, in Jandala I met a class of twenty-five young women attending a college extension centre providing an education in dressmaking. One student, wearing the traditional red *chura* (bracelets) to indicate her betrothal, had entered into a marital agreement with a NRI from Leicester in England (her aunt had made the arrangements), and the young woman was completing her education while waiting for her visa. At the end of the discussion my interpreter informed me that most of her classmates were keen to follow her example.[9]

From theses stories it is clear that matches between NRIs and young women in Punjab are subject to a number of pressures emerging from family needs, status, and the desire for suitability in matrimony. The normal desire of parents to secure a suitable and promising match for their child may often be eclipsed by the overpowering allure of international migration. This has led to the development of an uneven field, where power is unequally allocated to the NRI. Indeed, in District Hoshiarpur, in the Doaba region of Punjab, the District Commissioner stated that marriage complaints were the most common NRI-related concerns brought to the attention of the District Police Chief, with over 500 individual complaints in 1999.[10] The Indian legal system, though it does have provisions to deal with such cases, is seen as less inclined to treat women's concerns justly or in a suitable time frame. Indeed the issue of the abuse Indian women have experienced through marriages arranged with NRIs has become such a concern that it was specifically identified in an Indian Government sponsored High Level Committee investigation into the Indian Diaspora. The committee voiced their concern and recommended that the Indian state, prior to issuing marriage registrations, demand affidavits from the NRI groom attesting to their current marital status.[11] The problem of state inaction is not only linked to India, indeed the concern for adequate state action on the part of the promotion and protection of women's rights generally needs to be seen as a wider systemic problem. Canadian enforcement agencies have recently dragged their feet over the case of an Indo-Canadian woman and her brother who Indian authorities have accused of ordering the murder of her daughter who married a lower caste man from her mother's village in Punjab. Police authorities in India have requested the extradition of the woman and her brother from Canada, but have received little or no assistance from Canadian police authorities that have stated that such crimes are beyond their jurisdiction.[12] A transnational gendered focus demands that rather than contain the issue of patriarchy in the south, that is, India, we become more attuned to how its endemic and systemic nature and distribution permits such spatial intersections and reinforcements to occur.

In these examples I have focused on transnational marriage practices related to Punjab, but in order to do so I have had to broaden my focus to include evidence from multiple places and sub-disciplines. Such integrative approaches escape the geographically limited view of area studies by arguing that 'problems', in this case the role of patriarchy, span both developed and developing countries.

CONCLUSION

Despite geography's tradition of synthesis in research and explanation, we have been late to engage with transnational methods and concepts that provide integrative tools for the investigation of international migration and the resulting social and spatial practices that have emerged. I hypothesize that the fragmented nature of human geography has lead to a division of interests that has blinkered our ability to perceive how global movements of people, capital, ideas, and goods have shaped social practices, especially those linked to demographic processes such as marriage migration and family formation. But, despite the usefulness of a transnational approach for encouraging this synthesis, how gender operates in transnational exchanges is still relatively under-explored. Specifically, examinations of the 'private' sphere of reproduction, such as marriage, family migration, and fertility practices, provide opportunities that allow us to refocus on the power and mobility of gendered inequalities, and the way in which they intersect with wider structural transformations in the sphere of economic production. However, we also need to understand that women are not just passive victims in this process, and have tried here to address the systemic realities of patriarchal practices globally through various political processes both in India and overseas. Indeed, some highly successful examples of political change have been achieved in Canada that relate specifically to transnational marriage networks and the rights of women. Indo-Canadian women, via the work of immigrant serving agencies, have successfully lobbied to amend immigration policy in Canada to limit the ability of men to sponsor subsequent partners if they have any criminal charges linked to domestic violence or are in default of court ordered child support or alimony payments (Walton-Roberts 2004).

Transnational contexts influence social practices at the scale of the individual, but also force a connection with issues of power in various manifestations, be it patriarchy or capitalism. This includes focusing on how borders differentially influence human mobility and the cultural solutions communities create in order to resist or exploit such barriers. My field observations reveal that the pre-existing dense social networks between Canada and India provide opportunities for mobility but, in the case of spousal migration, the process is marked by gendered inequality and the transnational extension of certain patriarchal practices. The patriarchal practices evident in northern India have served to reinforce the position of women in society generally and in marriage processes in particular, both in India and overseas. Structural effects are seen both in the dominance of patriarchy, but also through other powerful tendencies, such as the role global consumerism plays in intensifying the traditional practice of dowry and changes in marriage practices that facilitate rapid agreements to be arranged between NRIs and families in Punjab. During Sikh transnational marriage negotiations, males tend to represent the embodiment of 'modern' western wealth and power, whereas women are constructed in more bounded, 'traditional' roles and ultimately more subservient to the wishes of their families. Women are undoubtedly the most vulnerable subjects in this transnational marriage process and exemplify why it is important to highlight the 'gendered geographies of power' evident in such interactions. This also highlights how transnational practices are not always celebratory demonstrations of immigrant agency, but can also act as a mode of transmission for the expansion and perpetuation (though often refashioned) of traditional gendered hierarchies.

NOTES

* This paper is a reprinted version of M. Walton-Roberts (2004), 'Transnational migration theory in population geography: Gendered immigrant networks between Canada and India.' *Population Space and Place*, 10, 361–73. Copyright 2004, John Wiley & Sons Limited. Reproduced with permission.

This research has been made possible through funding from the Indo-Canadian Shastri Institute, Social Sciences and Humanities Research Council of Canada and the Vancouver Centre of Excellence for Research on Immigration and Integration in the Metropolis. A version of this paper was originally presented at the Inaugural International Population Geographies conference in St Andrews, Scotland. The author's presentation in the conference was financed through a SSHRC Institutional Grant awarded to Wilfrid Laurier University. I would also like to thank two anonymous reviewers for their insightful comments on an earlier draft of this paper.

1. Non Resident Indians is the term used by the Indian Government to identify Indian citizens who reside outside India, and it is also used to refer to people of Indian origin (PIOs) who have acquired the citizenship of other countries. See http://indiandiaspora.nic.in/ accessed October 2003.

2. Ostensibly my research focused on wider trade, remittances and immigrant networks between India and Canada and led to over seventy interviews with various immigrant and government officials being conducted between March 1998 and March 2000 in Vancouver Canada and Delhi and Punjab, India. This paper contains a selection of these interviews and observations as they pertain to issues of marriage and migration in order to highlight the processes behind marriage networks between Vancouver Canada and Punjab India. While this was not a specific area of investigation in the research design, the importance of the issue became apparent through the course of my fieldwork.

3. All names are pseudonyms.

4. Interview Phagwara, 28 January 2000.

5. 4 December 1999, Palahi, Punjab.

6. Field visits and interview 18 and 20 November 1999.

7. This is a complex issue, since even in India the woman is removed from her family and natal village. Isolation more generally appears to be an experience women endure after marriage, and alliances with other women in her husband's family, such as mother-in-law and her brother-in-laws' wives, are often more conflictual than supportive (Das 1993). Indeed the experience of isolation is symbolized by the women's festival *Teeyan*, where women are permitted to return to their parents' village to join festivities and reconnect with family and other women from their village in order to share their experiences. My impression of this gathering is that it provides space endorsed for the sharing of complaints about in-laws through song, dance, and skits (satirical plays). My introduction to this festival was through Vancouver, where one of the main Indo-Canadian immigrant serving agencies launched a replica of the festival for Indo-Canadian women, which has become hugely successful with attendance regularly in excess of one thousand women.

8. Field visit to Guru Nanak Dev College, Nagoda, District Jalandhar Punjab, December 1999.

9. The centre in Jandala, Distict Jalandhar, was connected to the Rural Polytechnic in Palahi, District Kapurthala, visited December 1999.

10. Interview 19 February 2000. The District Commissioner suggested that in other districts in Doaba land disputes were the most common NRI-related complaints, but the lower price of land in Hoshiarpur meant matrimonial cases were the most common NRI-related complaints.

11. Press release 8 January 2002, http://www.indiandiaspora.nic.in/press release.htm, accessed October 2003.

12. http://www.cbc.ca/fifth/main_brideupdate.html, accessed 8 November 2002.

REFERENCES

Abraham, M. (2000). *Speaking the Unspeakable: Marital Violence among South Asian Immigrants in the United States*, New Brunswick: Rutgers University Press.

Arnold, F., S. Kishor and T.K. Roy (2002). 'Sex-selective Abortions in India', *Population and Development Review*, Vol. 28, pp. 759–85.

Arokiasamy, P. (2002). 'Gender preference and contraceptive use and fertility in India: Regional and Development Influences', *International Journal of Population Geography*, Vol. 8, pp. 49–67.

Bailey, A. (2001). 'Turning Transnational: Notes on the Theorisation of International Migration', *International Journal of Population Geography*, Vol. 7, pp. 413–28.

Bailey, A., R. Wright, A. Mountz, and I. Miyares (2002). '(Re)producing Salvadoran Transnational Geographies', *Annals of the Association of American Geographers*, Vol. 92, pp. 125–44.

Bal, G. (1997). 'Migration of Sikh Women to Canada: A Social Construction of Gender', *Guru Nanak Journal of Sociology*, Vol. 18, pp. 97–112.

Ballard, R. (1990). 'Migration and Kinship: The Differential Effect of Marriage Rules on the Processes of Punjabi Migration to Britain', in C. Peach, C. Clarke, S. Vertovec (eds), *South Asians Overseas*, Cambridge: Cambridge University Press, pp. 219–49.

Basch, L., N.G. Schiller, C. Szanton Blanc (1994). *Nations Unbound: Transnational Projects, Postcolonial Predicaments, and Deterritorialized Nation-States*, Pennsylvania: Gordon and Breach Science Publishers.

Bhabha, J. and S. Shutter (1994). *Women's Movement: Women Under Nationality and Refugee Law*, Stoke on Trent: Trentham Books.

Bhat, P.N.M. and S.S. Halli (1999). 'Demography of Brideprice and Dowry: Causes and Consequences of the Indian Marriage Squeeze', *Population Studies*, Vol. 53, pp. 129–48.

Boyle, P. and K. Halfacree (1999). *Migration and Gender in the Developed World*, London and New York: Routledge.

Bramham, Daphne (1996). 'India's Women Fight to End Deadly Dowry Demands', *Vancouver Sun*, 13 May, p. 11.

Brown, L., F. Pavri, and V. Lawson (1998). 'Gender, Migration and the Organization of Work Under Economic Devolution: Ecuador, 1982–90', *International Journal of Population Geography*, Vol. 4, pp. 259–74.

Citizenship and Immigration Canada (2001). Landing Immigrant Data Base.

Cumings, B. (1998). 'Boundary Displacements: Area Studies and International Studies During and After the Cold War', in C. Simpson (ed.), *Universities and Empire: Money and Politics in the Social Sciences During the Cold War*, New York: The New Press, pp. 159–88.

Das, V. (1993). 'Masks and faces: An essay on Punjabi Kinship', in P. Uberoi (ed.), *Family Kinship and Marriage in India*, Delhi: Oxford University Press, pp. 198–224.

Das Gupta, M. (1987). 'Selective Discrimination against Female Children in India', *Population and Development Review*, Vol. 13, pp. 77–100.

Divakaruni, D. (2000). 'Uncertain Objects of Desire', *Atlantic Monthly*, Vol. 285, No. 3. Accessed at http://www.theatlantic.com/issues/2000/03/divakaruni.htm

Escobar, A. (1995). *Encountering Development: The Making and Unmaking of the Third World*, Princeton: Princeton University Press.

Fair, C. (1996). 'Female Foeticide among Vancouver Sikhs: Recontextualising Sex Selection in the North American Diaspora', *International Journal of Punjab Studies*, Vol. 3, pp. 1–44.

Findlay, M. and Graham, E. (1991). 'The Challenge Facing Population Geography', *Progress in Human Geography*, Vol. 15, pp. 149–62.

Ford Foundation (1999) *Crossing Borders: Revitalizing Area Studies*. Ford Foundation. Accessed at http://international.uiowa.edu/centers/crossing-borders/resources.asp

Ford, N. and S. Kittisuksathit (1996). 'Mobility, Love and Vulnerability: Sexual Lifestyles of Young and Single Factory Workers in Thailand', *International Journal of Population Geography*, Vol. 2, pp. 23–33.

Gillespie, M. (1995). *Television, Ethnicity and Cultural Change*, London: Routledge.

Graham, E. (1999). 'Breaking Out: The Opportunities and Challenges of Multi-method Research in Population Geography', *Professional Geographer*, Vol. 51, pp. 76–89.

Graham. E. and P. Boyle (2001). '(Re)theorizing Population Geography: Mapping the Unfamiliar,' *International Journal of Population Geography*, Vol. 7, pp. 398–394.

Gupta, S.C. (1986). 'Sex Preference and Protein Calorie Malnutrition,' *The Journal of Family Welfare*, Vol. 32, No. 3, pp. 59–64.

Hershman, P. (1981). *Punjab Kinship and Marriage*, ed. Hilary Standing, Delhi: Hindustan Publishing Corporation.

High Level Committee on the Indian Diaspora, Report Issued under the Department of External Affairs, Government of India, January 2002. http://indiandiaspora.nic.in/contents.htm accessed 23 May 2007.

Howard, C. (1999). 'A Suitable Girl', *Elm Street*, October, pp. 80–92.

Hugo, G. (1996). 'Asia on the Move: Research challenges for Population Geography', *International Journal of Population Geography*, Vol. 2, pp. 95–118.

Hyndman, J. and M. Walton-Roberts (2000). 'Interrogating Borders: A Transnational Approach to Refugee Research in Vancouver', *The Canadian Geographer*, Vol. 44, pp. 244–58.

Johnston, H.J.M. 1984. *The East Indians in Canada*, Ottawa: Canadian Historical Association.

Joshi, P. (2000). 'A Suitable Boy?', *Marie Clare* (UK edition), July 2000, pp. 133–5.

Jyoti, S.K. (1983). *Marriage Practices of the Sikhs*, New Delhi: Deep and Deep Publications.

Kishwar, M. (1989), 'Dowry and Inheritance Rights', *Economic and Political Weekly*, Vol. 14, pp. 587–8.

Leslie, J. (1998). 'Dowry, "dowry deaths" and Violence Against Women: A Journey of Discovery', in W. Menski (ed.), *South Asians and the Dowry Problem*, Stoke on Trent: Trentham Books Limited, pp. 21–36.

Lievens, J. (1999). 'Family-forming Migration from Turkey and Morocco to Belgium: The Demand for Partners from the Countries of Origin', *International Migration Review*, Vol. 33, pp. 715–44.

Livingstone, D. (1992). 'A Brief History of Geography', in H. Viles, A. Goudie, and A. Rogers (eds), *The Student's Companion to Geography*, Oxford: Blackwell, pp. 27–35.

Mahler, S. and P. Pessar (2001). 'Gendered Geographies of Power: Analyzing Gender Across Transnational Spaces', *Identities*, Vol. 7, pp. 441–59.

Menski, W. (ed.) (1998). *South Asians and the Dowry Problem*. Stoke on Trent: Trentham Books Limited.

Mountz, A. and R. Wright (1996). 'Daily Life in the Transnational Migrant Community of San Agustin, Oaxaca and Poughkeepsie, New York', *Diaspora*, Vol. 5, pp. 403–28.

Nager, R. (1998). 'Communal Discourses, Marriage, and the Politics of Gendered Social Boundaries among South Asian immigrants in Tanzania', *Gender, Place and Culture*, Vol. 5, pp. 117–39.

Ong, A. (1999). *Flexible Citizenship: The Cultural Logics of Transnationality*, Durham and London: Duke University Press, 1999.

Puri, J. (1999). *Woman, Body, Desire in Post-Colonial India: Narratives of Gender and Sexuality*, London: Routledge.

Rouse, R. (1991). 'Mexican Migration and the Social Spaces of Postmodernity', *Diaspora*, Vol. 1, pp. 8–23.

Sachs, S. (2001). '"Clinics" pitch to Indian Émigrés: It's a Boy', *New York Times*, 15 August.

Schurmer-Smith, P. (2000). *India: Globalization and Change*, Arnold: London.

Shah, P. (1993). 'Female foeticide', *Seminar*, Vol. 410, pp. 42–4.

Sharma, U. (1993). 'Dowry in North India: Its Consequences for Women', in Patricia Uberoi (ed.), *Family, Kinship and Marriage in India*, Delhi: Oxford University Press, pp. 341–56.

Singh, P. (2000). 'In-Laws Behind 80 p.c. of Suicides', *Punjab Tribune*, 9 August.

Singh, N. (1999). 'What after Desertion?' *Sunday Punjab Tribune*, 5 December.

Skeldon, R. (1995). 'The Challenge Facing Migration Research: A Case for Greater Awareness', *Progress in Human Geography*, Vol. 19, pp. 91–6.

Smith, D. and A. Bailey (2001). 'Transnationalism, Ethnicity and the Family: Toward a Life Course Framework', Paper presented at the Inaugural International Population Geographies conference in St Andrews, Scotland, July.

Srinivas, M.N. (1989). 'Some Reflections on Dowry', in M.N Srinivas (ed.), *The Cohesive Role of Sanskritization and Other Essays*, Delhi: Oxford University Press.

Stalker, P. (2000). *Workers Without Frontiers: The Impact of Globalization on International Migration*, London: Rienner.

Talwar, R. (2000). '11 Dowry deaths in 1999', *Punjab Tribune*, 11 February, p. 5.

Tee, Karen Ai-Lyn (1996). *Between Two Cultures: Exploring the Voices of First and Second Generation South Asian Women*, Vancouver: Unpublished PhD Thesis, Simon Fraser University.

Times of India (2001). 'Indians in US using Sex Selection Procedures', 16 August.

Uberoi, P. ed. (1993). *Family Kinship and Marriage in India*, Delhi: Oxford University Press.

Walton-Roberts, M. (2004). 'Rescaling Citizenship: Gendering Canadian Immigration Policy', *Political Geography*, Vol. 23, No. 3, pp. 265–81.

White, Paul and Peter Jackson (1995), '(Re)theorising Population Geography', *International Journal of Population Geography*, Vol. 1, pp. 111–23

Willis, K. and B. Yeoh, eds, (2000). *Gender and Migration*. The International Library of Studies on Migration, 10. Cheltenham: Edward Elgar Publishing.

Wong, M. (2000). 'Ghanaian Women in Toronto's Labour Market: Negotiating Gendered Roles and Transnational Household Strategies', *Canadian Ethnic Studies*, Vol. 32, pp. 45–74.

Transnational Sikh Women's Working Lives
Place and the Life Course

Kanwal Mand

> Women's aspirations for education, career and marriage, in many cases their reluctance to accept the responsibility for childcare and elder care, all have implications for the ways in which households are constituted and have knock on effects for contemporary migration trends
>
> —Phizacklea 2000: 127.

Feminists have highlighted women's productive and reproductive activities to be inextricably bound to the household, which in turn organizes and influences the way in which women live their lives within them (Moore 1988; Sharma 1986; Whitehead 1981). Building on this earlier literature, current accounts on gender and migration further underscores the centrality of women in the creation and maintenance of households. As Alicea states: 'Subsistence work, which is work that creates and sustains physical life and psychological well-being, includes what Di Leonardo (1992) calls the "work of kinship", a concept important for understanding Puerto Rican women's role in creating transnational families and households' (Alicea 2000: 314). The work of kinship is traditionally perceived to be women's work involving activities such as gift-giving (Werbner 1990), the provision of money, food and care for the elderly and children (Alicea 2000; Gardner 2002), and visiting key social relations (Mahler 2000; Gardner 2002). Two predominant frameworks have been utilized to explore women's role in the experience of migration: in keeping with household decisions involving primarily the migration of men, women's experiences have been explored as those 'left behind'; more recently, women's movement as economic migrants has come to the fore driven by global demand for flexible labour. Gendered identities and activities play an important role in migration decisions at the household level while at state-level policies governing migration are increasingly gendered.

However, the distinction that women are 'left behind' or follow male migrants (husbands) versus their migration as economic migrants fails to capture some of the nuances of gender and migration. In this article I explore the theme of Punjabi Sikh[1] women's work as part of transnational households, and, focus on them taking up paid work outside the house, illustrating the value ascribed to these activities as contextual. I argue that women's activities are related to the perception held of places and their stage in the life course and is linked to household economics and status.

We will also see that women's options for work are influenced by migration histories, that is length of stay in a locality, or, command over the language. Whilst working in the public context could provide a degree of autonomy, particularly in the context of migration, Sikh women conceptualized their movement based on their identities as wives and mothers. Indeed, Sikh women have not moved either historically or in contemporary times across national boundaries to Tanzania or Britain for the purposes of earning a wage. However, as we shall see through the experiences of Satpal and her sisters-in-law, taking up paid employment in Britain becomes a norm and one that is related to household needs. South Asian women traditionally are on the move regionally or transnationally owing to the predominant norm of patrilocal residence which results in women having differing access to symbolic and material resources; this in turn influences their negotiations around travel. The second half of the paper takes up this theme and focuses on women's negotiations around travel and links these to material resources and status in households.[2]

SIKH WOMEN'S MIGRATION AND THE LIFE COURSE

As mentioned above, Sikh women's migration has tended to be as part of families in their roles as mothers and wives. Utilizing the notion of the life course is more appropriate than stating an age as it brings to focus 'roles and stages through which we pass as culturally embedded' (Gardner 2002: 19). The stage at which a woman arrived in Britain, both in terms of her life course and marital status, influences her ability to access material and social support in the British context. For example, women who arrived in Britain following their marriages to male migrants from the 1950s onwards have had a different relationship to Britain than transnational widows whose mobility between places is linked to a husband's death, the dispersal of their children, siblings and wider kin (Mand 2005). Additionally, although in recent years Sikh women are more likely now to be travelling for the purposes of education and subsequent employment, the women who were part of this research moved primarily as mothers, wives, or widows.

Ethnographic accounts on South Asian women stress that marriage and becoming mothers are pivotal moments in the course of women's lives and correspondingly influence how women are positioned within natal and husband's households. Moreover, Vatuk (1995) outlines the life course as a useful framework for understanding South Asian women's changing positions in the household and wider society, as one which stresses 'transitions [as] related to the development cycle of the family [and] are... important in defining major periods of a woman's life...' (Vatuk 1995: 293). Furthermore, women's location within the life course impacts the types of activities that they undertake and therefore creates distinctions between women within a household. As Vatuk remarks, 'the continuity of women's accustomed work roles, so closely associated with reproduction and the domestic domain, presents an advantage to women in the middle and old age, even as it frequently works against their well-being at the early phases of their life course' (ibid.: 301). This is a notion that has also been highlighted by Kandiyoti in her notion of 'patriarchal bargain' whereby women's power is said to increase as they get older particularly in relation to younger women in the context of extended households (Kandiyoti 1997, quoted in Gardner 2002: 149).

SIKH MOBILITY BETWEEN TANZANIA, PUNJAB, AND BRITAIN

The arrival of Sikhs from Punjab to East Africa was as recruited labour by the British colonial government. Although few Sikhs remained in East Africa following the completion of their contractual obligations (Bhachu 1985), the promise of economic opportunities meant that many arrived as 'free migrants' using their kin networks. Predominantly, it was Ramgarhia Sikhs who arrived as part of the 'free' migration and found that their skills in masonry and carpentry were in demand. In contrast, for Jat Sikhs, the traditional occupation of farming and landowning was not possible as under colonial rule Africans and Asians were excluded from land ownership. Instead, during these early days in Tanzania, Jat Sikh men tended to establish businesses in trading, transportation, construction as well as playing a key role in setting up institutions such as temples and educational and health care facilities. In this early phase of migration these men would return to Punjab in order to marry, following which they would return to Tanzania while their wives stayed with their kin in Punjab. The significance of gender in the experience of migration arises early in the narratives of men and women (Mand 2006). For women, movement is intrinsically related to their stage in the life course as marriage means they move first to husbands' households in Punjab (according to the norm of patrilocal residence), where they would await visits from their husbands and subsequently migrate to Tanzania.

The majority of elderly Sikh men I spoke with had been in Tanzania from the late 1930s onwards. Aside from marriage, maintaining links with Punjab were important because these men presumed an eventual return. An eventual return was in part due to the concept of the African space as being unsuitable for women and children (Nagar 1995). Such notions were also part of the narrative for early migrants arriving from Punjab directly to the UK during the 1960s (Anwar 1979). By the 1950s many women had begun to travel to Tanzania and larger numbers settled in urban areas of Tanzania. Women's role in reproducing social identities was pivotal as remaining with their husband's kin they were expected to incorporate 'the ways of the [husband's] family' and later reproduce these in Tanzania.

Significantly, the movement for Tanzania to Britain altered the standard pattern of male migration and women being 'left behind'. In contrast to direct migrants, for these families coming from Tanzania, migration to Britain either involved the entire family (although this is more the case for those migrating from Kenya) or it was women and children who migrated to Britain while men stayed behind in Tanzania. In a few cases, men did come up to take up work in the British context as part of a household strategy, as we shall see in the case of Satinder's husband. Nonetheless, an important shift had occurred. Women moved, while men tended to stay behind in Tanzania or return after a short period in Britain. The reasons why men stayed behind are closely related to the ways in which the African public space is conceptualized as being an arena unsuitable for women to work in, a continuation of an earlier premise, and at the same time in light of gender roles, whereby men are seen to be the primary breadwinners. Although events following Independence from colonial rule in neighbouring countries were more dramatic, entailing the much documented expulsion of Asians from Uganda, the situation in Tanzania differed. The newly elected socialist President Nyerere encouraged Asians, and we can say, quite categorically men, to stay on given their central role in the economy, in spite of many of them holding British overseas citizenship[3] (Mand 2004).

The arrival of Sikhs from East African countries and their reconstruction of an identity and social networks based on their 'East Africaness' has been documented by Bhachu (1985). Bhachu's research provides a detailed background although it differs from this research in that the families I worked with continued to maintain property, social and symbolic links with the Punjab and Tanzania (Mand 2004). A chief motivator for this maintenance of links is due to the development cycle of the household, while movement of members is closely related to their position in the life course and gender identity.

CHANGES IN SOUTH ASIAN WOMEN'S MIGRATION

Although early South Asian migration to Britain accounted for women's migration on the basis of 'family reunification' (Ballard and Ballard 1977), changes in global relations of production and consumption have meant that possibilities of work and migration has shifted, resulting in what some commentators have called the 'feminization of migration' (Gamburd 2000; Kabeer 2000). Kabeer's (2000) comparison of Bangladeshi women's lives and employment in Dhaka and in Britain marks a new mode of inquiry into South Asian women migrants as it emphasizes the economic aspects of South Asian women's migration, and its relationship to the global labour market. Therefore, whilst it has been uncommon for Sikh women to migrate for the purposes of earning a wage 'abroad', other South Asian women are migrating to places for the primary purpose of earning a living (Gamburd 2000; Siddiqui 2001). For example, Bangladeshi women are involved as labour migrants to the Middle East and Far East (Siddiqui 2001). Siddiqui's work illustrates that women's involvement as labour migrants impacts social relations within and between households as well as gender identities and roles at 'home' and 'abroad'. Furthermore, she highlights the role of state legislation as it curtails or enables women to migrate for economic reasons (ibid.). At the same time, women's paid labour in the subcontinent is increasingly acceptable albeit highly stratified according to caste and class (Caplan 1985). Gamburd highlights that Sri Lankan women's migration for the purposes of work remains physically and literally associated with the domestic sphere, particularly in that they care for their employers' children on the basis of their own identities as mothers. Therefore, Gamburd presents the 'importance of viewing housework and childcare as work, whether performed at home or abroad' (Gamburd 2000: 41).

What remains pivotal when exploring South Asian women's migration, whether it be conceptualized on the basis of their economic or social roles, is that women's lives are embedded within the household. Rather than being a stark disruption between economic and social reproduction, the notions that surround gender in South Asia results in women's work outside the house is being conceptualized as an extension of their gender roles. Meanwhile, while such norms are dynamic, state policies exacerbate gender norms found in migrant groups through their policies (Gardner 2002). As a result, women's involvement

as independent 'economic' migrants has been overlooked in
the literature; the complexities of legality and migration have
meant that for women to migrate 'legally from country to
country [they are] more likely to migrate *not* for the purposes
of work' (Phizacklea 2000: 122, emphasis mine). Phizacklea
calls for the recognition of institutions such as social networks
and households as, 'mediating between individual migrants and
the larger structural context, [which] are deeply implicated in
gendered ideologies and practices' (ibid.: 123).

The literature that develops the interrelationship between
women's work, the nation-state and transnationalism is predominantly based on analysis of South American transnationalism.
For example, writing about El Salvadorian transnationalism,
Fouroun and Glick-Schiller note that the mutual construction
of gender and national identities takes place in both public and
private domains (Fouroun and Glick-Schiller 2001: 542). They
go on to state that the 'extent to which the family and home
simultaneously are defined as women's domains and the site
of national honour and virtue, when women do women's work,
they become committed to the ideas and imagery that build the
nation' (ibid.). Hence, there are several discourses that position
women's work along gender ideals; in other words, women as
nurturers and as being committed to the establishment of the
family and or nation-state. Therefore, while migrant women
may gain a degree of independence from men through earnings
they 'continue to value the promise of male economic protection
[patriarchal family system] ...as it adds income earners [and] extends resources. Another appeal ...is the status related privileges
that are promised to them [women]...' (Kibria 2000: 189).

SIKH WOMEN'S LABOUR: THE TANZANIAN CONTEXT

It is uncharacteristic to find Sikh women working outside the
house in Tanzania. In a few cases where women are involved in
working outside the house, in the public arena involving liaison
with other Asian and African men, their work is portrayed as the
result of a 'sorry' situation. For example, one woman's husband
had suffered a disabling stroke and she had no sons, which
meant she ran their hardware store in the city centre; another
woman ran transportation businesses after her husband had a

debilitating illness and therefore could not control the businesses himself. A third widowed woman worked in her family's store. By and large, however, the predominant contact Sikh women have with non-Asian men is restricted to the domestic context, where they engage with African male domestic workers and sellers of household goods. Other Asian women, particularly Muslim women from the Ismaili and Ithna-Asheri communities, can be found working in 'family' businesses and public institutions where they deal with the local population. In more administrative sectors, it is not uncommon to find Goan women working alongside Asians, Africans, and Europeans (Nagar 1995). While the focus of this paper is not on religious identity, gender, and the experience of a place, there are undoubtedly some overlaps that affect Sikh women's work outside the home in the Tanzanian context. The visibility of Goan and Muslim women's presence in the 'public' labour market is partly related to the common (Catholic and Muslim) religious identities that they share along with sections of the African population. Historically, Tanzanian urban spaces have been highly segregated with Asians living within centres and Africans living at the edges of towns and cities. While some of these residential patterns have altered over the course of time, larger numbers of Asians still remain in the centre of the capital city; the majority of the Sikh population lives within the temple (or gurdwara) compound. Therefore, members of the Sikh community are in close proximity with one another and the temple is a focal point involving women of all caste and class groups. Although large numbers of Sikh women attend the temple in British cities and towns, amongst the transnational families I observed, their work and household chores meant that women's lives did not necessarily revolve around the temple as they would have done in Tanzania. However, this is not the case for elderly women, as they would often attend the temple where meeting with other Sikh women was an important social experience.

The urban spaces of Tanzania, historically have been delineated along racial lines whereby particular areas are marked as being dangerous, notably for women, which impacts South Asian women's mobility and hence potential access to resources. Transnational Sikh women with whom I worked with in Tanzania and Britain reported a feeling of potential surveillance from multiple others stating, 'here [Tanzania] our people [*apna lok*] are watching'. Such notions of surveillance and limitations on what one can do and experience was not so readily voiced by women in Britain, although strong kinship networks operate between families from Tanzania. The British context, however, affords greater anonymity.

In rare cases I observed Sikh women involved in buying from Arab stores in 'non-Asian' areas and selling them in Asian homes and temples, although more often women would return with goods from India and sell them to others. Overall though, working in the public sphere in Tanzania is discouraged and many young women are often found at home awaiting a marriage proposal. The status of the household and its position within the local Sikh community can be a further deterrent in women's mobility within Tanzania and particularly in the field of paid labour. This is because working women reflect negatively on the household men's ability to materially support the members. As Donner reflects in the case of Bengali women in Calcutta, working outside the household is limited to men because norms and 'restrictions on female mobility and women's economic activities are explained in terms of wider morality' (Donner 1999: 286). I found that the discourse of morality, in Tanzania, related to women's spatial mobility within the locality; this had an impact on their economic activities. These discourses should be located within wider historical and social processes. For example, South Asian men have occupied privileged economic positions under colonialism, leading to higher class status which meant that women did not need to work.

However, this class privilege has not been the experience of South Asians in Britain, where women working outside the domestic context does not reflect negatively on the status of the household. Working women in Tanzania are commonly perceived to be African, whilst in Britain it is white women as well as some Asian women who work. In Britain, the issues of morality and employment are differently conceptualized (cf. Nagar 1995). What has become clearer with the multi-sited approach to exploring Sikh transnationalism is that ideals about gender are dynamic, altering according to place. As we will hear from Kushi, working in Britain is part of being a 'good' wife who enables her husband to meet household needs. To this effect, women's mobility within Tanzania is constrained and is in contradiction to their transnational mobility.

Significantly in Tanzania, three Sikh women interviewed had undertaken degree programmes before marriage and migration from Punjab. One had recently become involved in part-time teaching of the 'mother tongue' at the 'international school' in Tanzania. This work of teaching the 'mother tongue' is significant as it demonstrates the issue of women's identities as cultural reproducers. Furthermore, the part-time nature of the work meant that women's earnings did not directly challenge male provision.

Women's engagement in paid labour, outside the domestic context should therefore be analysed in terms of what women do, under what circumstances, and why and where their activities alter. Although Sikh women in Tanzania may be involved in money-generating work, these activities do not occur in the public (African) domain but within the context of the family businesses, the house, and in the reproduction of 'culture' through teaching. Writing about middle-class Bengali households, Donner notes that when women are not in paid labour, particularly in the public sphere, it is an indicator of a higher 'status of a lineage' (Donner 1999: 286). This is certainly the case for the majority of Sikh households within Tanzania and is unmarked by class or caste distinctions. Therefore, whilst Sikh women work in the British locality, their embodiment of the household's status is more rigid in Tanzania. This suggests that localities and household organization play a role in the ways in which women's identities are conceptualized and the value placed on their activities.

ASIAN WOMEN WORKERS IN BRITAIN

Working in the public context is a necessary feature of life in the UK owing to the high cost of living in Britain. Sikh women's presence in the British labour market has historically been noted to be relatively high[4] (Office of Population Census and Survey [OPCS] 1991). Furthermore, Asian women's activism in the workplace has been noted as being part of British labour history, as Asian women played a central role in the strike concerning working conditions and racism witnessed in the three-month

strike at the Imperial typewriters factory in Leicester in 1974
(Parmar 1982). These images of Asian women were in stark
opposition to their representation within popular discourse as
passive and subordinated within the South Asian family (ibid.).
The 1991 census findings state that Indian women are 8 per
cent more likely to be in full-time employment than their white
counterparts, with 4 per cent in professional positions compared
to 2 per cent of their white counterparts (OPCS 1991: 26; Ahmed
et al. 2003). In spite of the high proportion of Sikh women in the
British labour market, this is not the case for all women of South
Asian origin, whereby engagement in the labour market is partly
influenced by religious and class identity, migration history,
and educational achievements (Ahmed et al. 2003). Therefore,
substantial differences in the experience of employment and
education exist amongst and between South Asian groups in
Britain (Ballard 2002). Ballard notes that Gujaratis arriving from
East Africa (and we could also add Sikhs, see Bhachu 1985) to
Britain have experienced a greater degree of social mobility in
the British context in comparison to Bangladeshis and Pakistanis
from Mirpur. Several interrelated factors influence the socio-
economic positions occupied by South Asian migrant groups.
These relate to a prior migration history and processes of family
reunification (for example, amongst Bangladeshis this process
occurred much later than for Sikhs), caste and class positions,
as well as cultural norms surrounding marriage and kinship
reciprocity. In terms of education, Ballard notes that British-born
Asians, including the Chinese community, are 'out performing'
the white majority; professions such as law and medicine are
favoured by Asian Indian groups (Ballard 2002, 2001).

Migrant women in Britain are also involved in labour
according to gender norms within the workplace and in the
household (Westwood and Bhachu 1988). This was how Satpal
(whose story we will hear more of below) reasoned her position
in relation to household and paid labour:

…no matter how hard one works at home there is no acknowledgement of
it. If one works outside then that is seen as work, and when you have your
own money you can buy at whatever price you want to pay. Although the
husband gives, it is my own earning… [to] buy my daughter whatever she
wants [Satpal, east London 1999].

Women's experiences of employment reveal the distinction between public and private to be blurred and contextual. Therefore,
while women's activities are valuable for the household and thus
accrue status, there are ideological distinctions that demarcate
and relegate men's and women's activities according to a public
/ private divide that assigns them differing value (Moore 1988).
The blurred distinction between public and private domains
and women's labour, as central for the household, is contradictory as illustrated in South Asian women's experiences of labour
in 'ethnic' ('private' businesses) out in the 'public' context of
Britain (Westwood and Bhachu, 1988; Parmar 1982).

Following changes in the labour market in Britain from the
1960s, ethnic businesses, such as South Asian-owned clothing,
jewellery, grocery stores, or travel agencies have been a key
component in the economic mobility experienced by migrant
groups. Within such business enterprises, South Asian women
have been present either on the front line working alongside
male kinsmen or behind the scenes (Ballard 2002; Westwood
and Bhachu 1988; Parmar 1982). As Phizacklea reveals, ethnic
business enterprises recruit women's labour on the basis of their
gender and kinship relationships; as a result they are vested
with responsibilities and can be 'subordinated to very similar
patriarchal control mechanisms in the workplace as in the
home' (Phizacklea 1988: 31). One of the key reasons why small
businesses became popular was due to the threat for women
of racism that was believed to compound their vulnerability.
Women's work within family or community-owned businesses
was perceived to be a 'safe' place for them. However, women
stand to lose in such arrangements in spite of their productivity
as migrant labour; 'due to patriarchal relations women's labour
is subordinated to male labour, cheapened and kept that way'
(Westwood and Bhachu 1988: 4).

What these early investigations highlight is the intersection
between identity and ethnicity. These studies focused on the
ways in which women's migration histories, class, ethnic identity,
and point of departure played a mediating role, in the context
of migration, in their experience of working outside the home
(Westwood and Bhachu 1988; Bhachu 1991).

TRANSNATIONAL SIKH WOMEN WORKERS

Satpal: We used to have a woman who used to help in the kitchen.[5] One day my mother had gone out and she'd asked me to clean up; the woman who lived nearby had gone home. There were a couple of plates and dishes lying around so I thought I'd start washing them 'up'. The woman came running home. 'Please don't wash the pans and pots', she said, 'leave them, and don't ruin your hands like mine. Your mother won't be happy to see that I let you do all this'. I was just thinking about her when I was at the [food packing] factory, looking at my hands and thinking…what a difference in life. She was concerned about my hands. I was freezing at the factory, lifting heavy things. We never thought we'd have to do such things. Over there we employ servants…and here we go out and do labouring. I felt quite tearful yesterday. I was thinking about the kind of work that I was doing. It was all right to do sewing work that was all sitting down and not touch [cold meat] like this [Satpal, east London 1999].

Satpal, a twenty-eight-year-old woman had migrated from Punjab following marriage to a Sikh migrant from Tanzania and was living in East London. She gave me this account on her return from a morning shift at the cold food-packing factory where she had recently begun working. Satpal relayed her feelings whilst preparing the evening meal for her family members living in the UK who are part of a transnational household with residences in Tanzania, Punjab, and England. In England, Satpal lives alongside her husband, sister, and brother-in-law, three nephews, a niece and, at times, her elderly mother-in-law. Satpal is the youngest daughter-in-law and has an eight-year-old daughter.

Like other women who came from Punjab and Tanzania, Satpal had never worked outside the domestic context before her arrival in Britain. Although Satpal works in Britain, she is aware that in Tanzania she would not be involved in paid work, whilst in her 'native' Punjab, Satpal recalls many of her contemporaries as being involved in professional vocations. Despite educational and professional qualifications, the experiences of Sikh women who are members of transnational households in terms of paid labour outside the domestic context are directly related to the place. For it is only in Britain, as opposed to the Tanzanian context, that larger numbers of women are almost always involved in the labour market.

In the case of transnational Sikh women like Satpal, employment is taken up during their stays in Britain from Tanzania and

Punjab. As we shall see below, undertaking paid employment is dependent on women's stage in the life cycle and marital status, which in turn informs the basis of women's relationship with the 'public' context of paid work. Furthermore, Satpal's situation will illustrate that despite women's work outside the household, they are still expected to perform other activities related to their gendered roles. In the context of transnationalism, this requires them to be flexible, enabling them to travel to and from households in different geographical localities.

The type of employment undertaken by Sikh transmigrant women in Britain is dependent on the time spent in a locality. Additionally, the type of work undertaken by women is influenced by their educational achievements, and in particular, their command over the local language. To a large extent, although many of these transmigrant women had attended school in Punjab, they now work in East London as seamstresses and cashiers for supermarkets; in West London many work in and around Heathrow Airport, particularly in the catering industry. In contrast, women who have been resident in Britain following marriage and migration from Tanzania, are often found in clerical posts at the airport or working within government welfare agencies. For a few women for whom residence in Britain is too brief, or where employment outside the house is not possible as they are responsible for the care of children or the elderly, women sometimes manage to raise an income through selling of gold and cloth that they have brought from their point of departure.

LABOURS OF LOVE: HOUSE AND PAID WORK

Satinder and Kushi are Satpal's sisters-in-law; all three are married to three brothers. Satinder is also Satpal's cousin, twice removed, and is referred to as the eldest daughter-in-law of the house as her husband is also the eldest brother in the household. Before marriage, Kushi, Satinder, and Satpal lived in Punjab; Kushi and Satinder were educated to the age of sixteen in their respective villages. Satpal on the other hand, unlike the other two, was educated beyond the age of eighteen, as before marriage she had begun attending a local college in the city where she lived as part of a nuclear family. Kushi is the most mobile of the three sisters-in-law. She married in India and then migrated to Tanzania, after which she temporarily relocated with her husband from Tanzania to Britain. Although her husband returned to Tanzania, Kushi remained for some time with their sons in Britain. Kushi's current mobility spans across three sites, as she visits her natal kin in Punjab, spends periods in Tanzania with her husband, as well as in Britain where her three children attend school or university.

Of the three sisters-in-laws, Satinder has never travelled to or dwelt at the households residence in Tanzania. She also does not feel the need to travel there. Satinder is the oldest of the daughters-in-law and her husband has maintained a steady job with London Underground from the time of his arrival in Britain in the late 1950s. Instead of visiting the family in Tanzania, Satinder had professed a desire to go to visit her natal kin in Punjab, or, her brother who had recently migrated to the United States from Punjab.

Following her marriage, Satinder's residence has always been in Britain. She began working shortly after the birth of her first child undertaking piecemeal or 'piece work', whereby seamstresses are paid on the basis of the garments they sew as opposed to a fixed or hourly rate. After having her baby and with the arrival of her husband's kin from Tanzania, Satinder increased her workload, which was made feasible with the aid of a pregnant Kushi[6] who would look after the children and the house. The two women, Satinder and pregnant Kushi, shared the piecemeal work alongside the household work and childcare. Kushi recalled those days when she and Satinder worked and lived in East London.

We would wake up at six in the morning and feed the children and my son was attending a nearby school so one of us would take him to school. The other one would start working on the machine. We took it in turns one on the machine the other would do the khar da kam (the work of house). The both of us had an understanding [Kushi, Tanzania 2000].

At this time the women kept their wages, which increased when Satinder began working at a '*desi*' (Indian) factory and was given cash on a weekly basis. Shortly thereafter Kushi joined her, while their mother-in-law and husband's unmarried sisters cared for the children. During this time Kushi gave her wages to the mother-in-law in return for an allowance. The wages were necessary to aid the household's growing budget, and, for marriage expenses for the sisters and the youngest brother-in-law (Satpal's husband). Kushi did not resent giving her money to her mother-in-law, rather she stressed that her husband reimbursed her generously 'seeing how good [she] was in giving money to Mama... you know a man is also pleased when a woman works, it does help him in sharing the responsibilities'.

Individually, both women stressed bad working conditions, low pay, and the intensity of workloads as the standard recollection of Indian employers. Their criticism of the 'desi' factory reconfirms the notion that working within 'ethnic' businesses can result in women being exploited while at the same time unable to express the injustices experienced. Kushi and Satinder then moved on to sewing at an 'English factory' that altered the way resources were handled by the women. While working at the 'English factory', Satinder stopped giving her earnings to her mother-in-law; her wages instead went into her own bank account. By now the household's financial demands had decreased, as the sisters were married and the male members had resumed working in Tanzania. Kushi fondly recalls the time spent at the 'English factory' as it opened up new experiences, in terms of contact with non-Indian women, and that their labour was suitably reimbursed. Additionally, being paid into their own bank accounts afforded the women more control over their wages.

...Those white ladies would smoke their cigarettes and make us laugh; we would take a break and in the canteen drink tea and talk. My boss was so happy with my work that he thought I was an expert (laughs), but I had sixteen years experience! I really enjoyed working there and the year I returned from India I worked in the factory for two months...they gave me the job as they knew my work and it was a time when so many were on summer holidays so I got some work [Kushi, Tanzania 2000].

In the early 1990s, Satinder's cousin, Satpal, came to the UK in order to marry Satinder's younger brother-in-law. The wedding was an opportunity for those members of the family, including Kushi, who was in Tanzania to return to the UK. Upon arrival, Kushi took up a job in the 'English factory'. Like Satinder, Satpal began working a year after her marriage as a seamstress, although not at home on a piece meal basis. Instead, she worked outside the house for a local Indian employer. After a year she gave up her job and relocated to Tanzania for nine

months. On her return back to Britain she did not work outside
the home as she was expected to undertake household work
owing to Satinder's departure to Punjab to visit her paternal
kin. During this time Satpal became pregnant and following the
birth of her daughter, she stayed at home in Britain for three
more years.

Living in England for the last seven years, with a year spent in
Tanzania and a return visit to India for a period of six months,
has meant that Satpal has found it difficult to find and maintain a
job in Britain. In part, this is because of her stage in the life cycle
and the household development cycle; by the time that Satpal
had her child, Kushi and Satinder's children were teenagers and
childcare was less of a priority for them. Satpal's work at the
cold food packaging factory was a last resort and her discomfort
is relayed in the story of her hands that poignantly expresses
the experience of marriage and migration and its relationship
to women's work within and outside the household. Satpal's
position is compounded by her position in the household
hierarchy wherein she is the youngest sister-in-law and has
worked the least and, so far only for 'Indian' employers. This
has meant that her exposure to English people has remained
limited and has impacted her knowledge and proficiency in
English, making it difficult for her to find work. Furthermore,
Satpal needed to find employment that allowed her to drop and
pick up her daughter from primary school, and her lack of a
means of transport further compounded her already restricted
employment chances.

Bhachu's work has highlighted that women's engagement in
paid labour bears a direct relationship to the 'traditionalisation
[sic] of particular female related cultural values ...but also the
renegotiations of the sexual division of labour' (Bhachu 1988:
79). Bhachu found that the women's paid labour impacted
notions surrounding masculine and feminine identities with
'men being more involved in the household because of women's
move into the labour market' (ibid.). These changes were,
according to Bhachu, apparent in East African households and
'the features...related to changes in gender roles and family
structure are accentuated in Britain, because [of] women's
control over productive resources' (ibid.: 90). Therefore, earning
a wage leads to changes in gender relations within households

and between its members whilst also enabling women to pursue and invest in activities and practices that they deem significant, for example, the translation of economic resources into dowry items (Bhachu 1991).

Bhachu's findings are contrary to my own, as amongst transnational Sikh households holding links between Punjab, Tanzania, and Britain, I found that the division of labour continues to be based along gender lines. Nonetheless, what is significant, albeit unexplored in Bhachu's work on 'twice migrants' from Punjab to East Africa and then on to Britain, is the significance of Britain as a space deemed suitable for women to work in. At the same time, the transnational households of this research reveal that place is important and that women's work continues to be both literally and symbolically associated with the household's needs. Owing to the predominance of their activities, arenas such as sewing, cleaning, catering, and general service provision, their work is seen to be an extension of their gender roles. However, as we have seen that Satpal and Kushi's mobility across the three geographical sites contravenes the notion that women simply follow male migrants as their work both inside and outside the house results in a flexibility that renders them more mobile. Meanwhile, household hierarchy, the relative longer residence and greater exposure to working outside the house and ethnic businesses bears an impact on the negotiations that Satinder can and does make regarding her mobility.

In the section above I have highlighted that women travel on the basis of their gender identities, based on caring roles and intra-household relations. At the same time, women's dwelling in travel (Clifford 1997), particularly in Britain, means that they undertake paid labour in the local economy. Therefore, what follows is an exploration of transmigrant women's negotiations about travel based on their engagement in skilled and unskilled manual labour. Let us now look more closely at the ways in which women's employment and stage in the life course influences their travel to and from places.

FAMILIAL JOURNEYS AND WOMEN'S DESIRES

We are all planning to take a trip to Africa mid next year, all of us for a week or so and then we will go away and explore Africa. I would like to meet my father-in-law, I know very little about him. I know very little about Africa: When I ask, they [her husband and mother-in-law] tell me it is like India but I think it can't be! What about all the red earth, the jungles and all those Jamaicans and kala (blacks)? I know that Tabora is the family village and that Africa is a very dangerous place and when we go to travel, independently, we will stay close to the village where the families stay so there can be help when we need it. I don't want to get raped or murdered out there. I would like to hire a car and travel with my family. I don't want to spend all my time in the family [Reena, east London 2000].

The desire to travel to Africa is expressed by Reena, a twenty-two-year-old British-born Sikh woman who lives in a joint household in East London, alongside her husband's mother, brother, and sister-in-law. Reena was working in a local take-away and said that she had not wanted to continue further education because she had 'always wanted to get married'. Reena subsequently married her husband, a twice-migrant from Tanzania living in the UK and had recently attended the marriage of her brother-in-law in India. Previously, Reena had been to India with her parents although she had never been to Africa; nor had her husband since his migration to Britain as a child. Some members of her husband's family in Tanzania were in contact, but, owing to the divorce between Reena's mother and father-in-law, bonds with Tanzania had weakened.

Reena begins her future plans by highlighting the context of travel to Africa, on the basis of her being part of an extended family. The visit falls within the remit of a family holiday as well as the meeting with an estranged member (her father-in-law). Reena's reference to the African town as the family village tightens the association of Africa as a familial place. These associations are based on the descriptions offered to her by her husband and his kin who speak of Africa and India as being similar places. However, Reena questions this on the basis of inhabitants and geography whilst raising her own expectations for travel as going beyond the familial context. Therefore, although she highlights family as an important factor for the experience of Africa, she correspondingly seeks independence from the family for the experience of travel in 'dangerous Africa'. In spite of the potential of dramatic events as reasons for staying close to the family and village (town), Reena expresses her desire to utilize this opportunity to experience Africa at both the level of tourism and within the nuclear family. Therefore, Reena's demarcation of being 'with my family' and not always 'in the family' are pivotal reminders of the ways in which place is experienced on the basis of gender, generation, position within households, and the direction of the journeys taken. The perceived threats of being in the African landscape, vocalized by Reena's suggestions about the 'other' and getting raped, further illustrate the ways in which Sikh women's mobility is curtailed in the African context. Travelling and dwelling in India differs in so far as there is the notion that locals are *apna* (ours), although in many cases migrants speak about the ways in which locals in India are unscrupulous in their dealings with foreigners.

Writing about returnees to Bangladesh, Sallie Westwood notes that women's travel back to Bangladesh as 'more grounded in familial relations and kin-based practices of everyday life which some saw as a constraint on their movement...' (Westwood forthcoming: 21–2). On the other hand, Westwood notes that young Bangladeshi men are able to explore their complex relationship to the land of their parents, on the basis that they are able to travel beyond the confines of familial and familiar places. Westwood's account clearly illustrates the significance of gender and the impact this has on conceptualization and experience of place. In addition, her analysis highlights the perception of places and travel as transforming in that 'returnees to Sylhet no longer want to spend their time in Sylhet just visiting relatives... but wanted, instead something more of a holiday in which they spent their time shopping, eating out and generally enjoying the place rather like tourists do' (ibid.: 12). To this effect Westwood highlights local entrepreneurial investments in returnees from Britain by creating suitable spaces to capitalise on their British-based counterparts' travel by constructing shopping malls and places for entertainment. These notions of returnees as consumers, in Sylhet, gives expression to the 'culture of migrancy' which not only highlights the basis of culture and economics, but also the ways in which tourism and generational differences arise in the desires of returnees (ibid.: 16–21).

Like second generation Sylhetis described by Westwood (ibid.), Reena's desire is to experience Africa on the basis of being a tourist. Her gaze towards Africa is couched in consumption terms, although she is aware that the context of her travel is as a married woman who is on journey which is familial. The touristic experience of travel stresses consumption ranging from the preparations undertaken before travel, such as guide books, maps, and the perception of places as objects for consumption (Kaur and Hutnyk 1999; Housee 1999; Gardner 2002; Westwood forthcoming).

The importance of place of departure, individual position within the household and, women's own interests in undertaking travel was also highlighted by Kirpal who refused to travel for her nephew's marriage in Tanzania. Kirpal is in her mid-forties and has been living in the UK since the late 1970s, when she migrated from Tanzania for the purposes of marriage. Subsequently, Kirpal separated from her husband and deals 'all alone with financial tensions'. These financial factors meant that Kirpal was offered, along with her children, tickets from her natal kin to attend the marriage in Tanzania. However, Kirpal noted that the offer of money for travel to the wedding would have meant that the experience of being in Africa would have been restricted to the event.

I had not been well and made an appointment for the hospital and you know that the waiting lists are so long and I could not miss out on the opportunity. They were all very cross with me, they wanted me to go [for a family wedding] and I sent D [eldest child]. It must have been hard for her but I thought she should see that place. She had not been since she was a little girl. I did not want to go and then I would have been stuck in the wedding. When I go, I want to see all the sites and visit my own childhood places and see the animals and hotels. Weddings are full of tension. [You] spend all that money and lose money here not working...I am sewing and the operation was for my hand [Kirpal, west London 2000].

Reena is a British-born Sikh woman and hence worked in a public setting before and after marriage, whilst for Kirpal the notion of non-domestic work as an activity undertaken by women followed her migration and subsequent marriage in the UK. Like Reena, Kirpal highlights the desire to travel to Africa as a tourist as different from experiencing the place on the basis of family, marriage, education, and employment. Both women at different points in their life cycles, and, having different familial contexts, reveal the association of women's travel within familial obligations and gendered activities (Malkin 1998). However, both women are able to vocalize and actualize travel plans because of their access to material resources gained through employment outside the domestic context in Britain. Interestingly, Kirpal's travel to Tanzania would mean a return to the place where she had 'grown up' and developed networks that are beyond the context of the family, and, are significant factors in her decision not to travel.

CONCLUSION

In this article I have explored Sikh women's movement to Britain as brides and wives while also focusing on their engagement in the paid labour market. I have demonstrated that paid labour enables women to negotiate their travel to and from different translocalities. We have also seen that women's access to material resources is influenced by their stage in the life course and the norms associated with particular places. Further, their work in the labour market is experienced as and conceptualized to be an extension of their gender identities. At the same time the needs of a household within which women's lives are embedded, are also overlain with hierarchy, thereby denoting different positions to women within the same family. The dynamic nature of household decision-making and the employment of women needs to be contextualized within wider structures as Kushi's and Satinder's employment history in the garment industry reflect. Where they were once employed through hidden economies (doing piece work), through their move to the 'English' factory, we can see changes in the wider structure which results in them having better employment conditions and feeling more 'valued' by their employees (cf. Kabeer 2000).

We have seen how place, in terms of the location and duration of residence women have, bears an impact on the options for women in the paid economy. This in turn is dependent on household organization. As we have seen, one of the features of transnational households is the ways in which its members are on the move, between places, in accordance with their gender.

These women's locations within the household and paid economy highlight their greater flexibility as their skills are more readily transposable. This translates to greater mobility across places for women on the basis of their gender identities and roles and further strengthens their centrality in the constitution and organization of the transnational household. Without the travel of women and their activities it is difficult for the household to become established and subsequently expand across places. The movement of women as brides, wives, or mothers is central to their experience of mobility and correspondingly shifts according to perceptions of place and wider social, political, and economic processes, not forgetting the needs of the household.

Notes

1. Throughout the paper I refer to my informants as Sikhs. This is because they would often stress that they were Sikh as opposed to Punjabi, a label they often associated with being Hindu-Punjabi.

2. This article is based on doctoral research conducted amongst ten Jat Sikh households maintaining links with Punjab, Tanzania, and Britain. Owing to the geographic dispersal of the households a multi-sited approach was taken to fieldwork using multiple methods (Mand, forthcoming).

3. Many Asians held such documentation and this was one of the major features in the process of Africanization following Independence.

4. For a general discussion on the differences amongst South Asian women in relation to employment see Ahmad *et al.* 2003.

5. Satpal is referring to her natal home in Punjab.

6. Although no longer valid as a result of changing immigration rules, a return to Britain for the birth of children was common during the 1980s and based on the belief that the newborn would be eligible for British citizenship.

References

Ahmed, F., T. Modood, and S. Lissenburgh (2003). *South Asian Women and Employment in Britain. The Interaction of Gender and Ethnicity,* London: Policy Studies Institute.

Alicea, M. (2000). '"A Chambered Nautilus": The Contradictory Nature of Puerto Rican's Women's Role in the Special Construction of a Transnational Community', in K. Willis and A.B. Yeoh (eds), *Gender and Migration,* Cheltenham: Edward Elgar Publishing Limited, pp. 301–30.

Anwar, M. (1979). *The Myth of Return: Pakistanis in Britain,* London: Heinemann Educational.

Ballard, R. (2001). 'Upward Mobility: The Socio-economic and Educational Achievements of Britain's Visible Minorities', at http://66.102.9.104/search?q=cache:I2sKt0WlmX0J:www.art.man.ac.uk/CASAS/pdfpapers/mobility.pdf+casas+upward+mobility&hl=en&ct=clnk&cd=1&gl=uk, accessed 10 May 2007.

—— (2002). 'The South Asian Presence in Britain and its Transnational Connections', at http://66.102.9.104/search?q=cache:yjScTaO9pIEJ:www.art.man.ac.uk/CASAS/pdfpapers/sasians2001.pdf+casas+the+

south+Asian+presence&hl=en&ct=clnk&cd=1&gl=uk, accessed 10 May 2007.

Ballard, R. and C. Ballard (1977). 'The Sikhs: The Development of South Asian Settlements in Britain', in J.L. Watson (ed.), *Between Two Cultures: Migrants and Minorities in Britain*, Oxford: Basil Blackwell, pp. 21–56.

Bhachu, P. (1985). *Twice Migrants. East African Sikh Settlers in Britain*, London: Tavistock.

—— (1988). 'Apni Marzi Kardhi. Home and Work: Sikh Women in Britain', in S. Westwood and P. Bhachu (eds), *Enterprising Women. Ethnicity, Economy and Gender Relations*, London / New York: Routledge, pp. 76–102.

—— (1991). 'Culture, Ethnicity and Class Among Punjabi Women in 1990s Britain', *New Community*, Vol. 17, No. 3, pp. 401–12.

Caplan, P. (1985). *Class and Gender in India: Women and their Organisations in a South Indian City*, London: Tavistock.

Clifford, J. (1997). *Routes: Travel and Transformation in the Late Twentieth Century.* Cambridge/ Massachusetts: Harvard University Press.

di Leonardo, M. (1992). 'The Female World of Cards and Holidays: Women, Families and the Work of Kinship', in B. Thorne and M. Yalom (eds), *Rethinking the Family: Some Feminist Questions*, Boston: Northeastern University Press, pp. 246–61.

Donner, F.H. (1999). 'Women and Gold: Gender and Urbanisation in contemporary Bengal', Unpublished DPhil Dissertation: London School of Economics.

Fouroun, G. and N. Glick-Schiller (2001). 'All in the Family: Gender, Transnational Migration, and the Nation-State', *Identities: Global Studies in Culture and Power*, Vol. 7, No. 4, pp. 539–76.

Gamburd, R. (2000). *The Kitchen Spoon's Handle: Transnationalism and Sri Lankan Migrant Housemaids*, Ithaca and London: Cornell University Press.

Gardner, K. (2002). *Age, Narrative, Migration. The Life Course and Life Histories of Bengali Elders in London*, Oxford: Berg.

Housee, S. (1999). 'Journey Through Life. The Self in Travel', in R. Kaur, and J. Hutnyk (eds), *Travel Worlds. Journeys in Contemporary Cultural Politics*, London and New York: Zed Books, pp. 137–54.

Kabeer, N. (2000). *The Power to Choose: Bangladeshi women and Labour Market Decisions in London and Dhaka*, London and New York: Verso.

Kandiyoti, D. (1997). 'Bargaining with Patriarchy', in N. Visvananthan (ed.), *The Women, Gender and Development Reader*, London: Zed Press, pp. 86–92.

Kaur, R. and J. Hutnyk (1999). 'Introduction', in *Travel Worlds: Journeys in Contemporary Cultural Politics*, in R. Kaur and J. Hutnyk (eds), London / New York: Zed Books, pp. 1–13.

Kibria, N. (2000). 'Power, Patriarchy, and Gender Conflict in the Vietnamese Immigrant Community', in K. Willis and A.B. Yeoh (eds), *Gender and Migration*, Cheltenham: Edward Elgar Publishing Limited, pp. 177–92.

Mahler, S.J. (2000). 'Constructing International Relations: The Role of Transnational Migrants and Other Non-state Actors', *Identities*, Vol. 7, pp. 197–232.

Malkin, V. (1998). 'Gender, Status and Modernity in a Transnational Migrant Circuit', Paper presented at the ICCR International Conference on Transnationalism, Manchester, 16–18 May.

Mand, K. (2004). 'Gendered Places, Transnational Lives: Sikh Women in Tanzania, Britain and Indian Punjab', unpublished DPhil dissertation: The University of Sussex.

—— (2005). 'Marriage and Migration at the End Stages', *Indian Journal of Gender Studies. Special issue: Marriage and Migration in Asia*, Vol. 12, Nos. 2 and 3, May-December, pp. 407–25.

—— (2006). 'Gender, Ethnicity and Social Relations in the Narratives of Elderly Sikh Men and Women', in *Ethnic and Racial Studies. Special Issue on Social Capital, Migration and Transnational Families*, Vol. 29, No. 6, pp. 1057–71.

—— (forthcoming). 'Researching Lives in Motion: Multi-sighted Strategies in a Transnational Context', in S. Coleman and P. Vom Hellerman (eds), *Multi-sited Ethnography: Problems and Possibilities in the Translocation of Research Method*, London: Routledge.

Moore, H. (1988). *Feminism and Anthropology*, London: Routledge.

Nagar, R. (1995). 'Making and Breaking Boundaries: Identity Politics among South Asians in Post Colonial Dar es Salaam', Unpublished DPhil Dissertation: The University of Minnesota.

Office of Population Census and Survey (OPCS) (1991). *Labour Force Survey*. Series No. 8. London: HMSO.

Parmar, P. (1982). 'Gender, Race and Class: Asian women in Resistance', in *The Empire Strikes Back. Race and Racism in 70s Britain*, Centre for Contemporary Cultural Studies. University of Birmingham: Hutchinson Press, pp. 236–75.

Phizacklea, A. (1988). 'Entrepreneurship, Ethnicity, and Gender', in S. Westwood and P. Bhachu (eds), *Enterprising Women: Ethnicity, Economy and Gender Relations*, London and New York: Routledge, pp. 20–34.

—— (2000). 'The Politics of Belonging. Sex Work, Domestic Work: Trans-national Household Strategies', in S. Westwood and A. Phizacklea (eds), *Trans-nationalism and the Politics of Belonging*, New York: Routledge, pp. 120–45.

Rojek, C. and J. Urry (eds) (1997). *Transformations of Travel and Theory*, London: Routledge.

Sharma, U. (1986). *Women, Work and Property in North West India*, London: Tavistock.

Siddiqui, T. (2001). *Transcending Boundaries: Labour Migration of Women from Bangladesh*, Dhaka: University Press.

Vatuk, S. (1995). 'The Indian Woman in Later Life: Some Social and Cultural Considerations', in M. Das Gupta and L.C. Chen, (eds), *Women's Health in India: Risk and Vulnerability*, Bombay: Oxford University Press, pp. 289–306.

Werbner, P. (1990). *The Migration Process: Capital, Gifts and Offerings among British Pakistanis*, Oxford: Berg Publications

Westwood, S. (Forthcoming). 'Makeover Migrants: Tourism and Diasporic Investments in Changing Places.'

Westwood, S. and P. Bhachu (eds) (1988). *Enterprising Women: Ethnicity, Economy and Gender Relations,* London and New York: Routledge.

Whitehead, A. (1981). '"I'm Hungry Mum": The Politics of Domestic Budgeting', in K. Young, C. Wolkowitz and R. McCullagh (eds), *Of Marriage and the Market: Women's Subordination Internationally and its Lessons,* London: Routledge, pp. 93–116.

Contributors

PURNIMA DHAVAN is Assistant Professor in the History Department at the University of Washington, Seattle. She is currently working on a book manuscript entitled 'From Sparrows into Hawks: The Making of Khalsa Culture, 1709–1799' which explores the debates, collaboration, and conflict among Sikh peasants, soldiers, and intellectuals that transformed a new martial community in the eighteenth century.

CONSTANCE ELSBERG is Professor of Anthropology and Sociology at Northern Virginia Community College in Alexandria, Virginia. Her publications include *Graceful Women: Gender and Identity in an American Sikh Community* (2003) and 'Healthy Happy Holy Organization/Sikh Dharma,' in *Encyclopedia of Religion* (2004).

C. CHRISTINE FAIR is Assistant Professor at Georgetown University's Security Studies Program in the Edmund A. Walsh School of Foreign Service. Previously she was a senior political scientist at the RAND Corporation, a political affairs officer at the United Nations Assistance Mission to Afghanistan, and a senior research associate with the United States Institute of Peace in the Center for Conflict Analysis and Prevention. She specializes in South Asian political and military affairs. She has authored several books including *The Madrassah Challenge: Militancy and Religious Education in Pakistan* (2009) and co-edited *Treading on Hallowed Ground: Counterinsurgency Operations in Sacred Spaces* (2008). She is member of the Council on Foreign Relations and the International Institute for Strategic Studies.

INDERPAL GREWAL is Professor of Women's, Gender, and Sexuality Studies at Yale University, and senior faculty in the South Asia Council and the American Studies Program. Among her several publications is *Transnational America: Feminisms, Diasporas, Neoliberalisms* (2005) and the co-edited *Gender in a Transnational World: Introduction to Women's Studies* (2001). She has jointly edited a special issue of *Signs* (2001) on 'Gender and Globalization'; and is currently working on the relation between feminist practices and security discourses in the US and India.

DORIS R. JAKOBSH is Associate Professor in Religious Studies at the University of Waterloo, Canada. She has published *Relocating Gender in Sikh History: Transformation, Meaning and Identity* (2003) and several articles on women in Sikhism. She is currently working on Sikh identity construction and the internet as well as a volume on Sikhism to be published in 2010.

JAGBIR JHUTTI-JOHAL is Lecturer in Sikh Studies at the School of Philosophy, Theology and Religion, Birmingham University. Her major areas of interest with reference to the Sikh Diaspora include gender issues, Sikh theology, and its application in a multicultural society and ethics and religion in medicine. She is also a member of the Centre for Family Law and Policy at the University of Oxford.

PREETI KAPUR is Associate Professor in Psychology at Daulat Ram College for Women, University of Delhi. She teaches social psychology and has published several papers on women's identity. She is currently working on a project pertaining to the study of 'self and identity' among Sikh women.

ANSHU MALHOTRA is Reader in the Department of History, Faculty of Social Sciences, University of Delhi. Her publications include *Gender, Caste, and Religious Identities: Restructuring Class in Colonial Punjab* (2002). Her current research interests focus on the history of gender and religious sensibilities from the early to mid nineteenth century Punjab.

KANWAL MAND is Research Fellow at the University of Sussex. Her doctoral thesis examined the relationship between marriage, migration and the creation and establishment of transnational Punjabi households spanning Tanzania, Punjab in India and London. She has published several articles on the Sikh diaspora in edited

MICHELLE MASKIELL is Associate Professor, Department of History and Philosophy, Montana State University. She is a renowned historian of labour, gender, and textiles in Northwestern India and Pakistan and has published articles in several journals.

GIRISHWAR MISRA is Professor and former Head of the Department of Psychology at University of Delhi. His areas of interest are cultural psychology, self and identity, emotions and health behaviour. His publications include *Applied Social Psychology in India*, *Contributions to Psychology in India*, and *Perspectives on Indigenous Psychology*.

NICOLA MOONEY teaches anthropology in the department of Social, Cultural and Media Studies at the University of the Fraser Valley, and is an Associate of UFV's Centre for Indo-Canadian Studies. Her forthcoming book is *Rural Nostalgias and Transnational Dreams: Identity and Modernity among Jat Sikhs*.

KAMALA ELIZABETH NAYAR is lecturer in South Asian Studies at Kwantlen University, British Columbia. Her publications include *The Socially Involved Renunciate: Guru Nanak's Discourse to the Nath Yogis* (2007); *The Sikh Diaspora in Vancouver: Three Generations Amid Tradition, Modernity and Multiculturalism* (2004) and several articles on the Sikh community in Western Canada. Her book *Hayagriva in South India: Complexity and Selectivity of a Pan-Indian Hindu Deity* (2004) is an extensive textual study on Indian religions.

ELEANOR NESBITT is Professor in Religions and Education, University of Warwick. Her publications include *Sikhism A Very Short Introduction* (2005), *Intercultural Education: Ethnographic and Religious Approaches* (2004), and *Interfaith Pilgrims* (2003). She is currently researching children's religious identity formation in mixed-faith families.

ROBIN RINEHART is Associate Professor and Head of the Religious Studies department, and chair of the Asian Studies

Program at Lafayette College, Easton, Pennsylvania, USA. She is the author of *One Lifetime, Many Lives: The Experience of Modern Hindu Hagiography* (1999), editor of *Contemporary Hinduism: Ritual, Culture, and Practice* (2004), *Debating the Dasam Granth* (forthcoming), and author of numerous articles on Hindu, Sufi, and Sikh literature of the Punjab.

NIKKY-GUNINDER KAUR SINGH holds the Crawford Family Professor of Religious Studies Chair at Colby College in Maine, USA. Her interests focus on poetics and feminist issues. She has published extensively in the field of Sikhism, including her books *The Birth of the Khalsa: A Feminist RE-Memory of Sikh Identity* (2005), *The Feminine Principle in the Sikh Vision of the Transcendent* (1993), *Sikhism* (1993), *The Name of My Beloved: Verses of the Sikh Gurus* (2004), and *Metaphysics and Physics of the Guru Granth Sahib* (1981).

MARGARET WALTON-ROBERTS is Associate Professor in the Geography and Environmental Studies Department at Wilfrid Laurier University, Canada. Her research interests focus on Canadian immigration and cultural diversity, how ethnic and gender differences shape settlement experiences, especially with reference to Indian immigration to Canada, processes of community formation across transnational landscapes, and more recently in regard to immigrant settlement in rural and small urban regions across Canada.